Design for
Environment

Other McGraw-Hill Books of Related Interest

Design for Environment

Creating Eco-Efficient Products and Processes

Joseph Fiksel Editor

Principal and Vice President
Decision Focus Incorporated
Mountain View, California

McGraw-Hill

New York   San Francisco   Washington, D.C.   Auckland   Bogotá
Caracas   Lisbon   London   Madrid   Mexico City   Milan
Montreal   New Delhi   San Juan   Singapore
Sydney   Tokyo   Toronto

Library of Congress Cataloging-in-Publication Data

Design for environment : creating eco-efficient products and processes
/ Joseph Fiksel, editor
    p.   cm.
  ISBN 0-07-020972-3 (alk. paper)
   1. Design, Industrial—Environmental aspects. 2. Industrial
management—Environmental aspects. I. Fiksel, Joseph
TS171.4.D478 1996
745.2—dc20
                                   95-32585
                                      CIP

McGraw-Hill

A Division of The McGraw·Hill Companies

  2 3 4 5 6 7 8 9 0 DOC/DOC 9 0 0 9 8 7 6

ISBN 0-07-020972-3

The sponsoring editor for this book was Zoe G. Foundotos, the editing supervisor was Paul R. Sobel, and the production supervisor was Suzanne W. B. Rapcavage. It was set in Century Schoolbook by Donald A. Feldman of McGraw-Hill's Professional Book Group composition unit.

Printed and bound by R. R. Donnelley & Sons Company.

Things derive their being and nature by mutual dependence and are nothing in themselves.

—Nagarjuna, Buddhist philosopher, lst Century AD

Isolated material particles are abstractions, their properties being definable and observable only through their interaction with other systems.

—Niels Bohr, atomic physicist, 20th Century AD

Contents

Part 3   Walking the Talk: Pioneer Stories

Contributors

Braden R. Allenby, Ph.D., *Research Vice President, Technology and the Environment, AT&T Engineering Research Center, Basking Ridge, New Jersey* (CHAP. 11)

Pat Bartholomew, *Director of Environmental Affairs, Baxter Healthcare Corporation, Deerfield, Illinois* (CHAP. 18)

Cliff Bast, *Corporate Product Stewardship Manager, Hewlett-Packard Company, Palo Alto, California* (CHAP. 13)

Deborah L. Boger *Office of Pollution Prevention and Toxics, U.S. Environmental Protection Agency, Washington, D.C.* (CHAP. 22)

Anne B. Brinkley, *Staff Engineer, Engineering Center for Environmentally Concious Products, IBM Corporation, Research Triangle Park, North Carolina* (CHAP. 12)

David Cohan, Ph.D., *Vice President, Decision Focus Incorporated, Mountain View, California* (CHAP. 10)

Kenneth R. Dickerson, *Senior Vice President, External Affairs, Atlantic Rickfield Company, Los Angeles, California* (CHAP. 17)

Joseph Fiksel, Ph.D., *Vice President, Decision Focus Incorporated, Mountain View, California* (CHAPS. 1, 2, 3, 4, 5, 6, 7, 8, 9, 27)

Nicholas Fotis, *Rexam Medical Packaging, Mundelein, Illinois* (CHAP. 18)

Michael Gershowitz, *Research Analyst, WMX Technologies, Inc., Washington, D.C.* (CHAP. 20)

Leah V. Haygood, *Director, Environmental Planning and Programs, WMX Technologies, Inc., Washington, D.C.* (CHAP. 20)

Carl L. Henn, CPL, CFP, *Senior Vice President, Concord Energy, Inc., Bernardsville, New Jersey* (CHAP. 26)

Barbara S. Hill, *Manager, Product Safety Technology, IBM Corporation, Somers, New York* (CHAP. 12)

Tom Korpalski, *Environmental Programs Manager, Computer Products Organization, Hewlett-Packard Company, Boise, Idaho* (CHAP. 13)

Ernest Lowe, *Managing Partner, Indigo Development, Oakland, California* (CHAP. 25)

Peter Melhus, *Director, Corporate Environmental Quality, Pacific Gas & Electric, San Francisco, California* (CHAP. 16)

Claudia M. O'Brien, *Office of Pollution Prevention and Toxics, U.S. Environmental Protection Agency, Washington, D.C.* (CHAP. 22)

Lisa Petrilli,   *Senior Product Manager, Baxter Healthcare Corporation, Deerfield, Illinois* (CHAP. 18)

Greg Pitts,   *Director, Environmental Programs, Microelectronics and Computer Technology Corporation, Austin, Texas* (CHAP. 14)

Frank P. Popoff,   *Chairman and Chief Executive Officer, The Dow Chemical Company, Midland, Michigan* (CHAP. 21)

Claude G. Poncelet, Ph.D.,   *Manager, Corporate Environmental Quality, Pacific Gas and Electric Company, San Francisco, California* (CHAP. 16)

Edward L. Quevedo, Esq.,   *Wise & Shepard, Counsellors at Law, Palo Alto, California* (CHAP. 24)

Jerry Schoening,   *Director, Environmental Health & Safety, Applied Materials, Inc., Santa Clara, California* (CHAP. 15)

Robert Shelton,   *Director, Environmental, Health & Safety Management, Arthur D. Little, Inc., San Francisco, California* (CHAP. 23)

Sandra Woods,   *Vice President, Chief Environmental Officer, Coors Brewing Company, Golden, Colorado* (CHAP. 19)

Preface

Dr. Seuss tells the story of the Lorax, one of my children's favorite parables. The *truffula* trees are destroyed by greedy capitalists in order to manufacture *thneeds*, and they wantonly pollute the environment until they exhaust all nature's resources. The Lorax is a forest-dwelling spirit who vainly cries "I speak for the trees!". Our children are growing up with these images and derive values that are sensitive to environmental destruction. A scrap of litter on the street offends them deeply.

In fact, our industrial organizations are no longer villains. A new generation of managers has embraced the Lorax's values and surprised those cynics who view capitalists as inherently self-serving. Leading U.S. corporations began to adopt progressive environmental policies even during the conservative reign of the last Republican administration. They have understood that environmental responsibility makes good business sense.

Design for Environment is a concept whose time has come. It is not the product of shrill environmental extremists demanding that industrial development be frozen, nor does it originate in the sentimental fantasies of nature-lovers. Rather, it is a deliberate, thoughtful, and mature effort by both government and industry to acknowledge the importance of environmental preservation while supporting industrial growth. Over the last few years, the rate at which environmental concerns have moved from the political fringe to the mainstream has been at least as astonishing as the sudden dismantling of the Soviet Union.

This book originated as a labor of love, corresponding to a new phase of my professional career. For years, I had worked in the area of environmental exposure and risk analysis, focusing on the impacts of chemical releases. I rarely thought about the design of the products and processes that generated those releases. Later, as manager of a DARPA project on concurrent engineering, I began to appreciate the immense power of designers to influence environmental outcomes. When I finally integrated my environmental knowledge with this concurrent engineering philosophy, the concept of DFE struck me with the force of a revelation. Apparently, as I soon discovered, I was not alone. Within a matter of a few years, DFE grew from an unknown term to a frequently overused industry buzzword.

One indicator of the rising importance of DFE is the number of professional and industry conferences that have included it as a major theme. In the year that I spent assembling this book, from June 1993 to June 1994, such conferences were held by the Institute for Electrical and Electronic Engineers, the American Chemical Society, the American Institute of Chemical Engineers, the Air and Waste Management Society, the Management Roundtable, the Global Environmental Management Initiative, the Microelectronics and Computer Consortium, and so on. I am sure there are many more that I left out. Yet in spite of all the hue and cry, DFE remains an elusive concept. We know it when we see it, but few can define it operationally.

The purpose of this book is to affirm the legitimacy of DFE as both a management approach and an engineering discipline. Being a lifelong engineer and mathematician, I believe that effective implementation of Design for Environment requires the development of practical design metrics, guidelines, and verification methods. I further believe that it must be deployed within an integrated system framework in order to provide useful guidance for decision-making during fast-cycle product development. With the help of many professional colleagues, I have assembled here a collection of writings that I hope will provide a useful point of reference for those who adopt the practice of DFE.

I wish to thank Warner North, William Balson, David Cohan, and especially Ken Wapman of Decision Focus Incorporated for their helpful collaboration, Tina Nuss provided invaluable administrative support throughout this project. I am also grateful for the efforts of the many contributors to this book, who gave of their valuable time to make this a fully-rounded work.

I dedicate this book to my wife Diane, whose steadfast idealism and faith have inspired me and given me strength and purpose, and to my sons, Justin, Cameron and Brandon, who hopefully will inherit a sustainable future.

Joseph Fiksel

Introduction

Joseph Fiksel, Ph.D.

Vice President
Decision Focus Incorporated
Mountain View, California

"[T]he traditional model of industrial activity—in which individual manufacturing processes take in raw materials and generate products to be sold plus waste to be disposed of—should be transformed into a more integrated model...the effluents of one process...serve as the raw materials for another process."

R. A. FROSCH AND N. E. GALLOPOULOS
Scientific American[1]

The Basic Premise

One generation ago, environmental quality was a little-known concept in the United States. Today we live in an age of heightened environmental awareness, fueled by public interest groups and the media. The processes involved in manufacturing and supporting most products may have adverse impacts on the environment, including the generation of waste, the disruption of ecosystems, and the depletion of natural resources. Current patterns of industrial development threaten to exceed the limits of sustainability in terms of resource utilization and waste management, and also pose potential threats to global climate, vegetation, and agriculture. According to the U.S. Environmental Protection Agency (EPA), about 12 billion tons of industrial wastes are generated annually in the United States, and over a third of this is hazardous waste. In addition, discarded products are rapidly expending scarce landfill capacity. For example, one study estimates that by the year 2005 about 150 million personal computers will have been sent to landfills.[2]

Unfortunately, our debates about environmental quality are frequently contentious—we become polarized around extremes, we allow environmental issues to become politicized, and we lose sight of the paucity of scientific information that is actually available. Environmentalists tend to be well intentioned but dogmatic in their mistrust of institutions and their reverence of pristine ecosystems. Regulators tend to be overwhelmed with the massive burden of their legislative mandate, and myopic in their implementation decisions. Businesspeople tend to be suspicious of the lot, and protective of their economic interests. The average citizen, bewildered by the barrage of propaganda, grows cynical and disenchanted. As a result, we become mired in disagreements and make little environmental progress. As the pundits say, "The only beneficiaries are the lawyers."

This book offers a more hopeful path. Our underlying premise is that environmental quality is compatible with industrial development. Rather than paying a steep price for environmental improvement, *corporations can redesign their industrial systems to achieve both environmental quality and economic efficiency.* This represents a radical departure from the traditional world view that considers environmental consciousness to be a burden upon industry. However, far from being speculative, this view is increasingly being embraced by leading global manufacturers in virtually every industry category. "Sustainable development" through eco-efficiency has become the rallying cry of a new breed of companies who see competitive advantage in conservation of resources and environmental stewardship. Part 3 of this book contains some reports of pioneering companies who have adopted this bold environmental vision.

Critics of the new corporate environmentalism have assailed this "win-win" philosophy as misleading, claiming that environmental costs will continue to outweigh the benefits.[3] Indeed, it is true that historic practices have left a large legacy of environmental restoration costs. It is also true that environmental performance improvement initiatives do not automatically produce financial benefits; they need to be evaluated in the same light as any other investments. Setting arbitrary pollution reduction goals may lead to expensive projects with diminishing returns. However, it is also true that a full consideration of environmental factors and trade-offs will reveal opportunities to simultaneously enhance customer satisfaction, profitability, and environmental performance. This will be amply demonstrated in later chapters.

What Is DFE?

The concept of *design for environment* (DFE) originated as recently as
1992, largely through the efforts of a handful of electronics firms that
were attempting to build environmental awareness into their product
development efforts. The American Electronics Association, under the
leadership of Brad Allenby, formed a task force on design for environment and produced a groundbreaking primer for the benefit of member companies.[4] Since that time, the level of interest has mushroomed, and the term has become a buzzword often connected to
corporate environmental stewardship or pollution prevention programs. This surge in popularity has created semantic confusion about
the meaning of DFE. For purposes of this book, we view DFE as a
specific collection of design practices aimed at creating eco-efficient
products and processes (see Chap. 5).

Design for environment is defined here as *systematic consideration
of design performance with respect to environmental, health, and safety objectives over the full product and process life cycle.*[5]

The practice of DFE is becoming essential in today's industrial
environment, as major firms recognize the importance of environmental responsibility to their long-term success. Their experiences reveal
that DFE provides competitive advantage by reducing the costs of
production and waste management, encouraging innovation in product simplification, and attracting new customers. The EPA has also
established several DFE initiatives to encourage reduction of pollution at the source (see Chap. 23).

What is driving these changes? For one thing, consumers have
become increasingly concerned about the environmental "friendliness" of the products that they purchase. Equally important, there
are a number of global trends that make it imperative for industrial
suppliers to become more aware of the environmental implications of
their product and process designs. The International Organization for
Standardization (ISO) is developing the ISO 14000 standards for
environmental management systems, analogous to the ISO 9000
series of quality management system standards. Many government
agencies, notably in the European Union, are taking aggressive steps
to assure that manufacturers are responsible for recovery of products
and materials at the end of their useful lives. At the same time, there
is a growing voluntary commitment on the part of major manufacturing firms to assure environmental responsibility for both their internal operations and their suppliers. This commitment is evident from
the flourishing of consortia such as the Global Environmental
Management Initiative and the Business Council for Sustainable
Development, as well as EPA-sponsored programs such as Green
Lights and 33/50 (see Chap. 3).

Conceptual Crossroads

DFE represents a conceptual crossroads—it is at the convergence of two thrusts that are transforming the nature of manufacturing throughout the world. As illustrated in Fig. 1.1, these two thrusts are enterprise integration and sustainable development.

Enterprise integration is the reengineering of business processes and information systems to improve teamwork and coordination across organizational boundaries, thereby increasing the effectiveness of the enterprise as a whole. The total-quality management movement has provided an important foundation for enterprise integration. More recently, *integrated product development* has been widely adopted as a strategy for "agile" manufacturing, allowing companies to release higher-quality products while reducing time to market.[6] As described in Chap. 6, integrated product development involves cross-functional design teams who consider the entire spectrum of quality factors, including safety, testability, manufacturability, reliability, and maintainability, throughout the product life cycle. Since environmental assurance is an important aspect of total quality, DFE fits naturally into this process.

Sustainable development is industrial progress that "meets the needs of the present without compromising the ability of future generations to meet their own needs."[7] The implied question of how to assure continued industrial growth without adverse ecological impacts was a major theme of the 1992 Earth Summit in Brazil. The concept of corporate environmental stewardship has provided a foundation for this thrust, and pollution prevention has become a common practice in industry. As described in Chap. 26, companies are now beginning to embrace "industrial ecology," which broadens their economic view of industrial management to include the natural ecosys-

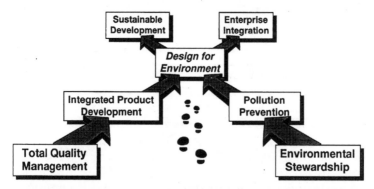

Figure 1.1 DFE represents a conceptual crossroad between the drive toward enterprise integration and the drive toward sustainable development.

tems in which they operate.[8] Figure 1.2 illustrates how traditional exchange value can be extended to include both man-made and natural capital. Instead of accounting purely for the labor and man-made materials that are inputs to production, a broader approach takes into account the value of natural resource inputs and the effect of waste outputs.[9]

DFE lies squarely at the intersection of these two thrusts. It represents a way to achieve sustainability while seeking competitive advantage. The scope of DFE, construed broadly, can encompass a variety of overlapping disciplines, including:

- Occupational health and safety
- Consumer health and safety
- Ecological integrity and resource protection
- Pollution prevention and toxic use reduction
- Transportability (safety and energy use)
- Waste reduction or minimization
- Disassembly and disposability
- Recyclability and remanufacturability

Historically, these issues have been managed by environmental, health, and safety groups that tended to be isolated from the mainstream in terms of both the strategic and the operational aspects of a business. However, as discussed in Chaps. 4 and 5, the role and positioning of environmental management groups are shifting, and environmental issues previously considered arcane are now emerging as part of a comprehensive business strategy.

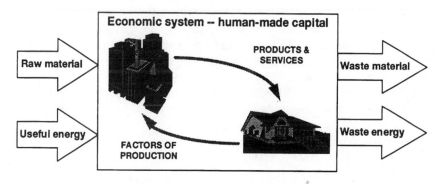

Figure 1.2 Broadening traditional economics to include the industrial ecosystem. (*Adapted from Ref. 8.*)

Thus, the dawning of DFE has resulted in active collaboration among company groups that rarely had contact in the past—environmental managers and product development managers. This book describes the exciting opportunities that are made possible by this unprecedented collaboration.

Implementation Challenges

Global companies, especially those based in Europe and Japan, are moving aggressively to integrate environmentally conscious technology and products into their strategies for future competitiveness. The strategic importance of DFE and examples of DFE practice are described in the excellent U.S. Office of Technology Assessment report, *Green Products by Design: Choices for a Cleaner Environment.*[10] In the United States, a number of progressive U.S. manufacturing companies such as AT&T and Procter & Gamble have begun to implement environmental quality programs aimed at continuous improvement in key measures of environmental performance.

As some of these pioneers have discovered, to perform design for environment consistently and effectively is challenging for several reasons:

- The necessary environmental expertise is not widely available among product development engineers.

- The complex and open-ended nature of environmental phenomena makes them difficult to analyze.

- The economic systems in which products are produced, used, and recycled are much more difficult to understand and control than the products themselves.

Despite the many examples of successful DFE efforts described in this book, the current state of DFE practice can be characterized as mainly opportunistic. Well-motivated and well-informed teams may be able to identify product improvements that are environmentally beneficial or that reduce life-cycle costs. However, in order to establish DFE as an integral component of the product development process, systematic methods and processes must be introduced into the daily work of development teams.

Companies that wish to implement DFE need to carefully consider the following issues:

Business motivations

- Do we have one or more business units for whom DFE appears to be a competitive factor?

- Have our customers expressed strong concerns about the environmental performance of our products or manufacturing operations?

- Do we envision regulatory changes or new standards that will influence our ability to profitably produce, distribute, and support our products?

Environmental posture

- Do our environmental policy and mission statement support the practice of DFE?

- Are we prepared to shift from a compliance-driven to a proactive environmental management strategy (or have we already done so)?

- Have we established corporate or divisional environmental improvement goals?

- How might our DFE initiative relate to existing industry programs (e.g., Responsible Care)?

- What is the overall impact of environmental excellence upon our company or industry image?

Organization characteristics

- Are we planning (or have we begun) to implement an environmental management system (EMS) that is well integrated with our existing management systems?

- Do we practice concurrent (simultaneous) engineering in our new-product development, using cross-functional teams?

- Do we have a system for managing product and process quality that can be extended to incorporate environmental attributes?

- Do we have the right organizational resources in line positions to support environmental and product stewardship?

- Do we have appropriate accountability and reward systems to provide incentives for meeting environmental improvement goals?

Existing experience

- What accomplishments have we made in "green" design, and what practical issues and barriers have we encountered?

- Have we performed any life-cycle assessments for products and/or facilities?

- Have we established programs and expertise in material recycling, resource conservation, waste reduction, or asset recovery?

- Have we implemented any initiatives in pollution prevention and environmentally conscious manufacturing?
- Have we attempted to introduce environmental quality measurement and management systems into our operations?
- Have we developed any useful enabling technologies for DFE, such as computer-based modeling or decision support tools?

Strategic goals

- Can we describe a business case that indicates DFE will contribute to our profitability or business development?
- Can we identify desirable environmental improvements in specific products or processes?
- Have we considered key partnerships or alliances with suppliers or customers that are needed to pursue DFE opportunities?
- Is it valuable for us to enhance environmental awareness among our employees, customers, suppliers, communities, or other stakeholders?
- Are we prepared to move toward life-cycle environmental accounting systems that use an activity-based structure to reveal "true" costs and benefits?

Many of the above themes are addressed in the following chapters. In particular, Part 3 of this book describes the experiences of 10 leading U.S. companies that have addressed these challenges successfully.

DFE Examples

The following two design scenarios illustrate the application of DFE to a product design decision and a process design decision, respectively.[10] Although fictitious, they reflect realistic technological alternatives based on actual case histories.

Consumer electronic product design

This example illustrates how DFE principles could be applied during the design of a consumer electronic product for global markets. Because of European take-back regulations, the design team must be concerned with the design issues that affect the end-of-life costs, including product disassembly and recovery of high-value materials and components. The team has two primary design goals: to minimize the product's total life-cycle cost and to increase the recycled-material content of the product.

The design team has identified several opportunities to accomplish their goals. First, they will reduce the number of different materials that are used in the product. This results in several benefits:

- Reduced raw material costs associated with purchases of higher volumes of fewer materials
- Reduced inventory requirements
- Lower labor costs for material separation at end of life
- Increased material salvage value associated with higher volumes and reduced handling and transaction costs

The design team has also identified a recycled material for the product housing that satisfies all engineering requirements, although it is modestly more expensive than the alternative virgin material. As a related benefit, this new material can again be recycled, increasing the product's overall recyclability.

Comparing the life-cycle costs associated with the new design with those for the original design highlights the economic benefits (see Table 1.1). A cost saving of $30 per unit, while seemingly modest, translates to millions of dollars over the life of the product.

Heat-transfer process design

This second DFE example applies similar concepts to the design of a process in a manufacturing facility. A company is reviewing options for replacing heat-transfer fluids that are used in injection-molding applications. Currently, heat-transfer fluids are purchased on the basis of the requirements of the application, product availability, and initial purchase cost. Worker concerns about adverse health impacts, recent product price increases, and the availability of several new products have motivated the company to reevaluate heat-transfer fluids. In selecting a heat-transfer fluid, the company has the following goals:

TABLE 1.1   Summary of Product Design Improvements

	Original design	New design
Costs per unit		
Material inputs	$100	$110
Manufacturing and assembly	$150	$150
Sales and service	$50	$50
Disassembly	$35	$15
Salvage value	($20)	($40)
Total life-cycle cost	$315	$285
Recycled content	25%	60%

- Minimize the total life-cycle costs
- Decrease the volume of heat-transfer fluids incinerated or land-filled
- Reduce adverse impacts to worker health

Heat-transfer fluids typically have different purchase costs, disposal costs, and useful lives. In addition, because of fundamental differences in their physical and chemical characteristics, the operating and maintenance costs (e.g., inspection costs, system repair costs, and worker training costs) can also differ.

Table 1.2 illustrates an analysis of several alternative types of fluid. While prefluorinated fluids are more costly initially, they have a longer expected lifetime (35 years), lower operating and maintenance costs, and much lower disposal costs (since they are recyclable) than other alternatives. These lower costs more than make up for the initial capital costs incurred to modify the heat exchangers. This life-cycle cost perspective shows that, on an annualized basis, prefluorinated fluids have significantly lower costs.

There are environmental benefits as well. Because prefluorinated fluids can be recycled, their use virtually eliminates the need to landfill or incinerate spent material. Furthermore, they are inert, nonhazardous, and nontoxic, thus minimizing concerns about risks to workers' health and potential environmental liabilities.

Using This Book

This book describes the basic principles of DFE, and outlines the steps necessary to make DFE a practical component of integrated product development. For those companies who see the wisdom of DFE, and wish to embark on a new path, this book provides a guide to the design and development of environmentally responsible products and processes. Consider it a road map to sustainable development.

Part 1, "Answering the Call," describes the emergence of corporate environmental consciousness in the United States, including the transition from regulatory compliance to environmental stewardship and

TABLE 1.2 Comparison of Alternative Heat-Transfer Fluids

	Capital and acquisition costs	Operating and maintenance costs	Disposal costs	Life-cycle costs	Annual (PV)
Mineral oil	$275	$4,531	$130	$4,936	$3,705
Aromatic hydrocarbon	$750	$6,023	$113	$6,886	$2,769
Prefluorinated fluid	$18,500	$4,344	$1	$22,845	$2,369

the recent flurry of voluntary environmental programs sponsored by government, industry, or both.

Part 2, "Seeing the Forest," describes the concepts and methodology of DFE, including performance metrics, guidelines, and supporting tools, and explains how DFE fits within the broader paradigm of concurrent engineering for new-product development.

Part 3, "Walking the Talk," consists of a collection of contributed chapters from some of the best-known environmentally progressive companies in the United States, each describing their approach to DFE and the lessons that they have learned.

Part 4, "Charting the Course," concludes with contributions from experts in a number of different professional fields, providing a glimpse into the future of DFE from the perspectives of management, law, industrial ecology, and global product stewardship.

Readers familiar with the background in Part 1 may wish to read only Chap. 2 and then skip directly to Part 2, which sets forth the important principles and practices of DFE.

References

1. R. A. Frosch and N. E. Gallopoulos, "Strategies for Manufacturing," *Scientific American,* September 1989, pp. 144–152.
2. Carnegie Mellon University, Department of Social and Decision Sciences, *Design Issues in Waste Management,* Pittsburgh, PA, December 1991.
3. Walley and B. Whitehead, "It's Not Easy Being Green," *Harvard Business Review,* May 1994, pp. 46–52.
4. American Electronics Association, "The Hows and Whys of Design for Environment," Washington, DC, November 1992.
5. J. Fiksel, "Design for Environment: The New Quality Imperative," *Corporate Environmental Strategy,* vol. 1, no. 3, December 1993.
6. W. J. Peet and K. J. Hladik, "Organizing for Global Product Development," *Electronic Business,* March 6, 1989, pp. 62–64.
7. World Commission on Environment and Development, *Our Common Future,* Oxford University Press, 1987.
8. E. Lowe, "Industrial Ecology, an Organizing Framework for Environmental Management," *Total Quality Environmental Management,* vol. 3, no. 1, Autumn 1993.
9. H. E. Daly, "The Perils of Free Trade," *Scientific American,* November 1993, pp. 50–57.
10. Office of Technology Assessment, *Green Products by Design: Choices for a Cleaner Environment,* OTA-E-541, October 1992, p. 116.
11. J. Fiksel and K. Wapman, "How to Design for Environment and Minimize Life Cycle Costs," *Proc. IEEE Symposium on Electronics and the Environment,* San Francisco, CA, May 1994.

Answering the Call:
The Green Frontier

2

Motivating Forces

Joseph Fiksel

"The stewardship of the environment is a domain on the near side of metaphysics where all reflective persons can surely find common ground....An enduring environmental ethic will aim to preserve not only the health and freedom of our species, but access to the world in which the human spirit was born."

EDWARD O. WILSON
The Diversity of Life[1]

A Rediscovery of Ancient Values

In the latter decades of this remarkable twentieth century, the relationship of humans to the environment has become a prominent subject in our social dialogue. Some trace the origins of this awareness to the publication of *Silent Spring* by Rachel Carson.[2] Many other writers and political figures have contributed to the rising tide of environmental consciousness. For example, E. F. Schumacher preached a new humanistic economics in *Small Is Beautiful*.[3] Theodore Roszak decried our alienation from nature in *Where the Wasteland Ends*.[4] Barry Commoner, in a series of books, argued persuasively for the development of new industrial technologies based on an understanding of ecological principles. Many of those who listened to these voices have now grown up to occupy positions of power and leadership. Today, interest groups such as the Environmental Defense Fund and the Natural

Resources Defense Council have developed considerable influence and lobbying power. In fact, an opposition movement has sprung up as a sort of "backlash" against these environmentalist factions.[5]

While it sometimes has a fanatical ring, the passion of the environmental movement appears to be genuine, born from a profound realization of our intimate connections with the ecosystem that surrounds us. In fact, environmentalists are simply rediscovering an ancient mode of thought that can be traced back to the pagan beliefs of early civilizations. Ancient peoples revered the land and respected other creatures. Our "western" culture has taken a considerable detour in its cognitive development, increasingly dominated in the centuries since the Renaissance by a philosophical and scientific tradition that viewed the universe as an orderly mechanism which we could analyze logically and conquer through our intellectual powers. The seventeenth-century philosopher Descartes' famous utterance, "I think, therefore I am," is perhaps the ultimate denial of our biological origins.

As twentieth-century scientists progressed beyond the tidy theories of Newtonian physics, and began to probe the mysteries of quantum physics, they acquired humility and in some cases became downright spiritual. For example, Fritjof Capra, the physicist turned philosopher who authored the renowned book *The Tao of Physics,* wrote the following description of a "systems view" of life:

> The earth...is a living system; it functions not just *like* an organism but actually seems to *be* an organism—Gaia, a living planetary being. Her properties and activities cannot be predicted from the sum of her parts; every one of her tissues is linked to every other tissue and all of them are mutually independent; her many pathways of communication are highly complex and non-linear; her form has evolved over billions of years and continues to evolve. These observations were made within a scientific context, but they go far beyond science. Like many other aspects of the new paradigm, they reflect a profound ecological awareness that is ultimately spiritual.[6]

Many laypeople have experienced the same sort of revelations. Having been cut off from their organic roots, they experience a great sense of reverence at finding them again.

In his influential book *Earth in the Balance,* Vice President Al Gore aptly describes the crisis of the spirit that has insulated our civilization from environmental awareness. He quotes the words of the American Indian, Chief Seattle, upon ceding his tribal lands to the U.S. government:[7]

> If we sell you our land, remember that the air is precious to us, that the air shares its spirit with all the life that it supports...if we sell you our

land, you must keep it apart and sacred, a place where man can go to taste the wind that is sweetened by the meadow flowers....This we know: the earth does not belong to man, man belongs to the earth. Man did not weave the web of life, he is merely a strand in it.

As history can attest, his message was largely ignored. Those few who foresaw the unfortunate side effects of industrial development—pollution, wilderness destruction, soil erosion—often adopted a Malthusian outlook, predicting catastrophic consequences if we did not mend our ways. Some encouraged a back-to-nature, "small is beautiful" approach as the only means of salvation.

In fact, Malthus' predictions of worldwide famine were incorrect because he did not foresee the incredible impact of technological change upon human productivity. The internal combustion engine, the telephone, the transistor—these and other inventions revolutionized our ability to generate economic value. However, we cannot take false comfort in our ability to pursue unfettered economic growth. Many economists today are acknowledging the need to seek a more sustainable equilibrium. In 1992 a team of global modelers updated the famous Club of Rome study, *The Limits to Growth,* which was released 20 years earlier. They concluded that:[8]

- Pollution and resource usage have already surpassed sustainable levels.

- We need drastic decreases in population growth and material consumption, and increased efficiency of material and energy usage.

- A sustainable society is still technically and economically possible.

While their study methods have been questioned, their conclusions are widely accepted. For example, in Sweden the "Natural Step" Foundation has gained commitment from a large number of major corporations to actively pursue sustainable manufacturing strategies. The PROMISE methodology of life-cycle design has achieved similar successes in The Netherlands. Just as the technological revolution helped mankind to disprove the doomsayers of the past, design for environment will be a key technology that enables our civilization to achieve sustainable development and preserve the best aspects of our present way of life for future generations.

From the DFE perspective, the utopia of the future is not a world of primitive lifestyles and small, independent tribal communities. It is an eco-efficient global village, where anthropogenic waste materials from each industrial process are ingeniously consumed as inputs to other processes, and we maintain a sophisticated, carefully designed balance with the natural resources that surround us.

The Global Agenda

To better understand the origins of DFE, we need to examine the global changes in environmental consciousness that swept through the international community over the last decade. The Earth Summit of 1992 (officially known as the United Nations Conference on Environment and Development) was a landmark event that represented the culmination of many years of discussion and debate in various nations. The dimensions of the debate at the 1992 summit, held in Rio de Janeiro, transcended national and industrial boundaries, touching upon issues such as export of pollution to developing countries, international equity of environmental regulations, and sustainability of population and industrial growth in the face of limited planetary resources.[9] A number of agreements about international cooperation were produced at the Rio summit, along with voluminous documentation. For purposes of this book, there are a few fundamental principles worth noting among the 27 principles of the Rio Declaration (the numbering is this author's).

1. Development today must not undermine the development and environment needs of present and future generations.

2. Nations shall use the precautionary approach to protect the environment. Where there are threats of serious or irreversible damage, scientific uncertainty shall not be used to postpone cost-effective measures to prevent environmental degradation.

3. In order to achieve sustainable development, environmental protection shall constitute an integral part of the development process, and cannot be considered in isolation from it.

4. The polluter should, in principle, bear the cost of pollution.

Principle 1 summarizes the basic tenet of sustainable development, that we should not compromise the quality of life for our descendants. This principle is as indisputable as "motherhood and apple pie," and is the foundation for most of the subsequent principles.

Principle 2 suggests a conservative posture toward uncertain environmental impacts, and we have already seen this posture manifested in regulatory responses to issues such as carcinogens in food products and, more recently, global climate change, i.e., the warming effect of CFCs and other "greenhouse gases." This principle is closely tied to traditional "command and control" notions of environmental protection, and has often been resisted by the business community for justifiable reasons. There are numerous examples of regulation which erred on the side of caution.

Principle 3 articulates the seeds of a new approach, wherein environmental concerns are *integrated* into the development process. This

book argues that the *only* way to meet the other principles in an economically viable fashion is to accomplish such an integration at the
earliest stages of product and process development.

Principle 4 represents the "stick" which has forced many reluctant
businesspeople to confront environmental issues. The threat of government decisionmakers assigning pollution taxes to selected industrial sectors is certainly a forceful "wake-up call." When the Clinton
administration floated a proposal for a "carbon tax" in 1993, it resulted in vociferous lobbying on the part of industries that felt they would
be unfairly penalized. Although that proposal was eventually
quashed, there are many similar approaches gaining support in other
nations, including extension of the notion of producer responsibility to
waste recovery, and "product take-back" regulations.

Max Baucus, Chairman of the Senate Committee on Environment
and Public Works, gave a glimpse of future legislative trends in the
United States when he stated in 1993:

> "The cornerstone of my strategy rests on the principle that...anyone who
> sells a product should also be responsible for the product when it becomes
> waste. Thus, the costs associated with collecting, sorting, transporting,
> reprocessing, recycling and returning materials back into commerce can
> be internalized and reflected in the price of the product." Indeed, another
> document from the Rio summit, Agenda 21, lays out a blueprint for
> implementing the "polluter pays" principle.

To reduce the rate of solid and hazardous waste generated, it recommends setting targets for specific waste reductions in industrial
processes and promotion of "cleaner" production methods as well as
recycling of wastes. It also recommends government support for
research and development into environmentally sound technologies in
order to stimulate businesses to practice sustainable development.
This is exactly the approach taken by the U.S. government through a
program administered by the Advanced Research Projects Agency
(ARPA), and the U.S. Congress has passed legislation to establish a
more formal funding program for environmental technologies.

The Response of Industry

The sweeping goals of Agenda 21 were accompanied by equally ambitious estimates of multi-billion-dollar investments required by developed nations to support the agenda. However, apart from any government subsidies and incentives, there has been a quiet revolution in
industry attitudes toward the environmental issues raised in Rio. A
significant factor in this revolution was the formation of the Business
Council on Sustainable Development (BCSD), an international group
of business leaders formed in 1990 to develop a global perspective on

sustainable development (see Chap. 3). Their book, *Changing Course,* is an important manifesto describing the both the challenges and the opportunities for profitability associated with sustainable development.[10]

As shown in Chap. 4, sustainable development is a logical outgrowth of industry practices, such as resource conservation and environmental stewardship, that have been ongoing for years. More recently, there has been an upsurge in pollution prevention and waste minimization among leading manufacturing firms, such as AT&T and 3M. These efforts seek to replace "end-of-pipe" pollution control methods with more cost effective process design changes, such as reducing the quantities of toxic materials used or produced as by-products. What is new is the elevation of these concepts to a level of strategic importance unprecedented in the past. Environmental issues, long considered peripheral, have rapidly entered the mainstream of business strategic thinking.

The leading firms that leaped onto the environmental bandwagon are captained by visionaries who believe in a sustainable and profitable future. In North America, these enlightened individuals include Samuel Johnson of SC Johnson Wax, Frank Popoff of Dow Chemical (author of Chap. 22), and Maurice Strong of Ontario Hydro. But visionaries are always a minority, and only when their vision proves credible do the more pragmatic members of the community begin to pay attention. In the space of only a few years, the awakening of environmental responsibility has spread phenomenally. There are good reasons for this—companies are receiving strong signals from all of their stakeholders that environmental stewardship is an essential business function. The driving forces that influence the adoption of DFE by corporations, illustrated in Fig. 2.1, include the following:

- *Customer awareness:* Retail customers are increasingly concerned about the environmental quality of the products that they use, and

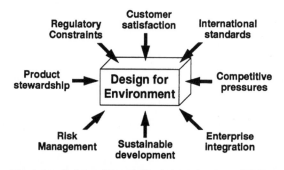

Figure 2.1   Driving forces influencing adoption of DFE.

major corporations are beginning to systematically review the environmental performance of their suppliers.

- *Eco-labeling programs:* A number of eco-labeling initiatives, which rate the environmental sensitivity of products, have arisen both in the United States and abroad (see Chap. 3), and the European Union is moving toward an eco-labeling standard.

- *Product differentiation:* Product designs that consider environmental issues will generally be superior in terms of elegance, energy efficiency, and cost of ownership, and can frequently sway a purchase decision if price and performance are comparable.

- *Profitability improvement:* A "green" approach to the design of products and processes can have a significant impact on product line profitability through savings in manufacturing and other operating costs, as well as through increased market share.

- *Regulatory pressures:* Both in the United States and abroad, government regulations regarding the environmental impacts of products and production processes are becoming more stringent, especially as regards the disposal and recycling of products at the end of their useful life (see Chap. 3).

- *International standards:* Many leading U.S. manufacturers are participating in a worldwide effort, coordinated by the International Organization for Standardization (ISO), to establish standards for environmental stewardship over the full product life cycle (see Chap. 3).

- *Employee satisfaction:* Employees and their families are increasingly conscious of their responsibility to the environment, and incorporation of such values into business activities contributes to their positive feelings about their workplace.

Perhaps the most important factor in changing industry attitudes has been the realization that paying attention to environmental responsibility can actually increase profitability. Reducing pollution at the source and designing products and processes in ways that enhance environmental quality generally result in higher productivity and reduced operating costs, and may also increase market share.

References

1. E. O. Wilson, *The Diversity of Life,* HarperCollins, New York, 1992.
2. R. Carson, *Silent Spring,* Houghton Mifflin, Boston, 1962.
3. E. F. Schumacher, *Small Is Beautiful,* Harper & Row, New York, 1973.
4. T. Roszak, *Where the Wasteland Ends,* Doubleday, New York, 1972.
5. Dixie Lee Ray with Lou Guzzo, *Environmental Overkill; Whatever Happened to Common Sense?* Harper Collins, New York, 1993.

6. F. Capra, *The Turning Point,* Simon and Schuster, New York, 1982, p. 285.
7. D. H. Meadows, D. L. Meadows, and J. Randers, *Beyond the Limits,* Chelsea Green Publishing Company, Post Mills, VT, 1992.
8. Stephan Schmidheiny with the Business Council on Sustainable Development, *Changing Course: A Global Business Perspective on Development and the Environment,* MIT Press, Cambridge, MA, 1992.
9. Al Gore, *Earth in the Balance: Ecology and the Human Spirit,* Houghton Mifflin, Boston, 1993.
10. M. Keating, *Agenda for Change,* Centre for Our Common Future, Geneva, 1993.

3

Towards Sustainable Development

Joseph Fiksel

"Treat the earth well. It was not given to you by your parents. It was lent to you by your children."

Kenyan proverb

Introduction

The dramatic emergence of the concept of sustainable development and the bold adoption of this concept by the business community marked the first wave in a transformation of industry attitudes toward environmental responsibility. This first wave was essentially an awakening of environmental awareness. The second wave, which began in the first half of the 1990s, involves a codification of principles—a vital prerequisite to the realization of any vision. In order for businesses to embrace environmental responsibility, they need to establish standards of performance and codes of practice.

This chapter describes how organizations around the world are grappling with this challenge. Having seen the light, they are now attempting to write down the gospel truths. Unsurprisingly, this turns out to be no easy exercise. Among the many nations and communities of the world, there is a wide diversity of views on what it means to be environmentally responsible, sustainable, or eco-efficient.

How Clean Is Green?*

In the days when environmental risk management was the prevailing paradigm, government and business officials frequently debated the question "How clean is clean?" This alludes to the difficult problem of setting contaminant limits in environmental remediation, when such limits may be measured in parts per billion. Assuming that the objective of cleanup is to limit human health risk or ecological risk, then the above question translates to "What level of residual risk can we accept?" Since zero risk is virtually impossible, some cutoff point was needed to avoid spending absurd amounts for pollution control and cleanup. For example, the U.S. Environmental Protection Agency (EPA) has often used the level of a 1 in 1 million lifetime risk of cancer as a regulatory threshold. One of the most frustrating aspects of dealing with the "How clean is clean?" question has been our inability to measure low levels of risk empirically. Instead, risk analysis practitioners are compelled to use dubious mathematical extrapolations (see Chap. 9), so that measuring "cleanness" became a somewhat hypothetical exercise.

Today, a similar question arises in a different context: namely, "How green is green?" The appellation "green" is often associated with extreme political views, but when applied to a product or a company it connotes environmental responsibility. However, "greenness" is even more difficult to measure than risk; in fact, it is a multidimensional set of characteristics that include risks, consumption rates, and many other less quantifiable attributes. The bewildering field of ecolabeling is discussed later in this chapter, and Chap. 7 discusses how companies have dealt with the challenges of environmental performance measurement. Establishing meaningful standards of comparison for competing products is even more daunting than comparing hypothetical risks.

Finally, a new riddle can be posed: namely, "How clean is green?" In other words, when we speak of "green" design or "clean" manufacturing, what level of pollution or waste reduction should we strive for? There are definitely two camps. Some believe that zero waste is an attainable goal, as demonstrated in cases of industrial symbiosis where one firm's wastes are another firm's feedstocks (see Chap. 26). Others argue that by the laws of thermodynamics we can only prolong, but not prevent, the inevitable progress of entropy which causes

---

*Although the words "green" and "clean" do occasionally appear in this book, they are best avoided because of their colloquial usage. Once the advertising and public relations community adopts a word, it may as well be deleted from science and engineering texts. Therefore, we prefer more precise terms such as "eco-efficient" and "sustainable," which, at least for the present, are less susceptible to misuse.

matter to decay into waste. In either case, companies are increasingly forced to confront this question as they deliberate over what voluntary goals to set for future reductions in emissions and waste.

Governmental Initiatives and Partnerships

A promising emergent theme in the environmental management arena is the increasing willingness of governments and industry groups to enter into voluntary collaboration for purposes of environmental improvement. The traditional "command and control" approach of regulatory agencies has been burdensome and ineffective, while experiments with voluntary initiatives have proved extremely successful.

Toxic Release Inventory (TRI)

One motivation for the rise in voluntary programs may have been the surprising response of industry to the EPA's Toxic Release Inventory (TRI) reporting requirements, under Title III of the Superfund Amendments and Reauthorization Act (SARA). By merely requiring companies to report their hazardous material releases to the public, the EPA gave managers an incentive to reduce them. Before long, companies had established TRI reduction as a standard corporate objective, and overall releases decreased by roughly 40% from the baseline year of 1988 through 1992. This clearly demonstrated the power of measuring environmental performance (see Chap. 7). In 1994, the EPA announced plans to widen the scope of the TRI program, including doubling the number of substances tracked and extending the requirements to nonmanufacturing sectors and federal facilities.

Pollution Prevention Act

This 1990 legislation directed the EPA to develop a national pollution prevention strategy, which is administered by the Office of Pollution Prevention and Toxics (OPPT). The act set forth the well-known "pollution prevention hierarchy," which recommends first trying source reduction, then recycling, and finally waste treatment as alternatives to disposal. It also encouraged a multimedia, life-cycle approach that would cut across EPA's traditional regulatory programs. Chapter 23 describes at length the OPPT's pioneering Design for Environment program, which is based completely on voluntary partnerships.

Since then, a host of innovative programs have been launched by the EPA and other agencies that rely mainly on industry cooperation rather than regulatory coercion. The following are examples of other governmental initiatives that have produced significant environmental benefits.

Voluntary programs and marketplace incentives

Green Lights.   Possibly the best-known environmental program in the United States, the EPA's Green Lights program is predicated upon the environmental value of energy efficiency. Energy conservation is one of the most attractive approaches to pollution prevention, because it is both easy to implement and results in direct cost savings. According to the EPA, every kilowatt-hour of electricity not used prevents the emission of 1.5 lb of CO_2, 5.8 g of SO_2, and 2.5 g of No_x. Companies enroll in the Green Lights program by committing to installing energy-efficient lighting at their facilities.

The EPA has launched other similar programs, including Green Buildings, which encourages energy-efficient equipment use, and Golden Carrot, which sponsored a competition for an energy-efficient refrigerator (won by Whirlpool).

Energy Star.   The EPA developed this program to encourage energy conservation in electronic devices. It sets maximum power levels for devices such as personal computers, and requires automatic power-down features. Products which meet the requirements have the right to display an Energy Star logo. The program has been extremely successful, especially since the federal government has incorporated Energy Star into its procurement guidelines.

Climate Wi$e and Waste Wi$e.   Climate Wise and Waste Wi$e are voluntary programs developed by the EPA to reduce greenhouse gas emissions and municipal solid waste, respectively. Participants have achieved significant cost savings through greater efficiency.

Environmental Leadership Program.   This EPA program is a voluntary initiative that invites manufacturing firms to apply for recognition by the agency as an environmental leader. Companies that apply must satisfy a number of criteria, including the existence of a DFE program. Related EPA initiatives include Project XL and the Common Sense Initiative.

33/50.   This voluntary EPA program encouraged companies to commit to reducing their TRI releases of 17 selected toxic substances an average of 33% by the year 1993, and 50% by the year 1995. Over 400 companies have signed up for the program, representing a reduction commitment of about 335 million lb of industrial toxics.

CONEG challenge.   The Coalition of Northeastern Governors (CONEG) issued a challenge to the Fortune 200 manufacturing organizations to identify how much packaging material they used annually, set voluntary targets for reduction, and report back annually on their progress. Initially, only 29 companies accepted the challenge.

Environmentally preferable products.   In October 1993, President Clinton issued an executive order directing federal agencies to purchase "environmentally preferable" products, and assigned the EPA the task of issuing guidance on how to identify such products. In February of 1994, the EPA issued a concept paper which set forth a general framework for defining *environmentally preferable*. This paper expressed two core principles: that key environmental attributes of products must be disclosed, and that product evaluation should adopt a holistic, life-cycle approach.

Subsequently, in April of 1994, the EPA recommended procurement guidelines for purchases of recycled-content products. The list of products includes engine coolants, construction materials, paperboard, plastic pipe, geotextiles, cement and concrete, carpet, floor tiles, traffic cones, running tracks, mulch, and office supplies. Obviously, the purchasing clout of the federal government provides a strong incentive for manufacturers to "green" their products.

International Environmental Standards

Along with the government initiatives described above, a major motivation for DFE has been the emergence of international standards that prescribe how companies should manage their environmental performance. Although compliance with such standards is voluntary, companies generally cannot afford to ignore them. The forerunner of these environmental standards was the ISO 9000 series of quality management standards, which have achieved remarkable worldwide success. Certification under ISO 9000 has become a *sine qua non* for international trade in industrial goods. Industrial customers feel secure in knowing that their suppliers' quality practices are certified, and therefore feel less obliged to audit them carefully. While certification involves some costs, the end result is greater productivity for all concerned.

A similar rationale holds for the development of environmental standards. To the extent that companies are concerned about their own environmental performance, they will also want assurance that their suppliers are practicing environmental stewardship and pollution prevention. Certification, in theory, provides an efficient means for verifying a company's commitment to environmental management. However, it is important to note that, as in ISO 9000, certification cannot guarantee the actual *level* of performance, but only the existence of a management system designed to enhance that *level*.

The scope of environmental standards is far broader and more complex than that of quality standards. While the latter relate only to the quality of deliverable products, the former span all of the interactions between a company, its physical environment, and its stakeholders, including customers, stockholders, regulators, suppliers, communities, interest groups, and employees. Moreover, cultural attitudes, policies, and legal requirements regarding environmental protection vary greatly from one nation to another. Therefore, the challenges of achieving international consensus on an ISO 9000–like standard should not be underestimated.

Table 3.1 provides a partial list of emerging standards and regulations in various countries. Several of the more prominent initiatives are discussed below.

International Organization for Standardization (ISO) TC207

In 1991, the ISO formed the Strategic Advisory Group on the Environment (SAGE) to consider whether it should pursue the development of environmental management standards (known as Series 14000). The response of SAGE was affirmative, resulting in the formation of Technical Committee 207 (TC207). This committee has, in turn, established several working groups to address different aspects of standards, including:

- Environmental management systems
- Environmental performance evaluation
- Environmental auditing
- Eco-labeling
- Life-cycle analysis
- Environmental aspects of product standards

One area of controversy in standards development is the issue of information disclosure. Many companies are concerned about protecting the confidentiality of environmental performance data that are collected for internal management purposes. If the existence of such data is known, it may be difficult to resist their disclosure to regulatory agencies or the public.

British Standards Institute (BS 7750)

In the United Kingdom, the BS 7750 standard was published in March 1992, and has already gained a strong following. Analogous to quality standards such as ISO 9000, BS 7750 does not set levels of compliance, but merely prescribes the process elements needed for environmental management. Figure 3.1 illustrates these process elements as well as the successive stages of environmental management systems (EMS) implementation that companies are expected to follow.

TABLE 3.1 Examples of International Environmental Initiatives

Country	Description of initiative	Date
United States	EPA—Clean Air Act: Eliminate ozone-depleting chemicals.	5/15/93
United States	EPA—Energy Star: Energy efficiency for electronic devices.	6/17/93
United States	State laws (12) on toxic heavy metals: Maximum of 100 ppm of lead, mercury, cadmium, or hexavalent chromium in packaging.	Compliance by 1994
Unites States, Germany, European Union, Norway, Japan, Sweden	Battery take-back or disposal laws: Bans, restriction, labeling, or take-back laws.	1993
Germany, France, Austria	Packaging take-back: Transport, intermediate, and sales packaging; "green dot" Duales System in Germany.	January 1993
Germany	Draft Electronic Waste Ordinance: Product take-back and recycling.	Probably 1995
Germany, European Union	Eco-labeling for environmental friendliness based on specified product and process criteria.	Proposal made in 1992
Denmark	Action Plan for Waste and Recycling (voluntary).	End of 1994
Sweden	Ecocycle Bill: Producer responsibility for eco-efficiency in resource usage.	January 1994
The Netherlands	Take-back and recycling legislation for white and brown goods.	January 1995
United Kingdom	BSI 7750: Certification for environmental management systems similar to ISO 9000.	Mid-1993
United Kingdom	GS13 British Telecom spec: Similar to BS 7750.	1992
European Union	Eco-audit: Similar to ISO 9000 and BS 7750.	1997?
European Union	EC Directive 91/C 46/08: Ban on polybrominated diphenyl ethers (PBDEs), polybromobiphenyls, polybromodiphenyls, dioxins, or dibenzofuranes in plastic parts.	1/1/95
European Union, Sweden	Bans and/or restrictions on heavy metal content: cadmium, selenium, mercury, chromium, lead.	1993
Canada	A requirement to sell to government agencies; part of the procurement specifications.	1993

Figure 3.1 Stages of environmental management systems (EMS) implementation and required elements per BS 7750.

Influenced by the U.K. experience, a host of other countries, including Canada, Ireland, France, The Netherlands, and South Africa, have developed their own national standards for EMS which are very similar to BS 7750. Moreover, the European Union plans to implement its European Eco-Management and Audit Scheme (EMAS) in 1995 on a voluntary basis. It is expected to resemble BS 7750 in many respects.

Canadian Standards Association (CSA)

The Canadian Standards Association (CSA) has been active in promulgating standards for environmental improvement and in coordinating dialogue among government, industry, and citizens' groups in Canada. In 1994 the CSA issued a new draft EMS standard, as well as a draft DFE standard. The latter sets forth a series of core principles analogous to the major guidelines presented in Chap. 8, and then, corresponding to each core principle, provides a series of questions that designers should consider for each stage of the product life cycle.

Japanese initiatives

In 1989 the Japanese government established a Council of Ministers for Global Environmental Conservation, which established broad policy goals and gave rise to a host of follow-up initiatives by individual ministries. In 1993, a new Basic Environmental Law was passed which introduced the concept of "environmental load" as a measure of sustainability. There has been a flurry of activity in Japanese companies addressing the use of DFE and life-cycle analysis techniques, and Japanese representatives have been active participants in the ISO TC207 process.

Product Eco-labeling: Caveat Emptor

A contributing factor to the ascendancy of DFE is the proliferation of eco-labeling initiatives in the developed countries. While it remains unclear how consumers will respond to them, many manufacturers are concerned about the potential marketing advantages or detriments associated with eco-labels.

One area of concern is the potential for restraint of trade. For example, the European Union (EU) has issued a set of eco-labeling requirements which could substantially impede the sale of foreign products in Europe. They require products to be manufactured by a state of the art process and to comply with EU regulations. It is unclear whether the forthcoming ISO standard will emulate this approach or adopt a less stringent posture.

In addition, many countries have developed their own eco-labeling programs, as illustrated in Fig. 3.2. The burden of complying with all of their differing requirements is certainly a disincentive to manufacturers. Some are hopeful that a universal standard will emerge, perhaps from ISO, that will serve to "harmonize" all of these different labels. It remains to be seen whether individual nations will be prepared to cooperate with such a harmonization process.

A recent EPA survey of eco-labeling identified five major categories of programs:[1]

■ Seal of approval	Identifies products as being environmentally responsible without specifying details (e.g., Blue Cross)
■ Single-attribute certification	Provides independent verification of a particular environmental performance measure
■ Report card	Provides information about a comprehensive set of environmental performance measures (e.g., Green Cross)
■ Information disclosure	Imposes mandatory requirements for disclosing environmental impact data
■ Hazard warnings	Imposes mandatory requirements for providing information about product hazards

Among the first three categories, there is much debate about whether consumers are willing and able to make informed choices about prod-

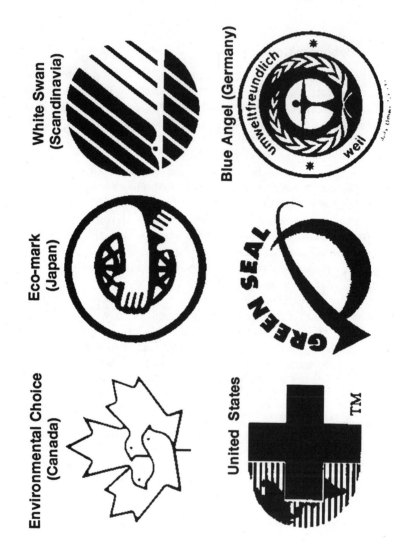

Figure 3.2 Examples of eco-labels.

ucts based on quantification of unfamiliar environmental metrics. At the same time, the U.S. Federal Trade Commission (FTC) has introduced environmental marketing guidelines to prevent confusion among consumers regarding "green" marketing claims.

While consumer values may be one motivation for DFE, it is a mistake to view DFE as synonymous with green marketing. In particular, many of the goals of DFE relate to efficiency of resource usage in manufacturing and distribution, in which case the benefits will accrue mainly to the producer, not the consumer. Thus, DFE is valuable as an integral part of product and process design, whether or not marketing managers decide that they want to convey an environmental "message" about benefits to their customers.

References

1. U.S. Environmental Protection Agency, *Status Report on the Use of Environmental Labels Worldwide*, EPA 742-R-9-93-001, Washington, DC, September 1993.

4

Corporate Environmental Responsibility

Joseph Fiksel

"Anticipating the coming industrial transformation and rethinking corporate roles on a large scale—the relationships to other firms, to customers and to society and the planet as a whole—can help companies to survive and thrive as agents of sustainable development."

Xerox Corporation advertisement

The Evolutionary Ladder

The activities of the Business Council for Sustainable Development (BCSD) described in Chap. 2 represent the initiatives of a small vanguard of progressive corporations. In terms of attitudes toward environmental responsibility, the rest of the business world falls along a broad spectrum ranging from apathetic to passionate. A prominent consulting firm recently estimated the distribution of worldwide companies among three categories that represent different stages of evolution:[1]

- 10 to 15% are in stage 1, characterized as *Problem Solving*. These companies have a traditional, reactive approach to environmental problems, and view regulatory compliance as a burdensome cost of doing business.

- 70 to 80% are in stage 2, characterized as *Managing for Compliance.* These companies attempt to be more effective in coordinating their environmental management efforts, but are still mainly compliance-oriented.

- 10 to 15% are in stage 3, characterized as *Managing for Assurance.* These companies are more far-seeing, and have adopted risk management as a rational means of balancing potential future environmental liabilities against costs.

Unfortunately, this classification scheme fails to capture the further evolution that has occurred within leading companies that have moved beyond stage 3. At least two additional stages can be distinguished:

- Stage 4, characterized as *Managing for Eco-efficiency,* includes companies who have recognized that pollution prevention is more cost effective than pollution control, and are seeking opportunities to become more environmentally efficient through waste minimization, source reduction, and other approaches. Notable examples include 3M, Procter & Gamble, and AT&T.

- Stage 5, characterized as *Fully Integrated,* includes companies that have adopted environmental quality as just one dimension of total quality, to be managed in an integrated fashion. It is questionable whether any company today has truly attained stage 5. However, many of the more enlightened stage 4 companies have established this as their ultimate vision, once their senior management has realized that environmental excellence is essential to profitability and competitive advantage.

The challenge of fully integrated environmental management is to discover innovative environmental solutions that maximize profitability and shareholder value. This requires a "paradigm shift" from a focus on controlling pollution and hazardous emissions to a global concern about the entire product life cycle. In this advanced stage of evolution, environmental management at last emerges from the shadows and claims its rightful seat at the corporate decisionmaking table.

From Risk to Reward

Those companies that have climbed the evolutionary ladder described above have experienced great satisfaction at moving away from a risk-based focus on theoretical probabilities to a quality-based focus on concrete, measurable accomplishments. Risk management is essentially a cost avoidance practice, and is peripheral to the core strategy of a manufacturing firm. Quality management, on the other hand, is central to competitive strategy, and those who find creative ways to improve both product quality and environmental performance have found the experience highly rewarding, both intellectually and monetarily.

Figure 4.1 shows, using marginal economic analysis, how the environmental management decisionmaking paradigm has evolved from an initial focus on minimizing liability (stage 3), to a more constructive focus on operating efficiency through pollution prevention (stage 4), and finally to an integrated life-cycle management approach (stage 5):

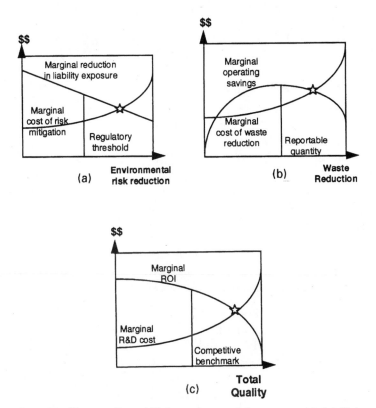

Figure 4.1 The paradigm shift in environmental management. (*a*) Risk management: discretionary spending on waste management and pollution control to achieve an acceptably low level of corporate liability exposure. (*b*) Pollution prevention: opportunistic investment in process improvements to reduce toxic material use, minimize waste, and increase efficiency. (*c*) Life-cycle management: systematic management of assets and design of products and processes to maximize profitability while assuring total life-cycle quality, including environmental quality.

- In stage 3, companies are largely concerned with identifying and mitigating sources of risk that may result in financial liability. They will make risk control expenditures to the extent that the next marginal dollar of expenditure does not exceed the corresponding reduction in potential liability, although the latter is difficult to assess due to the presence of large uncertainties. This approach may lead companies to move "beyond compliance"—for example, if there are significant residual risks associated with emissions that are exempt or below the regulatory threshold.

- In stage 4, companies are largely concerned with identifying opportunities for improving efficiency while reducing waste and emissions. On a case-by-case basis, they will invest in pollution prevention opportunities to the extent that the next marginal dollar of expenditure does not exceed the corresponding savings in operating costs. Eventually they tend to reach a point of diminishing returns where it is not cost effective to continue reducing waste using existing technologies. However, new product and process technologies may change the economics to the point where zero-waste or closed-loop recycling is attainable.

- In stage 5, companies are largely concerned with assuring stakeholder satisfaction and environmental quality over the complete life cycle of their products and facilities. This leads them to move from an opportunistic approach to a systematic approach, with environmental considerations factored into virtually all decisions. In fact, environmental decisionmaking is no longer a separate exercise—it becomes an integral part of business decisionmaking. These companies will invest in additional R&D, including environmental improvements, to the extent that they earn an adequate return on investment. If they are able to leverage their skills and technologies to profitably achieve superior quality, environmental or otherwise, this will constitute a competitive advantage.

The elegance of the stage 5 approach lies in the fact that that waste reduction and risk reduction are natural consequences of a drive toward total quality. The "voice of the customer" and the economic signals of the marketplace will guide the product development process to focus on appropriate targets of opportunity. In this context, designing for the environment has nothing to do with moral righteousness or social altruism. It is just good business sense.

With the above conceptual framework as background, the following sections describe some of the specific initiatives that individual companies and industry associations have taken to realize the stage 5 vision. Additional, more specific accounts of company experiences are provided in Part 3 of this book.

Product Stewardship Programs

The twin concepts of *product stewardship* and *environmental steward-ship* arose from a recognition by companies in the chemical industry and other industries that a defensive posture toward environmental issues no longer made sense. Rather than engaging in continual con-frontations with regulatory agencies and citizen groups, they decided it was important to affirm their values and articulate a constructive approach toward environmental safety and health. The notion of stewardship involves an ethical commitment by businesses to integri-ty and care in the management of their assets and products, extend-ing to all phases of manufacturing and distribution. In the United Kingdom, a similar concept has evolved called "duty of care."

Responsible care

The first industry to develop a comprehensive stewardship program was the chemical industry, under the auspices of the Chemical Manufacturers' Association. In view of the negative publicity sur-rounding the catastrophic Bhopal release and similar incidents around the world, restoration of its credibility and environmental image became an important priority for this industry. As a result, the industry developed the Responsible Care™ program, which has become a model code of practice for industries. The program includes a product stewardship code which enunciates a number of manage-ment principles describing appropriate behavior for companies in both protecting and communicating with their stakeholders. One important principle relevant to DFE is Principle 7—Product and Process Design Improvement, which states that a company wishing to practice product stewardship "establishes and maintains a system that makes health, safety and environmental impacts—including the use of energy and natural resources—key considerations in designing, developing and improving products."

Table 4.1 shows an example of a product stewardship checklist that was developed by DuPont, which the company distributes freely.

Ironically, although the chemical industry was the first to codify the product stewardship concept, chemical manufacturers have been slow to adopt DFE. Many of them are still caught up in the defensive mindset represented by stages 2 and 3 of our evolutionary ladder, and still tend to perceive environmental issues as a net burden on compa-ny resources. Only a few, such as Dow Chemical, have made any prac-tical attempts to move beyond risk management and adopt an inte-grated life-cycle approach to environmental decisionmaking. In contrast, newer industries such as the electronics sector, unencum-bered by historical liabilities, have embraced DFE wholeheartedly.

TABLE 4.1   Product Stewardship Checklist Developed by DuPont

What are the principal safety, health, and environmental (SHE) hazards?

What competitive products may be substituted for ours? What are their SHE hazards? What advantages do we have?

Does the customer have our MSDS and product information?

Product and Packaging Use

How does the customer use the product? For what purpose? Are there unique or new users?

Do any uses or handling raise potential SHE concerns?

Do the customer's employees have access to product information?

Are the customer's employees using recommended personal protective equipment?

Are recommended protective systems, including local ventilation, in place?

Has the customer done workplace monitoring? Should this be done?

Is the product stored properly? Storage tanks labeled? Spill containment facilities, e.g., dikes?

Does the customer have emergency response procedures in place?

What happens to product packaging? Is it reduced, reused, recycled?

Product Issues

Have there been any incidents involving our product? What was learned?

Have allegations been made regarding health effects of the product? Environmental effects?

Any other issues associated with the product?

Product Emissions and Disposal

Does any of the product become waste? Regulated hazardous waste? How is it disposed?

Is any of the product discharged to a wastewater treatment system? What is its fate?

Are there any air emissions from the product's use or disposal? What is their fate?

How do the discharges/emissions affect customer permits, compliance?

How can we continuously reduce all emissions and waste?

Distributor Questions

Does the distributor open and repackage or blend our product? If so, answer all questions above for the distributor.

Does the distributor provide product information to all customers? How do we know this?

Does the distributor visit customers to confirm proper use and disposal?

Other

Can we help in SHE? (waste management and minimization; SHE training)

Does the potential exist for exposure to downstream users of our product? If so, answer first 20 questions in checklist for downstream users.

Another industry with characteristics similar to the chemical industry is the oil and gas industry. In fact, many large oil and gas corporations have chemical divisions and therefore participate in both industries. The American Petroleum Institute framed a program similar to Responsible Care, which they call Strategies for Today's Environmental Partnership (STEP).

Total-quality environmental management

As described in Chap. 1, DFE represents the convergence of two fundamental thrusts, one based on environmental stewardship and the other based on the total-quality management (TQM) movement, in which measurement of progress is a fundamental canon.

When these two fields collided, the result was a blinding revelation: that environmental progress could be obtained in the same way as other performance improvements, that is, by establishing quantitative metrics and rewarding employees for meeting or exceeding targets. Thus was born the practice of *total-quality environmental management* (TQEM). Already a scholarly journal called *TQEM* has been launched, and many other new journals have appeared that address the same general subject.

Total-quality environmental management can be defined as *the identification, assessment, and continuous improvement of environmental attributes that contribute to the total quality of a company's products and operations.* Thus, TQEM is to the TQM process as DFE is to the product development process. Since these processes are closely intertwined in most companies, there is considerable overlap between DFE and TQEM.

An important force in the adoption of TQEM has been the Global Environmental Management Initiative (GEMI), a consortium of leading companies that sponsors an annual conference as well as many task force activities. GEMI has published an environmental self-assessment protocol, and is developing other guidance documents for environmental reporting and green accounting.

Other initiatives

- The Coalition for Environmentally Responsible Economies (CERES) has developed a set of principles for environmental stewardship, which have been endorsed by a number of large companies and many smaller ones. A summary of these principles appears as Table 4.2. The most notable signatories to date are Sun Oil Company and American Electric Power. In addition, GM has announced its adherence to a set of principles which are very close in substance to the CERES principles.

TABLE 4.2   CERES Principles

Protection of the Biosphere
   Eliminate harmful releases
   Safeguard habitats and biodiversity

Sustainable Use of Natural Resources
   Sustain renewables (water, soil, forest)
   Conserve nonrenewables

Reduction and Disposal of Wastes
   Source reduction and recycling
   Safe handling and disposal

Energy Conservation
   Conservation
   Energy efficiency
   Environmentally safe energy sources

Risk Reduction
   Minimize employee and community risks
   Safe technologies, facilities, procedures
   Preparation for emergencies

Safe Products and Services
   Reduce or eliminate environmental damage and safety hazards
   Inform customers about environmental impacts and safe use

Environmental Restoration
   Correct existing hazardous conditions
   Redress injuries or environmental damage

Informing the Public
   Inform those affected by hazardous conditions
   Maintain dialogue with communities
   Do not penalize employees for reporting problems

Management Commitment
   Ensure top management is informed and responsible
   Consider environmental commitment in selecting directors

Audits and Reports
   Conduct annual self-evaluation
   Create environmental audit procedures
   Complete CERES report and make available to public

- In 1991, the International Chamber of Commerce introduced a Business Charter for Sustainable Development (BCSD), which has been endorsed by over 600 companies around the world. These principles are listed in Table 4.3.

The following are examples of other international business consortia or environmental initiatives, which, like BCSD and GEMI, are helping their members work toward sustainable development:

- Corporate EH&S Roundtable
- Industry Cooperative for Ozone Layer Protection (ICOLP)

TABLE 4.3   International Chamber of Commerce Business Charter for Sustainable Development: Principles for Environmental Management

1. Corporate Priority

2. Integrated Management
   Integrate policies, programs, and practices into each business
3. Process of Improvement

4. Employee Education

5. Prior Assessment
   Assess environmental impacts prior to starting a project and prior to decommissioning a site

6. Products and Services
   No undue environmental impact
   Safe in intended use
   Efficient in consumption of energy and resources
   Can be recycled, reused, or safely disposed

7. Customer Advice

8. Facilities and Operations
   Efficient use of energy and materials
   Sustainable use of renewable resources
   Minimization of adverse environmental impact and waste generation
   Safe and responsible disposal of wastes

9. Research

10. Precautionary Approach
    Modify the manufacture, marketing, or use of products or services consistent with scientific understanding to prevent environmental degradation

11. Contractors and Suppliers

12. Emergency Preparedness

13. Transfer of Technology

14. Contributing to the Common Effort

15. Openness to Concerns

16. Compliance and Reporting

- International Network for Environmental Management
- National Association for Environmental Management
- World Environment Center
- World Industry Council for the Environment

In addition, there are many other associations and nonprofit organizations contributing to this powerful movement.

Environmental Reporting

In this age of environmental consciousness, it has become fashionable for companies to issue annual environmental reports. The intended audiences for such reports include stockholders, public interest groups, customers, regulators, and anyone else who takes an interest in environmental issues. Many companies have shifted rapidly from giving almost no mention to the environment in their annual reports to producing glossy, full-color brochures (usually printed on recycled paper) describing their achievements in waste reduction, biodiversity protection, and other aspects of environmental responsibility. These reports are more than propaganda pieces. They represent a meaningful effort to articulate an environmental policy and corresponding corporate environmental objectives and to track progress against these objectives.

Not long ago, most companies were reluctant to disclose any environmental data for fear that it might be misused. However, several regulatory initiatives by the U.S. Environmental Protection Agency (EPA) helped to start the process of disclosure. The right-to-know provisions of Title III of the Superfund Amendments and Reauthorization Act (SARA) required manufacturers to communicate to local communities regarding hazardous materials and safety measures. In addition, as mentioned in Chap. 3, the Toxic Release Inventory (TRI) provisions of SARA forced manufacturers to report any significant quantities of listed substances that they store or use. This simple requirement had the surprising effect of inducing many manufacturers to aggressively reduce their TRI inventories. The mere act of measurement and reporting created incentives for voluntary actions that will ultimately reduce waste and pollution.

With the emergence of TQEM, environmental performance measurement has become a key aspect of environmental management. Many companies have decided that, if they are going to be serious about continuous environmental improvement, they might as well reap the benefits of publicizing their successes. This has led to much debate about what to measure and what to report. In Part 2, we address the question of how to select and apply environmental metrics. When used for internal tracking purposes, metrics are simply useful management tools. However, when used for external reporting, they require more careful consideration of possible misinterpretation or misuse.

In 1993 a group of 10 international companies collaborated on the Public Environmental Reporting Initiative (PERI). They developed a set of guidelines recommending the organization and content of an environmental report. Recommended topics included:

- Company profile (size, scope)
- Environmental policy
- Environmental management (systems, goals)
- Environmental releases (e.g., TRI)

  Emissions by medium and hazardous waste disposition

  Companywide targets for reduction, and progress made

- Environmental risk management (audits, plans)
- Environmental compliance (violations, if any)
- Product stewardship and life-cycle management

  Pollution prevention and design for environment

  Customer and supplier coordination programs

  Employee recognition (incentives)

  Stakeholder involvement (outreach)

The most challenging part of these guidelines is the section on product stewardship and life-cycle management; the guidelines are quite vague about the recommended content. This is the area in which DFE can produce significant benefits, but the art of defining and measuring these benefits is still embryonic.

References

1. J. L. Greeno, "Corporate Environmental Excellence and Stewardship," in R. V. Kolluru (ed.), *Environmental Strategies Handbook,* McGraw-Hill, New York, 1994.

Seeing the Forest:
The Art and
Science of DFE

5

Conceptual Principles of DFE

Joseph Fiksel

"Corporations that achieve ever more efficiency while preventing pollution through good housekeeping, materials substitution, cleaner technologies, and cleaner products and that strive for more efficient use and recovery of resources can be called eco-efficient."

Declaration of the Business Council on Sustainable Development[1]

Eco-efficiency is a term that does not yet appear in dictionaries, but has already gained considerable force in shaping the environmental policies and practices of leading corporations. The Business Council on Sustainable Development (BCSD) sounded a trumpet call with their 1992 manifesto, *"Changing Course."*[1] Because of the credibility of the global companies that constitute BCSD's membership, their message has had a substantial influence on the strategic thinking of company executives around the world. BCSD's concept of eco-efficiency suggests an important link between resource efficiency (which leads to productivity and profitability) and environmental responsibility.

Eco-efficiency makes business sense. Through eliminating waste and using resources more wisely, eco-efficient companies can reduce costs and become more competitive. Moreover, as environmental performance standards become commonplace, eco-efficient companies will gain advantages in penetrating new markets and increasing their share of existing markets. Given this compelling logic, the obvious question is "OK, so how do we become eco-efficient?" To answer that question, this chapter begins to examine the business practices that companies have adopted to increase their eco-efficiency. Later chapters address more detailed questions of how to quantify the eco-efficiency of products and processes.

It is helpful to group the approaches to eco-efficiency suggested by BCSD into three successively broader categories, as shown in Fig. 5.1 and listed below.

1. *Cleaner processes:*   Modifying production processes and technologies so that they generate less pollution and waste. This approach assumes that the product definition is already fixed.

2. *Cleaner products:*   Modifying the design and material composition of products so that they generate less pollution and waste throughout their life cycle. Since manufacturing is but one stage in the life cycle, this approach includes development of cleaner processes, but allows for more fundamental changes in the product itself.

3. *Sustainable resource use:*   Modifying the production system as a whole, including relationships with suppliers and customers, so that fewer material and energy resources are consumed per unit of value produced. Since reduction in pollution and waste is but one way to reduce resource usage, this approach includes cleaner products and processes, but allows for broader technical and economic innovations that are often described as "industrial ecology" (see Chap. 26).

Design for environment (DFE) was defined in Chap. 1 as "systematic consideration of design performance with respect to environmental,

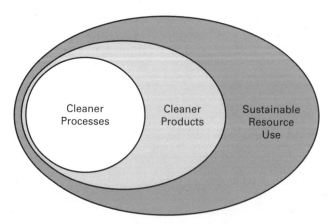

Figure 5.1 Approaches to achieving eco-efficiency.

health, and safety objectives over the full product life cycle." Thus, DFE is a design practice that embraces all three of the BCSD approaches. Moreover, it addresses the traditional concerns of health and safety management, to the extent that they are important product design considerations. In short, *DFE is the design of safe and eco-efficient products.*

Because of this broad definition, the scope of DFE encompasses a variety of disciplines, including environmental risk management, product safety, occupational health and safety, pollution prevention, ecology and resource conservation, accident prevention, and waste management. Figure 5.2 shows a hierarchical breakdown of DFE disciplines, most of which are routinely practiced by manufacturing firms.

Integration of DFE-related disciplines is crucial to successful development of eco-efficient products. Companies that have historically separated their health scientists, environmental engineers, and process safety engineers into different groups are finding it cumbersome to utilize these resources effectively. Such fragmentation will be all the more problematic when the environmental, health, and safety function becomes a participant in fast-moving product development projects. Moreover, these types of specialists need to collaborate with specialists in procurement, manufacturing, service, and other areas as part of an integrated product development team. (See Chap. 6.)

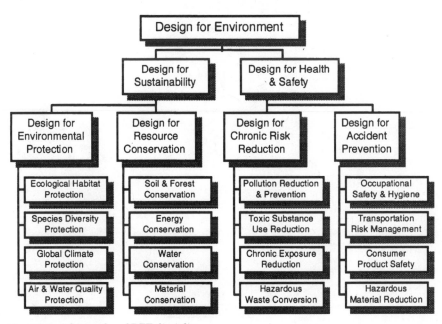

Figure 5.2 A hierarchy of DFE disciplines.

By the same token, an awareness of the product life cycle is critical to the practice of DFE. As shown in Chap. 6, there are many different interpretations of *life cycle,* depending upon what viewpoint is taken—process or product, physical or commercial. Figure 5.3 shows an example of the physical life cycle for durable goods such as refrigerators or personal computers. The flow arrows represent transformation and exchange of materials and energy, while the boxes represent economic agents or processes responsible for these flows. From this perspective, the purpose of DFE is to minimize the flows of energy and materials from the center of the diagram (i.e., depletion of resources), minimize the flow of wastes into the center of the diagram, and maximize the cyclical flow of materials around the perimeter of the diagram.

Cleaner Processes: Pollution Prevention

The pollution prevention movement represents the first significant step along the road to sustainability. In the United States, the Pollution Prevention Act of 1990 has helped to stimulate this movement (see Chap. 3), but a great deal of successful pollution prevention work has been performed by companies on a voluntary basis. The best-known corporate pollution prevention program is the Pollution

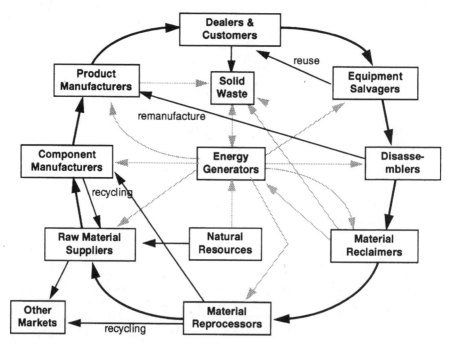

Figure 5.3 An example of a physical life-cycle model for assembled durable products.

Prevention Pays (3P) program conducted by 3M Corporation, described below. Many other similar programs with clever names have achieved impressive results, including Chevron's SMART (Save Money and Reduce Toxics), Dow Chemical's WRAP (see Chap. 22) and Coors' SCRAP (see Chap. 20).

There are four major categories of pollution prevention:

- Good housekeeping practices to ensure that resources are utilized efficiently and that preventable material losses are not occurring through leakage or excessive use

- Material substitution to reduce or eliminate the presence of undesirable substances such as heavy metals, carcinogens, or CFCs

- Manufacturing process changes to simplify production technologies, reduce water and energy use, or introduce closed-loop recycling

- Resource recovery to capture waste materials and reuse them either as inputs to other manufacturing processes or for secondary applications

Examples of pollution prevention programs

- 3M is an acknowledged leader in DFE. Their Pollution Prevention Pays (3P) program was established in 1975, and since then has achieved elimination of over 600,000 lb of air emissions, effluents, and solid waste, with a savings of over $500 million in capital and operating costs. The 3P policy was to select projects for funding that were voluntarily proposed by employees. The selection criteria were that the project must (1) reduce or eliminate existing or potential pollutants, (2) increase the efficiency of energy or other resource use, (3) employ some technical innovation, and (4) result in monetary benefit. In 1989, the company announced new goals for the year 2000: to reduce releases to all media by 90% and solid wastes by 50%. The 3P program has been renamed 3P Plus, and has shifted from a voluntary to a formalized approach built into the incentive systems. Also, in 1991, 3M introduced a new environmental improvement program called Challenge '95.[2]

- A number of good examples of profitable pollution prevention were among the demonstration projects sponsored by the President's Commission on Environmental Quality, which invited voluntary participation from industry.[3] In Columbus, Ohio, an engineering team at AT&T's telecommunications equipment manufacturing plant found a way to eliminate the use of a known toxic chemical (1,1,1-trichloroethane, or TCA) by the end of 1993, while achieving a projected annual savings of $200,000. In Beaumont, Texas, a similar team at a DuPont chemical plant was able to reduce ammonium sulfate emissions due to acrylonitrile manufacturing from 100 million to 40 million lb per year, and slashed annual manufacturing costs by $1 million with no capital investment required. In Mehoopany, Pennsylvania, a Procter & Gamble manufacturing plant which produces tissue, paper towels, and diapers implemented a comprehensive program to minimize solid wastes, resulting in annual estimated savings of $25 million.

Cleaner Products: Beyond Pollution Prevention

While pollution prevention has received a great deal of support and praise from environmental advocates, the way it is currently practiced has a number of inherent limitations:

- It tends to incrementally refine production processes as they currently exist, rather than rethinking their fundamental technology and design.
- It tends to focus on unidimensional measures of improvement (such as waste volume) rather than adopting a comprehensive view of environmental performance.
- It tends to "cherry-pick" by improving processes that were not optimized for efficiency; therefore these gains are not repeatable.
- It tends to be performed on a case-by-case basis, rather than being integrated into a company's business strategy.

Thus, current efforts at pollution prevention are only a first step—albeit a commendable one—along the path to sustainable development. They represent a shift in thinking from "end-of-the-pipe" waste treatment to "in-the-pipe" materials management. They also break through the traditional conflict between profitability and environmental protection. However, by the time pollution prevention is initiated, the investments in capital equipment have already been made, and the basic process parameters are already established. If pollution prevention thinking can be shifted back into the design cycle, before the products are specified and the plants are constructed, it can have an order of magnitude greater impact on eco-efficiency. This is essentially the purpose of DFE.

Elements of DFE

DFE seeks to discover product innovations that will result in reduced pollution and waste at any or all stages of the life cycle, while satisfying other cost and performance objectives. DFE cannot be practiced in isolation—it must be balanced against other design considerations to optimize a design. In order for DFE to be integrated effectively into a new-product development process, the following key elements are required:

- Eco-efficiency *metrics,* driven by fundamental customer needs or corporate goals, to support environmental performance measurement
- Eco-efficient *design practices,* based on in-depth understanding of relevant technologies and supported by engineering guidelines
- Eco-efficiency *analysis methods* to assess proposed designs with respect to the above metrics and to analyze cost and quality trade-offs

In addition, it is important for design teams to have an *information infrastructure* that supports the ongoing application of DFE metrics, practices, and analysis methods. These elements are discussed individually below.

Metrics

A variety of eco-efficiency metrics, or environmental performance measures, are used in various industries, reflecting industry-specific environmental issues. Many of these metrics have been adopted by eco-labeling programs both in the European Union and the United States. Examples of different types of metrics include toxic use measures (total kilograms of solvents purchased per unit of production), resource utilization measures (total energy consumed during the product life cycle), environmental emission measures (greenhouse gases and ozone-depleting substances released per unit of production), and waste minimization measures (percent of product materials recovered at end of life), to name a few. A more exhaustive list is provided in Chap. 7.

The choice of high-level environmental metrics is extremely important, in that it determines what types of signals are sent to engineering and manufacturing staff responsible for meeting operational goals. In addition, it determines the available options for communicating company performance to outside audiences. Once eco-efficiency goals have been expressed in terms of specific metrics, the next step in product development is to decompose these metrics into quantitative parameters that can be estimated and tracked for a particular product design. This process is discussed further in Chap. 7.

Practices

There are a variety of specific DFE practices associated with eco-efficient design. Ideally, a single design innovation may contribute to achieving several different types of goals. For example, reducing the mass of a product can result in (1) energy and material use reduction, which contributes to resource conservation, and (2) pollutant emission reduction, which contributes to health and safety.

The system boundaries associated with DFE are broader than those in the customary definition of a product "system." Rather than merely considering how the product interacts with its physical environment, one must consider the entire value-added chain—upstream processes involved in producing the components, raw materials, and energy to fabricate the product, as well as downstream processes involved in its distribution, use, and disposal. One must also consider how by-products or releases from these processes may transmute, migrate, and affect humans or the environment.

Listed below are some of the more common DFE practices in industry today:

- *Material substitution:* Replacing product constituents with substitute materials that are superior in terms of increased recyclability, reduced energy content, etc.

- *Waste source reduction:* Reducing the mass of the product or of its packaging, thus reducing the resulting quantity of waste matter per product unit

- *Substance use reduction:* Reducing or eliminating the types and amounts of undesirable substances (e.g., toxics or CFCs) that are either incorporated into the product or used in its manufacturing process

- *Energy use reduction:* Reducing the energy required to produce, transport, store, maintain, use, recycle, or dispose of the product and its packaging

- *Life extension:* Prolonging the useful life of a product or its components, thus reducing the associated waste stream (see below under "design for reusability")

- *Design for separability and disassembly:* Simplifying product disassembly and material recovery using techniques such as snap fastening of components and color coding of plastics

- *Design for recyclability:* Ensuring both high recycled content in product materials and maximum recycling, i.e., minimum waste, at end of product life

- *Design for disposability:* Assuring that all nonrecyclable materials and components can be safely and efficiently disposed (e.g., ink/pigment restrictions)

- *Design for reusability:* Enabling some components of a product to be recovered, refurbished, and reused

- *Design for remanufacture:*   Enabling recovery of postindustrial or postconsumer waste for recycling as input to the manufacture of new products

- *Design for energy recovery:*   Extraction of energy from waste materials, e.g., through incineration

A more detailed discussion of these and other practices, including generic engineering guidelines, is provided in Chap. 8. Figure 5.4 illustrates a number of opportunities to apply these types of practices in the development and manufacturing of electronic devices. While the functional flow diagrams for other industries will differ in their details, similar DFE opportunities can be found in every industry.

Part 3 of this book shows how DFE has been practiced by a wide range of companies from process-intensive industries such as electric power generation (Chap. 16) and petroleum refining (Chap. 17) to high-volume discrete manufacturing industries such as computers (Chap. 12), hospital supplies (Chap. 18), and beverages (Chap. 20).

Analysis methods

Finally, to "close the loop" in the development process, analysis methods are needed to assess the degree of improvement expected from a new design with respect to the eco-efficiency metrics of interest. Analysis methods may range from focused estimation of parameters (e.g., market surveys of expected recycling rates) to full-scale life-cycle assessment of environmental impacts. They may also include parametric relationships that show the interactions between environmental metrics and other cost or performance metrics such as reliability and durability.

Analysis methods generally are used by design teams in four different ways:

- *Screening methods* are used to narrow design choices among a set of alternatives; examples include threshold limits for chemical properties such as biodegradability, and material selection priority lists based on recyclability.

- *Assessment methods* are used to predict the expected performance of designs with respect to particular objectives; examples include calculation of expected material recovery rates, or prediction of environmental concentrations associated with specified emission levels. Assessment methods may range from simple qualitative indices to sophisticated numerical simulation models that predict environmental consequences. A number of methods have been developed for *life-cycle assessment,* enabling "cradle-to-grave" analysis of the flows of energy and materials throughout the life cycle of a product.[4]

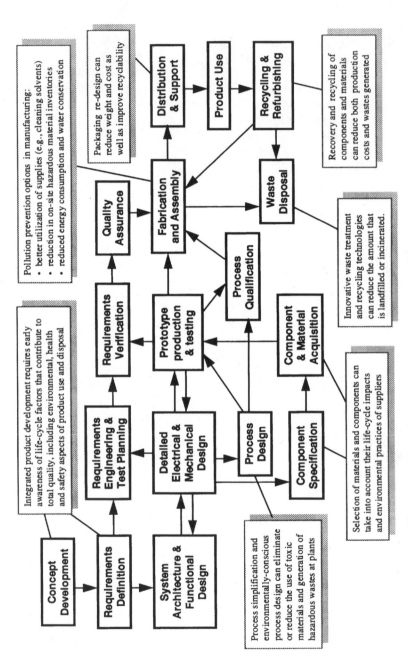

Figure 5.4 Examples of DFE opportunities in the electronics industry.

- *Trade-off methods* are used to compare the expected cost and performance of several alternative design approaches with respect to one or more attributes of interest. Such methods may include "what-if" simulations, quality-function matrices, or parametric analyses that draw upon various assessment methods described above.

- *Decisionmaking methods* are used to help design teams select from among alternatives when the trade-offs are complex or when large uncertainties are present; examples include analytic hierarchy techniques, expert advisory systems, decision analysis, and other optimization methods.

A full treatment of these many approaches is beyond the scope of this book. However, Chap. 9 provides a more detailed discussion of selected environmental performance assessment methods, along with examples of their application.

Information Infrastructure

Like any other engineering practice, DFE requires enabling tools that support the processes described above. There are at least three primary types of capabilities necessary for effective integration of DFE into product development:

- On-line design guidance
- Predictive assessment tools
- Integration with CAE/CAD framework

On-line design guidance

Design guidance represents a body of knowledge accumulated by a design organization regarding its key technologies and design approaches, including lessons learned from both successes and failures. For purposes of DFE, design guidance can provide assistance in several aspects of product development, including:

- Selecting appropriate DFE practices and metrics based on overall product goals
- Identifying interactions and trade-offs among eco-efficiency, cost, performance, manufacturability, maintainability, and other quality factors, so that candidate designs may be evaluated systematically
- Assigning relative importance to various categories of environmental impacts (e.g., toxic material emissions may have widely varying impacts depending upon their persistence, environmental fate, and ultimate concentrations relative to ambient baselines)

■ Recording in a "corporate memory" the objectives, design histories, and rationales for decisions regarding environmental characteristics of prior products

The actual form of on-line design guidance may range from a simple hypertext system containing cross-referenced rules of thumb to interactive "expert" systems that help to explore trade-offs among alternative designs or technologies. While paper-based design manuals have some value, computer-based DFE guidance is more compatible with today's fast-paced, high-performance cross-disciplinary team approach. On-line guidance allows direct, real-time retrieval and maintenance of DFE knowledge by engineers and other professionals engaged in product development.

Predictive assessment tools

In concurrent engineering, the use of predictive tools for evaluating product performance is important to assure coverage of all product requirements and to identify design flaws or omissions.[5] In particular, DFE requires automated tools because of the complexity of environmental issues associated even with simple products. As discussed in Chap. 9, many existing DFE programs are limited to the use of simple checklists or single-dimensional metrics, which provide little insight into the true *value* of product improvements. Instead, design teams require the ability to close the loop by receiving feedback regarding the benefits of design changes. Examples of performance assessment applications include:

■ Assessment of anticipated waste streams and emission rates based on information about product composition

■ Modeling of end-of-life costs for a product line based on available economic and operational data

■ Profiling of life-cycle environmental and financial implications of design alternatives

■ Rating of overall environmental performance for a candidate design

A number of companies have developed internal systems that provide these types of capabilities, although they are seldom fully integrated into the design automation environment. For example, Chap. 11 describes a Green Index software tool developed by AT&T to assess a product's overall environmental performance. Hughes Aircraft has implemented a similar system called the Green Notes Environmental Rating and Measurement System, which is used to automatically provide ratings as designers develop their product and process specifications.[6]

Integration with CAE/CAD framework

One of the pitfalls of computer-aided engineering is the tendency for different disciplines to develop their own specialized tools. As described in Chap. 6, this can impede integrated product development. To avoid this "islands of automation" syndrome, it is important that DFE tools be implemented in a way that facilitates data exchange and interoperability with other CAE/CAD tools. The preferred solution is to adopt a "framework" architecture in which all tools share common data models and interface specifications, thus allowing incremental extension and maintenance of the toolkit with tools from multiple vendors as well as custom applications.

A Vision for the Future

A suggested architecture for an information infrastructure that supports a systems approach to DFE is shown in Fig. 5.5. The basic data on products, processes, and industry characteristics need to be maintained in a separate database, which must be updated periodically as the industry evolves. Product developers will provide information about product design alternatives and strategy options as well as the different quality criteria to be considered. In return they will receive information and advice about possible outcomes, and evaluations that indicate which strategies are most favorable.

The infrastructure includes several computational models:

- A dynamic market model to assess the impacts of each design option upon industry and consumer activities, including purchase and use patterns

- A life-cycle assessment model to project the energy, materials, and release levels associated with these activity levels

- A multimedia environmental model to assess (if necessary) the exposures or impacts resulting from these releases

- A decision support model (potentially incorporating expert system technology) to evaluate choices in the face of uncertainty, and to consider what technical and business strategies the company might adopt in response to different market or competitive scenarios

Note that this infrastructure can be integrated with a CAE/CAD system in which users operate upon design descriptions. In that case, the CAE/CAD system would provide the primary human interface, and

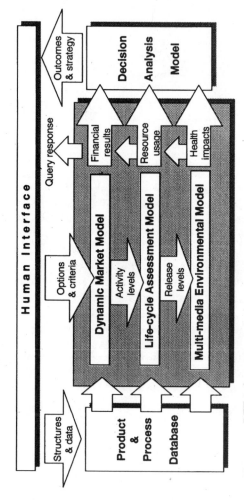

Figure 5.5   DFE information infrastructure.

access to the DFE infrastructure would be accomplished through a simple command overlay and programmatic interfaces. A designer could simply invoke a view of a design, trigger an environmental performance evaluation, respond to queries for data or assumptions, and automatically receive the life-cycle analysis results.

This type of conceptual framework enables the integration of cost, performance, manufacturability, maintainability, and other quality factors together with environmental considerations so that alternative designs can be uniformly compared. Moreover, it is capable of supporting business decisionmaking because it allows the representation of market dynamics, competitive actions, and associated uncertainties, and thus enables the assessment of strategic options with respect to alternative future scenarios.

At present there are a number of ongoing research efforts addressing various aspects of this framework:

- Carnegie-Mellon University (CMU) has developed a tool called *ReStar* which supports design for disassembly, and is currently marketed by Envirosoft. This tool runs only on workstations and is narrowly focused on one aspect of DFE. CMU is continuing its research in this area.

- The National Center for Manufacturing Sciences (NCMS) has recently launched a Green Design Advisor project with the support of several companies, but commercial results are probably at least five years away.[7]

- A number of companies, including Franklin Associates and Woodward Clyde Associates, have developed PC tools for life-cycle environmental assessment, but these tools are mainly devoted to computing material and energy flows based on linear flow models.

- Several major manufacturing companies, such as AT&T and Xerox, have reported that they are pursuing in-house efforts to develop intelligent design advisors for DFE. It is unlikely that their results will be commercially available in the foreseeable future.

Full implementation of such an infrastructure is not to be undertaken lightly. It involves many technical and organizational challenges. However, it provides a road map for the kind of life-cycle thinking and analytic processes that are necessary to truly integrate environmental and business strategies. Even partial automation of this infrastructure, if performed judiciously, can yield significant benefits to a product development organization.

References

1. Stephan Schmidheiny with the Business Council on Sustainable Development, *Changing Course: A Global Business Perspective on Development and the Environment,* MIT Press, Cambridge, MA, 1992.
2. T. W. Zosel, "Pollution Prevention Pays: the 3M Approach," *Proc. 1st International Congress on Environmentally-Conscious Design & Manufacturing,* Management Roundtable, Boston, 1992.
3. President's Commission on Environmental Quality, *Total Quality Management: A Framework for Pollution Prevention,* Washington, DC, January 1993.
4. J. A. Fava, R. Denison, B. Jones, M. A. Curran, B. Vigon, S. Selke, and J. Barnum (eds.), *A Technical Framework for Life Cycle Assessments,* Society of Environmental Toxicology and Chemistry, Washington, DC, 1991.
5. A. Rosenblatt and G. F. Watson, "Concurrent Engineering," IEEE Spectrum, July 1991, pp. 22–37.
6. C. Schutzenberger, "An Electronic, On-line Database for Quantitative Environmental Assessment of New Designs," *Proc. International Symposium on Electronics and the Environment,* May 1994, IEEE, Piscataway, NJ.
7. M. Wixom, "The NCMS Green Design Advisor, A CAE Tool for Environmentally Conscious Design," *Proc. International Symposium on Electronics and the Environment,* May 1994, IEEE, Piscataway, NJ.

6

Product and Process Development

Joseph Fiksel

Integrated Product Development

Manufacturing firms in the United States have almost universally recognized the need to reconsider traditional methods of product development and introduction. With increasing competitive pressures and rapidly changing markets, reduction in product development cycle time has become an essential goal. Equally important is the goal of continuous improvement in product quality and responsiveness to the "voice of the customer." Many firms have introduced new management methods designed to accelerate time to market and improve overall quality, largely through organizational changes. (Unfortunately, as discussed below, these changes are frequently hampered by lack of integration in the available information tools and resources.)

The National Research Council recently issued a pamphlet called *Improving Engineering Design* which effectively summarizes the prevailing wisdom of modern product development.[1] It cites four requirements for using design as a source of competitive advantage:

1. Commit to continuous improvement both of products and of design and production processes.

2. Establish a corporate product realization process (PRP) supported by top management.

3. Develop and/or adopt and integrate advanced design practices into the PRP.

4. Create a supportive design environment.

Moreover, it defines an effective PRP as incorporating the following steps:

- Define customer needs and product performance requirements.
- Plan for product evolution beyond the current design.
- Plan concurrently for design and manufacturing.
- Design the product and its manufacturing processes with full consideration of the entire product life cycle, including distribution, support, maintenance, recycling, and disposal.
- Produce the product and monitor product and processes.

In this spirit, the term *integrated product development* describes a process that has been adopted by most progressive manufacturing firms, even though they may have different names for it.[2] We define *integrated product development* (IPD) as follows: *a process whereby all functional groups (e.g., engineering, manufacturing, marketing, etc.) that are involved in a product life cycle participate as a team in the early understanding and resolution of key product development issues including quality, manufacturability, reliability, maintainability, environment, and safety.*

Integrated product development does not tolerate the traditional "sequential engineering" approach, in which a design is developed and refined in successive stages by different engineering groups (design, layout, test, etc.), with each group "throwing results over the wall" to the next group. Instead, companies that have adopted IPD use the approach of "concurrent engineering" (CE) or simultaneous engineering, in which the different engineering disciplines work in a parallel, coordinated fashion to address life-cycle requirements.[3]

The motivation for IPD is extremely strong when one considers the economics of product development. For example, in the automotive and electronics industry, it has been shown that up to 80% of product life-cycle costs are committed during the concept and preliminary design stages, and that the cost of design changes increases steeply as a product proceeds into full-scale development and prototyping.[1,4] The implication is that product developers should use concurrent engineering to examine a design from multiple perspectives and to anticipate potential problems or opportunities. By getting it right the first time, they will avoid costly changes and delays due to design iterations. This expectation has been borne out in companies that have utilized concurrent engineering methods. For example, a number of companies have implemented design for assembly and other so-called DFX approaches that introduce considerations of manufacturability at an early point in product development, thus reducing both the product cost and the duration of the development cycle.[5]

Organizing for Environmental Excellence

As described in Chap. 1, *enterprise integration* is the reengineering of business processes and information systems to improve teamwork and coordination across organizational boundaries, thereby increasing the effectiveness of the enterprise as a whole. In this context, IPD has been widely adopted as a strategy for "agile" manufacturing, allowing companies to release higher-quality products while reducing time to market.

Since environmental performance is becoming an important aspect of total quality, DFE fits naturally into the IPD process. DFE is essentially an application of the above IPD approach to environmental performance. The basic imperative of DFE is undeniably valid: "Get it right the first time." In other words, anticipate environmental quality issues during design, thus avoiding costly changes in the future. However, in order to put this principle into systematic practice, a substantial organizational commitment is required.

Despite the many examples of successful DFE efforts described in this book, the current state of practice can be characterized as mainly opportunistic. Most of the early successes in environmental quality improvement are the result of companies finding the "low-hanging fruit"—projects for which benefits were evident and barriers were few. In order for environmental quality management to mature and be integrated into company practices, two types of permanent change are needed:

- Organizational norms must be established that encourage superior environmental performance. This requires evolving from a broad corporate "mission statement" to setting achievable environmental improvement goals and to making employees accountable for meeting or exceeding these goals.
- Business processes must be modified to accommodate environmental consciousness. This requires integrating environmental quality metrics and assessment tools into engineering practices, as well as developing accounting systems that recognize environmental costs and benefits.

Companies that have implemented environmental quality programs cite a number of barriers that make implementation more challenging:[6]

- Resources are limited for starting new projects.

- Organizational and cultural inertia tends to favor "business as usual."

- Environmental issues are poorly understood among both managers and employees.

- Existing accounting systems are inadequate for reflecting environmental value.

- Design teams have a fear of compromising product quality or production efficiency.

To overcome these challenges requires both effective communication and an appropriate implementation strategy.

Key steps to take when introducing DFE

Chapter 24 discusses at greater length the organizational and strategic issues associated with introducing DFE. In brief, to establish a successful DFE program, there are a number of key steps that a company should follow:

Program definition

- Establish top-management commitment to legitimize the program.

- Invite inputs from external stakeholders, including regulators, customers, and communities.

- Fit the program to the existing organizational structure and cross-functional teams.

- Assure adequate staff training, incentives, and empowerment.

DFE implementation

- Establish appropriate DFE metrics and measurement tools.

- Assess the baseline environmental quality of existing products and processes.

- Develop improvement alternatives and select priorities, using systematic methods.

- Implement environmental quality improvements and measure the results relative to baseline.

Continuous improvement

- Integrate the new technologies and lessons learned into other products and processes.

- Institutionalize the metrics, guidelines, and other tools using computer support as appropriate.

- Communicate the beneficial results of DFE actions to stakeholders.

- Recognize and reward both team and individual accomplishments.

Once DFE becomes an integral part of total-quality management, it will help reveal new opportunities for companies to reduce life-cycle costs and improve overall product quality and profitability, while assuring that they are meeting their commitment to environmental stewardship.

Applying Concurrent Engineering

Chapter 5 described the main elements of DFE: metrics, practice guidelines, and analysis methods. These are the essential elements of any concurrent engineering discipline. For example, consider the design process for printed circuit boards, which has become highly systematized in order to enable rapid time to market. Among the many "ilities" addressed in this field is design for reliability (DFR). The corresponding elements are as follows:

- A common metric for DFR is "mean time between failures" (MTBF).

- A typical DFR practice guideline is "Allow adequate spacing for components with high power consumption."

- A typical analysis tool for design verification is a thermal simulation program which estimates the overall MTBF for a given board layout.

Finally, design trade-offs involving DFR are usually addressed through conceptual devices such as quality-function-deployment (QFD) matrices.

Just as DFR is supported by reliability tools, DFE must be supported by eco-efficiency tools. Figure 6.1 illustrates how such tools can be deployed to support achievement of rapid cycle time by an IPD team. The process begins with the analysis of customer needs and the establishment of product requirements. In a true concurrent engineering approach, requirements address not only product performance but also manufacturing, service, and other downstream issues including environmental quality.[7] Like any other objectives, environmental objectives are established using measurable and verifiable performance metrics.

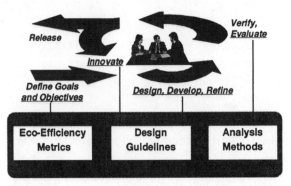

Figure 6.1 The process of integrated product development (IPD).

In general, a *requirement* can be defined as a description of a set of testable conditions applicable to products or processes. A requirement is said to be *satisfied* by a product (or process) if a test or observation reveals that the described conditions are met by that product (or process). The conditions may be represented in various forms, including:

- Behavioral: e.g., "system shall shut down when left idle"
- Qualitative: e.g., "shall be *stable* in extreme heat"
- Quantitative: e.g., *"width* < *(inner radius)* * 1.9 inches"
- Pictorial: e.g., "shall resemble this zigzag pattern"
- Logical: e.g., *"process type* shall only be *acid* or *thermal"*

The requirements management process consists of three main functions that are performed repeatedly in an iterative fashion. These are requirements *analysis,* requirements *tracking,* and requirements *verification.* Each of these functions is described below:

- *Requirements analysis* is the process of interpreting customer needs and deriving explicit requirements that can be understood and interpreted by people and/or computer programs. It is usually carried out by a select group of program managers, chief engineers, and senior project engineers. Complex designs can have thousands of requirements, which are often represented in a hierarchical fashion.

- *Requirements tracking* involves continuous interchange and negotiation within a project team regarding conflicting and changing objectives. Design decisions must be weighed in terms of a variety of factors, including project risk, schedule, cost constraints, and performance goals. An organizing scheme such as a *traceability hierarchy* is helpful in locating specific types of requirements, navigating through large volumes of requirements, and adding new ones at appropriate points.

- *Requirements verification* is the process of evaluating whether a product design complies with a designated set of requirements. This can be accomplished through actual testing of a prototype or at an earlier stage through predictive methods. Concurrent engineering teaches that the earlier in the design process verification can be performed, the more likely it is that design flaws will be detected before a large prototyping investment has been made.

After requirements have been defined, the product development cycle begins in earnest. As the team works on developing a detailed design, they employ *guidelines* drawn from each of the relevant design disciplines, e.g., manufacturability. While automated aids such as expert systems can facilitate the DFX practices, the innovative capabilities of human engineers are the key to success at this stage. Once an initial design has been formulated, it is possible to begin design *verification*; the earlier this takes place, the sooner the team will recognize design shortcomings and take steps to overcome them. As mentioned above, early and systematic design verification is critical to reducing both the number of design iterations and the time to market.

The use of automated systems at the verification stage is helpful to assure coverage of all product requirements and to identify design flaws or omissions. In particular, DFE requires a verification system because of the complexity of environmental issues associated even with simple products. Many existing pollution prevention programs are limited to the use of simple checklists or single-dimensional metrics, which provide little insight into the true value of product improvements. Instead, design teams need to the ability to close the loop by receiving feedback regarding the measurable benefits of proposed design changes.

Finally, in a truly integrated approach, DFE must be balanced against other cost and quality factors that influence design trade-off decisions. This is the most challenging part of the process, because of the need to simultaneously consider so many different criteria. While not mandatory, it is useful to have a well-structured *decision framework* that supports the exploration of trade-offs and uncertainties with respect to the original product requirements. The mark of a successful team is the ability to innovate under pressure, rather than compromising product quality. A "win-win" outcome is the introduction of environmentally beneficial innovations that also improve the cost and performance of the product when viewed as part of an overall system.

The Need for Better Tools

One of the barriers to concurrent engineering, especially in high-technology industries, is the reliance of engineers on design and manufacturing automation tools that do not allow cross-functional integration. Although many CAE/CAD tools exist that support the detailed work of individual engineers, there is still a great need for tools that help to evaluate trade-offs, provide design advice, and capture the accumulated experience of development teams. New types of information technology, such as "intelligent assistant" design tools, can facilitate a company's transformation from traditional ways of doing business to a more concurrent approach, and can provide ongoing support for IPD. Chapter 5 presented a vision of an information infrastructure that can fill this need.

Currently most companies use some form of automated support for product development. However, the available tools do not provide adequate DFX support during the product design and development process. The existing products and technologies presently in use fall into two major groups, general-purpose and specialized tools.

- General-purpose tools include text processors, spreadsheet tools, and database management systems, used mainly to collect and track design-related information.
- Specialized tools include CAE/CAD systems for systems engineering, design characterization, modeling, simulation, and requirements verification.

Most product developers must rely on some combination of general-purpose tools with internally developed custom tools to satisfy all of their DFX needs. This approach has the following weaknesses:

- Places most of the burden of vigilance on the users
- Requires frequent manual data transfer among tools
- Lacks a uniform, generalized structure for DFX
- Does not support concurrent, distributed users
- Creates a significant maintenance burden

As mentioned in Chap. 2, companies that are able to practice DFE stand to gain a substantial competitive advantage through improvements in cost efficiency and product differentiation. Some leading companies are developing DFE programs, and fully intend to capitalize on cost-effective opportunities to improve their environmental performance. For example, IBM has established a Center for Environmentally Conscious Product Design. Yet many companies have not progressed beyond the conceptual stage, and it is unlikely that they will be developing concrete methods or comprehensive software tools in the near future.

Only when DFE principles can be encoded into software tools will eco-efficient design become accessible to the vast majority of companies that are extremely busy meeting the needs of their various stakeholders and do not have the time or resources for developing new processes and systems. These companies are primarily interested in practical applications, and the extent to which they can improve their business performance.

Product and Process Life Cycles

The term *life cycle,* now so much in vogue, bears closer examination than it usually reviews. It turns out that one person's definition of life cycle may be quite different from another's. Consider the following widely differing interpretations:

1. *Business life cycle:* The product life cycle is a sequence of activity phases including the creation of a product concept, its development, launch, production, maintenance, maturity, reevaluation, and renewal in the form of a next-generation product. Similarly, the process life cycle is a sequence of activity phases including the development of facility and process designs, architecture and construction, operation and maintenance, and eventual upgrading or retirement.

2. *Physical life cycle:* The product life cycle is a sequence of transformations in materials and energy that includes extraction and processing of materials, product manufacture and assembly, distribution, use, and recovery or recycling of product materials. Similarly, the process life cycle is a sequence of transformations in materials and energy that includes extraction and processing of materials used for process equipment and supplies, process operation and control, equipment cleaning and maintenance, and waste disposal or recovery.

Note that a single process may be involved in producing a variety of different products, while producing a single product may involve a variety of different processes. Like most of this book, the following discussion focuses on the *product* life cycle.

As depicted in Fig. 6.2, these dual life cycles are orthogonal yet interwoven, and it is easy to understand how they might be confused.

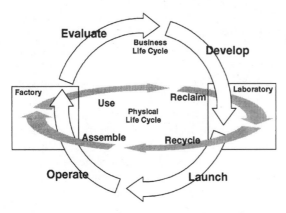

Figure 6.2 Dual life cycles associated with a product.

They intersect in at least two physical settings—in the laboratory where product and process concepts are created, and in the factory where full-scale production is performed. Yet they are very different in several respects:

- The *time scale* of the business life cycle is determined by the rate of technological change and other market conditions that affect product obsolescence; the time scale of the physical life cycle is determined by the length of service of a typical product unit, which may range from days or weeks for consumable products to years or decades for durable goods.

- The *responsibility* for the business life cycle and the business impacts (profits or losses incurred) is borne fully by the producing company; the responsibility for the physical life cycle and the associated impacts is distributed among many companies or individuals involved at different stages of transformation, and in some cases the responsibility for adverse impacts may be ambiguous (e.g., liability for waste disposal).

- The *continuity* of the business cycle depends upon the ability of a company to innovate by developing and delivering new product concepts that serve the needs of its markets; the continuity of the physical cycle depends upon the ability of various interested parties, potentially including the manufacturer, to refurbish used products or to recover the materials and energy content of discarded products and convert them to productive uses.

From a conventional product development perspective, interpretation 1 is the more meaningful one since it provides a framework for making business decisions regarding desirable product features and cost or effort trade-offs. The concurrent engineering approach described above has always been based on this model of the business life cycle, with "ilities" associated with different phases. On the other hand, the notion of the physical life cycle, interpretation 2, has been the focus of recent efforts at environmental labeling, standard setting, and performance evaluation.

It is no wonder then, that product teams are often puzzled by the new calculus of life-cycle assessment (LCA), which seeks to quantify the "cradle-to-grave" impacts of the physical life cycle. (Chapter 9 describes this approach and discusses its merits.) While it is relevant to sustainability, this type of life-cycle assessment may be quite unrelated to the business decisions addressed by product development groups, in which life-cycle analysis focuses on cost and performance trade-offs. For example, the increased cost of making a product more durable may be offset by reduced warranty costs. LCA results regarding environmental burdens, to the extent they reflect customer needs or corporate objectives, may certainly be factored into this type of business analysis, but the design decision framework must have a return-on-investment perspective. Chapter 10 explores at greater length the integrated life-cycle management (ILCM) approach, whereby financial, environmental, and performance issues can be treated in a unified framework.

References

1. National Research Council, *Improving Engineering Design: Designing for Competitive Advantage,* National Academy Press, Washington, DC, 1991.
2. W. J. Peet and K. J. Hladik, "Organizing for Global Product Development," *Electronic Business,* March 6, 1989, pp. 62–64.
3. S. Evanczuk, "Concurrent Engineering: The New Look of Design," *High Performance Systems,* April 1990.
4. O. Port, "A Smarter Way to Manufacture," *Business Week,* April 30, 1990.
5. G. Boothroyd, W. Knight, and P. Dewhurst, "Estimating the Costs of Printed Circuit Board Assemblies," *Printed Circuit Design,* vol. 6, no. 6, June 1989.
6. President's Commission on Environmental Quality, *Total Quality Management: A Framework for Pollution Prevention,* Washington, DC, January 1993.
7. J. Fiksel and F. Hayes-Roth, "Computer-Aided Requirements Management," *Concurrent Engineering Research and Applications,* vol. 1, no. 2, June 1993, pp. 83–92.

7

Environmental Performance Metrics

Joseph Fiksel

Introduction

The ability to evaluate environmental performance in objective, measurable terms is a key component of an effective DFE capability. As described in Chap. 5, environmental performance metrics are essential to support goal setting, monitoring, and continuous improvement in the design of products and processes.

Performance measurement has become a mantra of modern management, embraced by nearly ever major school of thought including total-quality management, business process reengineering, high-performance teams, and value-based management. "You can't manage what you can't measure" is an inescapable fact. Moreover, measuring individual and team performance with regard to specific objectives generally leads to significant improvements without the need for close oversight.

As discussed in Chap. 3, a number of the industrialized nations, as well as the International Organization for Standardization (ISO), through its Technical Committee 207, are introducing environmental management standards which specify the required elements of an environmental management system (EMS). In every one of these schemes, performance measurement is regarded as a principal component of the EMS.

This chapter describes environmental performance measurement tools and procedures, particularly as they relate to the practice of DFE. One of the key challenges of performance measurement is to incorporate a life-cycle view of environmental performance into operational metrics that can be easily computed and tracked.

Performance Improvement Challenges

During the economic recession of 1989–1992, many U.S. companies went through a painful period of downsizing and consolidation. The "reengineering" binge that swept the nation provided a rational framework for rethinking business processes to make them more efficient. Most companies emerged from this experience with a leaner, more productive work force and a fresh attitude. They recognized the need to do more with less, keeping in mind the concerns of all stakeholders: customers, shareholders, regulators, and interested communities. Improving the *performance* of existing resources—human, technological, and financial—became an important priority.

But what constitutes performance? Are traditional aggregate measures (e.g., return on net assets) sufficient to guide strategic and operating decisions? As companies explored this question, they rediscovered the performance improvement tools that had been successfully applied in total quality management (TQM). The TQM approach embeds an awareness of performance into an organization, so that employees receive correct signals regarding their contributions to corporate value. To apply TQM methods and achieve *continuous* improvement, a company must fulfill several preconditions:

- The important dimensions of performance need to be understood and characterized in terms of quantifiable metrics.

- Each individual in the company must have a means of relating their own objectives to the achievement of these metrics.

- A system must exist for tracking the achievement of performance targets and providing appropriate recognition to those responsible.

- As decisions are made at all levels of the company, a means must exist for understanding their impacts upon the affected performance metrics.

Thus, it is not sufficient to select and announce the metrics of interest. They must be operationalized through deliberate intervention into the organizational culture, processes, and reward systems.

Emerging Practices

A recent survey of key environmental executives, conducted by Decision Focus Incorporated, explored how leading companies are addressing environmental performance.[1] The 20 companies surveyed ranged from those for which manufacturing is primarily a *continuous-process operation,* including 3M, Amoco, DuPont, Merck, Intel, and Shell, to those for which manufacturing is primarily a *discrete-assembly operation,* including Boeing, Chrysler, Compaq, DEC, IBM, and Polaroid. Each executive was asked whether their company:

- Has a policy or mission statement regarding environmental responsibility
- Establishes quantitative targets or objectives for environmental improvement
- Rewards individuals and groups based upon environmental performance
- Uses environmental auditing and review procedures for facilities and products
- Employs environmental metrics in design, engineering, and quality management
- Integrates environmental awareness into business strategy and decisionmaking

The survey revealed a strong commitment on the part of these companies to achieving environmental excellence. However, a striking finding was that *while 55% of them claim to have integrated environmental awareness into their business strategy and decisionmaking, only 30% of them have actually included environmental metrics in their design engineering and quality management processes* (see Fig. 7.1).

The lack of implementation of quality metrics by 70% of the respondents presents a paradox, since without quality measurement it is

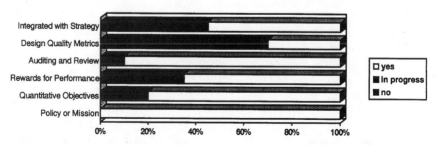

Figure 7.1 Environmental management practices at 20 major U.S. companies.

difficult or impossible to achieve continuous improvement in environmental performance. Broad objectives such as "50% reduction in total
waste generated by 1995" are certainly commendable, but it is difficult to achieve such objectives without operational metrics, accountability, and reward systems at the level of individual and team functional responsibilities. In particular, without a quantitative basis for
understanding the relative contribution of environmental quality to
profitability and customer satisfaction, it is difficult to make meaningful trade-off decisions during new-product development. These
results suggest that, while many of these companies have introduced
environmental awareness into their business strategies in a *qualitative* sense, they may still lack the analytical tools to evaluate the costs
and benefits of business decisions from an environmental perspective.

A common theme among the companies mentioned above is the
recognition that *environmental quality is just one aspect of total quality*. While seemingly obvious, this simple statement reflects a radical
change in attitude, and has profound implications in terms of a company's business processes. Instead of viewing environmental management as an unavoidable cost of doing business and treating it as an
overhead expense, these companies are beginning to view environmental management as an essential core function associated with
enterprise management, and to allocate funds to this function based
on its contribution to corporate value. This new perspective implies
two major changes in the business processes of an enterprise:

- Environmental performance metrics and assessment methods need
  to be integrated into engineering practices.
- Accounting systems need to be developed that explicitly recognize
  and track environmental costs and benefits.

This chapter focuses on how to introduce environmental performance
metrics. The development of assessment methods and environmental
accounting systems is discussed in Chaps. 9 and 10.

Environmental Performance Metrics

In the context of DFE, environmental performance metrics are parameters used to measure design improvement with respect to environmental goals. Because of their fundamental role in the development
process, quality metrics are essential to the successful practice of
DFE. Examples of environmental quality metrics that can be used to
establish design objectives include the following (note that these can
be measured in absolute terms or normalized with respect to product
units):

- *Energy usage metrics*
  Total energy consumed during the product life cycle
  Renewable energy consumed during the life cycle
  Power used during operation (for electrical products)

- *Water usage metrics*
  Total fresh water consumed during manufacturing
  Water consumption during product end use (for electrical products)

- *Material burden metrics*
  Toxic or hazardous materials used in production
  Total industrial waste generated during production
  Hazardous waste generated during production or use
  Air emissions and water effluents generated during production
  Greenhouse gases and ozone-depleting substances released over life cycle

- *Recovery and reuse metrics*
  Product disassembly and recovery time
  Percent of recyclable materials available at end of life
  Percent of product recovered and reused
  Purity of recyclable materials recovered
  Percent of recycled materials used as input to product

- *Source volume metrics*
  Product mass
  Useful operating life
  Percent of product disposed or incinerated
  Fraction of packaging or containers recycled

- *Exposure and risk metrics*
  Ambient concentrations of hazardous by-products in various media
  Estimated annual population incidence of adverse effects in humans or biota

- *Economic metrics*

  Average life-cycle cost incurred by the manufacturer

  Purchase and operating cost incurred by the customer

  Cost savings associated with design improvements

At the aggregate level, these metrics represent the overall performance of the manufacturing enterprise; they are sometimes called *primary* or *high-level metrics.* Typically they are driven either by a fundamental customer need or by important internal constraints (e.g., process capability). The relationship of primary metrics to product goals and objectives is illustrated in Table 7.1.

Primary metrics can be used to establish measurable overall objectives for a product development team. However, in order to be useful for quality improvement, primary metrics generally need to be decomposed into *operational metrics* which represent observable and controllable measures associated with a product or process. These operational metrics can be used not only to monitor continuous

TABLE 7.1   Environmental Goals and Corresponding Metrics

Goals	Examples of metrics	Examples of specific objectives
Reduce or eliminate waste	Pounds of emissions over the life cycle	Reduce life-cycle emissions by 30% annually
	Percent of product weight disposed in landfills	Reduce solid waste disposed to 1 pound per product unit
Develop "green," recyclable products	Percent of product weight recovered and recycled	Achieve 95% recycling
	Solid waste emissions	Eliminate end-of-life waste disposal
Reduce life-cycle cost of product	Manufacturing cost	Reduce total life-cycle cost to $7500 per product unit
	Distribution and support cost	
	End-of-life cost	Reduce end-of-life cost (or increase value) by 20%
Reduce cost of ownership for customers	Annualized purchase and operating cost ($)	Reduced to at most $500 per year
Conserve energy consumption over the life cycle	Total energy (BTUs) to produce one unit	Reduce to 1000 BTU
	Average power use	Reduce by 10% annually
		Power less than 30 W
Conserve natural resources by raising the recycled content	Percent by weight of product materials that is recycled	Achieve 20% or greater total recycled content
		Achieve 30% recycled plastics by weight

improvement but also to develop employee incentives and reward systems.

Operational metrics can be defined through an *enterprise model* that relates the performance of company assets and functional activities (e.g., fuel procurement) to the environmental performance of the company as a whole (e.g., hazardous air emissions). In particular, *product metrics* become operational when they are associated with a specific feature, module, or component of a design, and can therefore be estimated, tested, and verified. Similarly, operational *process metrics* represent observable and verifiable measures associated with particular operations and business processes (e.g., number of defects per million units produced). Figure 7.2 illustrates how operational metrics can be derived from primary metrics related to recyclability of durable goods.

There are several alternative uses for environmental performance metrics, and different types of metrics may be preferable for each use:

- *Performance-tracking metrics* are used internally to increase productivity and to assure that corporate objectives are fulfilled.

- *Decisionmaking metrics* are used to evaluate competing options when performance factors in addition to cost must be considered.

- *External reporting metrics* are used to disclose improvements in overall company performance to stakeholders.

Environmental performance measurement systems may address any or all of these uses. Because of the obvious data management challenges, it is clear that modern information technology will be an

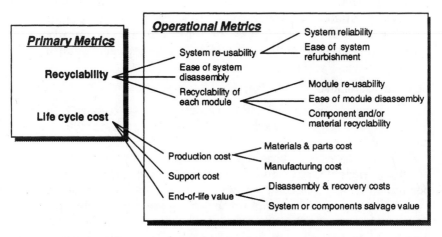

Figure 7.2 Example of decomposition of primary metrics into operational metrics related to product recycling.

important tool for implementing, computing, tracking, and converting these metrics to meet various needs. Chapter 5 has outlined the type of information infrastructure needed to support performance measurement and tracking.

Categories of Metrics

Environmental quality metrics can be classified according to the following three distinctions:

Qualitative vs. quantitative

Qualitative metrics are those that rely upon semantic distinctions based on observation and judgment. An example is the GEMI ESAP self-assessment protocol, which allows companies to assess the characteristics of their environmental management systems based on a generic rating system.[2] While it is possible to assign numerical values (or scores) to qualitative metrics, such numbers have no intrinsic significance. An advantage of qualitative metrics is that they impose a relatively small data collection burden and are easy to implement. A disadvantage is that they implicitly incorporate subjective information and therefore are difficult to validate.

Quantitative metrics are those that rely upon empirical data and derive numerical results that characterize performance in physical, financial, or other meaningful terms. An example is the Toxic Release Inventory (TRI) system mandated by the U.S. Environmental Protection Agency (EPA). The advantages of quantitative metrics are that they are objective, meaningful, and verifiable. A potential disadvantage is that the required data may be burdensome to gather or simply unavailable. Moreover, there are some environmental attributes, such as "public perception" or "environmental commitment," which are inherently qualitative and cannot be precisely quantified.

Absolute vs. relative

Absolute metrics are those that are defined with respect to a fixed measurement scale. An example is "total annual hazardous waste generated."

Relative metrics are those that are defined with respect to another metric or variable. An example is "total hazardous waste generated per unit produced." A common approach is to use *time-based relative metrics,* i.e. those which compute the change in a particular quantitative metric over a given time period; for example "percent reduction from 1994 to 1995 in total hazardous waste generated per unit produced."

The use of absolute metrics may lead to inappropriate comparisons of performance among two or more organizations, whereas relative metrics are generally less biased by differences among the organization characteristics. This potential for abuse of information has made many companies wary of reporting their environmental performance results.

Source vs. impact

With regard to environmental performance, *source metrics* are those that address the presumed root causes or origins of environmental consequences associated with an organization's activities. An example is the TRI, which measures the quantity of toxic materials released at a given site. An advantage of source metrics is that they are both readily observable and controllable. A disadvantage is that they are an indirect indicator of potential impacts and generally ignore differences in fate, transport, exposure, and effect pathways among different organizations.

Impact metrics are those that address the actual environmental consequences which may result from an organization's activities. An example is the use of exposure assessment and dose-response assessment to calculate the "increased cancer risk in the exposed population." While impact metrics have the obvious advantage of directly addressing the impacts of concern, the development of environmental impact metrics is generally challenging due to the technical and statistical uncertainties involved both in assessing impacts and in attributing them to specific sources (see Chap. 9).

In practice, the most efficient means of quality measurement is to select company-specific indicators (typically source-oriented) which are believed to be correlated with broad categories of environmental impacts. A common example is the measurement of total emissions of ozone-depleting substances, which are believed to be related to global climate change. Even though the magnitude (or even existence) of the relationship may be speculative, the use of a source metric allows companies and regulatory agencies to establish clear targets for improvement.

Example   3M has developed a measure of eco-efficiency called a *waste ratio* that is useful for application to manufacturing facilities.[3] It is calculated as follows:

$$\text{Waste ratio} = \frac{\text{waste}}{\text{product} + \text{by-product} + \text{waste}}$$

This is a *quantitative relative source metric,* since waste volume is measured relative to the total material output of the plant. In order to minimize this ratio, engineers can either convert waste to useful by-products or reduce the waste generated.

Applicability and Scope of Metrics

Environmental metrics ideally should be assessed with respect to the life cycle of the product or process being developed. Table 7.2 illustrates how various types of metrics are typically related to life-cycle stages. Each row represents a class of primary environmental metrics; the arrows represent the direction of desired improvement (up or down). An X in a given row and column indicates that the corresponding metric is relevant to the life-cycle stage.

In many cases, practical limitations of data resources or methodology may hinder the ability of a development team to evaluate all of the relevant cells. In other cases, companies may wish to exclude certain life-cycle stages from consideration because they are not relevant to business decisionmaking (see Chap. 10). Therefore, the intended scope and rationale for metrics should always be clarified. For example, rather than speaking of "energy use reduction," we should specify "reduction in energy use during manufacturing and distribution" or "reduction in power consumption during product end use."

Another important consideration in the selection of metrics is recognizing the interactions among environmental and other product and process metrics. For DFE to be truly integrated with product development, engineers must understand the synergies and trade-offs among environmental performance attributes and other design attributes. Specifically, product development teams should analyze the pairwise interactions between environmental metrics and those that relate to cost, performance, and customer satisfaction. In the "house of quality" approach commonly used in TQM (see Chap. 9), this is equivalent to examining the "roof" of the house.

Table 7.3 illustrates interactions that might be identified for a hypothetical consumer product such as a cleaning agent. Again, each row represents a class of primary environmental metrics; the arrows represent the direction of desired improvement (up or down). In this case, interactions are shown as either favorable (X) or potentially unfavorable (?). Note that it is also possible to indicate the degree or strength of interaction in qualitative terms. When applied to specific

TABLE 7.2   Relevance of Environmental Performance Metrics to Various Product Life-Cycle Stages

	Materials	Fabrication	Transport	End use	Disposal
Energy usage ↓	X	X	X	X	X
Water usage ↓	X	X		X	
Source volume ↓	X	X	X	X	X
Recycling and reuse ↑		X		X	X
Waste and emissions ↓	X	X	X	X	X
Recycled materials ↑	X	X			

TABLE 7.3   Example of Interactions Among Environmental Quality and Other Customer Benefits for a Consumer Product

	Performance	Cost	Safety	Convenience	Aesthetics
Energy usage ↓		X			
Water usage ↓		X		X	
Source volume ↓	?	X	?	X	
Recycling and reuse ↑		X		?	
Waste and emissions ↓	X	X	X	X	
Recycled materials ↑		?			?

products, this type of interaction matrix reveals some important insights. For example, one can readily see the synergies between life-cycle cost reduction and a number of environmental performance metrics. Likewise, one can identify environmental improvement options which may compromise other desirable features (e.g., recycled materials may have poorer aesthetic qualities than virgin materials).

Aggregation and Weighting Schemes

A common practice in environmental quality assessment is to use scaling or weighting techniques to aggregate various specific performance measures. For example, a frequently used approach to circumvent the challenges of environmental impact analysis is to rely upon source measures but to assign them priorities or weights based on an assessment of their relative importance, taking into consideration the available information about environmental impact pathways. Weighting schemes may be adopted to reflect a variety of different considerations, including:

- Values of different stakeholder groups (e.g., customers vs. community)

- Relative importance of environmental impacts (e.g., human health vs. ecology)

- Internal business priorities (e.g., strategic advantage)

While the aggregation of quality metrics may be desirable for purposes of simplifying decisionmaking, there are a number of problematic aspects to the use of weighting schemes for environmental metrics:

- There are usually implicit policies and value judgments embedded in the weighting system which are not apparent, yet may skew the results in unintended ways.

- Performance metrics are much more meaningful when considered separately, whereas the significance of improvement in an aggregated score is unclear.

- Aggregated measures invite comparisons among dissimilar products or facilities, while concealing important differences between such organizations.

By applying good practices, it is possible to avoid some of the above abuses or pitfalls; for example, a measurement system that captures the sources and rationales for all aggregated scores will allow later exploration and decomposition of the results, if necessary. A hierarchical approach toward decomposition, as illustrated in the classification of DFE methods in Chap. 8, would fulfill this need. In general, there is no universal weighting scheme to suit the needs of diverse organizations, and each company should develop a scheme that suits its business characteristics and priorities.

Examples of Environmental Performance Measurement

- Polaroid Corporation established a Toxic Use and Waste Reduction Program, with the goals of reducing the use of certain toxic materials per unit of production and the waste generated per unit of production by 10% per year over five years. To show their serious intent, the company adopted a policy that environmental performance would be equal to cost and quality in design trade-offs, and instituted an Environmental Accounting and Reporting System (EARS) to track data on improvement with regard to the goals. They developed a categorization of materials by degree of hazard to establish waste reduction priorities, and established a hierarchy of preferred waste management options. An example of their accomplishments was the introduction of catalyzed air oxidation for dye production, which eliminated the use of hexavalent chromium and saved $1 million per year in disposal costs.

- Ciba-Geigy, a global pharmaceuticals firm, has implemented a performance measurement and reporting system known as SEEP (Safety, Energy, and Environmental Performance). All major production sites must submit SEEP reports, with a total of 82 being submitted in 1992 from 17 different countries. The data are consolidated and used to produce a Corporate Environmental Report. Between 1990, when SEEP was initiated, and 1992, a number of performance improvements were realized; for example, SO_2 emissions were decreased by 43%, NO_x by 7%, and organic vapor emissions by 10%. Based on these results, Ciba-Geigy establishes annual site-specific targets for improvement.

References

1. J. Fiksel, "Quality Metrics in Design for Environment," *Total Quality Environmental Management,* vol. 3, no. 2, Winter 1993–1994, pp. 181–192.
2. Global Environmental Management Initiative, *Environmental Self-Assessment Program,* Washington, DC, September 1992.
3. T. W. Zosel, "Pollution Prevention Pays: The 3M Approach," *Proc. 1st International Congress on Environmentally-Conscious Design & Manufacturing,* Management Roundtable, Boston, 1992.

8

Practical
DFE Guidelines

Joseph Fiksel

*"If our products become unwanted or useless
material, they are...garbage. Our products deserve
a better fate....Garbage can be designed out of
a society."*

JOHN KUSZ
Safety-Kleen

As discussed in Chap. 5, the goal of DFE is to enable design teams to create eco-efficient products without compromising their cost, quality, and schedule constraints. An eco-efficient product is defined as a product that both minimizes adverse environmental impacts, and maximizes conservation of valuable resources throughout its life cycle. Chapter 6 has argued that, to be successful in this goal, DFE must be integrated seamlessly into the development process, from the analysis of customer needs and establishment of product requirements to the verification that these requirements have been fulfilled. The availability of guidelines for practicing DFE was identified as the second key element needed to support this process.

The Need for Guidelines

Once the product objectives have been defined, the product development cycle begins in earnest. It is an exploratory process during which ideas are generated, considered from various perspectives, and either pursued or rejected. As manufacturing companies have refined their product development processes, they have increasingly acknowledged the need for guidelines. There are at least two types of guidelines:

- *Prescriptive guidelines* are definite statements about what design-ers should or should not do, and are sometimes called *design rules*. There are many such guidelines related to environmental safety and health—for example, lists of banned materials.

- *Suggestive guidelines* represent accumulated knowledge, including best practices and lessons learned, but do not attempt to establish strict rules. They merely point in useful directions, or conversely, indicate directions that are probably not fruitful.

Virtually all of the DFE guidelines that we will discuss here are suggestive. There are several reasons for this: DFE is still embryonic, so that standards do not yet exist, and DFE involves many complex trade-offs so that general rules are difficult to find. The guidelines may be expressed in a variety of forms, ranging from verbal rules of thumb to multidimensional look-up tables to pictorial maps or dia-grams. There are a number of benefits derived from using guidelines, whether for DFE or any other DFX discipline:

- They encourage consistency among different development teams in areas where consistency is desirable, e.g., standard material-label-ing schemes.

- They promote continuity through the accumulation of knowledge ("lore") over successive design cycles, and allow that knowledge to be preserved and passed down.

- They lead to a more systematic design process that is less depen-dent upon the idiosyncrasies or particular biases of individual designers.

- They expand the scope of issues considered during design, allowing the team to anticipate downstream pitfalls or constraints that they may have ignored.

However, in a fast-paced product development environment, it is often difficult to ensure that product teams pay attention to guide-lines, especially if they are only suggestive and not strict require-ments. Various approaches are used to make developers aware of such guidelines, ranging from printed guidance manuals to on-line decision aids. To the extent that such tools can be built into the devel-opment process, they can be extremely effective in influencing prod-uct designs. An excellent example of successful introduction of DFX guidelines is the *design for manufacture and assembly* (DFMA) methodology originally developed by Boothroyd and Dewhurst at the University of Rhode Island. Their methodology has been encoded into software tools that are routinely used by major companies to simplify designs and hence reduce their assembly costs. Chapter 5 discusses in greater detail how decision support tools could play an analogous role for DFE.

Catalogue of DFE Guidelines

The following is a compilation of DFE guidelines that are commonly practiced by manufacturing firms in a variety of industries. While it is not comprehensive, it illustrates the range of practices that may be considered in DFE. To be truly useful to a particular company and product team, these types of guidelines need to be converted from the general statements listed below to more specific approaches that are applicable to the product(s) in question.

Table 8.1 summarizes the guidelines to be discussed below. There are several points to note about this list of guidelines.

- The list is by no means exhaustive, although it covers a majority of common industrial practices; new approaches are constantly being devised.

- The hierarchical classification scheme is somewhat arbitrary, since many of these practices are closely interrelated, as illustrated in Fig. 8.1.

- Each guideline may have impacts on one or more stages of the product life cycle, as illustrated in Table 8.2.

- There is considerable overlap with other DFX disciplines such as design for manufacture and assembly. Indeed, one strength of DFE is its synergy with other important design disciplines. For example, reducing the complexity of a design leads to fewer parts, lower assembly costs, and simpler disassembly.

Design for recovery and reuse

Design for material recovery.   To be recoverable with positive economic value, materials need to be as close as possible to the state of manufacturing feedstock. Material homogeneity, purity, and reprocessability are important considerations in determining their recovery value.

Composite materials (such as carbon fibers used in tennis racquets) were once prized for their superior mechanical properties. Ironically, today they have become problematic from an environmental point of

TABLE 8.1   Overview of DFE Practices

Design for recovery and reuse
  Design for material recovery
    Avoid composite materials
    Specify recyclable materials
    Use recyclable packaging
  Design for component recovery
    Design reusable containers
    Design for refurbishment
    Design for remanufacture
Design for disassembly
  Facilitate access to components
    Optimize disassembly sequence
    Design for easy removal
    Avoid embedded parts
  Simplify component interfaces
    Avoid springs, pulleys, harnesses
    Avoid adhesives and welds
    Avoid threaded fasteners
  Design for simplicity
    Reduce product complexity
    Reduce number of parts
    Design multifunctional parts
    Utilize common parts

Design for waste minimization
  Design for source reduction
    Reduce product dimensions
    Specify lighter-weight materials
    Design thinner enclosures
    Increase liquid concentration
    Reduce mass of components
    Reduce packaging weight
    Use electronic documentation
  Design for separability
    Facilitate identification of materials
    Use fewer types of materials
    Use similar or compatible materials
    Avoid material contaminants
  Design for waste recovery and reuse
  Design for waste incineration

Design for energy conservation
  Reduce energy use in production
  Reduce device power consumption
  Reduce energy use in distribution
    Reduce transportation distance
    Reduce transportation urgency
    Reduce shipping volume required
  Use renewable forms of energy

Design for material conservation
  Design multifunctional products
  Specify recycled materials
  Specify renewable materials
  Use remanufactured components
  Design for product longevity
    Extend performance life
    Design upgradeable components
    Design reusable platform
  Design for serviceability
  Design for durability
  Design for closed-loop recycling
  Design for packaging recovery
  Design reusable containers
  Develop leasing programs

Design for chronic risk reduction
  Reduce production releases
  Avoid toxic/hazardous substances
  Avoid ozone-depleting chemicals
  Use water-based technologies
  Assure product biodegradability
  Assure waste disposability

Design for accident prevention
  Avoid caustic and/or flammable
    materials
  Provide pressure relief
  Minimize leakage potential
  Use childproof closures
  Discourage consumer misuse

view. Most composite materials cannot be separated into their simpler and purer constituent materials and therefore are not recyclable except for purposes of waste incineration.

Recyclable materials include thermoplastics, engineering plastics, metals, and glass. As recycling technologies and materials science improve, we are reaching the point where recyclable materials can be found for virtually any application. Factors to consider in material selection include structural and aesthetic requirements as well as stability.

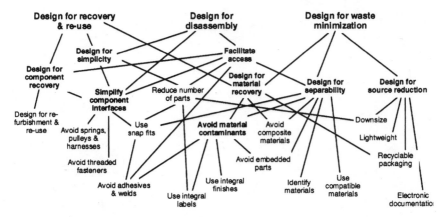

Figure 8.1   Interrelationships among DFE practices.

In general, the recyclability of a material depends on a number of factors:

- The economic attractiveness of recycling the material and the existence of end-use markets
- The volume, concentration, and purity of the recycled material
- The existence of recycling and separation technologies and an adequate recycling infrastructure

While beverage containers are commonly recycled by consumers, other types of materials are more difficult to recycle because of the lack of qualified recyclers. Without a recycling infrastructure, it is pointless to specify recyclable materials. Many manufacturers have addressed this barrier by forming alliances, such as the automotive industry's Vehicle Recycling Partnership.

Finally, it should be noted that recyclable materials need not be recycled materials. The latter are addressed below under "Design for Material Conservation."

Example   When Eastman Kodak was developing their new line of FunSaver Disposable Cameras, in 1989, they began to consciously design them for recyclability.[2] Using concurrent engineering, they were able to achieve an eight-month time-to-market cycle, even though the DFE issues posed a significant challenge. Under the system that they devised, photo finishers receive 5 cents per recycled camera frame as an incentive to return them to Kodak. The frame has color-coded parts which are separated and reground or reused at Kodak's special-purpose facility. In total, about 86% of the material in each unit is recycled, and over 5 million units have been recycled to date, implying that about 700,000 lb have been diverted from the waste stream. This is an excellent example of how a disposable product can be made environmentally responsible.

TABLE 8.2 Examples of DFE Guidelines That Can Influence Environmental Performance at Several Stages of the Product Life Cycle

Guideline	Stage in product life cycle				
	Procurement	Assembly	Distribution	Use/support	Recovery
Reduce number of distinct parts	*	*			*
Simplify component interfaces		*		*	*
Use similar or compatible materials	*				*
Use recyclable or recycled materials	*		*		*
Design for separability		*			*
Reduce packaging	*	*	*		*
Reduce mass of components	*	*	*		
Downsize products		*	*	*	
Design upgradeable components				*	*
Design recoverable components	*			*	*

Design for component recovery. In cases where product technology becomes obsolete rapidly, entire systems can be refurbished and resold. For example, there are thriving secondary markets for automobiles and personal computers. If the entire system is either not operable or not marketable, the next priority is to disassemble it and try to recover valuable components (see "Design for Disassembly" below). Although most salvaged components are resold to secondary markets, to the extent that refurbished components can be remanufactured into new products this will contribute to the achievement of *closed-loop recycling.*

Design considerations are important in determining the end-of-life value of various components. Product developers can increase this value in a number of ways:

- Designing components that are reusable for purposes of closed-loop manufacturing

- Designing components that are reusable for secondary applications due to their generic functionality, flexibility, or programmability

- Facilitating the nondestructive removal of the component—for example, surface-mounted chips are difficult to recover because their tiny leads become bent

- Designing the component in a way that speeds diagnosis and refurbishment

With the advent of take-back legislation in Europe (see Chap. 4), most manufacturers have established some type of solution to product recovery, either through in-house asset recovery programs or through turnkey arrangements with third-party firms.

> **Example** Xerox Corporation's Asset Recycle Management (ARM) program is recognized as one of the nation's most advanced asset recovery programs. A stated goal of Xerox's DFE effort, managed by Dr. Jack Azar, was to design products with minimum adverse environmental impact. ARM is a worldwide strategic initiative with the objective of achieving profitable utilization of unserviceable parts and equipment consistent with environmental goals. They have implemented a number of techniques including design for disassembly, recyclability, and commonality of parts. Currently they reclaim and remanufacture about 1 million finished parts per year, including toner cartridges and other components, amounting to an annual value of about $200 million.[3]

Design for disassembly

Facilitate access to components. The purpose of design for disassembly is to assure that a product system can be disassembled at minimum cost and effort. This is an important prerequisite to other end-of-life considerations such as component separability and recyclability. If you can't get access to a component, no matter how valuable, then you cannot recover it.

The extent to which a unit, module, assembly, or component should be disassembled depends not only on the costs of disassembly, separation, inspection, sorting, and refurbishment, but also on its reuse, resale, or salvage values. For example, it may not be cost-effective to disassemble products that contain many different, difficult to identify materials. Similarly, if components, assemblies, and modules cannot be reused or refurbished, and if they contain largely nonrecyclable materials, little disassembly is warranted.

The sequence of assembly and the extent to which a product is disassembled can be represented hierarchically by a *disassembly tree,* as shown in Fig. 8.2, which identifies all major modules and components in the product. There are a sequence of choices in order of priority to be made at each step in the sequence—resell, refurbish and resell, disassemble, or reduce to waste. Using mathematical optimization techniques, it is possible to maximize the net value recovered through product disassembly, based on information about the likely condition of the components, material and component salvage values, and average disassembly times.

At any stage of disassembly, the ability to remove a component or part is a key consideration. For example, parts that are embedded cannot be recovered easily for reuse. Moreover, if a part is embedded in an incompatible material, it makes it difficult to recycle the assembly. If the design does not allow for easily separable parts, then embedded parts should be constructed of recyclable and compatible materials.

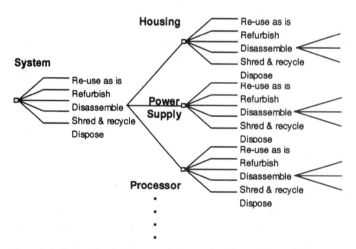

Figure 8.2   Example of a disassembly tree for electronic products.

Simplify component interfaces. Disassembly involves the sequential removal of components, and therefore the technologies used for the interfaces directly influence the ease of disassembly. The following guidelines will contribute to speeding up disassembly process and recovering a larger proportion of system components:

- Avoid springs, pulleys, and harnesses which complicate the disassembly process.

- Minimize the use of adhesives and welds between components which may be separated or between incompatible materials. Adhesives introduce contaminants, can detract from quality due to the potential for bond failure, and increase the costs associated with disassembly. If adhesives are required, try to use adhesives that are compatible with the joined materials.

- Use snap fits to join components where possible. Snap fits involve an undercut on one part engaging a molded lip on a mating part to retain an assembly. Snap fits are relatively inexpensive to manufacture, and have attractive mechanical properties.

- Avoid threaded fasteners (screws), if possible, because they increase assembly and disassembly costs.

- Use alternative bonding methods such as solvent bonding or ultrasonic bonding. Such methods may be acceptable for bonding parts made from the same material and which will not be separated at end of life.

- Spring clips or speed clips can be an inexpensive and effective way of joining parts and materials. They permit easy assembly and disassembly, and do not introduce contaminants.

Example NCR Canada's Imaging Systems Division, in Waterloo, Ontario, pioneered a program which they called Ecologically Responsible Design (ERD). Their 7731 personal image processor incorporated a number of environmental improvements, including product feature consolidation and differentiation, design for disassembly through material identification, and a packaging recycling method explained by a customer information sheet. To support their design efforts they adopted a checklist approach, with guidelines for purifying parts and easing disassembly. They also interfaced with other NCR groups such as corporate packaging to improve reuse, corporate publications to promote recycled materials, and corporate industrial design to achieve reduction in CFC use.[4]

Example Volkswagen has operated a recycling plant since 1990, at which cars are dismantled, liquids are drained, and wastes are separated for reprocessing; for example, some of the plastics are recycled into new automobile bumpers. Through design changes such as elimination of threaded fasteners and part count reduction, they have been able to significantly reduce disassembly time.

Design for simplicity.   Design elegance has long been a desirable attribute of products. For example, during the 1930s, the Bauhaus school of design formalized its criteria of elegance in terms of minimalism and functional orientation. With the advent of environmental consciousness, elegance in the form of simplicity has acquired a strong added motivation. Simplicity usually leads to lower manufacturing cost, lower material mass, greater durability, and easier disassembly for purposes of maintenance or asset recovery. There are several ways in which designers can try to achieve greater simplicity:

- Reducing the complexity of the product enclosures and assemblies in terms of their geometric and spatial design, as well as the complexity of their functional operation

- Reducing the number of distinct parts that are incorporated into a design; this is a well-known technique in the field of design for manufacture and assembly

- Designing multifunctional parts that serve a variety of purposes, e.g., using a single type of fastener for all assemblies

- Utilizing common parts in a number of different designs, representing either different models in a product family or successive product generations

Example   Kyocera Electronics has recently introduced a new printer called Ecosys which eliminates the need for a disposable or recyclable toner cartridge. The printer uses a self-cleaning printing drum coated with superhard amorphous silicon. With this more elegant design, users need only add toner to maintain the device.

Design for waste minimization

Design for source reduction.   Source reduction is routinely practiced as the most desirable alternative in the pollution prevention hierarchy. Reducing the mass of a product is the surest and most direct way to achieve waste reduction, and usually results in lower life-cycle costs as well. In many industries, notably electronics, the mass of products has been steadily decreasing due to consumer demand and technological advances. In other industries, such as food and beverages, the mass of the product itself is inflexible, and ingenious methods must be found to reduce the mass of containers and packaging. The following is a list of guidelines representing the most common source reduction practices:

- Reduce the product's physical dimensions.
- Specify lighter-weight materials as substitutes.

- Design thinner enclosures with existing materials.
- Increase the concentration in liquid products.
- Reduce the mass of key components.
- Reduce the weight or complexity of packaging.
- Use electronic documentation instead of paper.

Example Procter & Gamble's Laundry and Cleaning Products Division has been a pioneer in developing new product forms which reduce solid waste. They have introduced ultraconcentrated detergents which have rapidly grown in market share.

Example The ultimate in source reduction is represented by the fledgling science of nanotechnology, which seeks to develop products on a molecular scale.

Design for separability. Separability of incompatible materials and components is an important characteristic in determining the overall recyclability of a design. As noted under "Design for Disassembly," adhesives and welds should be avoided to assure separability. However, even after disassembly is complete, materials need to be sorted into different categories for purposes of recycling. A key strategy for separability, and an inexpensive one, is to facilitate identification of materials by means of coding or marking. For example, the International Organization for Standardization (ISO) has developed a generic identification and marking standard, ISO 11469, for plastic products. The goal of the standard is to help identify plastic products for purposes of handling, waste recovery, or disposal.

The labor costs associated with identifying, separating, sorting, and handling materials increase as the number of materials increase. Designing with fewer different materials both facilitates identification and results in larger volumes for each material, potentially increasing the salvage value that can be obtained. By the same token, using similar or compatible materials reduces the amount of separation effort required.

Avoid material contaminants. There are a number of potential contaminants that cannot easily be separated from product or packaging materials. Examples include adhesives, inks, paints, pigments, staples, and labels. Many manufacturers have begun to use integral finishes instead of painted finishes. This has advantages in terms of both lower manufacturing cost and recyclability.

While discrete labels are sometimes necessary, integral labels are preferable from an environmental point of view. Discrete labels are often made of incompatible materials and introduce contaminants (e.g., adhesives, paper, inks). They must be completely removed before a part can be recycled, which greatly increases the material separation cost.

Alternatives to discrete labels include molded-in or embossed labels. If discrete labels are necessary, it is best to avoid printed labels, or to use compatible inks. Discrete labels can be manufactured from the same material as the base part and attached without use of adhesives.

Design for waste recovery and reuse.   Waste is produced at every point in the life cycle of a product. The actual waste associated with the discarded product at end of life may be only a fraction of the waste generated by the manufacture, use, and disposal of a product. As an extreme example, the Microelectronics and Computer Technology Corporation (MCC) estimated that the production of a single semiconductor device weighing about 10 g generates approximately 7 lb of hazardous waste and 82 lb of nonhazardous waste (see Chap. 14). New environmental technologies are being developed that can recover useful materials from wastes. By considering such opportunities during product design, engineers are able to maximize the value extracted from waste materials.

While the above guidelines address recovery and reuse of product materials, an important aspect of pollution prevention is waste minimization for by-products and consumables that are generated during manufacturing, distribution, and use of the product (e.g., batteries).

Example International Tire Collection Corporation has developed a pyrolytic conversion process to recover gasoline, kerosene, diesel fuel, and carbon black from discarded tires which might otherwise sit in unsightly and hazardous refuse heaps.[5]

Example A number of electric utilities have begun to recover useful materials from their flue gas scrubber residue. For example, Southern Indiana Gas & Electric (SIGECO) recovers gypsum, which is sold as feedstock for wallboard manufacture. New York State Electric & Gas (NYSEG) recovers calcium chloride, which is used as an ice and snow melting agent.

Design for waste incineration.   The lowest form of material recovery is converting waste to energy, usually by incineration. However, this is still preferable to landfilling from an environmental perspective, and in some cases from a cost perspective as well. Waste-to-energy facilities can be found in many parts of the country that incinerate municipal solid waste, biomass (e.g., wood chips), or other wastes (e.g., automotive tires, railroad ties, utility poles) to generate steam and produce energy in the form of electricity. Hazardous wastes are typically not accepted for conversion to energy.

Because of capacity constraints, many municipalities have not entered into long-term contracts with large industrial waste generators. Although most municipally owned waste-to-energy facilities can accommodate small volumes (e.g., less than 100 tons per week) of additional waste, larger volumes can be problematic. However, if the material can be delivered during periods of high local energy demand at a time when alternative fuels are not available, municipalities may be willing to accommodate large industrial generators. Many facilities are located on rail spurs, so that transportation by truck or rail is feasible. To minimize transportation costs, many waste generators densify and bale their material before shipping.

Design for energy conservation

Reduce energy use in production. Energy conservation is one of the most attractive approaches to pollution prevention, because it is both easy to implement and results in direct cost savings. According to the U.S. Environmental Protection Agency (EPA), which sponsors the Green Lights and Energy Star programs (see Chap. 5), every kilowatt-hour of electricity not used prevents the emission of 1.5 lb of CO_2, 5.8 g of SO_2 and 2.5 g of NO_x. Therefore, designing energy-efficient production processes is a key DFE strategy.

Reduce device power consumption. The U.S. federal government has been aggressive in promoting energy efficiency of electronic devices. The Energy Star program has been credited with accelerating the reduction of power consumption, and in 1993 the General Services Administration added a boost by announcing that the government would seek to procure "environmentally preferable" products. There are also a number of initiatives in the European Union that emulate Energy Star.

Reduced power consumption in computers and peripherals is accomplished by means of *power management features* that power down a unit when it has not been used for some length of time. Such features have already become standard equipment on laptops.

In other types of products, energy efficiency is achieved through developing more efficient motors and reducing the energy load. For example, power use in refrigerators has declined by 30%, encouraged in part by the "demand-side management" energy conservation efforts of electric utilities.

Reduce energy use in distribution. An often overlooked aspect of energy use is the distribution chain of products, including shipments from component vendors to manufacturers or assemblers, from manufacturers to distribution centers or retail stores, and from these intermediate points to customers. It is not uncommon for a product to go through a half dozen shipment stages by various modes before arriving at its ultimate destination. Each leg of such a journey may entail significant cost as well as energy consumption; the most extreme case is shipping a missing part by courier to meet a delivery deadline.

Although the planning of distribution logistics is not normally considered a design activity, it is certainly an important part of integrated product development. Indeed, there are certain aspects of a product's physical design, including shape, thermal tolerance, and vibration tolerance, that limit the available distribution options.

The following are examples of guidelines representing common practices for increasing distribution efficiency:

- Reduce the total transportation distance for a product or its components—e.g., by shipping modules that are outsourced directly from the supplier to the final customer.

- Reduce the transportation urgency by allowing sufficient lead time to utilize low-cost bulk shipment.

- Reduce the shipping volume required by redesigning the product geometry, packaging volume, or stacking configuration so that less space is wasted.

- Reduce special temperature requirements or other shipping constraints that consume energy.   .

Use renewable forms of energy.   One approach to sustainable development is substitution of renewable energy resources such as solar power and hydropower for nonrenewable resources such as fossil fuels. Resources are considered renewable if the rate at which they are replenished is sufficient to compensate for their depletion. However, life-cycle analyses have indicated that the full impact of power generation by some "renewable" forms, such as solar, may be equivalent to those of nonrenewable forms if one takes into account the capital- and labor-intensive activities required to construct the necessary equipment and facilities.

Design for material conservation

Design multifunctional products.   Products which have multiple uses are by nature eco-efficient, in that the same amount of material achieves a higher level of functionality. The greater the proportion of time during a product life that the product is actually in use, the greater the ratio of value delivered to resources consumed. There are essentially two types of multiple functionality:

- *Parallel functions,* in which the same product may simultaneously serve several different purposes (e.g., a video camera that also serves as a playback device)

- *Sequential functions,* in which a product is retired from its primary use and then applied to a secondary and tertiary use (see example under "Resource Cascading" below)

Specify recycled materials. An important aspect of sustainable development is the conservation of nonrenewable resources. Manufacturing firms have long been in the habit of specifying virgin materials that are well characterized because they were manufactured through a precise process with known feedstocks. Recently, many firms have begun to encourage the use of more "environmentally conscious" materials that have significant levels (25 to 100%) of recycled content. This is feasible to the extent that substitution of recycled materials with potential impurities is cost effective and does not compromise the quality of the final product.

Metals are easily recycled, because they can be purified in a molten state. However, for engineering thermoplastics, the thermomechanical properties and color tolerances associated with recycled resins may be significantly compromised. One approach is to utilize virgin materials only for critical components and recycled materials for less demanding applications such as base assemblies.

Specify renewable materials. Instead of recycling nonrenewable materials, an alternative approach to sustainable development is substitution of renewable materials. Materials are considered renewable if the rates at which they are replenished are sufficient to compensate for their depletion. For example, materials developed through agriculture are renewable. Examples of products that use renewable materials include soy inks and wood products.

Use remanufactured components. Products manufactured with refurbished components can potentially have the same level of quality as ones manufactured with brand new components. Unfortunately, the Federal Trade Commission's disclosure rules are somewhat limiting in this regard. To the extent that remanufacturing is feasible, it makes design for component recovery a more attractive strategy (see above).

Design for product longevity. The longer the life of a product, the more eco-efficient it is, since the same amount of material delivers a larger amount of economic value. To the extent that manufacturers can maintain profitability, they may be willing to increase product life, charge a premium, and accept a drop in sales volume. From a consumer point of view, longer-lived products are generally more desirable because of convenience and cost savings.

There are some products whose life expectancy (measured in hours of operability or duty cycles) is much longer than their actual duration of primary use, due to technological obsolescence. Personal computers are a notable example.

Apart from the life extension for the product as a whole, another way to achieve longevity is to extend the life of product components. There are at least two ways to accomplish this:

- Design upgradeable components
- Design a reusable platform

Increased longevity implies a need for greater durability, which may require denser materials and stronger fastening methods. Interestingly, these objectives conflict with the design criteria used in designing for disassembly, separability, and waste minimization. You can't have it both ways. Designers need to understand the life-cycle cost and environmental trade-offs between durability and recoverability.

Design for closed-loop recycling.   Where possible, closed-loop recovery of materials and components enhances the value of strategies such as using recycled materials and remanufactured components. Establishing a closed-loop infrastructure provides greater assurance about uniformity, homogeneity, and reliability of the recycled assets.

Design for packaging recovery.   In the field of industrial packaging, great strides have been made in developing methods and technologies for the recovery, recycling, and reuse of packaging materials. For example, the Green Dot system in Europe established a broad packaging take-back infrastructure, but they have experienced management difficulties.

Design reusable containers.   Disposal of used containers is a major source of solid waste. Significant cost savings and material efficiency can be achieved by designing containers that can be recovered and reused for the same application. Industrial suppliers can redesign the shipping containers in which they deliver materials and components so that they can be recycled and used repeatedly. Consumers can learn to purchase concentrated refills for their spray bottles and detergents. The antique refillable milk bottle is a classic example of this approach, which we are now rediscovering.

> **Example** Safety Kleen is a company that specializes in the management of industrial solvents, including distribution, recovery, and recycling. They were able to save $1.8 million by redesigning the containers used to recover waste solvents from dry-cleaning plants. They redesigned the container from a steel drum that needed replacement every 1.5 times to a durable plastic container that could be used about 20 times and then converted to energy through incineration.

Develop leasing programs.   A radical alternative approach to product manufacturing and distribution is to introduce a "leased product" concept in which the manufacturer retains ownership of and responsibility for the physical product. (See, for example, Chap. 18.) This approach allows greater control over recycling and waste minimization, and may also provide greater customer satisfaction.

Design for chronic risk reduction

Reduce production releases. Designing "cleaner" processes is a more effective means of pollution prevention than merely retrofitting existing processes. Process engineers have discovered a variety of methods for reducing or eliminating undesirable emissions.

> **Example** Volkswagen, the German automobile manufacturer, decided to eliminate solvent-based paints rather than try to tighten volatile organic compound (VOC) emission controls. They have invested over $1 billion in water-based paint technology at several major plants, and have reduced the solvent content from about 80% to 10%. At this point they are using water-based paints as a base coat, but soon expect to substitute them for top coats as well. In addition to VOC reduction, VW's approach improves working conditions and improves paint quality.

> **Example** Stanley Tools is a nationally known manufacturer of quality hardware, including tape measures. In 1991, they were seeking an alternative to chrome plating for the ABS plastic tape enclosure. Their objectives were to lower hazardous occupational exposures and reduce waste products, while duplicating or enhancing the appearance and wear of chrome plate. After some experimentation, they developed a vacuum-activated coating process which used several coats: an ultrathin presputter stainless steel layer; a clear, UV-curable paint layer; and metallic vapor deposition with the final clear coat. This approach sharply reduced their solid waste, VOC, and wastewater releases. It also reduced the scrap rate and increased profitability. Added benefits were that it eliminated litigation over chrome-flaking injuries, and allowed them to operate a clean facility without fumes.[7]

Avoid undesirable substances. Many companies have developed lists of materials to be avoided due to their regulatory status or known health and environmental hazards. For example, materials containing certain flame retardants (e.g., PBDOs) may be restricted from normal recycling channels due to toxicity concerns. Several European countries are in the process of adopting such regulations, and alternative flame retardants should be explored.

Unfortunately, the continuing hysteria of public health advocates has led to some questionable policies regarding hazardous substances. The recent flurry of concern over a possible chlorine ban illustrates how vulnerable our economy is to haphazard regulation. By any objective measure, the economic value of chlorine and chlorine-based compounds appears to far outweigh the speculative low-level risks that are attributed to them.

> **Example** HENKEL, a German-based consumer products and specialty chemicals firm, made an early decision to eliminate phosphates from its detergents. Phosphates have been linked with eutrophication in lakes and rivers, which disrupts the aquatic ecosystem. After intensive R&D, the company discovered an effective substitute called Sasil. Their introduction of phosphate-free detergent in 1982 was highly successful, and by 1991 phosphate-free powders had a majority share of the Western European detergent markets.

Avoid ozone-depleting chemicals. The worldwide ban on CFCs that resulted from the Montreal Protocol, combined with the CFC labeling rules, have all but eliminated new uses of CFCs. However, substitute chemicals such as perfluorocarbons have similar properties, and may eventually be found to be culprits in ozone depletion. While there is much scientific controversy over the validity of such claims, manufacturers should carefully consider their process design choices and seek ways to eliminate suspect chemicals.

Use water-based technologies. The substitution of aqueous solvents for cleaning of parts and other industrial processes has become widespread. Through better control of mechanical and hydraulic factors, aqueous cleaning can be as effective as traditional methods that use more hazardous chlorinated solvents.

Assure product biodegradability. Formulation of products which degrade under typical disposal conditions is a common approach in cases where recycling is not feasible.

Assure waste disposability. Certain waste materials cannot be economically recovered and reprocessed. In these cases it is important that their physical form and hazardous constituents be controlled to assure safe and efficient disposal.

Design for accident prevention

Safety and accident prevention in both product and process design are important issues that should be addressed in conjunction with the above environmental issues. Traditionally, risk analysis techniques were applied to existing products and processes in order to identify potential hazards, quantify their significance, and determine how they might be mitigated. DFE provides an opportunity to apply these techniques during the design process, as a means of evaluating alternative design concepts and technologies. For example, hazards associated with the use of caustic or flammable materials can be minimized through designing out these materials or assuring that they are carefully contained. Similarly, explosive hazards can be avoided through innovations in chemical engineering. The following are examples of design guidelines that address process and/or product safety.

- Avoid caustic and/or flammable materials
- Provide pressure relief
- Minimize leakage potential
- Use childproof closures
- Discourage consumer misuse

Resource Cascading

One approach to DFE that seeks to maximize the utility of resource usage is based on the theory of *resource cascading*.[8] The aim of this approach, as illustrated in Fig. 8.3, is to find a sequence of resource uses that extracts as much economic value as possible from a given resource as it evolves from higher-quality to lower-quality forms.

For example, a batch of solvent used for degreasing in electronics manufacturing could, after a single use, be transferred to a metal cleaning operation. It could then be used in repeated cycles, until eventually being relegated to its lowest-quality use, as a paint solvent. Finally, through purification and recycling, the spent solvent could again be shifted back up the cascade chain to a higher-quality use.

Similarly, in a closed-loop cascading approach, plastic materials can be used first for cosmetic parts, secondly for internal structural parts, and finally for base parts in a particular manufacturing process, before being recycled into a commingled stream. By the laws of thermodynamics, all materials and energy reach an equilibrium state of maximum entropy, but resource cascading enables us to capture as much economic value as possible during this decline.

There are four basic principles associated with resource cascading:

1. *Appropriate fit:*   Reserve the highest-quality resources for the most demanding uses.

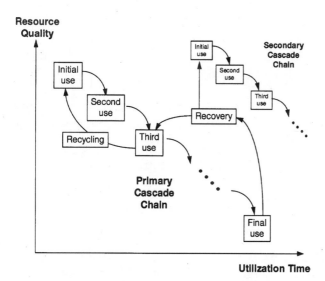

Figure 8.3   Resource cascading.

2. *Augmentation:* Increase the utility of a resource by extending utilization time or counteracting the decline of resource quality (e.g, through regeneration).

3. *Relinking:* At each conservative link in the cascade chain, consider shifting the resource to a secondary cascade chain where its utility may be greater (e.g., by using waste or by-products as feedstocks for other processes).

4. *Sustainability:* Assure that the rate of resource consumption is balanced with the rate of resource regeneration.

Note that augmentation and relinking invariably involve some expenditure of resources, so that decisions about alternative pathways should take into account the associated net utility. Examples of resource utility maximization efforts include:

- Impeding quality decline (e.g., adding preservatives)
- Supplementing quality losses (e.g., chemical replenishment)
- Increasing use intensity (e.g., sharing among multiple processes)
- Improving durability (e.g., protective coatings)
- Separation of a substance into basic resources (e.g., solvent filtration)
- Re-collection of dispersed material (e.g., cadmium reclamation from batteries)
- Regeneration of quality (e.g., thermal transformation)

While inorganic substances can often be relinked to the highest quality level through physical processes, organic materials must eventually be allowed to cascade through biochemical decomposition to the bottom of the chain, where they are regenerated into new life forms through solar energy.

The principles of resource cascading have been formulated only recently, but already they have been applied in diverse areas, for example:

- Reuse of biomass in agriculture and aquaculture
- Repeated use of chlorinated solvents for degreasing
- Recycling of plastic materials used for packaging
- Energy cascading in multistep alcohol distillation

Although it is tempting to consider "design for cascadability" as a product development discipline, there are a number of challenges to this approach. It is difficult to anticipate the requirements of subsequent links in the chain when designing an initial product. Moreover, understanding these subsequent links may require collaboration among designers in different companies. The quality and reliability of relinked or augmented products is difficult to predict. Finally, and perhaps most challenging, there is little economic incentive to motivate the extra effort and expense of designing cascaded processes unless the benefits of cascading accrue directly to the original manufacturer (e.g., recovery and refurbishment of used parts).

On the other hand, cascading of resources used in manufacturing processes is much more promising. Partnerships among multiple suppliers within a cascade chain are beginning to demonstrate the advantages of this approach.

Example A well-known example of cascading is a demonstration project operated jointly by Digital Equipment Corporation (DEC), GE Plastics, and Nailite, Inc., of Miami, Florida. Obsolete DEC computer products are recovered from customers and dismantled in a dedicated disassembly facility. The computer housings are shredded and the plastic is reprocessed and delivered to Nailite, who in turn produce roofing components and shingles using about 48% recycled material. These roofing products are installed on McDonald's restaurants, which appear to promise continued growth in demand. Thus, engineering resins which might otherwise be landfilled are cascaded to a second-tier use.

References

1. J. Kusz, "Is It Product Design or Is It Garbage Design?" *Design Perspectives,* Industrial Design Society of America, Great Falls, VA, December 1989.
2. A. Van de Moere, "Kodak's Design for Recyclability," *Proc. 1st International Congress on Environmentally-Conscious Design & Manufacturing,* Management Roundtable, Boston, 1992.
3. V. Berko-Boateng, J. Azar, E. DeJong, G. A. Yander, "Asset Recycle Management—A Total Approach to Product Design for the Environment," *Proc. IEEE Symposium on Electronics and the Environment,* Washington, DC, May 1993.
4. A. R. Hamilton, "Combining Technical Innovation with Ecologically Responsible Design: The Case of the NCR 7731 Personal Image Processor," *Pollution Prevention Review,* Winter 1992–1993.
5. *Environmentally Conscious Manufacturing Newsletter,* U.S. Department of Energy, Sandia National Laboratories, Albuquerque, NM, vol. 4, no. 2, July 1993.
6. *Business and the Environment Newsletter,* Cutter Publications, Arlington, MA, February 1994.
7. J. Maru, "Creating an Environmentally Friendly Coating System," *Proc. 1st International Congress on Environmentally-Conscious Design & Manufacturing,* Business Roundtable, Boston, 1992.
8. T. Sirkin and M. ten Houten, *Resource Cascading and the Cascade Chain: Tools for Appropriate and Sustainable Product Design,* Interfaculty Department of Environmental Sciences, University of Amsterdam, The Netherlands, 1993.

Methods for Assessing and Improving Environmental Performance

Joseph Fiksel

Introduction

In designing eco-efficient products, it is important to consider all stages of their life cycle, including raw material extraction, processing, transport, component manufacturing, product assembly, distribution, end use, service, disposal, and recycling. While product development teams need not analyze all of these life-cycle stages in exhaustive detail, they should be aware of those environmental issues, at any stage of the life cycle, that are relevant to either customer needs or technical and financial constraints.[1]

Moreover, as mentioned in Chap. 6, *analysis methods* are required to enable systematic assessment and quantification of environmental performance across the life cycle of a product or process. Assuming that metrics have been defined and objectives have been set, analysis methods can be used in several ways:

- To evaluate the degree to which a particular design meets cost or performance objectives and requirements

- To compare alternative designs and evaluate their relative merits
- To identify potential design improvements and evaluate their expected benefits

Although quantitative methods are preferable for purposes of continuous improvement and competitive benchmarking, in many cases quantification is difficult and qualitative methods have served adequately.

Examples of useful analysis methods that are commonly applied during product development by manufacturing firms include:

- Qualitative methods for assessing environmental performance of a product design throughout the life cycle
- Life-cycle assessment (LCA) methods for calculating the net energy or material flows associated with products
- Impact analysis methods for quantifying the potential environmental, health, safety, and economic consequences of environmental releases
- Environmental accounting methods for assessing the costs incurred either by the manufacturer, its customers, or other parties at various stages of the product life

The following sections briefly describe each category of methods, and Chap. 10 will address life-cycle analysis methods in greater detail.

Qualitative Methods

Qualitative assessment methods have a number of obvious advantages over quantitative methods—they are easier to apply, require minimal data, and can be useful in spite of large uncertainties. For many companies, such methods are the logical first step in implementing DFE because they can provide value without requiring large resource expenditures. Qualitative approaches have countless variations; below we illustrate two common types of methods: *checklists* and *matrices.*

Checklists

The simplest and most common qualitative assessment tool is a checklist of *criteria,* stated in the form of questions or points to consider. The use of checklists is often one of the first DFE initiatives undertaken by product development organizations because checklists require only modest resources to update and maintain, and are easy to understand and implement. Despite these advantages, checklists do have important limitations:

- They are qualitative in nature, even though it is possible to compute numeric scores. This means that they provide only crude measures of performance improvement. For example, a checklist might pose the question "Have you found ways to increase the fraction of waste converted into useful products?" A simple "yes" answer does not convey much information. Performance evaluation should take into account the baseline waste stream, the types of wastes, the difficulty of recycling, and the level of improvement achieved. (See Chap. 8.)

- They provide no guidance to product developers regarding the relative importance of different issues or the degree of effort that is warranted in addressing a specific issue. For example, is it more important to reduce source volume or to assure recyclability? Is a 10% reduction in waste a reasonable goal? How much of the R&D budget should be committed to achieving these goals? These are challenging questions that can only be answered through a more rigorous trade-off analysis. (See Chap. 10.)

- Checklists can actually reduce creativity by encouraging a false sense of complacency. People who have worked through the checklist in a mechanical fashion may feel that they have done all that is necessary to consider environmental issues. Thus they may fail to become sufficiently involved in DFE issues and may overlook important opportunities or problems that are not covered on the list.

Nevertheless, checklists are an effective starting point for encouraging organizations to think about environmental issues and begin taking positive actions. The following describes different types of checklists that are commonly used:

Material selection criteria. Perhaps the most common checklist device is a list of materials to be consulted by engineers when specifying parts. This can take two forms: a list of *preferred* materials based on environmental considerations, or a list of materials to be *avoided* because of regulatory restrictions and environmental concerns.

Supplier selection criteria. The environmental performance of a product or process is intimately tied to the materials and energy flows that characterize its life cycle. From the perspective of industrial ecology, products do not exist in isolation, but are part of the fabric of an industrial system which extends broadly in both time and space. For example, automobiles and computers are assembled from a variety of components that typically are manufactured by one set of suppliers and recovered or recycled by another set of contractors. Companies that are highly leveraged in this way have begun to review the environmental performance characteristics of their suppliers and contractors.

Product or process design criteria. Design checklists are essentially a formalization of guidelines like the ones discussed in Chap. 8. They usually consist of a series of questions or criteria that address specific DFE considerations, and are applied as a form of design review. The best time to use such checklists, of course, is during the concept development stage, but they are also useful as part of a milestone review to assure that the product team has considered relevant environmental concerns.

Matrices

Qualitative matrices are a useful technique for trade-off analysis in design decisions. They involve creating a matrix diagram in which the rows represent competing options or objectives and the columns represent design attributes. Again, there are many variations on this basic technique. While matrices have many of the same advantages and limitations as checklists, they do provide a means for evaluating trade-offs and representing more subtle interactions among design criteria.

One popular approach that employs such matrices is *quality function deployment* (QFD), which uses a "house of quality" model to make explicit the relationships between customer desires and product design parameters. This is essentially a matrix whose rows represent desirable properties of the product, and whose columns represent controllable and measurable parameters of the design; interactions between these parameters can be represented in the "roof" of the house. The QFD analysis can be performed recursively by further analyzing and dissecting each of these parameters. A number of PC-based tools are available for creating, displaying, and printing QFD matrices.

> **Example** Brad Allenby of AT&T, a well-known proponent of DFE, developed a qualitative matrix approach for environmental impact assessment as part of his Ph.D. thesis.[2] The approach arrays alternative technologies (rows) against life-cycle stages (columns), and indicates both the magnitude and uncertainty of the impact in each cell of the matrix through graphic devices. Without requiring detailed data or laborious calculations, this approach appears to offer useful insights into the environmental preferability of different technologies. For example, Allenby applied the matrix to assess three alternatives to lead solder in electronic devices—indium alloys, bismuth alloys, and conductive epoxies. The results suggested that, from a life-cycle perspective, lead is preferable to the alternatives because the latter tend to utilize more resources and generate more emissions in the extraction and processing stages.

Life-Cycle Assessment Methods

As mentioned in Chap. 4, the Society for Environmental Chemistry and Toxicology (SETAC), has developed a standard methodology for *life-cycle assessment* (LCA), defined as an objective process to:

- Develop an inventory of the environmental burdens associated with a product, process, or activity by identifying and quantifying energy and materials used and wastes released to the environment

- Assess the impact of those energy and materials uses and releases on the environment

- Evaluate and implement opportunities to effect environmental improvements

Although many companies have adopted LCA inventory methods, the latter two assessment stages are still in their infancy.

Critics have pointed out a number of serious limitations to the LCA methodology:

- Defining system boundaries for LCA is controversial.

- LCA is data-intensive and expensive to conduct.

- Inventory assessment alone is inadequate for meaningful comparison, yet impact assessment is fraught with scientific difficulties.

- LCA does not account for other, nonenvironmental aspects of product quality and cost.

- LCA cannot capture the dynamics of changing markets and technologies.

- LCA results may be inappropriate for use in eco-labeling.

While it is true that past work on LCA has suffered from data quality problems and a lack of consensus on methodology, SETAC and other organizations are now addressing these problems. Moreover, the International Organization for Standardization's (ISO's) Technical Committee 207 is developing general guidelines for LCA to support its proper application. With appropriate definition of system boundaries, LCA can be useful for identifying the environmental advantages or drawbacks of various design options, thus supporting product development decisions.

Companies that implement a full-scale DFE program will require an integrated life-cycle approach that adequately represents the differences among design approaches across the various life-cycle stages of products, that explicitly represents the inherent uncertainties regarding technical, economic, and regulatory factors, and that incorporates all relevant quality metrics.

Example   Procter & Gamble, one of the world's largest consumer products companies, has consistently applied LCA methods to assess environmental quality, especially in its laundry and paper products. P&G is renowned for having funded an early and controversial study which compared cloth diapers to disposable diapers, finding that disposables compared favorably in terms of life-cycle waste generated per diaper use. Recently, P&G analyzed the energy content of various cleaning products, and discovered that over 80% of the life-cycle energy use occurs in heating the water during use of the product. The company is now developing a cold-water detergent which will have significant energy conservation benefits.

Example   Table 9.1 shows the results of a partial LCA conducted by the Microelectronics and Computer Technology Corporation (MCC), and described more fully in Chap. 14. Despite its limitations, the study revealed a number of design thrusts that could significantly reduce the environmental burdens of workstation production, namely:

- Focus on reduced power consumption during end use and during manufacturing of printed wiring assemblies.

- Develop new manufacturing technologies for semiconductor devices that use less energy and resources and generate less waste material.

- Focus on weight reduction and recycling for display monitors.

Impact Analysis Methods

Within the LCA framework described above, the second and most challenging stage is the assessment of the impacts associated with environmental releases during the manufacture, transport, use, and disposal of products. These impacts may include environmental, health, or safety impacts upon humans and ecosystems as well as economic impacts such as land use restriction and resource depletion. Moreover, impacts may be local, regional, or global in nature. The assessment of impacts is problematic because we have a relatively poor understanding of the complex physical and chemical phenomena that determine the fate and effects of substances released to the environment. Despite a great amount of continuing scientific research, our knowledge remains fragmentary and largely theoretical.

Impact analysis is a vast subject, and many other books have been devoted to various impact analysis approaches. The following is a

TABLE 9.1   MCC Life-Cycle Environmental Assessment of a Computer Workstation*

	Semi-conductor devices	Semi-conductor packaging	Printed wiring assemblies	Display monitor	End use	Total
Energy (kWh)	285	60	1790	180	9100†	11,415
Product weight (lb)	0.02	1.2	3.5	50		55
Hazardous waste (lb)	7		40	2		49
Nonhazardous waste (lb)	82	1	6	1		90
Water (gal)	2800	10	4300	200		7310

*Excludes about 28% of material: disk drive, keyboard, housing, cables, packaging, etc. Also excludes upstream materials and associated processes.

†Based on total operating life of 35,000 h.

brief discussion of the most common methods that might be adopted for purposes of DFE implementation.

Conventional risk analysis methods

The term *risk* may be defined as follows: *a risk is the possibility of an adverse outcome associated with an event or activity.* Risk generally has two dimensions: the *likelihood* that an adverse outcome will actually occur, expressed as a probability, and the *magnitude* of the consequences expressed in terms which depend on the nature of the outcome (e.g., cost of ecological damage, incidence rate of disease). There are two classes of risk typically distinguished: acute risks associated with accidental events (e.g., spills), and chronic risks associated with ongoing activities (e.g., occupational exposures). Acute risks are frequently assessed in terms of a *risk profile,* which assigns a probability distribution to the range of risk magnitude. Chronic risks are usually assessed in terms of the expected incidence of specific outcomes over a given time period. In principle, however, these two classes of risk are part of a continuum, and can be assessed within a common framework.

Risk analysis is a widely accepted approach whereby risks can be anticipated, understood, and controlled. While there are many versions of this approach, a number of fundamental process steps are commonly practiced:

- *Risk identification* is the process of characterizing potential sources of risk (sometimes called *hazards*) in terms of their nature, mechanisms of action, and possible outcomes; it may also include priority setting to determine which risks merit greater attention.

- *Risk assessment* is the process of estimating quantitatively the likelihoods and/or magnitudes of selected risks that have been identified; this generally includes assessment of the uncertainty associated with the "best" estimates of risk.

- *Risk evaluation* is the process of assigning relative importance to risks that have been identified and/or quantified, based on regulatory, economic, social, or other factors that influence their acceptability to stakeholders.

- *Risk management* is the process of deciding how to avoid, mitigate, or otherwise control those risks that are deemed unacceptable; it generally involves a balancing of risks against the costs and benefits of mitigation alternatives.

- *Risk communication* is the process of understanding the concerns of stakeholders regarding identified risks, and explaining the results of risk assessment, evaluation, and management decisions in terms that are meaningful to those stakeholders.

Risk analysis is a complex subject, spanning a broad variety of risk sources, mechanisms, endpoints, and mathematical techniques. Despite the large amount of literature that has accumulated regarding risk analysis, its methods are still evolving due both to theoretical advances and new empirical findings. Fundamental limitations on what is knowable (e.g., the "true" impacts on human populations of chronic low-level exposures) will continue to force reliance on predictive models, so that scientific debate over risk assessment methods may never be fully resolved. As a consequence, decisionmaking regarding the mitigation of risks will continue to be challenged by the presence of significant assumptions and uncertainties in the available information.

Given these inevitable limitations, it is still possible to develop and apply an objective decisionmaking process that takes into account the degree of uncertainty in risk estimates, as well as the relative importance of the corresponding endpoints from the perspective of different stakeholders. Moreover, it is possible to factor this type of information into a risk-cost-benefit analysis such that the associated trade-offs can be explicitly communicated to a variety of interested parties. To pursue such an approach requires great attention to the quality, adequacy, and credibility of the information upon which analyses are based. This information encompasses the following:

- Types and magnitudes of risk *agents,* including hazardous materials and waste products as well as radiation

- Possible initiating *events* leading to unplanned releases, such as leaks, spills, fires, explosions, or deliberate human intrusion

- Fate and transport *mechanisms* that describe how released agents are dispersed in the environment and partitioned among air, water, soil, and other media, as well as how they are chemically and physically transformed

- Categories of *receptors* that may be exposed to released agents, including workers, community residents, sensitive populations (children, pregnant women, etc.), natural vegetation and wildlife, aquatic organisms, and domestic animals and crops

- Exposure *pathways,* or routes, whereby humans and other biota may be exposed to released agents or their by-products, including inhalation, uptake through direct contact, ingestion in water, and bioaccumulation in the food chain

Indexing and scoring methods

Rigorous use of risk analysis methods, while important for health and safety assurance, is impractical as a comprehensive tool to address all the different facets of environmental performance. For some effects, such as ecological impacts, the absence of adequate data and validated models makes quantitative risk assessment impossible. For other types of impacts, such as resource depletion, the risk assessment paradigm as a whole is inappropriate, and must be replaced by an economic cost-benefit evaluation framework. In either case, the complexities of quantitative impact analysis are considerable, and will be the subject of ongoing research for decades to come.

A necessary alternative is the application of indexing and scoring methods which use available data combined with subjective judgments to derive numerical ratings. These "scores" are seldom physically meaningful in an absolute sense, but can be used to distinguish the *relative* environmental impact of alternative approaches. Such methods, for example, have been used extensively in the Superfund hazard-ranking system for setting priorities on waste site remediation. Unfortunately, these methods have often been faulted for inaccuracy and failure to account for important site characteristics. By providing a mechanistic, repeatable algorithm, scoring methods can lead to false confidence in results which are at best approximate and occasionally outright wrong.

Example Volvo Car Corporation, with the help of the Federation of Swedish Industries, has implemented an indexing system called Environmental Priority Strategies (EPS) to provide feedback to product design teams regarding the overall environmental impacts of their designs. The system calculates an *environmental load value* (ELV) for any automotive part based on a specification of its material inputs and fabrication processes. For each such material and process type, the system provides a common measure of environmental impact, which is obtained by multiplying together various factors that rate the severity and importance of different types of effects. While the mechanics of the calculations are simple, the scope of effects included is extremely broad.

The Volvo EPS system is important if only because it is one of the earliest approaches actually used by designers to provide environmental performance comparisons. However, the apparent simplicity of the ELV numerical score masks a wealth of subtleties and assumptions that are concealed from the designer. It can be argued that EPS-like methods encourage "environmental ignorance" on the part of design teams. They have the obvious drawback that it is difficult for designers, without delving into the logic of the system, to obtain insights into what technical changes might result in an improved score.

Environmental Accounting Methods

It is widely recognized that most current accounting methods do not capture the costs or revenues associated with environmental management efforts in a useful way. Because environmental budgets are usually assigned to overhead accounts, DFE initiatives in product or process engineering organizations cannot easily be credited for their monetary benefits. On a broader scale, our accounting systems do not properly internalize the environmental impacts of product and process decisions. In particular, impacts upon resources such as materials, water, soil, or energy are difficult to evaluate because market value based on classical supply and demand mechanisms fails to reflect the true societal value of these resources.

As a consequence, under conventional accounting methods, it is usually difficult to justify the costs of environmental quality improvement, since their benefits are not directly quantified. However, by following the principles of activity-based costing, it is possible to capture the contribution of environmental improvements with regard to increased profitability. Recent work in the field of *total-cost assessment* has shown that when savings associated with reduced energy use, reduced waste management expenses, and salvage values of recycled materials are taken into account, environmental improvement projects become much more financially attractive.[3] Many companies, especially in Europe, have begun to practice this sort of "eco-balance" accounting routinely.

It is important to distinguish between environmental accounting "in the small," which provides an integrated corporate perspective on contributions to profitability, and environmental accounting "in the large," which seeks to develop appropriate prices for goods and services commensurate with their environmental importance. The former is already being practiced in some form by many firms, and is eminently feasible. The latter, also known as "full-cost pricing," is much more ambitious and controversial, and will require international political consensus to become realistic.

Example   Table 9.2 shows how an Austrian mineral water producer, Romerquelle, justified an investment in a container-recycling facility. From a direct-cost perspective, the additional costs due to capital depreciation, energy, and materials were close to $150,000. However, by taking into account the cost savings associated with reduced waste and the income from paper and plastic recycling, the net annual revenue was found to be $540,000.

The Challenges of Decisionmaking

The ultimate purpose of environmental performance assessment is to support decisions, whether business decisions by manufacturers or policy decisions by governmental and other organizations. It is important that such decisions be informed by a generic life-cycle framework which recognizes the multitude of impacts that may affect stakeholders. Decisions based on considerations that are too narrow (e.g., considering only initial costs, or focusing only on recyclability) are bound

TABLE 9.2 **Example of Environmental Accounting**

Depreciation	Energy	Quantity	Current cost	Total cost	Cost savings via waste reduction	Income from recycling products	Total income	Balance
Plastic recycling $5.6 K	160 kWh $17.9 K	526 tons	$1.6 K	$25.1 K	$92.0 K	$317.5 K	$409.5 K	+$384.5 K
Paper recycling —	66 kWh $7.4 K	307 tons (labels & cardboard)	$2.7 K	$10.1 K	$168.4 K	$740.0 K	$169.1 K	+$159.0 K
Purification $12.7 K	185 kWh $20.7 K	378 tons	$77.9 K	$111.2 K	$78.3 K	—	$78.3 K	−$32.9 K
Glass recycling —	—	519 tons	—	—	$24.7 K	$5.0 K	$29.7 K	+$29.7 K
Totals $18.3 K	412 kWh $45.9 K	1730 tons	$82.1 K	$146.3 K	$363.4 K	$323.3 K	$686.7 K	+$540.3 K

SOURCE: Romerquelle Mineral Waters, Austria, 1992.

to be flawed. On the other hand, decisions which attempt to factor in an overly broad range of outcomes (e.g., planetary health, societal welfare) are likely to become bogged down in uncertainty and confusion. There is an alarming tendency nowadays to judge environmental acceptability in terms of a "laundry list" of hypothetical impacts which can only be assessed through questionable subjective methods using arbitrary assumptions. A judicious middle point between these extremes is clearly desirable.

One useful means of pruning the complexity of a decision problem is to identify first-order impacts that really matter to the decision-making organization, and that are significantly influenced by the decision outcome. Chapter 10 expounds further on how appropriate bounding and sensitivity analysis methods can be used to reduce decisions to a manageable structure. There are a number of key questions that need to be asked:

- What is the *minimal* set of environmental metrics that are adequate to represent the design's environmental performance?

- For each metric, can the degree of environmental improvement associated with each design option be assessed in quantitative terms?

- Do side effects of performance improvement need to be explicitly considered; for example, might an emission reduction be offset by an increase in risk associated with the substitute technology (e.g., waste incineration)?

- Can the analysis focus only on the immediate impacts of the design change, or do systemwide risks associated with materials and energy requirements need to be taken into account?

- Is it necessary and feasible, either implicitly or explicitly, to assign relative importance ratings or monetary equivalents to noncommensurate types of impacts?

- Is there a unifying conceptual model that defines the activities for which both cost and environmental performance estimates are developed? If not, are the underlying models for cost and environmental assessment compatible?

- How is uncertainty in cost or environmental assessments represented and managed? Does the range of uncertainty cast doubt upon the validity of the decision process?

These are challenging questions which will force analysts to look beyond the mechanics of their standard methodologies and adapt to the needs of decisionmakers, who prefer simple insights to complex mathematical results.

References

1. G. A. Keoleian and D. Mereney, "Sustainable Development by Design: Review of Life Cycle Design and Related Approaches," *Proc. Air and Waste Management Association Annual Meeting,* Cincinnati, OH, May 1994.
2. B. R. Allenby, "Integrating Environment and Technology: Design for Environment," in B. R. Allenby and D. Richards (eds.), *The Greening of Industrial Ecosystems,* National Academy of Engineering, Washington, DC, 1993.
3. U.S. Environmental Protection Agency, *Total Cost Assessment,* Report no. EPA/741/R-92/002, Washington, DC, May 1992.

10

Integrated
Life-Cycle
Management*

David Cohan, Ph.D.

Vice President
Decision Focus Incorporated
Mountain View, California

Introduction

This chapter introduces the concepts and techniques of *integrated life-cycle management,* and illustrates how these techniques can be used by businesses to make concrete progress toward improving both environmental and economic performance. The essence of integrated life-cycle management (ILCM) is to focus explicitly on the real *decisions* firms make and on the specific economic and environmental performance *metrics* that are used to evaluate these business choices, while defining the *life-cycle boundary* in a way that is meaningful to the firm's decisions. As will be discussed, the range of potential applications of ILCM is broad, and some applications can span a wide variety of performance metrics and life-cycle stages. However, any successful application will be directly motivated by a specific set of business

---

*The material presented in this chapter is based on work carried out in collaboration with David Gess, a senior associate at Decision Focus Incorporated.

goals and business decisions, rather than by any abstract or theoretical notion of the appropriate life-cycle scope.

Many of the ILCM applications to date have focused on managing the full life-cycle *costs* associated with products and materials, and the processes and activities in which these products and materials are used. Decisions addressed have included product choice and process design decisions, among others, and the life-cycle boundary is typically defined to include all stages from which the firm may incur costs. We refer to this class of applications as *life-cycle cost management* (LCCM). Many of the examples discussed in this chapter are drawn from these applications.

ILCM emphasizes bringing a life-cycle perspective to business decisions, while always making sure that the life-cycle approach is a means to an end, and not an end in itself. The purpose of adopting a life-cycle perspective is to improve business performance in both economic and environmental dimensions. Achieving these goals requires maintaining a clear focus on concrete business decisions and business performance goals. In the ILCM approach, the nature of these business decisions and business goals drives the definition of life-cycle boundaries and the selection of life-cycle performance metrics, and the analysis process is guided by the need to make business decisions efficiently, as well as from a life-cycle perspective.

Motivation: A Life-Cycle Perspective Makes Sense

What are the motivations for life-cycle thinking in businesses today? And why is a decision-oriented approach the most productive way to bring life-cycle thinking into business planning and operations? The answers lie in the simultaneous trends of increasing competition and growing demands for environmental quality, and in the nature of business processes and practices themselves.

Increasing domestic and global competition is forcing companies to reduce costs and improve efficiency. This pattern is seen in both manufacturing and service industries, and in the most technologically sophisticated as well as the most prosaic. At the same time, increasing costs for waste disposal and emissions control, growing regulatory pressure, concern regarding liabilities, and increasing customer demands for environmental quality are providing powerful incentives for firms in virtually every industry to find opportunities to reduce or even eliminate the adverse environmental impacts associated with their operations. Companies are rapidly shifting from a reactive posture toward environmental concerns toward proactive environmental stewardship, with the goal of realizing concrete benefits to the firm's customers, employees, shareholders, and other stakeholders.

Motivated by these cost and environmental concerns, several techniques have been developed to exploit a very simple and intuitive concept: *every stage in the "life cycle" of a product or process has both costs and environmental impacts.* Some of these techniques, such as traditional life-cycle costing (LCC) as widely practiced in the defense industry, consider the direct capital and operating costs of producing, using, and maintaining products, or the analogous costs of operating manufacturing or service processes, but have typically ignored environmental costs. Other techniques, such as life-cycle assessment (LCA), assess the environmental impacts for all activities that take place over a product's full life cycle, "from cradle to grave," without linking these impacts to concrete business decisions or to other business considerations. So, while a life-cycle approach appears to make sense, how can such an approach really add value in competitive business environments?

We believe that a successful life-cycle approach must allow firms to explicitly consider both costs and environmental measures if it is to be effectively integrated into day-to-day business decisionmaking. Of equal importance, a life-cycle approach must be motivated by business decisions and business goals if it is to have practical value to businesses. Companies need a flexible life-cycle approach that can be tailored to meet their specific business, environmental, and other important goals. The approach should help the company efficiently assemble the appropriate life-cycle information and bring it to bear on their business decisions. The approach will also need to evolve over time as companies' goals and the business environment change.

Such a flexible, decision-oriented life-cycle approach can be applied to an enormous range of businesses and industries, from small firms to large, from the "cleanest" service industry to the oldest "smokestack" manufacturing operations, and from mass production to custom craftsmanship. By maintaining a consistent life-cycle perspective, while tailoring the actual implementation to fit each class of decision and the specific needs and characteristics of each firm, the ILCM approach can be effectively applied from the simplest product selection decisions to the most complex and challenging product design efforts or capital investment decisions.

Firms adopting such an approach have the potential to realize significant economic benefits through cost reduction or enhanced value of their products and services, while simultaneously improving their environmental performance. ILCM encourages communication and coordination across diverse functions within a firm, and is fully consistent with ongoing efforts focused on total-quality management (TQM). Furthermore, the life-cycle perspective, and the broad life-cycle thinking it encourages, will provide additional benefits to firms that are striving to reengineer their operations, breaking down arbitrary functional or organizational boundaries, and evaluating business processes as well as design and operating decisions from a firmwide, life-cycle point of view.

Integrated Life-Cycle Management

This section begins with a discussion of how ILCM is tailored to a firm's business decisions and business goals, while maintaining a fundamental life-cycle perspective. This notion of a flexible yet internally consistent life-cycle approach that can be tightly matched to a firm's specific needs is fundamental to any successful application of ILCM. Following the overview of the key dimensions along which the approach is customized, we present several specific ways in which ILCM may be implemented. In each case, the specific implementation will make sense when it fits a firm's strategic goals and can be focused on specific business decisions.

Tailoring ILCM to business goals and business decisions

ILCM is a comprehensive and flexible life-cycle framework for making planning, design, and operating decisions, explicitly considering costs and other fundamental business metrics together with environmental, health, and safety factors. Unlike other life-cycle approaches, ILCM focuses on a firm's business decisions, which, together with the firm's goals, guide the scope of the implementation. The scope is tailored in three key dimensions:

Life-cycle boundary: The scope of the life cycle is defined consistent with the firm's goals and the nature of the decisions being addressed. If appropriate, the life-cycle boundaries could be defined very broadly to encompass all of the stages from cradle to grave for a product or process. Alternatively, the life-cycle boundaries could be defined more narrowly to include only those stages that are controlled by the firm, or those stages that result in costs or other impacts on the firm. The key concept is that *there is no single "correct" definition of the life cycle.* Depending on the specific set of decisions, a given firm may well find it appropriate to use several different definitions of the scope or boundaries of the life cycle. Several examples will be presented below.

Metrics: Impacts and costs can be measured in a variety of ways (see Chap. 7). For some decisions, firms may want to assess the cost to the firm of all impacts in the defined life cycle. For other decisions, firms may want to consider other metrics, such as solid waste volume, air emissions, energy used, or health risks to exposed populations. Decisionmakers often need to make trade-offs among several metrics, such as cost and waste volume. One alternative may incur higher cost but produce lower waste compared to other alternatives, while another may result in lower cost with higher volume of a less hazardous waste. The selected metrics must be consistent with a firm's business goals, as well as with the scope of the life cycle as discussed above.

Alternatives: Using a decision-oriented life-cycle process only makes sense if there are real decisions. The alternatives may be obvious, or a firm may need to identify and create innovative options and then make choices among them. For example, alternatives can range from purchasing or waste disposal options to product substitution options to design alternatives to specific options for redesigning processes and systems. The key is to make sure that appropriate options are considered—options which are consistent with the decisions being addressed, and with the definition of the life-cycle boundaries.

For example, if a firm's goal is to minimize the environmental impacts of their manufacturing process, the decisionmaker may select a life-cycle boundary that starts with the upstream suppliers of the products they purchase, includes the manufacturing process and the disposal of any by-products, and ends with the environmental impacts of their wastes and emissions. The firm may choose an environmental metric, such as waste volume. The firm may assess the impacts of current operations, plus alternative processes that are likely to reduce the environmental impacts. The following sections provide examples of how ILCM can be tailored to meet a firm's specific business goals.

In addition to tailoring the life-cycle boundary, the choice of metrics, and the type of alternatives considered, any application of ILCM must also be tailored to fit a firm's business processes. This can often be the most difficult challenge of all, and in many cases the greatest value of the life-cycle approach is that it stimulates a firm to reevaluate and redesign key business processes to facilitate bringing an appropriate life-cycle perspective to business decisions. How firms can begin to meet this challenge is discussed later in this chapter, following the example life-cycle management analyses.

Applications of ILCM

This section describes several implementations of ILCM that are tailored to specific company goals with respect to life-cycle boundary, metrics, and alternatives.

Goal: To evaluate the environmental burdens of a product. The implementation of ILCM to meet this goal resembles life-cycle assessment (LCA), with an explicit focus on the firm's decisions that are driven by measures of the environmental burdens of a product (see Chap. 9). Consistent with standard LCA techniques, the firm would select a full cradle-to-grave life cycle. As illustrated in Fig. 10.1, the life cycle would begin with the extraction of raw materials, include the upstream supply chain, the firm's manufacturing processes, distribution to customers, use by customers, and ends when all products and by-products have returned to the earth. With regard to metrics, a firm may choose one or more of several measures, including raw material use, energy use, emissions quantity, waste quantity, human health risks, ecosystem indicators, or measures of the environmental impacts from these activities; some measures, of course, are more challenging to estimate than others.

From a business perspective, the traditional LCA approach has several potential drawbacks. This choice of life cycle typically does not correspond to the scope of a firm's influence of control. In addition, the choice of metrics does not include any cost estimates, which are a key input to business decisions. However, this implementation of ILCM can provide the life-cycle perspective of LCA approaches combined with the decision-oriented analysis process of ILCM.

Goal: To make purchasing and operating decisions based on the full costs to the company. This application of ILCM focuses on determining the full life-cycle costs associated with products and materials acquired and used by a firm, or with operations or processes within the firm. This approach, which, as noted above, we refer to as *life-cycle cost management* (LCCM), is being used by a number of companies to help improve their materials management and procurement processes, while achieving pollution prevention goals as well. Here, we draw the

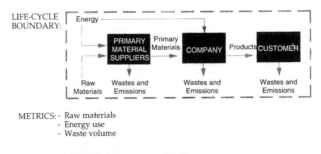

Figure 10.1 Life-cycle boundary used to understand and evaluate the environmental burdens of a product.

life-cycle boundary around those activities that may significantly affect a firm's bottom line and over which the firm has some control. As illustrated in Fig. 10.2, the life cycle typically begins when the company purchases a product or material, and ends when the material and all by-products have been disposed of, including any liabilities, record-keeping, or other potential costs that remain.

In this application of ILCM the primary metric used to compare alternative actions is life-cycle cost. Compared to traditional cost accounting, we include a more complete picture of true cost along two important dimensions: (1) cost throughout the life cycle over time and (2) indirect and uncertain costs. This is in addition to all the more obvious direct costs considered in traditional budgeting and accounting systems. *Direct costs* are the costs that are typically thought of as part of the cost of buying and using a product, or performing some task or operation. *Indirect costs* are real costs to the firm that appear on someone's budget, but which have not traditionally been attributed to a product or process (such as training, storage, waste disposal, legal, or record keeping). *Uncertain costs* are costs that may or may not be incurred and depend on a particular event (such as a spill, fire, or other accident, unanticipated failures, or unexpected legal action).

Although some of these costs may be difficult to estimate, better decisions (e.g., decisions that maximize value and minimize cost for the firm as a whole) will result when even rough approximations are included, as opposed to the costs being ignored. As discussed below, decision analysis techniques can be applied to effectively estimate the direct, indirect, and uncertain costs throughout the defined life cycle, and to use these estimates as a basis for improved business decisions. The next section describes LCCM in greater depth, as a concrete implementation of the overall ILCM approach.

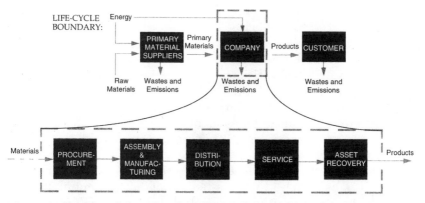

Figure 10.2 The life-cycle boundary for LCCM includes all life-cycle stages in which a firm may incur costs.

Goal: To determine the cost of ownership for customers. Some companies sell products in the market that are priced higher than their competitor's products, but actually provide lower overall cost to the purchaser. For example, although energy-efficient appliances may have a higher purchase price, they may provide the lowest-cost option for the customer compared to less efficient appliances when operating, maintenance, and other costs of ownership are taken into account. In these cases, firms may wish to estimate the true cost *to their customers* of each of the products available in the marketplace. To meet this goal, a firm can use a life-cycle boundary that begins when a consumer buys a product, includes the consumer's use of the product, and ends when the consumer disposes of the product. The firm would probably use cost as the primary metric, but could also include any other metric that would be useful in (or would influence) the purchase decisions made by their customers, whether other firms or individuals.

Goal: To design eco-efficient products without compromising cost, quality, or schedule constraints. In designing eco-efficient products, design teams want to consider both costs and environmental impacts, but for different life cycles. Similar to LCA, a design team that is applying DFE may wish to consider the environmental burdens for a product's cradle-to-grave life cycle shown in Fig. 10.1. However, from a cost perspective, the team may prefer to draw narrower life-cycle boundaries, taking into account only customers and first-tier suppliers.

Thus, using ILCM, firms can build integrated life-cycle management frameworks that are tailored to address their evolving business and environmental goals. An integrated approach allows decision-makers to evaluate trade-offs between cost and environmental outcomes, identify opportunities for improvement, and help meet the goals of improving both environmental stewardship and economic competitiveness. While remaining firmly anchored to real business decisions, the ILCM approach allows natural evolution in its implementation, while encouraging consistency across applications. For example, some firms may choose to begin with an LCCM process applied to procurement decisions, then later extend the approach to add environmental metrics and include a broader set of operating decisions. Other firms may choose to begin by assessing life-cycle environmental burdens as an element of a DFE program, then add life-cycle cost and process design or operating decisions to their ILCM efforts.

The next section focuses on LCCM, both as a specific example of ILCM that is being used by firms today, and as a potential starting point for some of the other implementations of ILCM discussed above.

Life-Cycle Cost Management

The primary goal of LCCM is to save money by making purchase, operating, and maintenance decisions based on the full life-cycle cost of a material, product, process, or service, which explicitly includes the costs of environmental, health, and safety issues. The scope of decisions and alternatives that can be addressed includes product and material selection and use, process design, waste management, and others.

Secondary goals often include achieving pollution prevention, source reduction, or waste minimization targets. In many cases, the alternative with the lowest life-cycle cost also provides an opportunity for pollution prevention. However in other cases, a firm is required to make trade-offs between cost and other goals. In these cases, ILCM provides the information firms require to make informed decisions that impact cost and pollution prevention goals.

Why are life-cycle costs important?

The true cost of any product or material that a company purchases is much more than simply its purchase price. That product or material will carry with it a host of costs associated with its acquisition, use, and ultimate disposal, including costs of storage, transportation, facilities, energy, labor, training, and record keeping, among others. Thus, the *life-cycle cost* of a product may be defined as the total cost that a firm incurs, from the time of purchase until the disposition of any wastes or by-products and beyond, as long as liabilities or other costs may remain.

Although major investment decisions often reflect total life-cycle costs, most firms make thousands of "small cost" decisions without life-cycle costs in mind. For example, many companies purchase and use hundreds or even thousands of chemicals, materials, and products as part of their everyday operations. These include materials and components used in their products, and solvents, paints, lubricants, preservatives, reagents, cleaning agents, batteries, lights, and many others used in manufacturing or service processes.

Many of these products and materials may have significant direct and indirect costs associated with their use or by-product disposal. These costs can add up to a large part of operating expenses and may result in future liabilities or other unpleasant surprises. Although each individual product specification or purchase decision may be small, when the same or similar choices are made again and again, the cumulative implications of the life-cycle costs may become significant. Taking the full cost of each product, material, or process into account when decisions are made can prevent making choices with excessive and avoidable costs due to training or use requirements, maintenance waste generation, or other factors.

The concept of life-cycle cost may be extended beyond products or materials to more complex components, systems, and processes by clearly defining each of the elements of a system, each of the steps in a process, and each stage in the life-cycle of materials used in the system or process, and then identifying each of the cost elements within the defined scope of the system or process. The same observations made above apply here as well: by taking full life-cycle costs into account, and identifying indirect as well as direct costs, firms have the potential to make design and operating decisions that can result in substantial long-term cost savings. Furthermore, in our experience, the options that minimize costs often minimize waste generation and other environmental impacts.

The key is to consider not only the life-cycle dimension, from initial planning and acquisition to ultimate disposal and beyond, but also the other important dimension, ranging from the most obvious direct costs, to the indirect costs (often obscured in overhead accounts) and potentially significant uncertain costs. These indirect and uncertain costs can often exceed the more apparent direct costs.

What are the costs?

What are the cost elements that must be considered if one is to estimate the complete life-cycle costs associated with a product or material, or with a component or system, or of a process or operation? It is easiest to envision what we mean by life-cycle cost if one thinks in terms of a purchased product or material; the extension to more complex systems or processes is straightforward.

The "full life cycle" of a product or material begins as a decision is evaluated and a choice is made to acquire the product or material, or to acquire a component or system containing the substance. Costs are then incurred throughout the acquisition process, during handling or storage prior to use, throughout the use of the product or substance or equipment, and due to disposal of any wastes or residuals. In many cases costs will be incurred *after* disposal as well. Cost components may be incurred *immediately,* e.g., at the time of purchase or use, or they may be *deferred,* such as certain record-keeping costs or future legal liabilities. In simple terms, we may define the life-cycle cost of a chemical or material as:

Life-cycle cost = Cost of acquisition　(Including direct purchase cost, handling or transportation costs, record keeping, etc.)

+ Cost of use　(Including the direct costs of use, associated labor and other materials costs,

	training and management costs, occupational liabilities, costs of waste minimization efforts, etc.)
+ Cost of disposal	(Including treatment costs, actual disposal costs, costs of record keeping and management, etc.)
+ Postdisposal cost	(Including long-term record keeping, potential legal liabilities, etc.)

Each of these cost categories may be further organized along another dimension, depending on the nature of the cost components. This dimension includes four general *types* of cost elements:

- *Direct costs* that will be incurred by a firm *with certainty.* These are the costs that are typically included when options are compared in conventional cost analysis. These costs are easily measured and are typically *attributed* to the products or materials under consideration, or to the processes or activities in which they are used, by standard accounting and budgeting systems.

- *Indirect costs* that will be incurred with certainty, but which usually are *not* attributed to or directly associated with a given chemical or material. These are costs such as handling and storage, training, permitting, legal services, and record keeping that are usually incurred due to the use of a given product or material, but which are typically not included in cost analyses. In other words, these costs are incurred by the firm, and show up on someone's budget, but typically not on the budget of those evaluating the decision.

- *Uncertain costs* that *may* be incurred by a firm, and can be either direct or indirect in the sense described above. These potential costs will involve real dollars to the firm, but are uncertain in magnitude and/or timing. These may include, for example, legal liabilities associated with use or disposal, or added disposal costs incurred due to new regulations.

- *Social costs,* such as *environmental externalities,* that are *not* directly incurred by a firm, but which the firm may choose to consider, or be directed to consider by a regulatory body, in choosing products or materials, or in evaluating process alternatives. Externalities include environment releases or impacts that are not reflected in the price of a product or otherwise borne by a firm using a product.

Examples of each type of cost element that may be incurred are shown in Table 10.1. Some of these cost elements are currently measured or tracked by many firms, while others are not. Others are measured, but are typically not considered when decisions are made

TABLE 10.1   Examples of Life-Cycle Cost Elements

Type of cost	Stage in life cycle			
	Acquisition	Use	Disposal	Postdisposal
Direct	Purchase Taxes Shipping Financing	Labor Equipment Maintenance Inspection	Transport Storage Recycling Treatment Disposal	Insurance
Indirect	Handling Storage Record keeping	Delivery to job site Training Industrial hygiene Regulatory compliance	Training EH&S	Record keeping Monitoring
Uncertain	Spills and accidents while handling or in storage	Spills and accidents while in use Equipment failure Occupational liabilities	Accidents or spills Compliance with new regulations	Legal liabilities due to site contamination

that will ultimately influence the cost outcomes. These include, for example, many of the indirect costs. Still others, particularly the uncertain and externality costs, are rarely addressed in typical day-to-day decisions regarding the acquisition, use, and disposal of chemicals and materials. Experience suggests that these latter costs, when taken into account, can significantly influence the comparison of chemical or material options.

Potential applications of LCCM

As suggested above, there is a broad scope of potential applications of LCCM. These include, but are not limited to, the following examples:

- Evaluation of new-product alternatives or evaluation of options for new applications in a materials management and procurement process

- Product standardization efforts by materials management or procurement functions, or by operating units

- Pollution prevention and waste minimization efforts, both to identify cost-effective options and to ensure that such efforts are consistent with business performance

- Process or operations management, whether in a manufacturing or service environment

- Fleet management, for firms that own or operate large vehicle fleets

■ Process design, whether for manufacturing processes or service operations

Several of these applications will be illustrated in examples discussed below.

Managing life-cycle costs: Putting the concepts into practice

This section describes a structured process for managing life-cycle costs, and serves as an example of the general decision analysis process used in any implementation of ILCM. In the specific context of LCCM, this process is designed to help companies

■ Identify classes of decisions to address

■ Target information gathering to support these decisions

■ Efficiently gather information and track costs

■ Use this information to make better product choice and process design decisions

■ Implement business processes to facilitate managing life-cycle costs

Although the concepts involved are straightforward and intuitive, our experience has shown that putting them into practice can be challenging for a variety of reasons. Information is widely dispersed throughout an organization. Some costs are highly uncertain. Budget accountability and decision responsibility are typically defined in ways that are inconsistent with a life-cycle management perspective. Consequently, the decision analysis approach is specifically designed to help companies efficiently assess life-cycle costs and use this information to facilitate making good decisions without investing excessive time and effort in the process.

The framework, or process, for managing life-cycle costs can be divided into three major parts:

1. Identify issues, opportunities, and decisions. A life-cycle approach can be used for making decisions ranging from purchasing paint to designing a complex manufacturing plant. This step involves identifying the product categories, processes, or activities to address using life-cycle cost methods, and setting initial priorities for analysis. As each topic or application is characterized, specific decisions should be identified; a life-cycle cost analysis (part 2) is needed for each interrelated set of options. In some cases, a particular topic (for example, procurement of batteries, or design of a new production line) will have several sets of decisions (for example, "Which battery type for flashlights?" "Which battery type for vehicles?" etc.), and hence will require several interrelated analyses.

2. Carry out a life-cycle cost analysis for each decision that has been identified. A life-cycle cost analysis examines each alternative course of action to identify the one with the lowest life-cycle cost. In addition, the analysis helps clarify how the life-cycle costs can vary given a range of alternative assumptions or uncertain outcomes, and identifies where these uncertainties may affect the ranking of the options.

An iterative approach is central to the life-cycle cost analysis methodology. Taking an iterative approach helps avoid wasting valuable resources in pursuit of irrelevant information. Each individual life-cycle cost analysis will proceed through a series of steps from defining alternatives to evaluating results. These steps include:

1. *Define the analysis:* This step includes identifying the alternatives to be evaluated, specifying the life-cycle stages for each alternative, and identifying the relevant cost elements for each life-cycle stage. This step also includes specifying what cost measure will be used to compare alternatives, ensuring a consistent comparison that accounts for differences in performance or efficiency.

2. *Estimate costs:* In this step, cost information is gathered for each alternative. Typically one begins by assigning a best guess and a range of estimates for each cost element, and converting the cost estimates into the cost measure specified in step 1. After completing subsequent steps, the analysis process will help indicate where additional or more refined cost estimates are needed.

3. *Calculate costs:* This step involves combining the best-guess cost estimates to get an assessment of the total life-cycle cost for each alternative. As part of this step, costs are calculated such that differences in performance or efficacy are taken into account, so that the life-cycle cost measures for each alternative are calculated with respect to a common basis or measure of performance. A preliminary identification of the alternative with the lowest life-cycle cost can be made, and detailed cost streams over time can be examined.

4. *Evaluate results:* This step is guided by *sensitivity analysis,* that is, by investigating whether the decision (i.e., the ranking of alternatives) changes as cost estimates vary throughout the range assigned to each. Carrying out this sensitivity analysis is a key to the entire decision analysis process, as the sensitivity results guide the subsequent steps in the analysis. Based on the sensitivity analysis results, it may be appropriate to invest more resources in estimating specific costs; to add or remove an alternative from consideration; to carry out an explicit probabilistic analysis; or to

recommend a decision without any additional analysis or data gathering.

3. Develop recommendations, make a decision, and implement the selected option. At this point, the results from the analysis should provide clear justification for a decision, even if there are uncertainties in the cost or performance estimates that remain unresolved; the sensitivity analysis will have demonstrated whether or not these uncertainties really matter to the decision. In addition, the analysis will provide documentation to explain why the decision is appropriate, as well as indicating how the decision might change if some of the key assumptions or cost elements were to change in the future.

Ideally, life-cycle cost information should be collected and used as part of everyday planning and operations. However, to gain initial experience with the approach, it is usually best to conduct a number of ad hoc analyses of specific products or processes. Typically, such analyses are carried out by small, cross-functional teams assembled specifically for that purpose. Such initial analyses can serve several objectives:

- Provide experience with life-cycle cost concepts and analysis techniques

- Provide insight into how LCCM can best be tailored to each particular company's practices

- Demonstrate the potential benefits and rewards of LCCM

Moving beyond the initial applications to a broader implementation of LCCM entails additional challenges. After presenting some concrete examples of LCCM applications, we will discuss lessons from practical experience that can help firms begin to make this transition.

Examples of LCCM Applications

This section presents several real-life examples in which LCCM techniques have been used by firms to make product, process, or pollution prevention management decisions. Building on this experience, several of these firms are moving toward broad implementation and operational use of LCCM in their planning and operations.

Example 1: Evaluating utility pole treatment chemicals and pole materials

Electric utilities and telephone companies use tens or even hundreds of thousands of utility poles in their distribution systems, with annual costs for pole purchases typically involving millions of dollars. Although other alternatives are beginning to be used, these poles have traditionally been made of wood. In order to prevent dry rot, wood poles need to be treated with a wood preservative. Creosote has been a common treatment for decades; more recently, other wood treatments have been used as well. One potentially attractive alternative involves treatment with chromated-copper arsenate (CCA).

However, any of the currently available treatments poses potential environmental considerations as well. These include the environmental consequences of the pole-treating operations, potential releases from the poles when in use (e.g., chemicals leaching into the soil surrounding the pole), and due to disposal of the poles when they fail or are otherwise taken out of service. These environmental concerns are already causing the cost of poles and of pole disposal to rise significantly, and pose uncertain costs for the future.

An electric utility that currently purchases and installs about 20,000 poles each year wanted to reevaluate their choice of pole treatment materials. In addition, they wanted to consider alternatives to wood poles, and to potentially consider the option of doing without poles altogether by placing lines underground. Given the range of potential alternatives and the environmental concerns, it made sense to assess the life-cycle cost of each of the potential alternatives, as well as for the current types of poles.

Focusing initially on one widely used class of distribution poles, we identified three types of treated-wood poles, along with steel, fiberglass, and concrete alternatives. We chose to compare the alternatives on the basis of dollars per mile of distribution line (levelized annual cost over the lifetime of the pole). Although dollars per pole (rather than per mile of line) might appear to be the obvious measure to use as a basis for comparing options, it turns out to be inadequate for comparing wood poles with other types of materials. This is because certain types of steel, concrete, and fiberglass poles have a longer spanning capability than do wood poles, and hence require fewer poles per mile (note, however, that when poles are being used as direct replacements for existing poles in existing lines, the life-cycle cost per pole *is* the appropriate metric; thus, we actually calculated both metrics.)

The life-cycle stages and principal cost elements for utility poles are summarized in Fig. 10.3. Prior to initiating the analysis, one of the major concerns of the firm's management was the potential disposal costs and uncertain future liabilities associated with the disposal of treated-wood poles. An additional concern was the potential costs of contamination of the soil at pole sites.

After defining the life cycle and the relevant cost elements, the team developed initial cost estimates for each of the items shown in

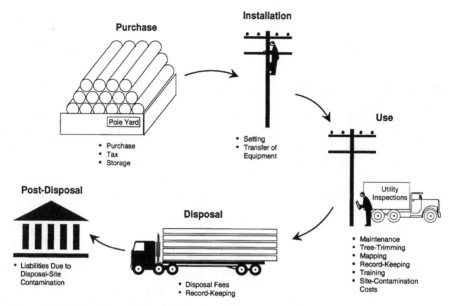

Figure 10.3 Life-cycle costs for utility poles.

Fig. 10.3, along with the lifetime of each pole type, the discount rate, and the inflation rate. Some of these costs are inherently uncertain, while for others the firm had only limited information; for all of these cost elements, we estimated a "best guess" value as well as low and high values that reflected the best and worst cases.

Our best-guess estimates indicated that one of the wood pole options was the lowest-cost alternative. However, we also learned that the lowest-cost option changed as we varied our assumptions about pole lifetime and purchase price. Therefore, we recommended that the company do more research on lifetimes and purchase prices before making a final decision. We also advised the company not to do any more research on other cost elements, because better information would not be likely to change their decision.

One surprise was that the disposal costs and potential liabilities did not turn out to be significant to the decision; even when these costs were set to their greatest possible values, the least-cost option did not change. One reason for this result is that the greatest cost risk is if a pole disposal site were to become a Superfund site. However, even though the costs of such an outcome would be large, they would be spread over so many poles that the cost per pole was negligible. Costs due to pole site contamination were more controversial, as there was significant disagreement as to the likelihood of these sites becoming a significant, and potentially costly, environmental issue. Based on current regulatory practices in their state, the firm chose to assume that these costs would not become significant, while also planning to monitor the situation, recognizing that the choice of pole types could well change if the state regulatory environment changed.

Based on the initial analysis, the firm chose to invest in further research on pole lifetimes, and to seek firm bids from suppliers of two of the alternatives. After refining the estimates of pole lifetimes, and using the bids to refine the purchase price estimates, the firm was able to proceed with their choice of pole type.

In addition to learning that disposal costs did not, in fact, drive the decision, the firm also found that the indirect costs associated with installing and maintaining the poles significantly exceeded the direct acquisition cost of the poles. This finding, together with the importance of pole lifetimes, has changed how the firm views pole purchase decisions in the future. Installation and maintenance cost, reliability, and the expected lifetime of the poles are now considered as key inputs to pole selection and use.

Example 2: Choosing batteries for backup power applications

A company wanted to understand the life-cycle costs of batteries and to develop a list of approved batteries for a number of specific uses. As part of organizing the study, we identified a list of candidate battery types and applications. We decided to evaluate the large batteries that provide emergency backup power at remote facilities first, followed by batteries that provide similar functions at the firm's central facilities and manufacturing plants.

As we defined the remote facility battery analysis, we identified two types of lead-acid battery alternatives (A and B) and a nickel-cadmium battery alternative. Because the company wanted to use the same battery for all of their remote facilities, we chose to compare alternatives based on the cost for all of the facilities, measured by the present value of the full life-cycle cost over the lifetime of the batteries. As in the utility pole example, battery disposal costs were a key concern driving the analysis, as well as concerns regarding maintenance and reliability. One group was pushing for the use of Ni-cad batteries as a long-life, reliable solution.

Following the LCCM decision analysis process, after defining the alternatives and the cost elements, we estimated a best guess and a range of values for each of the costs, along with estimates for the battery lifetime, discount rate, inflation rate, and the number of installations.

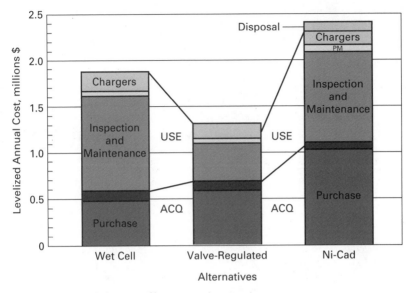

Figure 10.4 Life-cycle costs of battery options.

The best-guess cost estimates, shown in Fig. 10.4, indicate that one of the lead-acid batteries (value-regulated type A) has the lowest life-cycle cost. The Ni-cad option turned out to be higher-cost one under virtually any scenario. When looking at the range of uncertainty for each cost estimate, we learned that the most critical element was the maintenance cost for each battery type. This was important due to the remote location of the facilities; the labor time required to travel to the facilities to inspect and maintain the backup power systems meant that maintenance labor costs became one of the largest elements of the total life-cycle cost. Battery A appeared to be preferred because it was a particularly low-maintenance configuration. Reviewing the information available demonstrated that the decision between lead-acid types A and B would change only if the maintenance costs for battery A were very high, and significantly higher than for battery B. In this situation, battery B (wet cell) becomes the lowest-cost choice. The consensus among the company's battery experts was that the maintenance costs for battery A would never exceed those for battery B. Therefore, the company has decided to use battery type A at all of their remote facilities.

It is worth noting that a subsequent analysis addressing backup power batteries at central facilities led to a different decision, in favor of battery type B. In this case, maintenance personnel were making periodic visits, to inspect other equipment, to locations with backup power systems. Thus, the incremental costs of inspections were very small, and it was not worth paying the additional costs for high-reliability, low-maintenance batteries.

Example 3: Managing parts washers

A company wanted to purchase the lowest-cost solvents for their parts washers used in assembly and maintenance operations. As we began to define our alternatives, cost elements, and the overall life cycle, we realized that the firm might be able to achieve greater cost savings and reduced waste disposal liability by looking at a broader decision: should the company continue to lease their parts washers or should they own and service the parts washers in-house? The annual costs involved are considerable, because there are numerous parts washers in regular use at each of a dozen or so facilities.

In the parts washer example, the life-cycle costs are organized according to the following stages:

- *Acquisition:* Purchase costs for parts washers, spare parts, solvent, filters, and safety equipment; record-keeping costs

- *Use:* Parts-washer maintenance costs; solvent replacement costs, either by a vendor service or the company; potential spill cleanup costs; hazardous materials training costs

- *Disposal:* Waste analysis costs; disposal fees; disposal transportation (including paperwork)

- *Postdisposal:* Regulatory reporting costs; potential medical claims; potential disposal site contamination costs

Notice that the life cycle of parts washers, which spans 15 to 20 years, also includes separate life cycles of the solvents and filters used in the cleaning process, which span 6 to 12 months. This is an example of the general concept that the appropriate definition of a life cycle must be tailored to the specific class of decision, and that it may sometimes make sense to use multiple definitions.

Figure 10.5 shows the estimates of the annual life-cycle cost of one parts washer, levelized over its lifetime, for the two alternatives: (1) leasing the parts washers from a vendor with regular vendor service and (2) owning and maintaining their parts washers in-house; for reference, the figure also shows the equivalent cost of manual parts cleaning. Since the chart shows life-cycle cost broken down by stage, we can get a picture of which stages contribute the most to the life-cycle cost. Although owning their own parts washers has a higher acquisition cost, this option has the lowest overall cost and lower disposal cost. This is because the firm has greater control over the frequency of solvent replacement in the parts washers, as well as direct

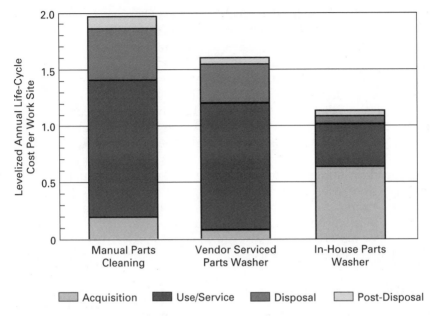

Figure 10.5   Life-cycle cost of one parts washer.

control over the disposal of the spent solvents; the firm judged that its disposal costs, including an allowance for potential environmental costs associated with disposal, were less than what they were currently being charged by the vendor service.

Implementing LCCM: Lessons Learned

In this section, we will discuss lessons from the above and other applications that may prove useful as firms begin to move to broader implementation of LCCM. Although these suggestions, as with the examples above, are focused on LCCM, many of the lessons are pertinent to the other applications of ILCM that were introduced earlier in this chapter.

Identifying opportunities for improvement

To increase the likelihood that an analysis will result in cost savings, companies may want to begin by evaluating products, processes, and activities for which current practices incur high costs that are not usually included in the decisionmaking process and which could potentially be avoided by choosing an alternative course of action. For example, a manufacturing process that requires the use of solvents may result in high disposal costs for the solvents as hazardous wastes. If the disposal costs of the solvents, and potential future liabilities associated with such disposal, were not considered when the company initially decided to use the manufacturing process, then this process may be a good candidate for evaluation on a life-cycle cost basis—especially if nonhazardous alternatives are potentially available.

If the initial subject of an analysis is a product which incurs particularly high training costs, waste disposal costs, or other high costs, the tendency is to look for another material which serves the same function at lower cost. In many cases, the largest savings may come not from product substitutions, but from changing the higher-level processes that use particular products. The creative development of alternatives might allow a function to be accomplished in a completely different way, eliminating the need for a specific high-cost product, chemical, or material. Therefore, one should consider evaluating higher-level alternatives as well as straightforward product substitution.

Efficiently estimating life-cycle costs

Because of poor information or inherently uncertain events, almost all cost information is uncertain to some degree. Some of the largest costs associated with products can come from unanticipated events. For example, price increases result in higher purchase costs; workplace accidents can result in medical liabilities; chemical spills can result in shutdowns and high cleanup costs; disposal site contamination may lead to large liabilities many years after disposal of wastes. All of these costs contribute to the total life-cycle cost of a product, and should be included in the analysis.

The LCCM framework explicitly allows one to represent uncertainty in the analysis. Sensitivity analysis can be used to speed the analysis by identifying which uncertainties are, in fact, significant. In this way, one can begin with broad estimates, with the understanding that sensitivity analysis later will determine where those estimates need to be improved. In many cases, uncertainties that initially seem to be impossible barriers turn out to be insignificant to the decision.

Modifying business processes to facilitate managing life-cycle costs

Modifications to company business processes—including accounting systems, information systems, incentives, personnel accountability, communication mechanisms, and information flows—can facilitate widespread, efficient use of LCCM on an ongoing basis.

Some of these modifications are aimed at improving communication and coordination between departments or functions in an organization. Managing life-cycle costs can help purchasing, engineering, operations, and waste management departments to share their concerns, work together to find cost-saving solutions, and achieve individual and shared goals.

Companies may want to encourage different methods of cost accounting for decisionmaking purposes. Many companies traditionally assign *fully allocated costs* to specific activities in the life cycle of a product, process, or activity. For example, inventory costs are often assigned to products on a fully allocated cost basis. What this means is that the total costs associated with inventory for all products, from rent for the warehouse to managers' salaries, are assigned or allocated to all of the items in inventory.

When making decisions about a specific product, we prefer to not use the fully allocated inventory cost as the basis for the decision because it may overstate the actual cost. For example, eliminating any one product would not reduce the rent for the warehouse or the managers' salaries. Instead, we prefer to use the *marginal* or *activity-based cost* for the product when making decisions about the specific product. In the inventory example, the marginal cost might be the cost of labor for unloading, stocking, and loading, plus any paperwork associated with that particular product, but not a portion of the utility bill or insurance costs. For higher-level decisions, the marginal cost may be the same as the fully allocated cost.

Managing life-cycle costs to achieve pollution prevention

Pollution prevention and waste minimization were the original motivations for implementing LCCM in most firms that are using the techniques today. Life-cycle cost analyses can effectively identify areas where pollution prevention is the optimal choice. They can serve to give companies a better understanding of the relative importance of the costs of disposing of associated waste, to justify the purchase of initially more expensive but ultimately cleaner materials, and to guide the design of systems or processes that reduce costs through minimizing wastes.

Both LCCM and pollution prevention measures can be used to achieve the same goals. They can be thought of as two perspectives on the same problem. While pollution prevention programs look at possible pollution prevention options and attempt to find those that would save dollars, LCCM helps identify cost-saving opportunities, many of which prevent pollution.

Waste disposal is not *always* the driving factor in costs, however. In some cases pollution prevention may not be the most cost-effective alternative. Even in these cases, information on life-cycle costs can be useful in developing a waste reduction program. Companies working toward waste reduction goals can use life-cycle cost information to help quantify the trade-offs between cost and waste minimization, to identify a least-cost set of options for reducing waste, or to help create alternative products or practices.

Conclusions

This chapter has introduced the broad concept of integrated life-cycle management as a comprehensive yet practical approach to incorporating life-cycle thinking in business decisions. A number of potential applications of ILCM were outlined. One important class of applications, referred to as life-cycle cost management, was discussed in detail. LCCM has already demonstrated significant value to the firms that are putting these techniques into practice. Combined with appropriate environmental performance metrics, LCCM is a logical first step toward achieving the vision of full, integrated life-cycle management.

Although many of the original applications of LCCM were motivated by pollution prevention or waste reduction goals, the approach is useful even when pollution prevention is not a central issue. LCCM can be used to identify and evaluate *any* opportunities for saving costs, including switching to more efficient products, reducing maintenance requirements, finding longer-lived equipment, and purchasing more efficient materials.

Beyond cost efficiency, LCCM can provide a number of other potential benefits, either directly or by augmenting complementary programs. Examples of these potential benefits and complementary efforts include:

Total-quality management: Life-cycle cost information provides a consistent way to measure improvements in performance. The LCCM process can facilitate quality programs and vice versa.

Improved materials management: LCCM can help to identify the most cost effective products for particular applications and to compile standardized purchasing guidelines, potentially reducing the number of product types stocked.

Improved internal communication: Estimating life-cycle costs requires the integration of information from many sources. Soliciting input about costs increases the communication between departments.

Improved public relations: Many of the savings that can result from life-cycle cost analysis arise from the reduction of wastes, emissions, and other environmental impacts relevant to public interests.

This vision for integrating environmental needs with business objectives into a single unifying framework is ambitious, but there are clear, practical steps that firms can take to begin moving toward that vision. An integrated environmental business management strategy must be tailored to meet the needs of each firm. However, it will typically include the following elements:

- All business decisions will be made using a life-cycle perspective that provides an understanding of both the business and environmental impacts of design, construction, and operating decisions.

- The life-cycle perspective will be driven by concrete business needs, rather than arbitrary academic criteria, and will reflect consideration of all pertinent impacts to all environmental media.

- Information systems will efficiently provide information on economic and environmental performance on an activity-oriented rather than a functional basis.

- Business processes will evolve so that accountability, responsibility, and incentives, as well as the organizational structure and information flows, all support the business and environmental goals of the company.

Walking the Talk: Pioneer Stories

The Conceptual Framework of DFE at AT&T

Braden Allenby, Ph.D.

Research Vice President, Technology and the Environment
AT&T Engineering Research Center
Basking Ridge, New Jersey

Introduction

AT&T shares the growing awareness among today's global corporations of the strategic value of incorporating environmental considerations into both manufacturing and product design. The company is continually working to improve the environmental performance of manufacturing and support operations, and is also beginning to integrate an understanding of environmental impacts into product design processes. Taken together, these actions are leading the company to develop a new competency called *strategic environmentalism.*

In some ways this approach is nothing new. The Bell System, as a vertically integrated monopoly, not only manufactured telephones and telecommunications equipment, but leased these products to consumers. Periodically, these products were returned to the company, then refurbished and reintroduced into commerce. At the end of their useful life, they were taken back and disassembled into their component parts for reuse, recycling, and disposal.[1] This wasn't done because recycling was on everyone's minds, but because it made good business sense.

When divestiture created the new AT&T in 1984, the economics supporting internal recycling systems changed, and the company had to develop a new approach to environmental concerns. Traditional compliance activities had to be augmented in order to meet increasingly stringent and detailed legal requirements such as those in the 1984 amendments to the Resource Conservation and Recovery Act (RCRA) and the Superfund Amendments and Reauthorization Act of 1986 (SARA). The company had to sort out its role in connection with developing international standards like the Montreal Protocol, and had to become even more responsive to the growing environmental concerns of employees, stockholders, and customers around the world.

In order to meet these pressures, and go beyond them to integrate environment and technology throughout its operations, the company has developed the concept of design for environment, or DFE. For AT&T, DFE is a proactive, anticipatory, and preventive operating and engineering design approach. The goal of DFE is to avoid potential environmental problems for a technology, process, service, or product over its total life cycle by addressing them during the product concept and design stages.[2] DFE is one of several components in AT&T's approach to concurrent engineering—DFX. The "X" in this design system stands for the desired product characteristic—manufacturability, safety, testability, etc.[3]

Concurrent engineering integrates manufacturing, marketing, safety, testing, environment, and other considerations at the earliest possible point in the design and development of products.[4] This approach is standard operating procedure at AT&T, with new engineering practice components such as DFE added as necessary. The DFE component is still evolving, and its initial focus is primarily on the relationship between product manufacturing and end-of-life considerations and the environment.

DFE provides the company with a comprehensive and integrated corporate approach to operating as an environmentally responsible company. AT&T's system for environmental change has both internal and external dimensions. Internally, it includes our environmental vision, how we are organized to focus on strategic environmental concerns, the current environmental goals towards which we are working, the developing information systems and tools that support DFE, and what we have learned about introducing DFE into our corporation. Externally, we are supported in our efforts to build a global environmental infrastructure through alliances and partnerships with industry, government, and educational groups.

AT&T's Environmental Goals

The initial drivers for AT&T's postdivestiture environmental activities were the goals announced at the shareowners' meeting in April of 1990. These goals provided very specific environmental targets. Even though, at first glance, these goals seem to focus on "end-of-pipe" solutions, as those charged with implementing them worked toward them we began to understand that we could not meet them simply by improving end-of-pipe technologies. This helped us recognize the benefits of moving toward DFE throughout the corporation. The goals and results are listed below. (Also see Figs. 11.1 through 11.5.)

- Phase out chlorofluorocarbon (CFC) emissions from manufacturing operations by year-end 1994. This goal was met in May of 1993— except for contracts with the Department of Defense that mandate the use (about 400 lb of emissions annually) of CFCs.

- Reduce reportable toxic air emissions 95% by year-end 1995. Reportable toxic air emissions in 1993 were 92% lower than they were in 1987.

- Decrease manufacturing-process waste disposal 25% by year-end 1994. In 1993 disposal of wastes from manufacturing processes had been decreased 57% from 1987 levels.

- Recycle 60% of paper by year-end 1994. This goal was exceeded in 1993 by recycling 63% of waste paper—about 48 million lb.

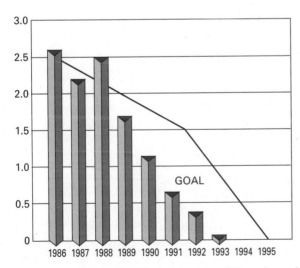

Figure 11.1   AT&T total CFC emissions (in millions of pounds).

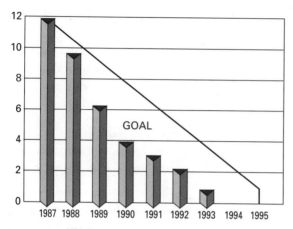

Figure 11.2   AT&T total reportable toxic air emissions (in millions of pounds).

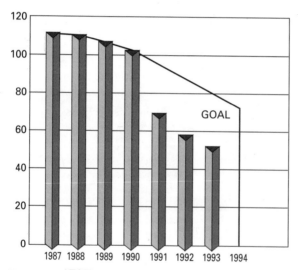

Figure 11.3   AT&T total manufacturing waste disposed (in millions of pounds).

- Reduce use of paper 15% by year-end 1994. As of 1993, use of paper had been reduced 28% from 1990 levels.

The report card is a good one, but these results would not have been possible without the total-quality management (TQM) approach that gives all employees a consistent blueprint to follow. TQM was the first tool used at AT&T to improve environmental performance.

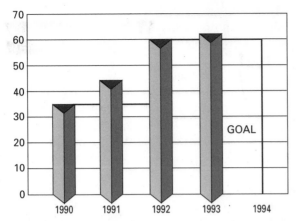

Figure 11.4   AT&T total paper recycling (percent of waste paper).

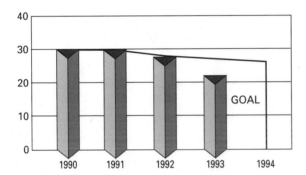

Figure 11.5   AT&T paper use (in thousands of tons).

Importance of Quality Methodologies

Quality methodology has always provided something of a shared blueprint for AT&T. The company's emphasis on quality has both preceded and informed its current focus on the environment. Whether we are working to maintain the most reliable telecommunications network in the world, to manufacture a new generation of switching and transmission equipment, or to rid our processes of ozone-depleting chemicals (ODCs), the quality blueprint teaches the same lessons. We have modified traditional total-quality management into *total-quality environmental management* (TQEM) just as we have added DF"E" to DF"X."

"Quality" has taught AT&T management that any defect is an inefficiency. We thus recognize, for example, that manufacturing waste is not an inevitable part of our business, but the result of inefficient processes that can be improved.

Quality methods also provide a more long-term, rational approach to managing environmental issues. They teach that scrambling to comply with the latest government standard should be replaced by learning to anticipate the future directions of the regulatory process. Since today's legal landfill can become tomorrow's Superfund site, and product-oriented environmental regulations can close markets overnight, complying with existing regulations in a reactive way is not in the best long-term interests of a business.

AT&T is also integrating environmental concerns into its business at every level, not just because it is the right thing to do, but because it is the smart thing to do. An emphasis on the environmental aspects of design can provide strategic advantages. It makes good business sense.

As the company's TQEM blueprint helped us meet our goals, it also helped us see that we had to move beyond goals to a clearer formulation of our vision and a more formal application of DFE.

AT&T Environmental Vision

The goals as stated in 1990 represented a kind of stake in the ground. They effectively focused activities and actions. However, in focusing on goals it is sometimes possible to lose sight of the larger picture.

Goals should lead in a specific direction. They should support consistent overarching values. In particular, where the environment is concerned, the "big picture" is of the utmost importance. In the long run, it isn't possible to save the trees until you understand the forest. In 1993, in an attempt to understand "the forest" and the company's place in it, a new environmental vision was developed for AT&T:

> AT&T's environmental vision is to be recognized by customers, employees, shareowners, and communities worldwide as a responsible company which fully integrates life cycle environmental consequences into each of our business decisions and activities. Designing for the environment is a key in distinguishing our processes, products, and services.

This vision statement was put together by AT&T experts from throughout the world—specialists in manufacturing, industrial ecology, environmental management, research, and development. Their initial efforts were reviewed by all of the company's business units—the groups responsible for implementation. The final vision statement provides a framework for DFE that makes clear the corporate commitment supporting the company's developing DFE activities and environmental partnerships. It is a cornerstone that makes it possible to continue building the rest of the infrastructure needed to define and meet AT&T's environmental goals.

AT&T's Organization

By itself, a vision will not produce any results. A corporate vision has to be real to the people who make the corporation work, its employees. However, the most well-intentioned people in the world cannot be fully effective until they are part of an organization that supplies them with the information they need to make decisions and a structure that gives them the creative freedom to implement the solutions they design.

AT&T has over 300,000 employees, 145 manufacturing facilities, and offices in 85 countries. The corporate organization provides for core functions such as human resources, public relations, and environment and safety (E&S) that are part of headquarters groups. These groups support the business units, which operate relatively autonomously to serve customers for long-distance services, for multimedia products, for switching equipment, microelectronics, and AT&T's other primary businesses.

A 1991 review of the corporate Environment and Safety (E&S) Organization identified the need to more closely connect the expertise of that headquarters group with the implementation efforts in the 20-plus business units. By 1993, each AT&T business unit and division had appointed an Environment & Safety Officer, and regular meetings and planning sessions had been established. Representatives of the corporate E&S Organization, the Law Organization, AT&T Bell Laboratories, and the E&S Officers in each business unit are included in this process. As simple as it may sound, just getting all the right people in the same room on a consistent basis is crucial to being able to understand and manage environmental matters at both macro and micro levels within the corporation.

The E&S Officers assure business unit compliance, review the integration of E&S imperatives into business plans, and suggest future corporate directions. The corporate E&S and Law organizations supply information about government regulations, systems to track compliance, and audits of business unit performance. Bell Laboratories representatives connect emerging technologies with the kinds of solutions needed by individual business units to meet corporate goals and fulfill the corporate vision. We believe that this kind of integrated organizational structure will maximize the creativity of individual business units as they identify the environmental requirements for their products, while at the same time connecting the business units into the larger environmental picture that comes together at the corporate level.

In addition to the E&S vice president, we have also added a research vice president for technology and environment who works with our research community, business units, Law Organization, E&S Officers, and corporate E&S Organization to coordinate activities through the AT&T DFE Coordinating Team. Under this umbrella group, issue-specific subteams have been established. The subteams and their functions are listed below:

- *Green Accounting:* Getting financial systems to allocate environmental costs on a product-by-product and process-specific basis

- *Energy:* Identifying the issues affecting operations and products, and supporting the development of energy-efficient products and operations

- *International Environmental Standards:* Helping contribute to the coming generation of international environmental performance standards

- *Supply Line Management:* Ensuring that the company is partnering with suppliers to obtain environmentally appropriate materials, components, and subassemblies for its products

- *Take-back:* Preparing AT&T for the changes that will be required by voluntary and mandatory return of products to their manufacturer at the end of their useful life

- *Life-Cycle Assessment and DFE:* Developing technical methods to aid in understanding the environmental impact of processes, operations, products, and services

- *External Relations:* Being active collaborators and leaders of industry, governmental, academic, and nonprofit environmental organizations

Integrating Technology and Environment— DFE at Work

Much of AT&T's success in reaching its environmental goals results from advances in technology. For example, these advances have supplied the alternatives needed to help eliminate the use of CFCs and reduce toxic air emissions. We believe that the environment may have no better friend than technology.

AT&T's policy on technology and the environment has as one goal that the company will

> utilize Design for Environment principles to design, develop, manufacture and market products, processes, and services worldwide with environmentally preferable life cycle properties; and promote achievement of environmental excellence designing every new generation of product,

process, and service to be environmentally preferable to the one it replaces.

No matter how compelling a corporate vision, no matter how effective a quality blueprint, and no matter how clear a policy to integrate technology and the environment, they are of no value unless teams of individuals are personally committed to making a difference in performance.

The extent of AT&T's success is due to employees around the world who take their environment and safety responsibilities personally. It is the enthusiasm of the engineers, clerks, factory staffs, installers, researchers, and managers on the front lines of the business that is making the real difference in performance. They are the ones who devise process and product improvements that have helped AT&T exceed its environmental goals while satisfying its customers and shareowners. This chapter illustrates a few of the actions taken by the people of AT&T in 1993 to improve their work environment and our world.

CFC elimination

The effort to eliminate ozone-depleting chemicals such as CFCs continues to teach us about the complexity of integrating environment and technology in our operations. The first lesson learned was that there is no single solution. The goal of eliminating CFCs in AT&T factories is being achieved by the implementation of multiple technologies, all of which raise their own sets of environmental, health, and safety issues.

Progress in CFC elimination is a global success story. AT&T invested more than $25 million to develop alternative technologies to CFCs. We began using new cleaning solutions derived from chemicals found in orange peels and cantaloupes. We developed a new family of solder pastes that can be cleaned with water. However, unlike other water-cleanable fluxes, these solder pastes produce no malodorous vapors, pose no problem with skin contact, and remain usable on the circuit board for up to a full day. We designed "no-clean" solutions using a low-solids fluxer and a new solder gun that makes cleaning solvents unnecessary because it prevents excess solder flux vapor from condensing on the circuit board surface. None of these solutions works for all of the company's manufacturing applications, but taken together they helped eliminate CFCs in AT&T's manufacturing operations worldwide.

Some of the replacement technologies for CFCs contribute (under certain conditions) to smog by resulting in the potential emission of volatile organic compounds (VOCs). Accordingly, work is now in progress on new generations of cleaning techniques such as carbon dioxide (CO_2) pellet blasting and liquid supercritical CO_2 cleaning that will not lead to emissions of VOCs. These promising technologies are relatively harmless to the atmosphere.

Liquid supercritical CO_2 when used as a solvent is particularly effective in cleaning precision parts with blind holes, pores, crevices, and small clearances. It also works well with products that cannot be exposed to water because of the danger of corrosion. After the cleaning process has been completed, more than 99% of the CO_2 that has been used can be recovered and reused.

CO_2 pellets (dry ice) when fed through a hose and nozzle in a high-pressure stream demonstrate success in a wide range of cleaning applications. The pellets, derived from waste CO_2 produced in chemical manufacturing processes, are effective at everything from blowing off dust to stripping paint. When the cleaning is complete, the CO_2 naturally separates from the residue it removed and returns to the atmosphere. This method of cleaning is now used in AT&T's Denver factory to clean test probes. Test data show that the cost savings from this single application should exceed $1 million over a three-year period per location.[5]

Toxic air emissions

In 1990, AT&T's Network Power Systems in Mesquite, Texas, was using 67,000 lb of CFCs, creating 35,000 lb of air emissions, and generating more than 33,000 lb of hazardous waste. In April of 1993, the governor of Texas recognized the plant for eliminating CFCs, for reducing air emissions to 1400 lb, and reducing hazardous wastes to 1000 lb.

What happened between 1990 and 1993 was that industrial pollution met a quality improvement team called The Toxic Avengers. This team used TQEM to identify every one of the plant's processes that produced pollution. They then enlisted the support of all 2400 employees, who scoured every inch of the one million square-foot facility to eliminate toxic emissions, CFCs, and hazardous waste.

Such reductions cannot, of course, be obtained routinely in different manufacturing facilities. Nonetheless, they demonstrate that a quality approach combined with the commitment of all employees can be a powerful tool both to enhance efficiency and prevent pollution.

Waste disposal

The fact that the company has far exceeded our goal in this area has not slowed efforts to continue reducing manufacturing-process waste disposal. Where manufacturing-process waste is concerned, AT&T follows two basic approaches: The first is to consider the "waste" a resource that we have not yet learned how to use. The second is to make DFE a standard operating procedure. DFE is helping AT&T design products in ways that will minimize the waste that they produce.

The Planet Protectors, the factory quality team in Mesquite, Texas, provides a valuable model. Organized to reduce waste disposal, this 14-member team worked with over 100 coordinators in their building to start a plantwide dialogue on reducing waste disposal. They helped make the reduction of refuse everyone's job.

They now recycle paper, plastics, and aluminum. They even buy all their paper janitorial supplies from the paper mill that recycles the plant's waste paper. Excess packaging materials go to local businesses to be reused, used eyeglasses go to the Lions Club, and wooden pallets wind up in employees' fencing, shelving, and backyard decks. This plant now recycles 96% of its identified recyclables, and in 1992 kept about 15 million tons of garbage out of the local landfill.

Recycling

One of the best examples of the results that can be obtained when an entire business unit gets behind recycling can be seen at AT&T— Paradyne where paper and cardboard recycling programs saved 4335 trees, 1.8 million gal of water, and 765 yd^3 of landfill space in 1993 alone (Fig. 11.6). For all recycling programs at Paradyne, the savings were about $90,000. From just this one, 2300-member business unit, that's almost $40 and nearly two trees per employee. It is important to note that these results came primarily from programs that were in place for only six months in 1993.

AT&T has continued its trend of increasing the rate of paper recycled and increasing the tons of recycled paper used. Efforts have also been particularly successful in New Jersey, where commitment to paper recycling and available recycling facilities have resulted in 92% of office waste paper being recycled.

Corporationwide, AT&T now prints almost all employee, customer, and shareowner communications on recycled paper. In addition, recycled paper is specified when purchasing writing tablets, folders, letterhead, memo paper, business cards, restroom supplies, and corrugated cartons.

Reduced use of paper

The goal of a paperless office certainly hasn't yet been reached, but we are making significant reductions in paper use. The scale of our business is so large that sometimes what seem like small changes can add up to large savings. AT&T worked with customers to design a con-

Figure 11.6   AT&T—Paradyne recycling program.

densed format for the bills of PRO WATSr business services. This change saved 3.2 million sheets of 8.5- by 11-in paper in 1992—about 16 tons. Also, the largest customers are now offered a monthly bill on computer disks; this replaces hundreds, and sometimes thousands, of pages for a single customer each month. The EasyLink Services business unit helps implement large-scale reductions in paper for all customers. EasyLink Services provides electronic messaging (AT&T Mail), electronic data interchange, fax applications, and information services.

Internal, high-volume use of electronic newsletters distributed through AT&T Mail began with the on-line publication *AT&T Today*. This electronic newsletter is mailed to 135,000 employees in the United States each day, and has now introduced European and Asian editions. Most AT&T business units have followed the lead of *AT&T Today* and begun electronic publications. In one communications services business unit, a bimonthly, eight-page, printed publication that cost $20,000 per issue and didn't satisfy readers was replaced by a weekly electronic newsletter costing $1500 per issue. The electronic news not only satisfies readers because it is up to the minute, it also saves paper.

Developing Support Systems—DFE Doesn't Just Include Technology, It Is Technology

Our challenge is to integrate the power of technology with the needs of the environment. In some instances, technologies that could serve environmental concerns already exist, but organizations are only just beginning to put them to use. Earlier this year, for example, we worked with the National Information Infrastructure Testbed Consortium to create a specialty environmental communications network. This network transfers information to researchers on global climate changes, tropical deforestation, and the effects of natural disasters at speeds of 45 megabits per second—about the information in 10 average-length books transmitted in one second. The network will become part of the information superhighway. It is a familiar technology, but this is one of its first environmental applications.

In other cases, there are ideas that have not yet been converted to commercial technologies. One example is the bioengineering of bacteria that will eat toxic heavy metals. A project investigating this promising means of recovering heavy metals from waste streams has been recently funded by an AT&T Industrial Ecology Faculty Fellowship grant to Spelman College.

In all cases, the strategic use of research and development resources at AT&T Bell Laboratories is helping integrate technology and environment. The laboratories are developing both the information systems that help the company make sound environmental decisions, and new technologies that show strategic promise and environmental value.

Information systems

DFE applications require accurate and available data that make informed choices possible. AT&T is developing a series of information systems that will make it easier to include environmental considerations in every phase of design activity. This cannot yet be done consistently because DFE requires both information and systems that haven't been developed, but progress has been made.

First, basic information is made available through the On-Line General Information Exchange System (OLGIES), which links E&S staff around the globe electronically and provides instant information about practices, guidelines, personnel, and documents.

Supplementing this general information are systems like CHEMIS—the Chemical Management Information System. CHEMIS tells us who uses what chemicals on a location-by-location basis throughout AT&T. The system is the foundation of our chemical management process, and makes it easier to comply with government regulations and to alert individual locations to new regulations.

The Basic Chemical Tracking System (BCT) monitors the use of chemicals at each AT&T location. This on-line system is fed by CHEMIS and is electronically linked to receiving and storeroom systems. It provides product- or ingredient-level information on quantity received, quantity in stock, quantity used, and where used. It also provides the detailed usage information required for reporting under the Superfund Amendments and Reauthorization Act (SARA), and produces the required reports.

These information systems, and others like them, have been used as the basis for factory applications that increase the ability to be responsive to environmental needs. They also help manage chemical use within the company to increase efficiency and lower cost.[6]

The Systems Analysis for Waste Minimization is an on-line system that tracks process material use and waste generation per unit of product manufactured. We expect this kind of tracking will help us comply with the next general round of national regulation in the United States. It is already required under the Toxic Use Reduction Act (TURA) in Massachusetts. With this system, the required state reports can be produced with the touch of a button, but more importantly we can learn how to minimize waste while meeting quality and cost objectives. This system also provides the data necessary to extend AT&T's management accounting systems to include product- and process-related environmental costs.

Design tools

The integration of the above information systems with application tools at all AT&T factories will help make "green" design a reality by providing the information needed to make informed, data-based decisions.

We have already used an "environmental advisor" software system to help design one of our phone sets. The environmental recommendations were developed through a software tool called the Green Index that made the final product better, both practically and environmentally.

The Green Index is an example of a working prototype used to raise the sophistication of DFE methodology for a new product. This software tool is used to assess "the sum of a product's design, manufacturing, packaging, use, and ultimate disposal parameters rated according to their environmental impact."[7]

The Green Index assigns an index number to various attributes, based on questions such as:

- Does the product use recycled material in its manufacture?
- Are any toxic or hazardous materials used in manufacturing the product?
- Is the product recyclable?
- Are plastics identified so consumers know how to dispose of them?

- Is the manual printed on recycled paper?

Each of the attributes receives a score based on the product design. The best possible score in each of several general areas such as physical design, electrical parts design, and packaging is 100.

After the first evaluation of a business phone set recently developed using the Green Index, the phone set scored 86.3 for physical design and 55.6 for electrical design. Analysis of the results indicated areas for improvement such as:

- Mark the plastic casing so that it can be easily recycled.
- Print the user's manual on recycled paper.
- Replace, to the extent possible, the tin–lead solder with an alternative interconnection technology such as a conductive adhesive or a nonlead solder.

After these changes were made, the score for physical design increased to 93.6 and the score for electrical design to 72.2. Clearly, there is not yet a complete enough grasp of environmental impact to make the Green Index an infallible tool, nor will any manufactured product have no impact on the environment. However, using the Green Index in connection with this product made AT&T's designers more aware of the attributes that reduce the negative environmental impact of the product.

When DFE tools like the Green Index are used in concert with the other modules in the DFX series like design for reliability, the result is an even more competitive product. Of course, all aspects of a product must be considered and balanced during the design process. For example, in the case of the business phone set, the conductive adhesive that now substitutes for some uses of tin–lead solder still needs to pass the "drop test," which measures how many times you can drop the phone, at so many feet above the ground, before it breaks.

Similar DFE tools are now being used in hardware development of the 5ESSr switch, in wireless design, and with some corded phones. In these instances, which are quite complex, we are still in the initial stages. We are working toward automated DFE tools that will integrate with computer-aided design (CAD) systems for designers. As more knowledge is brought to better information systems, the goal of sophisticated DFE gets closer.

Introducing Strategic Environmentalism into the Corporation

DFE is *strategic environmentalism*—that is, the understanding and application of environmental principles and practices within a company in such a way that they satisfy customer requirements, provide competitive advantages, and have a positive impact on shareholder value. This is easier said than done.

Fully implementing strategic environmentalism requires major changes in both the principles and practices of any company. Experience and data both teach that organizations resist change, and that resistance to change increases in rough proportion to the magnitude of the change demanded.[8]

The magnitude of the change necessary to implement strategic environmentalism is extremely high. One of the reasons we are facing environmental challenges today is that the public, regulators, and businesses have failed to recognize the complexity of the linkage between economic activity and environmental impact. Instead, we have tended to focus on specific areas like auto emissions or CFC emissions without sufficiently considering the earth as a unified environmental system. Once again, where the environment is concerned, it isn't possible to save the trees until you have seen (and understood) the forest.

We have found it helpful to segment our DFE activities into two categories: specific DFE (SDFE) and generic DFE (GDFE). Specific DFE (the Green Index, for example) is used at a micro (product or process) level in software design systems. Generic DFE is used at a macro (firm) level to implement concepts such as "green accounting systems." SDFE concerns the specifics of a single product's design. GDFE lays the foundation that makes it possible to modify the entire corporate culture. Both are necessary to implement strategic environmentalism.

Even though this is a tremendously complicated area, and even though we don't yet know all that we need to know to solve the problems that we face, it is possible to make incremental progress both in introducing SDFE and GDFE. The implementation of DFE in any company will depend on the specifics of its design process, and more broadly on its business culture. What follows is a summary of what has been learned at AT&T about applying DFE in the context of this company's corporate culture and design environments.

Introducing DFE

The more DFE looks like what you are already doing the better. At AT&T, a historic attention to quality has been an obvious connection to an emphasis on environmental factors in product design. More specifically, the integral role of concurrent engineering, with its separate modules for manufacturability, testability, etc., provided a framework that supported specific SDFE as yet another module in this series.

DFE requires teams of environmental (and other) professionals to translate environmental data into tools that design teams are already familiar with. AT&T's designers are comfortable with CAD tools, checklists, and standardized lists of components. Its environmental professionals, Bell Labs scientists, and engineers are working to develop the environmental components of these tools for the design teams. We have found that it does not work to try and turn designers into environmental experts, but it does work when environmental experts translate the necessary data into the formats designers already use.

A corporatewide "flash cut" to DFE will not work. Trying to introduce DFE in all its complexity at one time is bound to fail. Picking a few dimensions of DFE—for example, pollution prevention, recycling, or design for disassembly—smooths the introduction, and usually produces excellent, quantifiable results such as those AT&T has had with CFC elimination. We didn't begin work toward our CFC goal with DFE in mind, but we now see the CFC elimination process as a DFE testbed and as a basis for further progress and continuous improvement.

Introduce DFE as a test case in an area where success is relatively certain. The experience gained, as well as the environmentally preferable product produced, will be invaluable. But be careful—an initial failure with DFE will greatly increase resistance.

Introducing generic DFE (GDFE)

To implement GDFE fully, the entire culture of the organization has to be changed. Key elements in changing a culture to support GDFE include:

- The support and leadership of senior management.
- The development of a different kind of environmental professional. These are the people who will be expected to:

  Translate environmental data into designer-friendly tools

  Proactively identify materials such as heavy metals that are likely to become future targets of regulatory pressure

  Understand and manage environment as a strategic competency for the company—not simply an end-of-pipe, overhead engineering function

  Link with other internal organizations such as business units, public affairs, health affairs, public relations, and government affairs. These links should ensure official and unofficial feedback loops that inform design, direct business planning, and support the representation of the company's interests to customers and the government.

  Provide regular audits of performance for all internal organizations. The complexity and numbers of environmental and safety regulations are enormous. Reading, tracking, and applying these regulations is coordinated at AT&T by corporate E&S professionals. The internal audits that they perform for AT&T's businesses help ensure that AT&T's performance meets government regulations and standards. In 1993, the program for environment and safety audits at each AT&T location was expanded. The number of audits increased from 674 in 1992 to 825 in 1993. We are now using a computerized database to help each E&S Officer track their compliance plans.

- Attention to the environmental preferences of customers in a systematic, data-intensive way.

- The implementation of reward and recognition systems for environmental successes.

- The availability of education and training programs for DFE.

- The complete integration of vendors and suppliers into the DFE processes.

- An accounting system that assigns environmental costs to the products that generate them. As long as these costs are "lost" in corporate overheads, there will be little real incentive to change. We are just beginning to implement this kind of "green accounting" for the environment, as well as for safety. In 1994, for example, medical costs for workers' compensation are being allocated to individual business units on the basis of their claims. The appearance of this expense on business unit budget lines has already increased attention to safety and begun improving performance. Green accounting is closely linked with *activity-based costing* (ABC) as it is developing throughout AT&T.

- Active participation in industry, government, academic, and nonprofit groups that are addressing environmental principles, practices, and standards.

We anticipate that moving AT&T to a complete implementation of strategic environmentalism will require the resolution of countless issues yet to be identified, and will take between ten and twenty years.

Partnerships and alliances

Environmental solutions must ultimately be global solutions. It does no good, for example, for just one company to eliminate CFCs using proprietary substitutes. All companies and all industries must cooperate to reduce CFCs or the hole in the ozone will not close. Cooperation within and among industries, governments, researchers, educators, and individuals is the only way to keep the earth in a healthy balance.

AT&T is vigorously pursuing partnerships and cooperation to improve the environment. The environment is a problem that doesn't have a micro solution. No matter how effective its application to individual products, DFE can never be a stand-alone solution. Internal efforts to improve environmental performance can't reach their full potential until industry standards, government regulations, and an industrial ecology infrastructure support them.

Association highlights

AT&T was a charter member of the Industry Cooperative for Ozone Layer Protection (ICOLP) which began its work in advance of the 1987 Montreal Protocol to accelerate the development of alternatives to CFC solvents in electronics manufacturing. The company has made processes that it developed using alternative cleaning substances like terpenes (orange pulp derivatives) and n-butyl butyrate (cantaloupe derivative) available worldwide without any licensing fees.

In 1990, AT&T helped found the Global Environmental Management Initiative (GEMI), which is a partnership of 26 major corporations that works at improving the environmental performance of business. GEMI celebrated its fifth anniversary in 1995, and AT&T has continued to play a lead role in organizing conferences and other activities of this influential group.

AT&T is also active in the International Organization for Standardization (ISO) as it develops environmental standards that will become part of the ISO-9000 certification program for manufacturing and services.

In 1993, AT&T worked with Renew America to establish an award for the best use of information technology to advance environmental goals, and with Overseas Press Club of America to fund the Whitman Bassow Award for the best journalistic reporting from outside the United States on environmental issues.

Another one of AT&T's key partners, the American Electronics Association, has been extremely active in the DFE area. AT&T has provided leadership assistance to them and put together their primer titled *The Hows and Whys of Design for the Environment*; AT&T staff also authored several chapters of this book. Also, the work the AEA is doing through its Take-back Task Force reinforces our efforts to informally benchmark our progress against other firms. It is helping develop an industrywide position on take-back policies in anticipation of U.S. legislation encouraging such programs.

AT&T has similar programs and activities with many other organizations, including the Electronics Industry Association, the Computer and Business Equipment Manufacturing Association, the Institute of Electrical and Electronic Engineers, the Microelectronics and Computer Technology Corporation, the National Academy for Engineering, and the National Center for Manufacturing Sciences. The important point is that only by being tied into all of these groups, and others, can the company continue to develop appropriate macro solutions to environmental challenges, and to support the development of national, proactive environmental programs within industry and government.

Government cooperation highlights

AT&T is working with the EPA, as well as with environment and technology leaders in Congress, to help reduce the adversarial relationship between government and industry that has characterized much of the environmental regulations in the United States. AT&T is committed to a partnership in meeting common environmental goals.

AT&T is also tied into government initiatives through the Department of Defense and the Department of Energy to explore environmentally preferred electronics manufacturing technologies. An example is research being conducted jointly by AT&T and Sandia National Laboratories, a Department of Energy lab, to develop environmentally preferable substitutes for tin–lead solder.

Philanthropy and education highlights

The AT&T Foundation's 1993 environmental support went to twenty nonprofit organizations, and six universities for industrial ecology fellowships. *Industrial ecology* is an emerging field of study that seeks to eliminate or reduce environmental impacts of all economic activity. DFE supports this goal by considering environmental concerns at every stage of a product's life cycle—from design, to manufacture, to use, to disposal or reuse. This field integrates technology and environment in all economic activity and borrows from engineering, physical science, economics, management, and law.

The six AT&T Industrial Ecology Faculty Fellowships awarded in 1993 supported projects exploring the recycling potential of household plastics, devising methods to assess exposure to lead, developing microorganisms capable of removing toxic metals from sewage, reducing health risks in high-definition display technology, and developing formal industrial ecology study programs.

One of that year's AT&T Foundation nonprofit grants helped fund a conference organized by Renew America in Washington, D.C. This conference brings together representatives from the most successful environmental programs in the United States to share success stories.

Among the groups receiving awards from Renew America in 1993 were a sixth-grade class in Utah that lobbied the state for a youth tree-planting program, a Boston utility striving to reduce commercial electricity usage, and a ranch in Oregon that brings together ranchers, environmentalists, and government agencies to resolve rangeland disputes. The total funds approved by the AT&T Foundation for environmental concerns in 1993, as in 1992, exceeded $700,000.

Future Directions and Challenges

During the next decade, environmental issues should continue to grow in importance in relation to other public policy issues, and business operations will probably be conducted in a world that is increasingly perceived as resource-constrained. On the basis of existing efforts and developing policies, the following projections seem reasonable:

- There will probably be widespread implementation of postconsumer take-back. This will require significant evolution of the firm's E&S function. No amount of end-of-pipe technology will help firms comply with the full implementation of postconsumer product take-back requirements like those now being enacted in Germany, Japan, and elsewhere.[9]

- Product life-extension programs, including requirements for mandatory product remanufacture, recycling of components, and extreme restrictions on disposal of any material, will become common.

- The "functionality" economy will evolve. In this economy, consumers will be sold functions such as computer service, transportation, or telecommunications rather than products such as computers, cars, and phones. Leasing will increasingly replace purchase of products.

In line with current trends that reflect greater concern over the environmental impact of industrial practices, governments and nongovernmental environmental organizations will become far more deeply involved than they are now in choices of materials, technologies, process and product design, and corporate practices. There are several likely consequences of such a future for corporations such as AT&T:

- The nature of manufacturing will change considerably. Companies will have to become proficient at managing materials over their life cycle. They will also have to reorient their thinking from selling products to offering services.

- Customer focus based on the provision of function, rather than just products, will become a necessary prerequisite for forming long-term, individualized, high-value-added relationships among service suppliers and their customers.

- Significant changes in legal structures will have to be managed. For example, the legal liabilities and risks assumed by firms will change when they can no longer simply transfer the ownership of products to customers. Antitrust issues may arise as industry begins to implement product take-back systems.

- There is at least the possibility that, in an environmentally con-strained world, the traditional role of a private firm as a strictly profit-driven entity will be modified over time so that firms must give more consideration to social cost as well as financial cost in their operations.

- Manufacturing and industrial operations will increasingly become cooperative collaborations among industries, governments, indepen-dent environmental associations, and the public. Environmental solutions will be systemic and global rather than focused on a single issue such as clean air or clean water.

Telecommunications, or perhaps more accurately multimedia com-munications, is likely to have a unique place in this future. It is the business of our industry to bring people together without requiring the large expenditures of energy necessary for auto, train, or plane trans-portation. In a highly developed information society able to create vir-tual realities, it may be possible to bring people together in ways that are in greater harmony with the environment.

All of this is a vision for tomorrow. Today, we can begin the journey by using DFE as the foundation for the remaking of the corporation and the services it provides through the implementation of a strategic environmentalism.

References

1. Janine Sekutowski, "Design for Environment," *Proc. 3rd International Conference on Advanced Materials,* Aug. 31–Sept. 4, 1993, Tokyo.
2. Werner J. Glantsching, "Design for Environment and its Role in Environmentally Sound Manufacturing," U.S.-Japan Center for Technology Management Conference, March 25–26, 1993, Washington, D.C.
3. Braden Allenby, "The Hows and Whys of Design for the Environment," American Electronics Association, June 1993.
4. Werner J. Glantsching, "Design for Environment (DFE): A Systematic Approach to Green Design in a Concurrent Engineering Environment," *Proc. First International Congress on Environmentally Conscious Design and Manufacturing,* The Management Roundtable, May 4–5, 1992, Boston.
5. Peter H. Read et al., "In-Circuit Test Probe Fixture Cleaning with Solid CO2," Technical Memorandum, AT&T Bell Laboratories, December 15, 1993.

6. Braden Allenby, "A Systems Approach to Chemical Management by Manufacturing Firms in an Environmentally Constrained World," *Journal of Systems Integration,* 2:213–226, 1992.
7. Y. B. Zaks, "Environmental Rating Tool: Green Baseline Using 8503 BCS ISDN Terminal," Technical Memorandum, AT&T Bell Laboratories, August 18, 1992.
8. Braden Allenby, op. cit., Ref. 3.
9. Braden Allenby, "Testing Design for Environment: Should Lead Solder Be Used in Printed Wiring Board Assembly?" *SSA Journal,* September 1991.

Environmentally Conscious Products: An IBM Initiative

Anne B. Brinkley

Staff Engineer
Engineering Center for Environmentally Conscious
Products
IBM Corporation
Research Triangle Park, North Carolina

Barbara S. Hill

Manager, Product Safety Technology
IBM Corporation
Somers, New York

The IBM Corporation has a strong environmental, health, and safety foundation, with policies in these areas dating back to the early 1970s. The guiding principles were to provide a safe and healthful workplace, be responsible in the communities where the company does business, and extend our care to the global environment. This foundation led to the development of innovative programs to deal with a multitude of traditional environmental, health, and safety issues. The company's commitment frequently resulted in taking a more aggressive posture on program goals, implementation, and measurements.

As these programs and the information technology industry matured, the corporation looked beyond its traditional roles for ways of expressing its corporate stewardship towards the global environment. In the late 1980s, attention shifted from manufacturing-process issues to the information technology product itself. The concept of extended producer responsibility towards products was just beginning to form in Europe. Working from a stewardship perspective, IBM decided that another step forward was needed, and responsibility and commitment for long-term environmental aspects of products was added to the corporation's environmental affairs policy. In 1990 IBM issued a corporate policy letter stating its commitment to "develop, manufacture and market products that are safe for their intended use, efficient in their use of energy, protective of the environment and that can be recycled or disposed of safely."

This stewardship concept has evolved into a strategic environmental direction for IBM. The evolution took a somewhat different approach than the path taken with traditional environmental affairs issues, which tend to be regulation-driven. Key members of the corporation, representing worldwide operations, met to identify a "wish list" of design objectives. Then, through detailed discussions with product development teams, an objective and strategic design goals were set for the corporation's vision of *environmentally conscious products* (ECPs). The objective was to have IBM continuously improve products and processes to ensure the protection of the environment. The design goals were:

- Product contents must be capable of being recycled or reused at the end of product life.

- Products must use materials that have a recycled content and reutilized components.

- Products must be designed using ease-of-disassembly techniques.

- Product energy consumption must be reduced.

Several dependencies were identified during the planning phase with the development teams. These included access to technical guidance and research, education, and tools for the development engineer. In response, IBM established the Engineering Center for Environmentally Conscious Products at Research Triangle Park, North Carolina, as a center of competence for materials recycling and reutilization. The mission of the center, established in 1991, is to provide technical guidance, laboratory evaluation, and engineering support to promote the incorporation of environmental attributes in IBM products. The center serves IBM's divisions worldwide in the development of environmentally conscious products and works with the corporation's suppliers and brokers to enhance the recycling and reutilization of IBM products.

Due to the diversity of the IBM product lines, the product divisions were then responsible for assessing the strategic ECP goals within their product lines, and defining their own implementation strategies for the ECP program. Several ground rules were established, which included

1. Setting implementation dates to capture new-product development activities
2. Ensuring that the environmental design goals did not preempt other design goals that addressed characteristics such as functionality and safety
3. Placing priority on high-volume or commodity-type products
4. Taking into account the total product life costs

Choosing to Challenge

The ECP goals established by the corporate staff with the technical assistance of the Engineering Center for Environmentally Conscious Products team and key division staff set new targets for all product lines that prioritized desired environmental attributes, anticipated implementation dependencies, and sensitized product development organizations to the mounting environmental pressures of the global marketplace. The targets were aggressive and deliberately directed toward the design community. Without a delicate balance between the technically challenging and the impractical, the visionaries of the ECP program would have recruited few followers. But in fact, the troops rallied around a framework that provided the technical leadership, education, and innovation to transform their jobs, their attitudes, and their products into the instruments of stewardship.

In presenting the four design goals for the strategic direction of ECP development in 1991, the corporate staff paid obvious attention to dependencies presented by the state of the art. Specifically, the first goal, "Product contents must be capable of being recycled or reused at the end of product life," recognized that the infrastructure for materials recycling was not prepared to manage an influx of new materials from durable goods, particularly engineering materials. In defining its goal for future product recyclability, IBM accepted a leading role in the development of new internal and external processes and industry alliances to promote progress toward the goal of recyclable business machines. The dependencies associated with the first ECP design goal included:

- Availability of technical guidance documents or standards
- Materials composition of products
- Materials recycling research

- Current design practices/impediments
- Recycling and reuse infrastructures

The first dependency, upon guidance documents and standards, was addressed by IBM with the release of an internal corporate standard in March of 1992. The standard, titled "Coding and Recycling Thermoplastic Parts," was developed by the Engineering Center for Environmentally Conscious Products to enhance the capability to recycle or reuse plastics in our products. The standard requires the use of a coding system that identifies the specific thermoplastic comprising a given part. The coding system was based upon the German automotive standard symbology using "greater than" and "less than" signs (> <), with the resin identification noted in between the symbols. This symbology was later adopted for ISO 11469.* The coding is permanently affixed to the plastic parts, usually by molding directly into the part. There are three levels of identification:

1. The resin's acronym from ISO 1043†
2. IBM's internal material code
3. The resin's manufacturer and commercial trade name (optional)

A typical representation of the coding system for a polyvinyl chloride part is shown in Fig. 12.1.

The coding standard in IBM accomplished several things. It established a new design criterion for environmentally conscious products, and in so doing began a partnership between designers and materials engineers for product review of environmental attributes. It introduced the concept of standardized material identification to focus the industry at large on common problems of product recyclability. It provided a life-cycle cost incentive to comply with the ECP design goal because properly identified plastics could produce higher revenues for materials reclamation operations whether by IBM, an IBM vendor, a third-party recycler, or a material supplier. The coding system ensures that, for future products, the emerging recycling infrastructure has a tool to efficiently manage a waste stream of engineering thermoplastics.

An additional requirement of the coding standard was the formation of site-based teams with design and materials engineers at their core, to provide ECP support and education to developers. These teams created checklists from ECP design criteria. The checklists provided guidelines on regulated materials like ozone-depleting chemicals and

---

*International Standard ISO 11469: 1993(E), "Plastics—Generic identification and marking of plastic products."
†International Standard ISO 1043-1: 1987(E), "Plastics—Symbols."

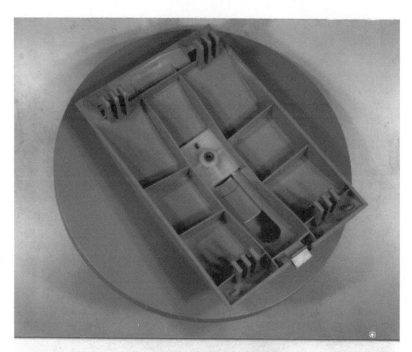

Figure 12.1 Photograph of a monitor pedestal base, highlighting the molded-in material identification: > PVC <.

batteries; fastening and joining technologies for ease of disassembly; electromagnetic shielding technologies; plastics finishing, coding, and recycling; power management; and resource minimization.

Another approach for enhancing potential recycling and reuse of IBM's product contents required evaluation of materials comprising high-volume products. The Engineering Center for Environmentally Conscious Products, being located in the one of the manufacturing facilities for IBM's personal computer products, began studies to demonstrate the feasibility of recycling different types of thermoplastics from personal computers.

Four material types were salvaged from known parts collected by IBM reutilization centers, which primarily reclaimed reusable service parts from scrap machines. The thermoplastics included modified polyphenylene ether, polycarbonate, polyvinyl chloride (PVC), and polycarbonate/acrylonitrile-butadiene-styrene (polycarbonate/ABS). Parts were collected, cleaned, ground, and molded into test specimens for evaluation by IBM, Underwriters Laboratories, and original resin manufacturers. Test results showed that polycarbonate, PVC, and polycarbonate/ABS specimens exhibited physical properties that met the specifications of their virgin counterparts.

Further work then demonstrated that recycled PVC could be remolded into monitor covers in concentrations of up to 100% recycled resin. Covers molded from 25%, 50%, and 100% recycled PVC passed all end-use test requirements. This fundamental research on field-returned materials confirmed the premise that end-of-life equipment contained materials capable of being reused and/or recycled. It also suggested the viability of the second ECP design goal, to use materials with recycled content in IBM products, and set the stage for joint IBM-supplier pilot recycling projects, a first link in interindustry planning for a recycling infrastructure.

Recycled Content

Achievement of the second ECP design goal, the use of materials that have recycled content, assumes the availability of a sufficient and acceptable feedstock for next-use applications. While metals recycling is an industry standard practice, a ready feedstock of engineering thermoplastic materials was an improbable occurrence when IBM charted this course. Implementation of recycled content in plastic parts for business machine applications required that IBM pursue two possibilities: (1) closed-loop recycling opportunities or (2) facilitating supplier development of new material grades with recycled content. In both endeavors, IBM has had success.

With the proven technical feasibility of recycling common thermoplastics from IBM's personal computer products, concurrent activities developed at IBM's Personal Computer Company locations in Greenock, Scotland, and Research Triangle Park, North Carolina, to support the incorporation of postconsumer plastic into a business machine application. The Greenock project actually began as a cost reduction effort for keyboards, the base cover of which was molded from PVC. Several factors contributed to the concept of cost reduction through material recycling. IBM was operating a limited, voluntary product take-back program in the United Kingdom. The vendor, who reduced scrapped equipment to buyable material streams, did not have a market for the recovered PVC. Landfill costs to IBM were mounting, as was public concern over PVC waste in Europe. PVC comprised half of all the polymer tonnage used by Greenock. IBM recognized that, with the collaboration of its vendor and PVC suppliers, each company had an opportunity to develop integrated solutions to problems that were insurmountable to the single companies.

Using the existing collection system, IBM and the Mann Organization jointly identified separation and qualification processes to ensure a consistent quality of screened feedstock from the reclamation facility. Hydro-Geon, a leading PVC manufacturer, developed processes to convert the screened feedstock into a new 100% postconsumer recycled grade that was made to the specification created by IBM. Greenock's in-house molding facility worked with Hydro-Geon to optimize the processability of the resultant grades, and finally IBM implemented the closed-loop process by purchasing the new grade of 100% recycled PVC for the original keyboard cover application. The achievement of this ECP design goal not only produced savings for IBM—22% off the PVC raw material cost—it was a breakthrough for the PVC polymer industry to demonstrate an economic and productive business opportunity in the information technology industry. The environmental benefits of reuse of waste and reduction of PVC as landfill are long-range benefits outside of IBM, with implications for improved environmental quality and protection.

The success of the Greenock program presents an opportunity to resolve IBM's European postconsumer PVC waste disposal problems. IBM Germany began participating in the program in 1993 to realize disposal cost avoidance of approximately $225 per ton. Recruiting international participants for the PVC recycling program would alleviate temporary shortages experienced with the keyboard operations, but recent bans on the export of waste within the European Union have created other obstacles for expansion of the project. IBM continues to work to influence the technical and regulatory initiatives throughout Europe that impact projects such as this.

In the United States, the Engineering Center for Environmentally Conscious Products contacted plastic resin suppliers to request and pursue the development of new polymer grades with recycled content.

A candidate application for recycled polycarbonate/ABS material was identified in system unit covers for new personal computers. On IBM's production timetable for the product, Miles Polymer Division responded to the challenge of meeting IBM's criteria: a 25% postconsumer polycarbonate/ABS, color-matched resin with physical properties equal to virgin at a cost savings over the virgin resin. Miles located a postconsumer waste stream, not only in the United States, but also in Europe, through its parent company in Leverkusen, Germany, for use in the United Kingdom, where the cover sets were to be molded. The worldwide synergy involving IBM laboratories, material suppliers, compounders, molders, and test houses was a critical hurdle in the rapid delivery of a polycarbonate/ABS computer cover with postconsumer recycled content. The project was an innovation for Miles Polymer Division also and has sparked further recycling services in their industry.

Leading the information technology industry to a new outlook on plastics recycling meant convincing agencies like Underwriters Laboratories (UL) that the time had come to support the movement toward environmentally conscious products. No other business machine manufacturer had approached UL about qualifying recycled material for use in business machines when IBM began the dialogue in 1992. There was never any question that products containing recycled material would need to meet the UL general product safety design and performance requirements. But UL had no procedure for evaluation of recycled plastic. Through joint studies with IBM, UL gained experience and confidence in the quality of test specimens for several recycled resins. Moreover, their testing of end-use requirements in IBM's proposed applications for the recycled materials proved that viable recycling programs could be a reality for equipment manufacturers. UL has now developed limited procedures for granting approval based on end-use testing of parts with recycled content. The Engineering Center for Environmentally Conscious Products continues to work with UL for further expansion of the procedures.

Pervasive implementation of IBM's goal to incorporate recycled content in its products is evident in many IBM divisions. The European operations of IBM, Digital Equipment Corporation, and Hewlett-Packard developed a collaborative initiative for software products in 1992. The effort resulted in recommendations for the standardization of paper and packaging components of these products, which included the use of recyclable materials, free of toxic or lead-based contaminants. In 1994, the IBM Software Manufacturing Solutions group, which is responsible for all software and publications products, consolidated its paper purchases and established contracts for volume purchase with a few limited sources for U.S.-manufactured products. The contracts changed procurement requirements to specify recycled content papers. Outside of the U.S. federal government, IBM is one of the largest users of text papers, purchasing several million pounds of paper each month. The implementation has provided a major economic benefit to IBM with annual savings exceeding $5 million, as well as providing a market for 1 million lb of postconsumer paper. IBM permits its print vendors to purchase the specified recycled paper for their other customers' orders, thus providing them a competitive edge over nonparticipants in the paper program. IBM benefits by increased volume/price leverage.

Establishing the program has led IBM into proactive involvement in other environmental areas. IBM is encouraging its paper and print vendors to institute environmental processes that reduce waste and improve air and water discharges. Agri-based (soy) inks and coatings are replacing petroleum-based inks. Vinyl binders for publications are being replaced with paperboard products that are more durable, have a better printing surface, and cost less. PVC shrink-wrap is being replaced with a recycled, chlorine-free polyolefin material. These examples demonstrate IBM's initiatives to promote environmental technology solutions in all aspects of its product lines.

The Packaging Program

IBM's Environmental Packaging Program started in 1990 when a team of internal packaging engineering experts was given the mission to develop and implement a worldwide environmental packaging program. The cornerstone of the program is an environmental packaging design guide developed by the team to proactively address worldwide environmental issues related to packaging materials. The guide is IBM's road map to implement its basic environmental packaging strategy of reduce, reuse, and recycle.

Today, IBM's Worldwide Distribution Engineering Services Department (WDES), located in Research Triangle Park, North Carolina, carries the responsibility to implement a formal environmental packaging program for the corporation. The design guide has been distributed to all worldwide packaging organizations to assist them in lessening the impact of IBM's packaging on the environment. IBM has shared this program and guide with many groups in industry, government, and academia.

The objectives of the environmental packaging program are reflected in packaging design goals that inspired parallel ECP initiatives:

- By-product elimination (e.g., CFCs, dioxins, heavy metals)
- Methods for reducing the amount of packaging required
- Increasing reusability of packaging designs

- Refurbishing and reusing versus purchasing new (e.g., pallets)
- Improving recycling through use of proper symbology identifications
- Improving recycling by requiring more recycled content

WDES has developed engineering specifications as additional tools to assist in the uniform, worldwide implementation of IBM's environmental packaging objectives. These specifications are indicated on packaging engineering drawings used for procurement of packaging materials and electronic parts from IBM suppliers. The specifications cover restricted heavy metals, prohibited blowing agents (CFCs), and the selection and identification of recyclable packaging materials.

As environmental packaging initiatives are monitored worldwide, compliance schedules developed by WDES ensure that IBM meets or exceeds targeted improvements established for the global packaging industry. From 1990 to 1993 IBM implemented the elimination of CFCs and polybrominated biphenyls/biphenyl ether flame retardants from its plastic packaging. Packaging designs eliminated commingled materials, and the postconsumer recycled content of packaging materials reached planned targets of 30% for corrugate, 25% for polystyrene, and 15% for polyethylene. The goal set for year-end 1994 was a minimum of 40% postconsumer recycled content in corrugate and a minimum of 15% recycled resin in plastics.

To help encourage implementation of the above initiatives, an annual competition was started by asking IBM packaging engineers to submit their environmental projects, which conformed to the corporate strategies, to WDES. The winners were selected based on how well the projects met the objectives of the guide and scheduled initiatives. From 1990 to 1992 over 180 environmental packaging projects saved IBM in excess of $33 million. The program has gained momentum, and increased work efforts are evidenced by the fact that, in 1993 alone, 120 projects were submitted with savings in excess of $30 million. Based on the program outlined above, IBM was awarded the first annual Coalition of Northeastern Governors' (CONEG) Challenge Award for source reduction on May 4, 1994.

Design for Disassembly

In the hierarchy of disposal strategies for products at end of life, reutilization is the highest form of waste avoidance. The reutilization of parts and subassemblies from "retired" or surplus products is the revenue-producing activity that currently sustains reutilization and materials recovery operations at IBM's disposal facilities. As a result of the computing industry's fast and frequent technology leaps, shorter product cycle times, and higher volumes of information technology equipment destined for replacement, continued efforts to manage recovery programs responsibly and economically depend upon new products that incorporate design-for-disassembly techniques. At IBM, design for disassembly is practiced through adherence to ECP checklists and design guides or Corporate Bulletins (IBM standards for internal use). These practices emphasize proper coding and identification of materials, avoidance of commingled materials, limited numbers of different materials, as well as encouraging snap-fit and other alternatives to adhesive or mechanical fastening.[1]

Design for disassembly not only facilitates the recovery of reusable parts, but it is the "make or break" proposition for product end-of-life economics. Consider the ramifications of the German packaging waste law issued in 1986. The guidelines were prioritized: avoidance of waste, recycling of waste (both material and thermal recycling), and disposal of waste. Draft legislation for electronic equipment waste in Germany has been proposed for several years based on similar priorities. Design for disassembly is a guideline of these impending requirements for electronic product disposal, which would mandate product take-back obligations by equipment manufacturers. Design-for-disassembly and design-for-recycling practices are imperative for viable programs to conform to the increasingly regulated marketplace.

IBM instituted voluntary product take-back programs in Europe as early as 1989, before the first such proposal appeared in draft legislation. The programs were initiated at the request of customers and have expanded to eight countries: Switzerland, Germany, Italy, the United Kingdom, Austria, France, Sweden, and The Netherlands. Each program is independent and may operate directly through IBM, an IBM subsidiary, or a vendor. Typically customers pay fees depending upon the type or weight of equipment being returned. These charges relate to the transportation or shipping costs. In Germany, for example, this charge can range from $30 for personal computers to $2400 for mainframes.

In general the return programs operate as follows. Products are delivered to a centralized location to be dismantled. Usable parts are segregated and returned to manufacturing. The other categories separated and independently handled are precious metals, cathode-ray tubes, plastics, ferrous and nonferrous metals, and hazardous wastes. Figure 12.2 depicts the average product waste streams from IBM Germany's disposal center operations in 1993. Scrap iron is the most significant commodity, at 60.4%. Plastics and nonferrous metals are seen at much lower volumes (9% and 8.5%, respectively), but it could be anticipated that these volumes will be increasing, as today's products reach end of life.

The combined 1993 volume from all return programs in Europe was over 16,000 tons. The average yield for recycling from those programs

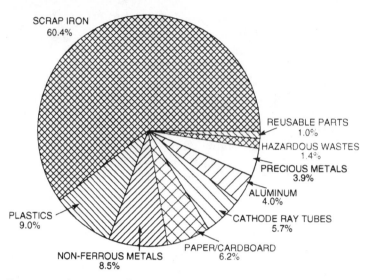

Figure 12.2 Average product waste stream composition for information technology products.

was approximately 70%. Although the majority of the volume of IBM's voluntary product take-back programs still comes from internal disposal, external customer participation has been increasing.

As these numbers increase, IBM's engineers and environmental professionals are working to qualify new vendors and technologies for environmentally responsible solutions to product waste disposal. Cathode-ray tubes (CRTs) are a case in point. As recently as 1992, CRTs presented one of the biggest barriers to achieving a high degree of waste recycling. Recent developments in recycling CRT glass in the United States have reduced the recycling charges such that recycling is now an economically viable option to landfilling. IBM explored several options for CRT disposal in the United States, including remanufacturing vendors, and ultimately chose to contract the recycling of tubes in the United States with a qualified company. In addition to diverting waste from hazardous landfills, this initiative also captures the plastic covers from the CRT units for potential closed-loop plastics-recycling applications.

Much remains to be done to improve the efficiencies of IBM's product disposal and reutilization centers. The identification of problems for end-of-life operations provides a feedback mechanism for product designers, bringing "cradle-to-grave" stewardship full circle. Recommendations to product development from the European centers include:

- Standardize and reduce number of screw types.
- Minimize stickers and labels; find new labeling methods.
- Integrate environmental criteria in purchasing specifications.
- Identify disassembly points on products.
- Improve environmental specifications in product environmental impact documents.
- Develop life-cycle assessment tools.

Product Energy Consumption

As the use of information technology products has grown, so have the concerns related to the environmental burdens associated with the amount of energy being consumed by these products. This is one area where technology and the environment have dovetailed to achieve an objective of reducing energy consumption. The development of portable computers, notebooks, and subnotebooks has led to innovative ways to provide efficient and effective power sources, as well as low-power states. In larger computer systems, power management also has strong design considerations. Even within component development, such as hard disk drives or chips, lower power objectives are being set.

In 1991, the U.S. Environmental Protection Agency (EPA) approached IBM to be one of their initial industry partners to define a voluntary program that would produce energy-efficient products. The program, known as the Energy Star program, began with personal computers and monitors. The objective to meet was a low-power state of 30 W or less for independent personal computer system units or monitors, and a low-power state of 60 W or less for integrated products, which have a monitor included in the computer casing and are not powered directly from a wall outlet. When the EPA launched Energy Star in 1992, IBM was ready with the PS/2 E®, which required much less energy than typical desktop systems. The PS/2 E® was one of the first Energy Star products announced within the industry. The system utilized a "sleep" or "power-down" mode that went into effect after a period of inactivity. In this mode, the monitor needed only 8 W and the system unit 27 W or less. Today, a wide variety of IBM products bear the Energy Star logo, and "sleep" modes are becoming routine for many of the products.

The recognized success of this program is challenging design teams to demonstrate energy reduction accomplishments in other product lines as well. One new development has been the IBM PowerPC® family of microprocessors. These products provide for four software-controllable power-saving modes. Three of the modes (nap, doze, and sleep) are static in nature, and progressively reduce the amount of power dissipated by the processor. The fourth is a dynamic power management mode that causes the functional units in the microprocessor to automatically enter a low-power mode when they are idle, without affecting operational performance, software execution, or external hardware. The technology of the large mainframe computers has been driving power consumption down as well. The new generation of products will achieve approximately a twofold improvement in energy efficiency by the year 2000, from previous products. This will be accomplished in part by migrating systems to CMOS (complementary metal oxide silicon) technology and from gaining efficiency from new power technologies.

Energy efficiency is one design-for-environment issue with clear association and acceptance in the marketplace. Customer interest in energy-efficient products has been mounting, and government efforts steering new environmentally preferable procurement practices attest to regulatory activities that will promote the marketability of products with specific environmental attributes. Part of IBM's overall ECP strategy includes advocating IBM and industry positions in the public policy arenas. Energy has become a challenge since many countries are defining their own unique requirements. IBM has been working with other industries, governments, and standards bodies in an effort to ensure that product energy issues are viewed with an international perspective. Because of the potential for marketplace barriers, energy concerns are one clear example where international harmonization would provide the best solution for industry, government, and the consumer alike.

Life-Cycle Assessment

The intent of *life-cycle assessment* (LCA) is to provide a method to quantitatively report the environmental impacts associated with an activity, product, or system. As a tool for "environmental metrics," its development and standardization become a basis for product and process comparisons that theoretically identify environmentally superior choices. Its potential influence in labeling environmental "leaders and losers" within a market or industry cannot be ignored. Because LCA supports a variety of global initiatives, such as environmental certification programs, full-cost accounting, and "green" procurement, it is emerging as a critical and common element of environmental management schemes.

The Engineering Center for Environmentally Conscious Products studied available LCA models and protocols and chose the LCA framework sponsored by SETAC (Society of Environmental Toxicology and Chemistry) for a test case exercise. IBM's objective for the test case was to evaluate the SETAC LCA technique at a part level, as well as a subassembly and product level, for the selection of materials and processes with minimum impact on the environment. A second objective of IBM's study was to determine if LCA data could be readily used by the IBM engineering community. Given the overwhelming complexity of information technology equipment for a complete LCA study, the center chose to compare processing choices for surface treatment and finishing operations of a sheet steel cover for a PS/2 model 95®.

Figure 12.3 shows the life-cycle system of the metal cover. The scope of IBM's test case LCA was to compare only those manufacturing-process alternatives available for specification by IBM engineers. That is, the LCA was limited to evaluation of the parallel options shown for steel coating and painting in Fig. 12.3. The test case used the Boustead model for inventory analysis of the vendors who performed the following surface treatments for sheet steel: electrogalvanizing, aluminizing, and galvannealing. For surface finishing, data was collected on powder coating versus waterborne paint operations. The ecoprofiles of these process options provided a significant contribution to LCA development for business machine applications.[2]

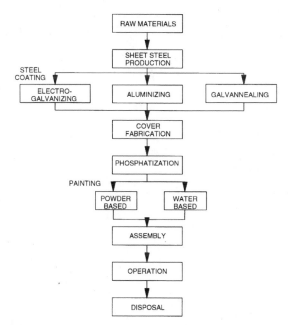

Figure 12.3 Diagram showing the manufacturing flow for the LCA test case cover.

In fact, the exercise did suggest environmental benefits in electro-galvanizing and powder coating the covers as opposed to the other process choices evaluated. In terms of meeting the original objectives for the IBM study, the lessons of the test case highlighted the limitations of the current state of development of LCA that make it impractical today as a design tool for the engineering community at large. The models employed for inventory analysis require enormous amounts of data on the process operations of IBM vendors. The data are sensitive and/or proprietary and have temporal and geographic dependencies. The location-specific nature of the inventory data may be the biggest drawback to the use of LCA by multinational companies. For example, the product used for the test case is manufactured by IBM in the United States, Mexico, Scotland, Australia, and Japan. The results of the test case obtained for vendors in the United States may have little relevance to any other production system for the same part. Comparable analyses, based on the other geographic locations, would be necessary for comprehensive assessment of the processing options. This level of analysis is not practical at the present time.

The incomplete state of methodology for the SETAC LCA framework also provides no consensus leading to a numerical assessment of environmental impacts in the "impact assessment" phase of LCA. Nevertheless, IBM is recommending to its product design teams that LCA can be used to facilitate choices between competing materials and processes when significant environmental savings are identified and no significant trade-offs of impact categories exist. A general "less is better" principle is still the best interpretation of inventory data, and the generation of ecoprofiles for major mechanical parts of IBM machines will be pursued. Only through the experience of working with the LCA process will quality data and methodology become a reality for valid and equitable application of LCA to information technology products.

Toward the Future

The integration of environmental considerations into the initial stages of product development has been critical to the evolution of environmentally conscious products. Without environmental design goals as part of a product designer's normal and routine decisionmaking process, progress and accomplishments will occur in a haphazard manner. The use of cross-functional teams that support the decision-making is essential as the design and engineering communities' areas of responsibility increase dramatically. IBM's Environmentally Conscious Products program has been successful in establishing clear and concise objectives for a designer to achieve, without being prescriptive. Innovation must have free rein, but since "the environment" can be boundless, objectives must provide the scope within which the designer can work.

The design of environmentally conscious products will evolve over time. It is apparent however, that there are dependencies that need to be overcome for true success. The dependencies face industry, government, and the consumer. The major hurdle is market incentives. Today, most of industry has pushed forward environmental design objectives on the basis of product stewardship. However, marketplace incentives, including customer demand and cost-effective recycling and reuse infrastructures, will be crucial for continued commitment. Traditional "command and control" regulation will not effectively move industry in this global business environment.

The issue of infrastructure is multifaceted. An underlying support structure both within and outside of a company is needed. Internal to a company's operations there needs to be a means to handle products at the end of their life and maximize recycling and reuse of materials and components. An external support structure must facilitate collection, segregation, and identification of second-use materials, as well as new applications for these materials. The external infrastructure is dependent on the synergy of the manufacturers, the material suppliers, reclamation centers, brokers, and customer demand. The automotive industry has successfully developed support infrastructures over time. Information technology and electronics products have different requirements that dictate unique disposition alternatives. Signs of this synergy in our industry are starting to develop, but need to be broadened quickly.

Besides the physical mechanisms needed to consider effective and efficient product take-back and recycling, there are other infrastructure issues. These include the availability of quality postconsumer materials and components for viable production, acceptance of such materials by certification agencies and test houses, and practical tools for designer and engineer to use in the decisionmaking process.

Government regulation is another dependency. Existing regulations often present barriers to implementation of the newer concepts of environmental product design. One example would be the regulatory definition of "waste." Conflicting definitions can restrict the movement of valuable postconsumer materials and components, making recycling and reuse nearly impossible. The global marketplace is supported by global development and manufacturing. Restrictions need to be minimized to allow for global solutions. Harmonizing international requirements will be essential for success. For a global company to meet a multitude of country or regional requirements, the intended benefits to the environment may be compromised by the added implementation burdens.

Among it all sits the consumer of the product. While focus is on the extended responsibility of the manufacturer, the consumer has a strong role to play as well. For the marketplace success of ECP, consumers must express a need for environmentally conscious products and support the product's development in their purchasing decisions. Full participation, particularly as end-of-life product return programs evolve, will be crucial for a successful closed loop. The issue of customer acceptance of products and parts that have been refurbished for reuse or recycled is of major concern. Tied to this is the issue of environmental marketing claims. Industry and the consumer need additional guidance on how environmental information can be responsibly communicated, to allow for informed purchasing decisions to be made.

These problems are not insurmountable. The team concept for the manufacturer, regulator, and user applies—with everyone accepting responsibilities, the tasks can be done. Only with synergy and changes in how traditional environmental issues are handled will these obstacles be overcome. Environmentally conscious products can have a successful future—-a healthy planet and our quality of life depend on it.

References

1. J. R. Kirby and I. L. Wadehra, "Designing Business Machines for Disassembly and Recycling," *Proc. IEEE 1993 International Symposium on Electronics and the Environment,* May 1993, p. 32.
2. A. Brinkley, C. Chafee, C. N. Cheung, J. R. Kirby, S. P. Rhodes, I. L. Wadehra, P. G. Watson, and M. Wolf, "Ecoprofile Studies of Fabrication Methods for IBM Computers: Sheet Metal Computer Cover," *Proc. IEEE International Symposium on Electronics and the Environment,* May 1994, p. 299.

13

Hewlett-Packard's Life Cycle-Oriented Product Stewardship Program

Cliff Bast

Corporate Product Stewardship Manager
Hewlett-Packard Company
Palo Alto, California

Tom Korpalski

Environmental Programs Manager
Computer Products Organization
Hewlett-Packard Company
Boise, Idaho

This chapter outlines the evolution of Hewlett-Packard's (HP's) program in "product stewardship," which focuses on assuring that HP's products and processes are environmentally responsible throughout their life cycles. The transition from an "end-of-pipe" to a "life-cycle management" perspective over the past two decades is examined, together with prominent examples of government's new leveraging of market forces to evoke more environmentally responsible behavior by industry.

Also described are the genesis of HP's current environmental management policy, HP's newly established global product stewardship network and management process, and some of the key accomplishments achieved at this early stage of program deployment. This chapter also explains how metrics (based on a pragmatic use of emerging life-cycle assessment concepts) are being used within HP's Computer Products Organization to drive product environmental design by targeting specific areas where designers can reduce the life-cycle impacts of their products on the environment.

From "End-of-Pipe" to "Pollution Prevention"

Environmental protection in the 1970s and first half of the 1980s focused principally on managing the "end-of-pipe" effluents from manufacturing facilities. During this period, corporate environmental management staffs grew to meet the ever increasing volume of regulatory requirements.

During the mid-eighties, forward-thinking companies recognized that the growth in regulations would continue in response to escalating public pressure for environmental protection. They concluded that a management approach emphasizing prevention over management of effluents and wastes was needed. This onset of pollution prevention thinking also precipitated recognition that responsibility for environmental management needed to be broadened to include functions outside of the professional environmental, health, and safety staff.

Early successes in pollution prevention

Both these changes in perspective have been positive for the environment, as it is now possible to harness the broader capabilities of other functions within companies to address issues that previously were chiefly the province of the environmental staff.

For example, the growing involvement of the manufacturing function has been key to achieving the substantial reductions in U.S. industry environmental emissions since 1986, as evidenced by the annual emissions reports published by the U.S. Environmental Protection Agency (EPA) as mandated by the Superfund Amendments and Reauthorization Act (SARA). At Hewlett-Packard (HP), "reported SARA emissions" have been reduced by 99% since 1987. Also, HP was one of the first companies to commit to EPA's voluntary toxic emissions reduction initiative (the so called 33-50 program), and, in fact, had attained EPA's 50% reduction goal by 1992.

Another prominent example has been the electronics industry's excellent progress in eliminating the use and emissions of ozone-depleting substances, principally chlorofluorocarbons (CFCs) and trichloroethane (TCA), in their worldwide manufacturing processes. At HP, use of these chemicals was virtually eliminated in our worldwide manufacturing processes by May 1993.

The key to the success of that program was that responsibility appropriately was assigned to the worldwide manufacturing function. Manufacturing's involvement was needed because the elimination effort required fundamental redesign of many of HP's manufacturing processes. HP's procurement function also played a key role in this program by communicating HP's expectation that our worldwide suppliers of parts and components also needed to eliminate use of these chemicals.

Emergence of "product stewardship" market forces

As we moved into the 1990s, new market forces have materialized which are precipitating another change in the way major corporations think about environmental management. In Europe especially, a philosophy of life-cycle management, or "product stewardship," is proving to be a major driving force for a host of legislative initiatives that are leveraging market forces to evoke more environmentally responsible behavior by industry.

At HP, product stewardship is seen as a philosophy and practice of designing products and their associated accessories and processes to prevent and/or minimize adverse health, safety, and ecological impacts throughout their life cycle, i.e., design, manufacture, distribution, use, take-back, disassembly, reuse, recycling, and ultimate disposition of constituent parts and materials. Thus, HP's environmental program has expanded its focus beyond the company's manufacturing facilities to also consider product shipment, use by the customer, and eventual disposition at the end of the product's useful life. Also taken into account are the possible environmental impacts that may occur "upstream" with respect to HP's suppliers' manufacture of materials, parts, and components used in HP's products.

This new product stewardship philosophy represents a major change in perspective and is bringing attention to the fact that much, and often most, of the environmental impacts associated with products occur beyond manufacturing facilities.

German "take-back" legislation

The product stewardship philosophy is behind two prominent examples of market-driven initiatives, one in Germany and the other in the United States. In Germany, beginning in 1993, manufacturers are now required by law to take back packaging materials returned by customers. Manufacturers who sell in Germany now have a "market-driven" incentive to reduce the volume of packaging as well as move to more environmentally friendly packaging materials (less friendly packaging materials are charged a higher tax per kilogram).

Germany also has proposed legislation that will require manufacturers to take back products when returned by the customer at the end of the product's life. Germany's proposal is perhaps the most significant development that has awakened industry leaders to think about their products in life-cycle management terms.

It is not an unreasonable assumption that many products in the "design hopper" today will face mandatory customer- or legislative-driven take-back requirements in major European markets by the time these products reach the end of their useful life. Thus, a number of companies like Hewlett-Packard are moving forward with programs which emphasize the need to design products in preparation for mandatory take-back.

EPA Energy Star program

Market forces are also being used very effectively to drive attention to product energy consumption and thereby achieve a reduction in air emissions and potential global warming impacts from associated energy generation. This is best exemplified by the widely acclaimed EPA Energy Star program for computers and printers.

The EPA's program allows manufacturers to voluntarily meet the program's requirements and thereby qualify to indicate conformance to Energy Star performance criteria in their product marketing literature. HP was among the first group of companies to sign on for the Energy Star computers and printers programs. The anticipated market impact of Energy Star materialized in October 1993, when President Bill Clinton issued an executive order requiring agencies of the federal government to purchase only computers and printers that meet the Energy Star requirements.

The Energy Star program is precipitating substantial attention to energy efficiency in product design without having to rely on the EPA's traditional "command and control" approach. This program has achieved a true "win-win" for customers, who save on energy costs; for companies, who can demonstrate environmental responsibility; and for the environment.

These two prominent examples of market-driven initiatives— German take-back laws and Energy Star—are among a growing list of similar developments that are motivating leading companies like HP to begin now to design products:

1. To make them easy to disassemble

2. To use components and materials that can be reused and/or recycled when the products reach the end of their useful life

3. To design products so as to minimize lifetime energy consumption during use by the customer

Evolution of HP's Product Stewardship Program

Environmental management policy

As life-cycle concepts began to permeate the thinking of HP's environmental management function, it became apparent that HP's environmental management policy needed to be revised. HP's policy objective, revised in 1992, now reads: "To provide products and services that are environmentally responsible throughout their life cycles and to conduct business operations worldwide in an environmentally responsible manner." Also adopted with HP's revised policy was a set of guiding principles that embrace the life-cycle management philosophy.

Environmental Management Steering Committee

To facilitate business management involvement in assuring company-wide implementation of HP's revised policy, in 1993 HP management established a new Environmental Management Steering Committee, whose mission is to "provide the strategic direction, policy development and objectives that support the implementation of HP's environmental management policy consistent with business needs and HP values."

The new Steering Committee consists of executive-level representatives of all HP's businesses and is facilitated by HP's corporate director of environmental management. The new Steering Committee is proving to be a major mechanism for facilitating business management involvement in assuring that life-cycle issues and concerns are incorporated into HP's business strategies and plans.

HP's revised policy made it clear that the trend toward broadening responsibility for environmental, health, and safety management beyond the professional staff was a permanent one. This is especially true for HP's product stewardship program, which focuses on implementing the "environmentally responsible products" portion of HP's policy. In fact, the goal of HP's product stewardship program is to assure that all HP's businesses design their products to be environmentally responsible throughout their life cycle by integrating product stewardship needs and objectives into their business strategies and plans.

Product stewardship program

In 1992, HP launched a product stewardship program within its Computer Products Organization (CPO). CPO was the logical choice for HP's initial efforts in product stewardship, since CPO produces HP's widely recognized LaserJet and PaintJet printers, and Vectra personal computers (PCs). CPO's products are produced in high volumes and therefore represent HP's most significant opportunity to reduce environmental impacts in the life-cycle design of our products.

With environmental market forces continuing to escalate, CPO decided to establish a full-time product stewardship program manager position. This new position had CPO-wide responsibility for facilitating communications and broad CPO product stewardship strategy development and deployment. CPO's program manager also has the role of interfacing with the corporate and geographic functions to define the support needed from these functions to meet CPO's needs.

CPO quickly recognized that product stewardship constituted a quintessential cross-functional issue, with no individual function having the clear mission and broad array of capabilities needed. This meant that there was no logical "owner" for the program, and, in fact, most functional groups were hesitant to take the lead for this emerging challenge.

Establishment of CPO division product stewards

CPO's solution was to ask each division product line general manager to designate a single "focal point" person to assume primary program responsibility. This person's role is to coordinate the activities of the various division functions to evaluate, understand, and assure an appropriate response to emerging product stewardship market forces that could have an impact on CPO's products. Within HP, these "focal point" employees have become known as "product stewards." CPO's product stewards were recruited from among the functional triad of R&D, manufacturing, and marketing, or another function closely affiliated with the product generation process, e.g., product quality. The decision to draw the "product stewards" from functions directly involved in the product generation process, we believe, is very key to the success of HP's program. Product stewards need to understand and be experienced with the division's "phase review" process for product design. They also need to be acquainted with the product development platform and where each project is in the design schedule.

CPO's program development "road map"

CPO's strategy was first to have their new program manager conduct on-site visits with his "customers," the CPO division product stewards, to understand their progress in advancing product stewardship and to inquire about their needs and concerns, including where and how the new program manager could use his new role to support their efforts.

CPO's program manager also worked in close partnership with HP's European region environmental manager, HP's U.S. environmental government affairs manager, and HP's corporate-level product stewardship manager, to evaluate the major market forces likely to affect CPO's businesses and to develop a list of recommended major objectives for CPO's program. These were reviewed with the general managers of CPO's various businesses, who approved their deployment throughout CPO.

Education of corporate and geographic staff functions

Concurrent with these activities, the same group worked together to acquaint the various corporate and geographic functions with product stewardship and its emerging business implications. The group reviewed the market forces, issues, and support needs being expressed by CPO's "product stewards," and helped each function understand that it was in a unique position to contribute to CPO's program. This early effort in educating each of the staff functions prepared each function to begin delivering support to CPO. Moreover, the support requested by CPO was representative of the support HP's other businesses were expected to request, once these other HP businesses began to launch their product stewardship programs.

CPO program progress

During this early partnership between CPO and the HP corporate and geographic functions, the following progress was achieved in advancing HP's product stewardship program:

- Establishment of mechanisms to track, evaluate, and communicate the business implications of global legislative and market developments

- Deployment of design for the environment guidelines for products and packaging (for products, this meant leveraging the experience of HP's product recovery centers in Roseville, California, and Grenoble, France, to define design practices that facilitate end-of-life disassembly, reuse, and recycling)

- Development/piloting of product environmental profile sheets
- Piloting a set of product stewardship metrics (see below)
- Development of an HP brochure entitled "HP's Commitment to the Environment," which describes HP's environmental management policy, programs, and performance progress for HP's customers, employees, and other HP stakeholders
- Development of first-generation environmental performance criteria for HP's suppliers

Expansion of Program to HP's Other Businesses

As HP was advancing CPO's program, concern began to mount that it was time for HP's other businesses also to direct their attention to product stewardship. Early in 1993, a team representing the HP European management team, CPO, and HP corporate presented a proposal to HP executive management. That proposal recommended that an HP global product stewardship network, or "virtual" organization, be established to help HP's other businesses launch their programs. HP's corporate function, the Product Processes Organization (PPO), which includes the corporate environmental management function, was chartered with the following mission: "In *partnership* with HP's geographic organizations and other corporate functions, provide a *strong facilitation platform* to the HP businesses and be *proactive* in elevating *awareness* and *leveraging* product stewardship *solutions* for *improved business results.*" The italicized words in this mission statement were chosen very carefully. What follows is an overview of examples of how HP's program addresses each key element in our mission.

HP's global product stewardship network

A global network has been established which acts as a "virtual" organization to address product stewardship issues. Each business has designated a single program focal point, analogous to CPO's program manager, with parallel responsibilities for program facilitation, coordination, and communication. Each of these group-level focal points has established product stewards at the product-line division level to "round out" the network within each business.

The corporate component of the partnership is fulfilled by a team of representatives from the corporate functions, including quality/product regulations; packaging engineering; procurement; environmental, health, and safety; electronic assembly development center; U.S. environmental government affairs, public relations, and marketing communications; and legal.

On the geographic side of the partnership, there are U.S. and European organizations involved with logistics and HP's aforementioned product recovery centers; European environmental government affairs; country management organizations (via HP's European Environmental Management Steering Committee); and the "Americas" field organization.

Each corporate and geographic function has one, or where appropriate, several focal points who understand their function's role(s) in supporting the product stewardship efforts of HP's businesses. As issues emerge, we can call upon these focal points to participate in rapidly mobilized, cross-functional teams to address each issue.

For example, teams have been established to address such issues as European product take-back, battery legislation, and the proposed Netherlands ban of certain brominated flame retardants in products, to name a few. These teams quickly develop situation analyses and recommend actions which are communicated to HP's businesses/product stewardship network for appropriate follow-up at the product-line level.

Strong facilitation platform

The strong facilitation platform is being provided in several ways, including:

- Regular briefings of HP executive and business management including HP's Environmental Management Steering Committees

- Regular workshops for the HP business program focal points/global network; meetings are held every three to four months and allow HP's businesses to review and calibrate direction for HP's strategies and staff functions' support activities

- HP business–driven support projects, the scope and funding of which is co-developed in partnership with HP's businesses

Proactive awareness

HP's global tracking and communication network is the key mechanism for assuring "early warnings" on legislative and market developments to facilitate advance planning and to avoid "blindsiding" of HP's businesses. HP also participates in programs like IEEE conferences and similar activities to keep HP's businesses informed of industry product stewardship trends and initiatives.

Leveraging solutions

The global network provides a communication link which facilitates HP-wide sharing and collaboration and provides a forum for HP's businesses to identify "high-leverage" projects which they want addressed centrally (e.g., global tracking). HP's other businesses are already leveraging the spadework accomplished in connection with launching CPO's program. Many of the tools (e.g., design for environment guidelines) developed to support CPO's initial program activities are now being directly employed by HP's other businesses.

Improved business results

This last key element of the mission statement is meant to underscore the important point that HP's product stewardship efforts should ultimately help HP's businesses achieve improved business results by helping to assure they meet the emerging product environmental performance expectations of HP's customers.

Although it is still relatively early in HP's program, CPO has released products with improved environmental features, including the HP Vectra PCs and LaserJet 4L printers. We expect that the program foundation described above will enable HP's businesses to continue introducing new products that will meet the expected increasing customer expectations for product environmental performance. We also believe that product stewardship will further advance HP's contributions to a better environment today and tomorrow.

CPO Use of Metrics to Drive Product Environmental Design

As described above, Hewlett-Packard defines product stewardship as the philosophy that the manufacturer of a product should be responsible for that product and all associated environmental (health and safety) impacts throughout the product life cycle related to design, manufacture, distribution, use, obsolescence, recovery, reuse, and disposal of the product and its components and related support products. The Computer Products Organization of Hewlett-Packard has launched a product stewardship program with an overall objective to provide products and services that are environmentally sound throughout their life cycle and to conduct operations worldwide in an environmentally responsible manner.

Driving forces for action

The driving forces for CPO's program initiative include:

- Customer/market expectations
- Legislative and regulatory initiatives
- Competitor actions
- HP company objectives

To begin with the last item, HP has always had a stated corporate objective to be a good, responsible citizen, and this objective is the foundation for all of its environmental and safety programs including product stewardship.

Competitor actions also help to drive product stewardship improvements and results. For example, if one computer maker introduces and successfully markets a line of energy-efficient personal computers, other manufacturers will try to improve on their product offerings.

A third driver is legislative and regulatory initiatives that do in some cases drive our actions. In particular, in the area of product stewardship, some initiatives in Europe, e.g., the German packaging initiative, have helped to define some areas of focus for our efforts.

The fourth, and perhaps most important driver, is customer and market needs and expectations. Customers are beginning to inquire about the environmental features and/or impacts of our products and processes. Examples include energy efficiency, packaging materials and recyclability, and ozone-depleting substances used in our manufacturing processes.

CPO's overall strategy to achieve its product stewardship objective is to integrate the concept and thinking into its normal business processes. That is, make it a way of life where all departments from R&D to marketing to manufacturing to distribution think about it, set objectives, and strive to improve products and processes. We believe this approach is the only way to be successful and meet our long-term goals, and also that the expertise and innovation of our product designers will help define more environmentally responsible solutions in the long term, not dictated solutions from others.

CPO product characteristics

CPO's product mix includes PCs/monitors, servers, printers, plotters, faxes, and scanners. The products are relatively complex, with a multifarious mix of materials, components, and subassemblies such as printed-circuit assemblies, fans, motors, cables, case plastic, and metal parts.

Materials, parts, and components suppliers are numerous and global in nature. The products are marketed and sold in highly competitive, global markets. The products and business as a whole are characterized by rapid technology changes, short product life cycles (including short development cycles), and narrow market windows. These product and business characteristics were an important consideration in deciding the approach and parameters to measure results and improvements relative to the objective.

Selecting a methodology and an approach

A set of metrics, or measurement tools, was needed to help drive product and process improvements and to provide management an easy method to review and measure progress. A cross-functional team (including representatives from R&D, marketing, manufacturing, quality, and environmental management) developed the methodology and approach. The team decided that any proposed methodology and actual metrics should meet several criteria:

- The approach should be simple (easy to use), pragmatic, timely (i.e., not require excessive time and analysis to develop and use), flexible, and noncontroversial. Otherwise, designers and others would be reluctant to use it due to time, cost, and other "design for" pressures.

- The parameters selected should be based on what the customer/ market and/or governmental/regulatory agencies currently use or are likely to target early on as measures of environmentally responsible products. These expectations should be coupled with feedback from HP product recovery centers on issues and needs regarding end-of-life handling of old, obsolete products.

- The parameters selected should be factors which product designers have the ability to directly influence and impact versus criteria outside their direct sphere of influence.

- The approach should be a starting point to launch improvements. It should not be a full life-cycle analysis (LCA) of all materials, components, etc., in the product.

The selected approach

Using the above criteria, the team selected key LCA parameters or elements to use as measures of the environmental responsibility of products, packaging, consumables, learning products, and manufacturing processes. The metrics are used to set product-specific objectives. Objectives can be set and results measured as a percentage improvement above a baseline product, package, or manufacturing process. Alternatively, specific target values or goals can be set for each parameter and actual results compared to the targeted value.

The metrics are divided into four areas:

- Materials conservation and waste reduction
- Energy efficiency
- Design for environment
- Manufacturing-process emissions

Each area has several parameters or elements to be considered and measured. The selected parameters are presented in Tables 13.1 and 13.2.

The parameters selected for the metrics are based on customer questions and requests, governmental initiatives, regulatory actions, proposed eco-labeling criteria, and end-of-life handling considerations. In addition, a simple desktop analysis by one printer product line revealed that energy use and consumables use by the end user were the dominant environmental impact parameters, followed by end-of-life disposition.

Some of the parameters do not apply to packaging, consumables, or learning products, and in certain cases, all of them may not apply to some types of products. Therefore, product lines must have flexibility and discretion in omitting those criteria that do not apply to their products. Similarly, metrics and an improvement goal may not be set for every product. Rather, only selected, key products may be targeted for improvements. In some cases, a product line might only target packaging or consumables for improvements for any one year based

TABLE 13.1   Product, Consumables, and Packaging Metrics

Metric/parameter	Value/measure
Materials Conservation and Waste Reduction Parameters	
Mass	Kilograms
Projected percent remanufactured or reused	Percent by weight
Projected percent recycled	Percent by weight
Energy-Efficiency Parameters	
Normal operating mode	Watts
"Sleep" mode	Watts
Off mode	Watts
DFE Parameters	
Variety of materials	Number of different materials
Plastics marked	(Yes or no)
Disassembly time	Minutes
Recycled-material content	Percent
Materials requiring special handling	Number of materials

TABLE 13.2   Manufacturing Process Metrics

Metric/parameter	Value/measure
Process emissions parameters	
SARA 313 emissions	Kilograms per year
Hazardous waste generated	Kilograms per year
Hazardous waste reused/recycled	Percent of waste
Solid waste generated	Kilograms per year
Solid waste reused/recycled	Percent of waste

on customer, market, and regulatory considerations. These specifics are left to the discretion of management and their product line teams.

No weighting of the selected parameters was attempted. That is, when determining an overall percentage improvement in a particular product, more weight is not given, for example, to energy efficiency versus recycled content. Instead, individual product lines will use the metrics along with customer, market, and regulatory data specific to their products to prioritize and focus their efforts. Weighting all the criteria equally, while arbitrary, is better than weighting some criteria over others in the absence of full life-cycle data to support the weighting decisions. Given current understanding of DFE issues, equal weighting is probably the best method to use at this time since improvements in any of the criteria will yield more environmentally responsible products and processes.

Measurement of several of the parameters related to end of life requires some type of assessment of the product, packaging, etc., prior to its end of life. These parameters include projected percentage of readily recyclable materials, projected percentage remanufactured or reused, disassembly time, and materials requiring special handling. A process has been established at HP's product recovery centers to perform these product assessments.

The formal metrics package was finalized and distributed in late 1993. New-product development teams have begun to use the metrics as one tool in defining new-product environmental objectives. Results from these efforts will be measurable in new products introduced during the mid-1990s.

Efforts by several product lines prior to the development of the formal metrics have yielded improvements in products, packaging, and manuals. Two examples, Vectra personal computers and the LaserJet 4L printer are presented in Tables 13.3 and 13.4. In addition, in May 1993 HP met its goal and eliminated all manufacturing uses of ozone-depleting substances. Ozone-depleting substances were one of the top SARA 313 emissions from HP sites in the United States. Overall, SARA 313 emissions have been reduced by 76% since 1987 at U.S. sites.

TABLE 13.3   Vectra Personal Computers Environmental Improvements—1993

Metric/parameter	Improvements*
Product	
Mass	7 kg, 45% improvement
Energy use	30 W, 40% improvement (EPA Energy Star compliant)
Variety/number of materials (case parts or box)	2 (pure plastic and steel), 60% improvement
Plastics marked	Yes, 100% improvement
Disassembly time (to subassembly/board level)	2 min, 35% improvement
Materials requiring special handling	No PBDE flame retardants; no heavy metal batteries (no batteries in some models)
Packaging	
Material	Nonbleached Kraft, EPS foam, no heavy metals in inks
Recyclability	100% recyclable
Recycled content	50% recycled cardboard
User manual	
Mass	150 pages, 60% improvement
Materials	Nonbleached paper, no wire-o binding
Recyclability	100% recyclable (no separation required)
Recycled content	50% recycled paper

*Percentage from 1988 baseline.

Life-Cycle Analysis: Observations and Future Considerations

LCA must be viewed in the context of customer and market needs and expectations. Customers are beginning to inquire about the environmental features and/or impacts of products and processes. However, research and real-world purchasing data also show that, while customers are beginning to show interest in "green" features and issues, their decision to buy is still based first on cost and performance—that is, what the product does and how well it does it. If price, function, and quality are all equal, then some customers are beginning to include "green" as a possible differentiator.

Coupling this customer preference for low-cost, high-quality products with the highly competitive and global marketplace, that at least the computer business operates in, implies that environmental improvements must take into consideration customer and market expectations and demands to be successful. For the concepts of product stewardship to be successful in the long term, they must also be economically sustainable. Said another way, "green" products which cost

TABLE 13.4   LaserJet 4L Printer Environmental Improvements

Metric/parameter	Improvements*
Product	
Mass	30% improvement
Energy use	Sleep mode—5 W, 85% improvement, (EPA Energy Star compliant)
Plastics marked	Yes, 100% improvement
Nuisance emissions	Eliminated ozone emissions
Consumables	
Mass	30% improvement
Recyclability/waste reduction	Toner cartridge shipped with printer (reduces packaging); economode for draft printing; uses 50% less toner, extends life; free toner cartridge return and recycling program
Paper	Supports a variety of recycled paper use
Packaging	
Mass	Bulk shipment to distribution centers saves packaging waste
Material	Nonbleached Kraft, EPS foam, no heavy metals in inks
Recyclability	100% recyclable
Recycled content	50% recycled cardboard
User manual	
Mass	66% improvement
Materials	No wire-o binding
Recyclability	100% recyclable (no separation required)
Recycled content	Recycled paper used

*Percent improvement over previous model.

more and/or do not perform to expectations will not sell. Therefore, caution and care must be exercised with any initiatives that would substitute government action or mandates for the support of the marketplace as evidenced by customer purchase decisions. If gaps exist between LCA real risks and/or impacts and market demands, consumer education and awareness must be shared by everyone, not forced by dictating requirements on manufacturers which do not reflect the real needs and desires of the marketplace. Business cannot be expected to deliver products that the market will not purchase.

Simple, pragmatic approaches to LCA are needed to get started, build momentum, and achieve early wins for the environment and business. Success will drive further improvements. It is currently impractical for individual companies to undertake complete LCA on complex products. The next level of LCA requires an approach that can be used and leveraged by businesses, including a consistent approach, a pragmatic, doable approach, and consensus data on relative environmental impacts of different materials, components, etc., including their weighting/importance to be used along with price and performance data in decisionmaking.

Acknowledgment

Our sincere appreciation to HP's Jean Claude Vanderstraeten, Cynthia Johnson, HP's Director of Environmental Management Don Summers, and members of HP's global product stewardship network for their continuing contributions to advancing HP's product stewardship programs. Thanks to the Hewlett-Packard employees who worked as part of the team in developing the metrics package, including Jane Bell, Jack Daugherty, Theo Dirksen, Denise Furet, Nancy Matela, Dennis McGavis, Hal Phillips, Doug Pollock, Bill Robison, and Brad True.

14

A Life-Cycle Assessment of a Computer Workstation*

MCC

Greg Pitts

Director, Environmental Programs
Microelectronics and Computer Technology
Corporation
Austin, Texas

Introduction

The Microelectronics and Computer Technology Corporation (MCC), one of the nation's leading technology development and commercialization organizations, is a consortium of nearly 100 corporations, public and nonprofit agencies, and universities. MCC provides a forum where industry, government, and academia can collaborate, leveraging investments and expertise in the development of high-risk, high-impact technology while reducing costly duplication of efforts. This collaborative environment provides an opportunity to cooperate on projects that are inherently multicompany or multiindustry. It also provides a setting for nurturing the creation and growth of new businesses to provide advanced technology products and services.

---

*This work is adapted from an industry-led study published by MCC and authored by many, entitled Environmental Consciousness: A Strategic Competitiveness Issue for the Electronics Industry, Microelectronics and Computer Technology Corporation, Austin, TX, March 1993, and is reprinted with permission from MCC.

The workstation life-cycle study

Beginning in late 1992, MCC undertook an effort to work with industry representatives to generate a life-cycle assessment of a computer workstation. This was the first step in an attempt to quantify and identify opportunities to simultaneously improve environmental performance, improve product performance, and reduce overall life-cycle costs of electronic products. A collaborative effort among dozens of companies, this unusual effort is expected to stimulate design for the environment (DFE) activities in the electronics industry.

The study did not strictly adhere to the developing methodologies for life-cycle analysis, which call for a three-step approach of inventory, impact, and improvement covering all aspects of a product's life, from cradle to grave. The slightly divergent approach taken in this study is in part due to the recognition that a complete life-cycle analysis for such a complex product could not be reasonably accomplished. Rather than further limit the scope of the study to more completely address the complete life cycle of only a few components, the broader approach provided a cross-cut view of the several electronics sectors. The study therefore concentrated on the key workstation components for which there was sufficient background knowledge and expertise available. Additionally, participants provided more qualitative information in order to develop a series of recommendations for action. The study focused on five electronics industry sectors: semiconductors, semiconductor packaging, printed wiring boards and computer assembly, computer systems, and displays. This chapter will outline the study methodology and results.

Study Background

Historically, environmental concerns have often not been addressed until the "end of the pipe," or until after the pollution is generated. Until recently, government agencies have focused on end-of-pipe regulatory solutions rather than a proactive effort aimed at pollution prevention and source reduction. Industry has responded with remediation programs, not adequately addressing source reduction or waste minimization. Furthermore, environmental issues have too often been addressed in a fragmented and adversarial manner. Industry, government, and the academic communities have not sufficiently collaborated in developing balanced policies, practices, and technologies. The result has been a lack of synergy and, more importantly, a loss of competitiveness in emerging global markets.

Global business implications cannot be overstated. As described in Chap. 3, several countries in Europe, such as Germany and Sweden, have responded aggressively to environmental concerns.* As one example, the German government has enacted legislation requiring manufacturers to take back products after their service life. These regulations have prompted manufacturers in other countries to think more carefully about environmental considerations and take action to reduce product impact on the environment.

With the advent of increasingly stringent regulations, both in the United States and abroad, many manufacturing organizations are incorporating environmental considerations into the design and manufacture of products. As described in earlier chapters, the DFE concept, often called "green design," refers to a design process which treats "environmental attributes...as design objectives, rather than constraints."[1] This approach to design will not only reduce the environmental impact of products, but will also improve industrial competitiveness by emphasizing efficient use of materials and energy while reducing costs associated with environmental compliance.†

Product designers must develop cooperative relationships with material suppliers, process engineers, and waste coordinators to use and dispose of materials in a way that minimizes environmental impact. To a large extent, this will require a shift in perception of the environment by top management from an external requirement to a business opportunity.[2]

An important premise of DFE is that "green design is likely to have its largest impact in the context of changing the overall systems in which products are manufactured, used and disposed, rather than changing the composition of products per se."[3] When attempting to assess the environmental impact of a particular product, it is important to recognize that the product itself is not necessarily the major contributor of environmental releases; more often, the manufacturing or disposal process contributes the greatest impact.

Effective responses require a systems approach. A systems approach refers to "an organized attempt at looking at the objectives, methods and results [of the design process] in their entirety rather than merely performing a limited set of activities which might appear to be based on a restricted...point of view....[It stresses] consideration

---

*Additional details about international trends are discussed in *Environmental Consciousness: A Strategic Competitiveness Issue for the Electronics and Computer Industry,* Summary Report, Microelectronics and Computer Technology Corporation, Austin, TX, March 1993.

†Environmental impact is not the only design criterion that manufacturers must adhere to when designing products. Consideration of performance, safety, quality, cost, reliability, and function are fundamental in the product design. Therefore, it is important to take a systems approach to product design that incorporates not only environmental characteristics, but other design factors as well.

of the [product] requirements over the entire span of system life,"[4] taking into account environmental considerations, and applying effective solutions throughout the product life cycle, especially during conceptual and design stages. In this context, product life cycle includes all aspects of a product's manufacture and use, beginning with design, through acquisition of raw materials and components used for manufacture to customer use, and concluding with disposal or recycling. Chapter 9 described the life-cycle assessment approach, which is a methodical way to view a product from an environmental perspective.[5]

In a traditional product approach, designers concentrate on the product itself. In a systems approach, the designer more consciously includes processes involved in the manufacture, use, and end-of-life disposition of the product during the design process. This has been a relatively new addition to some corporate strategies, and is reflected in approaches such as total-quality management (TQM) and flexible manufacturing.[6] In a systems approach, the product is connected to a broader infrastructure including materials, energy, and management of waste.

Study Description

Milestones

While other approaches exist for evaluating environmental impact, the focus adopted in this effort has been on a systems assessment of the product life cycle. Key milestones during the course of the study were as follows:

- A presentation to the Chief Technology Officers of the Computer Systems Policy Project (CSPP) by industry and the national laboratories in April 1992 resulted in a decision to pursue an environmental assessment targeted at the electronics and computer industries. MCC assumed responsibility for facilitating and coordinating the study.

- Building upon sponsorship and support from the U.S. Department of Energy, MCC worked with industry and government to develop a work plan, adopting the approach based on a "typical computer workstation."

- An Advisory Committee composed of industry, national laboratory, Department of Energy (DoE), and U.S. Environmental Protection Agency (EPA) representatives was formed to provide overall guidance of the effort.

- More than 100 participants from over 40 organizations participated in a workshop in Albuquerque, New Mexico, to launch "A Life Cycle Environmental Assessment of a Computer Workstation."

- Seven task forces were formed, and over the next several months each prepared a report. The reports were distributed for review and comment.

- A questionnaire was provided to task force leaders for gathering quantitative information regarding energy and material used and on wastewater and hazardous and nonhazardous by-products generated in products and processes. Answers to the questionnaire were analyzed and form the basis of the workstation analysis.

- A study coordinating committee reviewed task force reports to identify common findings and recommendations.

- All findings and recommendations were reviewed with task force leaders and the Advisory Committee (in group and individual meetings).

- The initial study concluded with a conference in Washington, D.C., in March of 1993.

Task force organization

As indicated, task force reports were generated as an outgrowth from the Albuquerque workshop and follow-up efforts. The task forces were organized as follows:

1. The manufacture of materials and their disposition, addressed by the Chemicals and Materials Task Force*

2. Wafer-level semiconductor manufacturing, including material usage and disposition, but not material manufacture, addressed by the Semiconductor Devices Task Force

3. First-level assembly from wafer dicing to molded package, addressed by the Semiconductor Packaging Task Force

4. Printed wiring board (PWB) fabrication and board assembly, including component issues, addressed by the Printed Wiring Boards/Computer Assemblies Task Force

---

*Although natural resource acquisition was part of the original charge to the Chemical and Materials Task Force, the task force decided not to include acquisition, noting that the acquisition of raw materials is primarily a function of the mining and extraction industry.

5. The manufacture, use, and disposition of displays, addressed by the Displays Task Force

6. Computer assembly, including internal peripherals such as power supplies, housings, drives, and enclosures, addressed by the Computer Systems Task Force

7. Education, from K-12 through continuing education, on-the-job training, and public awareness, addressed by the Education and Training Task Force

Within areas of life-cycle analysis, task forces considered the following common issues:

- Key environmental concerns including

   Source reduction

   Recyclability

   Treatment

   Disposition

   Energy

   Risk

- Current and future regulations, both domestic and foreign
- A systems approach to environmental cost and impact
- The marketing impact, including accessibility to future "green" markets
- Potential roadblocks
- Current technology efforts by industry, government and universities worldwide*

In addition, they reflected upon the following questions:

- What are the primary environmental issues this task force should address with regard to its technology area?
- What are the primary environmental costs?
- What are the primary global compliance concerns?
- What are the primary environmental constraints and/or issues in the marketplace?

---

*In practice, some teams viewed the assignment, in part, as the "identification of holes." That is, they identified areas in which either new efforts need to be started or current efforts require significant expansion. Efforts already well under way were not a focus for these teams.

- What are the top 10 issues this task force believes must be addressed?

Task force reports analysis

The task force reports were reviewed and analyzed to identify common and unique findings and recommendations. The findings were ranked in priority order and summarized as follows:

- A significant increase in collaboration, as well as more effective collaboration, is vital.
- The availability of high-quality quantitative data and information (including cost) is a must for good decisionmaking.
- Technology, education and training, incorporation of a systems orientation, and improved accounting systems are approximately equal in terms of importance.

Task force Leaders were asked to rank the top three recommendations for their respective team. The top recommendations across all of the teams are:

- Technology development is first and foremost and must be pursued.
- Education and training directed at, and provided to, multiple communities (public, customer, accountants, management, engineers, etc.) must be undertaken.
- Policy and regulatory incentives (such as investment credits, cost sharing, use of national laboratories) are vital to supporting competitiveness, and must be developed and implemented.
- Collaboration among multiple communities is critical (e.g., industry, government, academia, and the public).
- Accessible and high-quality data and information must be available and easy to use.

Data collection

In conjunction with the qualitative assessment, a systems analysis of the manufacture of a computer workstation was facilitated through a questionnaire completed by each of the task forces. One concern in dividing the computer workstation into discrete sectors was the potential loss of a systems perspective. To provide linkage, systems advisors from Sandia National Laboratory and Los Alamos National Laboratories contributed, coordinated, and gathered product and process data, working with the task forces.

The questionnaire was distributed to six of the task forces (the focus of the education and training task force made completion of the questionnaire inappropriate). The questionnaire, designed by the two systems analysts, collected data about materials and processes and provided a common evaluative framework from which to draw certain conclusions about current industry practices. Responses were used for integrating team findings and developing a set of recommendations to assist U.S. industry in achieving environmental goals. A four-part methodology was applied to establish an industry baseline, define critical areas, identify system constraints, and create action plans (or recommendations).

Industry baseline.   Current environmental practices must be identified (and baseline established) in order to understand what improvements are necessary. The following questions were addressed:

- How are computer workstations currently manufactured?
- What are the costs of computer workstation manufacturing?
- What materials are used in the manufacturing process?
- How much energy is used during the manufacturing of the computer workstation?
- How much waste is produced during the manufacturing of the computer workstation?
- What kinds of toxic materials are used in or produced from the manufacturing of a computer workstation?
- How are computer workstations currently disposed?
- What percentage is currently recycled?
- What percentage of a computer workstation can be recycled?
- What are current regulatory requirements?
- How are requirements expected to change in the next year? Next five years? Next ten years?

These questions helped determine the current impact of the electronics and computer industries on the environment. This impact was measured using multiple criteria, including:

- Amount of material used
- Efficiency of material and energy usage
- Amount of waste produced
- Amount of material reused or recycled

Although the working group was divided into seven task forces, it is important to remember that all seven groups were part of a single whole. While each production group dealt with its own issues of materials usage and waste production, the group remained aware of activities of the preceding and following production groups, as well as the entire system. To facilitate this, a questionnaire for evaluating current industry behavior and increasing understanding of the materials and processes used by each group was developed. The questionnaire was distributed to all task forces, except for the education team.* The results of these questionnaires were analyzed by the system advisors and used to create a snapshot of current industry practices and establish a system-level baseline.

Critical areas.   Once the above questions had been addressed, manufacturers could begin determining which aspects of the product's life cycle need the most improvement and develop priorities to target these areas. For example, processes and materials that result in the greatest negative environmental impact were addressed first.

System constraints.   The next step was the identification of constraints on the system. Such constraints included current and anticipated regulatory requirements, quality and performance specifications, technical limitations, and cost. Once these constraints and any others were identified, short- and long-term goals could be specified.

Action plan.   Information gathered in the previous three steps was combined and used to create an action plan. The following questions were addressed:

- What are reasonable (given cost and quality constraints), achievable (given technology limitations), and responsible (given regulatory requirements) goals?

- What materials and manufacturing processes must be altered to produce a computer that creates less impact on the environment?

- How can government help industry?

- How can educators and manufacturers inform the public, i.e., help the public become more aware of environmental issues?

- How can employees help identify waste minimization and other pollution prevention opportunities?

- How can engineers (product and process) most effectively incorporate techniques such as design for recycling or design for disassembly?

---

*The education group does not readily fit into the above framework. The main reason is that the final product of this group is service, not physical goods. Clearly, education is part of the current computer life-cycle infrastructure and should be characterized along with the tangible hardware cycle.

Once the data from the questionnaires were gathered, a workstation analysis was performed across the task forces. The responses to the questionnaires were somewhat abbreviated for several reasons. In general, material and energy consumption data were not readily available on a per part basis. Furthermore, in some instances, detailed production information was regarded as proprietary. The following categories of information were extracted for comparison of the identified computer manufacturing elements:

- Energy consumption
- Material usage
- Wastewater production
- Hazardous and nonhazardous waste production

The purpose of the questionnaire was to highlight the basic areas of environmental concern and place them in perspective. In terms of a computer life cycle, the results gathered from this questionnaire were by no means complete. Deliberate omissions were made so that the focus would rest on the manufacturing areas of greatest interest, expertise, and influence, such as semiconductor devices, semiconductor packaging, printed wiring boards, displays, and computer assemblies. As a result, the countless environmental transactions that occur upstream of the five manufacturing categories are not included and may or may not overshadow the concerns identified here. In particular, issues of material and component acquisition and manufacture were not addressed in the study.

Questionnaire responses were normalized in terms of a prescribed workstation configuration in order to facilitate comparisons among the five manufacturing categories. In this way, material, energy, and waste data associated with semiconductor device manufacture could be compared to the material, energy, and waste data associated with printed-wiring-board fabrication in a meaningful way for the particular product investigated. Each task force's response was based on furnishing the appropriate data for semiconductor devices, printed wiring boards, and other hardware for the workstation.

Overview of Results

Workstation description

For purposes of this analysis, a *workstation* is a high-end desktop computer. It is defined as one CPU (containing a motherboard, two interface cards, one hard drive, one floppy disk drive, one disk control card, one power supply, and associated cables and switches), one display, one keyboard, one mouse, cables, and a power strip. Presumably, displays, keyboards, disk drives, and power supplies all contain printed wiring boards, which contain packaged circuits, which in turn contain a semiconductor chip and so on. For the questionnaire and for comparison purposes, an average workstation was defined by the task force leaders to contain the following:

- One 6-in silicon wafer of product ($\sim$28 in^2)

- 220 integrated circuits (213 in plastic and 7 in ceramic packages)

- 517 in^2 (3.6 ft^2) of single-layer and multilayer printed wiring board (beginning with single-layer raw panel material of 23.25 ft^2)

- One monitor with a diagonal length of 20 in.

An analysis was performed by MCC of three workstations exhibiting performance characteristics similar to those of the hypothetical workstation, in order to assess the validity of the assumptions. A basic breakdown described the number of boards, noted the technology used, noted the type of packaging, and estimated the silicon area.

Three workstations were examined in detail: a DEC 3100, a Sun 3/60, and a Sun SPARC1. A Sun keyboard and mouse and a Sony 20-in monitor represented the balance of the workstation configuration for the study. Printers and other peripherals were not included. Each represented a viable workstation, with a wide range of technologies and state of evolution. A brief performance and configuration description is shown below in Table 14.1. A breakdown of the major components, their number, size, and volume, is shown in Table 14.2.

From the data in 14.2, it can be seen that a somewhat expected trend occurs. As technology advances (and silicon integration continues), the number of semiconductor devices decreases, silicon area decreases, and performance increases. For comparison of the CPUs, this excludes memory devices, which greatly affect the total silicon area and are highly configuration specific. Memory accounts for more than half the silicon area in a modern workstation.

Workstation analysis

The questionnaire results account for approximately 72% of the finished computer (by weight). The remaining 28% of the materials can be accounted for by the computer housing, keyboard, mouse, disk drives, power supply, and other miscellaneous parts. Note that many of these materials are beyond the knowledge of the participants of this study since they are typically furnished by outside suppliers. A study of greater depth would investigate all supplier levels. This level of detail was not warranted in this study since the myriad sublevels are

TABLE 14.1   Basic Performance and Configuration Data

	Make/model		
	Sun 3/60	DEC 3100	Sun SPARC1
Performance	~3 MIPs	~5 MIPs	~15 MIPs
Clock speed	25 MHz	25 MHz	25 MHz
Processor type	68020	RISC	RISC
Date of first manufacture	1987	1989	1989
Configuration	Video board, no hard drives or memory	200-M hard drive, 24-MB DRAM, video board	Two 100-M hard drives, 16 MB DRAM, video board

TABLE 14.2   Breakdown of Components in Three Workstation CPUs*

			Semiconductor Packages						
		Board area	Plastic			Ceramic			Silicon area
Workstation	Weight		Qty	Vol.	I/O	Qty.	Vol.	I/O	
DEC 3100	23.5	174	168	3.3	3730	9	1.4	550	2.86
Memory	—	55.8	240	4.9	4800	0	0	0	3.46
Sun 3/60	26	296.2	234	9.5	4714	28	2.5	1037	4.25
Keyboard	4.5	31.9	4	0.3	86	0	0	0	0.07
Mouse	0.3	8.1	1	0.1	22	0	0	0	0.02
Sun SPARC1	21	117.6	64	2.3	2280	7	1	439	1.73
Memory	—	47.6	144	3	2880	0	0	0	2.07

			Other Components			
		Board area	Interconnect		Passive/other	
Workstation	Weight		Qty.	I/O	Qty.	I/O
DEC 3100	23.5	174	25	1191	500	1196
Memory	—	55.8	0	0	240	480
Sun 3/60	26	296.2	52	2056	281	917
Keyboard	4.5	31.9	21	86	19	70
Mouse	0.3	8.1	11	23	14	35
Sun SPARC1	21	117.6	38	1004	85	190
Memory	—	47.6	0	0	0	0

*Area is in square inches. Volume is in cubic inches. Weight is in pounds.

probably beyond sufficient influence of the six task teams in the time available.

The following summarizes the scope of analysis in each manufacturing sector and use of the product:

- *Semiconductor device fabrication:* All materials and energy have been taken into account

- *Semiconductor packaging:* Does not account for the lead frames used in the process. These are purchased from an outside supplier.

- *Printed wiring boards:* Does not take into account all of the passive components used to assemble printed wiring boards, e.g., resistors, capacitors.

- *Displays:* Does not take into account the power supply, housings, brackets, cables, and fasteners used to complete the display terminal. These components are purchased from external suppliers. It is anticipated that they contribute a significant amount of materials and energy to the manufacturing process.

Computer systems, was by far the least documented manufacturing sector, since many components may be purchased from external suppliers. Figure 14.1 shows the components that were accounted for in the study.

Energy consumption

Energy consumption was compared for the useful life of the computer workstation and four stages of the manufacturing process, including semiconductor devices, semiconductor packaging, printed wiring board, and display. For the majority of the time that computers are turned on, they are not actively in use, and 30 to 40% are left running at night and on weekends. Workstations on local area networks are even more likely to be left on 24 hours a day. For comparative purposes, useful product life (before obsolescence) was estimated at four years, even though the anticipated reliability life is much longer. Energy use during the product life was, therefore, assumed to be

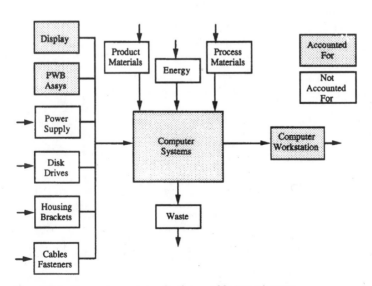

Figure 14.1   Computer systems final assembly input/output.

35,000 hours, based on 24 hours per day for four years; this number does not anticipate innovative measures to decrease energy use, such as lower-power components and "sleep states" when the computer is inactive. Table 14.3 is a breakdown of the energy consumed during these life-cycle stages.

By far the greatest amount of energy is consumed during computer use. While not all component and energy usage is accounted for, it is unlikely that the manufacturing energy consumption would exceed energy use during a normal lifetime. PWBs and computer assemblies appear to represent the largest manufacturing use of energy, while semiconductor device manufacturing, display fabrication, and semiconductor packaging use significantly less energy by comparison.

According to the EPA, computer systems are believed to account for 5% of commercial electricity consumption, and this may increase to 10% by the year 2000.[7] By comparison, lighting in the United States accounts for 20 to 25% of electricity consumption.[8] If we assume that computer usage will continue to increase, the potential annual energy consumption attributed to computers may indeed be higher than 10% in the future.

Material usage

The manufacture of a computer workstation requires input of both product and process materials. *Product materials* refer to the materials which will become part of the finished product. Excess product material may come from yield loss or by design, as in the case of the discarded die at the edge of a round wafer or panel loss in printed-wiring-board fabrication. Process materials are used as catalysts to the manufacturing process, and not in the finished product. Examples include cleaning solvents, photoresists, and process gases. Process

TABLE 14.3   Approximate Energy
Consumption of a Computer Workstation
during Production and Consumer Use*

Subcomponent	Energy (kWh)
Semiconductor devices	285
Semiconductor packaging	60
PWBs and assemblies	1790
Displays	180
Consumer use	9100

Energy in this table does not include that required to process upstream raw materials or used to manufacture other components of the computer, such as the disk drive, keyboards, etc. This figure includes 12.25 therms of natural gas (89 359 kWh) used for glass furnaces adjusted to reflect the current efficiency of electrical power generation (estimated at 35% efficiency).

water is treated separately and is not included with waste material. In Table 14.4, waste from used process materials and product material yield loss is combined since each eventually contributes to the waste stream.

The manufacture of both semiconductor devices and printed wiring boards requires the use of a significant amount of process material, relative to the finished product. Both of these products involve a number of lithographic, plating, and etching processes which require a significant use of chemicals and process materials. The manufacture of the display terminal represents the greatest contributor to the total weight of the workstation, but uses the least amount of process material per product. A very small amount of display material is wasted, as shown in Table 14.4.

Hazardous and nonhazardous waste production

As with many industrial processes, the manufacture of the computer workstation produces both hazardous and nonhazardous waste. A working definition of *hazardous waste* is "a solid waste or combination of wastes which, because of quantity, concentration, or physical, chemical, or infectious characteristics, may cause or significantly contribute to an increase of mortality or an increase in serious irreversible illness."[9]

Of total waste produced, hazardous waste (by current disposal standards) is a very significant component. Nevertheless, it should be noted that the U.S. electronics industry generates only 1.3% of the

TABLE 14.4   Approximate Material Usage during Computer Workstation Manufacture

Subcomponent	Final product (lb)	Waste material (lb)	Total material (lb)
Semiconductor devices	—*	89†	89
Semiconductor packaging	1	1	2
PWBs and assemblies	4	46	50
Display	50	3	53
Total	55	139	194

*Weight contribution of the semiconductor devices is negligible relative to the entire workstation.

†Liquid chemicals and sodium hydroxide (used for wastewater neutralization) contribute 63 and 25 lb, respectively, to this total figure; a state of the art factory has demonstrated manufacturing with 31 and 8.8 lb.

nation's reportable toxic wastes and emissions.* Printed wiring manufacture was identified as contributing the most hazardous waste during workstation manufacture, as illustrated by the data collected in Table 14.5. The printed-circuit-board industry accounts for about 0.26% of the annual industrial toxic chemical releases reported by the electronics industry.† Furthermore, extensive recovery efforts minimize the amount of hazardous waste actually sent to landfills. Table 14.5 contains a breakdown of the weight of the hazardous and nonhazardous wastes generated during four of the manufacturing stages.

Wastewater production

A significant amount of water is utilized during the manufacture of a computer workstation. Although semiconductor device manufacturing uses the most water per pound of finished product, the fabrication of printed wiring boards uses the most water per workstation. As shown in Table 14.6, the manufacture of printed wiring boards results in a substantial amount of wastewater.

Analysis conclusions

Upon examination of the data received from the task forces regarding consumption of energy and material and waste production, approximately 72% of the materials (finished product only) used in worksta-

---

*Based on a Bernouilli-based version of the Toxic Release Inventory from the EPA database, November 24, 1992, compiled from the state diskettes for SIC codes 3671 through 3679; 1990 data.
    †Ibid.

TABLE 14.5   Approximate Waste Generation from Workstation Manufacture

Subcomponent	Hazardous waste (lb)	Nonhazardous waste (lb)
Semiconductor devices	7*	82
Semiconductor packaging	—†	1‡
PWBs and assemblies	40	6
Display	2	1

*A state of the art factory has demonstrated manufacturing with the production of 2.5 lb of hazardous waste. For this figure, 85% (or 2.1 lb) is recycled back to the original chemical manufacturers or used as a fuel in another industry. The remaining 15% (or 0.4 lb) is incinerated. In addition, approximately 3200 cubic feet (250 pounds) per wafer of high-purity nitrogen, oxygen, and argon gases are not included. They are returned to the environment as extracted and were not considered waste.
    †Hazardous waste produced from semiconductor packaging is negligible.
    ‡Hazardous waste produced during the fabrication of PWBs is not sent to a landfill, but is sent to a metal recovery facility for recycling.

TABLE 14.6   Approximate Water Usage in Workstation Manufacture

Subcomponent	Water (gal)
Semiconductor devices	2800*†
Semiconductor packaging	10
PWBs and assemblies	4300‡
Display	200

*A state of the art factory has demonstrated manufacturing with 1000 gal.

†Deionized water represents 80% of this water usage, or 2272 gal.

‡The use of only 1400 gal of water has been demonstrated using state of the art water recovery technology.

TABLE 14.7   Final-Product Material Composition of the Workstation

Subcomponent	Weight (lb)*
Semiconductor devices	0.02
Semiconductor packaging	1.2
PWBs and assemblies	3.5
Display	50.
Unaccounted	21.

*Weight in this context refers to one workstation worth of finished product.

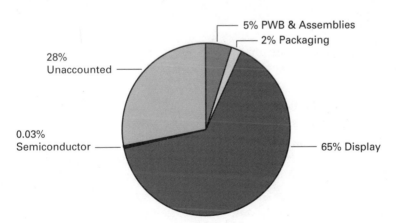

Figure 14.2 Final-product material composition of the workstation (by percentage of total weight).

tion manufacture were taken into account. As mentioned earlier, the remaining 28% were not considered in the scope of this study. Table 14.7 and Fig. 14.2 show the weight contribution of each workstation component to the final product (note that semiconductor devices are barely visible because of their relatively negligible contribution).

By weight, the display terminal and computer system are the largest contributors to the workstation and to ultimate disposal. However, as shown in Tables 14.3 through 14.6, these two manufacturing phases are not the greatest contributors to either the energy consumed or the wastes produced during the manufacture of the workstation.

Findings and recommendations from workstation analysis

The intent of the workstation analysis was to improve the understanding and perspective of the overall computer industry. Only relative conclusions can be drawn from this data. Since an absolute measure of environmental impact does not exist, one environmental option cannot absolutely outweigh another. The results of this analysis can be best used to identify opportunities for environmental improvement. The following conclusions were drawn from this study, and the following recommendations were offered:

- Energy consumed during the service life of the computer is substantial (relative to energy consumed during manufacturing).

  Recommendation: From an environmental standpoint, designing for reduced power consumption during operation may warrant higher priority than improving the energy efficiency of a specific manufacturing process.

- Energy consumption during printed wiring board fabrication is significant relative to the other manufacturing steps.

  Recommendation: Efforts to reduce energy usage are currently under way and should continue to be emphasized.

- Semiconductor devices enable today's workstations to perform their function. These small devices are the most efficient weight-reducing components of the computer, yet their manufacture uses comparatively large amounts of manufacturing resources.

  Recommendation: Continue to develop new manufacturing technologies that use lower amounts of utilities, process materials, and energy.

- Semiconductor device manufacturing and printed wiring board fabrication consume significant quantities of water relative to the other manufacturing sectors.

  Recommendation: Activities, such as recycling and reuse, which are currently under way in the industry, should continue to be pursued.

- Although fabrication of printed wiring boards generates the greatest amount of hazardous waste, this waste is sent to a facility for recovery. Semiconductor device manufacturing produces the greatest amount of nonhazardous waste (which results from acid neutralization and would otherwise be classified as hazardous waste).

  Recommendation: Continued efforts should be made to reduce both waste streams.

- The computer display is the greatest contributor to the total weight of the workstation.

  Recommendation: The display is an ideal candidate to initiate a comprehensive recycling program and research into new technologies.

- This study did not include the manufacturing of disk drives, power supplies, cables, housing, etc.; therefore, no conclusions can be drawn about these components and subsystems. However, one cannot assume that because these components do not appear in this report, the related environmental consequences are minimal. On the contrary, some of these "hidden" environmental impacts may actually be substantial relative to the concerns highlighted in this survey.

  Recommendation: Continued investigation of other components and subsystems of a computer workstation is recommended.

Future Directions

The publication and dissemination of this study has stimulated a number of activities within MCC, within the government, and in industry at large. As one part of a more comprehensive look at the opportunities for improvement in electronics manufacturing and products, the study has been very useful and effective. In fact, two companies, GeoSoft: The Company, and Resource Concepts—Environmental, have cited the study as the catalyst for their formation. Each is addressing an aspect of disposition and attempting to benefit from the reuse and the recycling of electronic products, respectively.

MCC embarked on a subsequent effort with industry leaders, trade associations, national labs, academia, and the government to develop an electronics industry environmental road map. This effort, which builds off the study, was initiated during the fall of 1993 at the Electronics and the Environment Roadmap Workshop held in Washington, DC, and hosted by MCC. The roadmap, published in December, 1994, is expected to provide the direction for the "greening" of the electronics industry during the next ten years by identifying activities and opportunities to reduce manufacturing and compliance costs, while simultaneously benefiting the environment. Technology roadmaps are one of the fundamental planning tools produced by an industry, displaying the full range of needs for future directions and establishing milestones for R&D activities necessary to turn plans into reality.

One industry-government partnership has already developed from these activities. As a part of the EPA's Environmental Technology Initiative, a DFE project was farmed to focus further study on printed wiring boards. The EPA based its decision to work with industry and environmentalists on the level of industry cooperation experienced during the initial study activity. This collaborative project compares various fabrication approaches and identifies alternative technologies. Investigation of these technologies will help to characterize the potential for them to benefit the environment while maintaining or improving cost and performance. In the future, similar collaborative efforts are expected within industry or as industry-government partnerships, thus distributing the costs of research and development and minimizing redundancy.

References

1. Office of Technology Assessment, *Green Products by Design: Choices for a Cleaner Environment,* OTA-E-541, U.S. Government Printing Office, Washington, DC, October 1992, p. 7.
2. Ibid., p. 9.
3. Ibid., p. 9.
4. Harold Chestnut, *Systems Engineering Methods,* Wiley, New York, 1967.
5. Society of Environmental Toxicology and Chemistry and SETAC Foundation for Environmental Education, Inc., *A Technical Framework for Life-Cycle Assessments,* SETAC Foundation, Washington, DC, January 1991, p. 1.
6. Lola M. Matysiak, "Design for Environment: An Analysis of German Recycling Legislation and Its Implications for Materials Trends and Corporate Strategies in the Automobile Industry," masters thesis, Massachusetts Institute of Technology, Cambridge, May 19, 1992, p. 52–54.
7. Brian J. Johnson, U.S. Environmental Protection Agency, Global Change Division, Energy Star Computers Briefing, Washington, DC, 202-233-9114.
8. Jerry Lawson and Bob Kwartin, "EPA's Green Lights Program: A Bright Investment in the Environment," *Pollution Prevention Review,* Summer 1991, p. 216.
9. *Environmental Engineering Dictionary,* 2d ed., 1992.

15

DFE in Semiconductor Equipment Design

Jerry Schoening

Director, Environmental Health and Safety
Applied Materials, Inc.
Santa Clara, California

Introduction

Since its formation approximately 25 years ago, Applied Materials Incorporated has always been a technology leader in the semiconductor wafer processing equipment industry—and in 1993 became the number one company in the world for sales in that industry. Consistent with its industry leadership, Applied Materials has taken a proactive position with regard to emerging environmental performance and regulatory compliance issues. In this area also, Applied Materials has established itself as a leader in the industry, responding to customer needs, participating in the development of related legislation and standards, and often meeting requirements prior to compliance dates.

Applied Materials has established a global policy to ensure protection of the environment at its plant locations and in its products. The following policy statements are taken from the Global Policy which is signed by the president of Applied Materials: It is our policy that

- The local management for each Applied Materials location will ensure that the requirements of all applicable environmental laws and regulations and the Applied Materials' Standards, whichever are most stringent, are met by the employees, facilities and operations.

- Applied Materials will strive to eliminate highly toxic materials from its processes, products and operations and/or replace them with suitable less toxic or non-toxic alternatives.

- Energy management programs will be implemented to minimize the usage of natural resources.

- Waste minimization programs will be implemented to reduce the amount of solid, liquid, toxic and/or non-toxic wastes. Recycling, redesign of processes and selection of more efficient processes will be investigated.

- Applied Materials will work to minimize its customers' environmental exposures by identifying and minimizing toxic by-products and effluents in its products.

- All spills, leaks and emissions that require reporting to a local or government agency, will be investigated as to the root cause. Action plans will be developed and implemented to prevent future incidents.

- Each location shall establish written policies and procedures as a means to implement this policy and audit for conformance.

This corporate policy is supported by detailed corporate standards for related items, which are contained in the corporate safety manual and implemented at all locations where they are applicable.

Applied Materials has always taken appropriate action as a responsible member of the community to ensure compliance with all applicable regulatory requirements. The semiconductor industry requires the use of regulated materials, and our processes generate hazardous waste. We have therefore found it necessary to develop, implement, and maintain safety and environmental programs to control the hazards inherent in this kind of operation and to meet the associated regulatory requirements. Examples of these programs follow:

Injury and Illness Prevention Program: This is the primary employee safety program document in the state of California. It requires that a formal program be implemented to include identification of responsibilities for safety, plans for communication with and from employees, employee compliance provisions, methods of hazard identification and evaluation, accident investigation program, method of ensuring correction of identified hazards, and a method for specifying and delivery of safety training to employees.

Hazards Communication Program: A program that requires the company to provide information to employees regarding the hazards of the chemicals they may encounter in the workplace. AMAT provides each new employee with safety training on chemical and other hazards. In addition, the training addresses the responsibilities of the employees and the management for safe working conditions.

RCRA Hazardous Waste Regulations: Applied Materials must properly store hazardous waste generated from its operations, and dispose of it as required by the Resource Conservation and Recovery Act (RCRA) regulations. Appropriate records must be kept and periodic reports to the government are required.

In addition to employee safety, Applied Materials' culture is very sensitive to the needs of our customers and to our responsibilities to the communities in which we live and work. These communities have been sensitized to the hazards of chemicals in our society by incidents such as the large chemical release in Bhopal, India, and have responded by putting pressure on the government to control the perceived hazards by regulation. The resulting increase in regulatory requirements has become a burden for our customers. They have experienced significant problems in managing the hazardous materials used in the industry, including the permits and the associated regulatory oversight. Applied Materials has recognized the importance of safety and environmental issues to our community and our customers and has responded by becoming more proactive in the environmental, safety, and health arena.

This decision to be proactive is reflected in the company's stated strategies, which include, in part:

- *People:* Attract, develop, empower, and retain Applied Materials people *with a safe and healthful work environment* that provides opportunities, recognizes their individual achievements, and treats each person with respect and trust.

- *Products:* Implement semiconductor wafer processes with innovative, reliable, *safe, and environmentally responsible* production equipment which provides our customers with enabling technology.

Applied Materials has become known in the industry as the leader in establishing safety and environmental performance standards for its equipment that go beyond the regulatory requirements. The company's goal is to provide the customer with a *total solution* to their problem when they order equipment. To do this, it has been necessary to become familiar with customers' safety and environmental needs, incorporate them as requirements in the design process, and assist in shaping the regulations that are being proposed to further regulate the industry.

One way of being proactive is through our involvement in industry associations, which has assisted in recognizing current issues and allowing the company to participate in the development of forthcoming requirements. The semiconductor industry has several strong trade associations that facilitate communication between the customer and supplier, and also act on behalf of the industry in shaping the regulatory framework within which manufacturers must work.

One example of this is the Santa Clara County Manufacturing Group, a coalition of companies located in Santa Clara County, California, organized to involve member companies in a cooperative effort with local government to identify and address major public policy issues affecting the economic health and quality of life in Santa Clara County. As part of Applied Materials' work with the Manufacturing Group, we participated in a committee composed of industry, city government, regulatory agencies, and consultants to develop the Toxic Gas Model Ordinance which is now incorporated as part of the Uniform Fire Code governing our operations. This relationship allowed us to assist in defining regulations which would protect the community from environmental hazards that could occur as a result of hazardous gas releases. The resultant regulation is recognized as a landmark effort because it provides the needed controls without over-regulating the industry or imposing requirements, at high cost, that have no direct benefit to the public.

Another example of a proactive role in the industry is Applied Materials' involvement in the Semiconductor Equipment and Materials International (SEMI). As part of its activities, SEMI develops guidelines to assist the industry in arriving at uniform ways of addressing common problems. Among the problems being addressed are environmental and equipment safety issues. Applied Materials has been active in the SEMI organization for ten years and has been a leader in many of the task forces dealing with safety and environmental activities.

Organization

The corporate Environmental, Safety and Health Department is organized under the group vice president of customer satisfaction along with the Corporate Quality Department. This is in recognition of the large part that quality and safety play in customer satisfaction. A recent customer survey indicates that the majority of our customers are either satisfied or very satisfied with the safety and environmental aspects of our equipment, showing that we have been successful at satisfying the customers' desire for safety.

Applied Materials has organized all of the environmental, safety, and health functions under one director. This was done to ensure maximum communication and synergy between the three related groups. We have recognized that during the design, development, and test of our equipment we experience the majority of the potential hazards that a customer would encounter in the use of our equipment. We are required to meet the same environmental regulations in our laboratories as our customers are required to meet in their "fabs."

Our personnel are exposed to the same hazards in the workplace as our customers' employees are in their factory. These environmental and occupational hazards must all be minimized during the design process. With all three functions in the same organization, the information collected by the environmental and occupational safety groups gets passed on to the product safety group for incorporation in the design as part of a process of continuous improvement.

All of the product development and engineering efforts are organized under the group vice-president of the Worldwide Products Organization. Within the engineering organization, a product safety engineer is assigned to each engineering project team. The product safety engineer is responsible for the identification and incorporation of safety and environmental design requirements into the design. Once the design and initial prototypes are completed, the design team is required to complete the characterization testing of the equipment to verify its safety features and possible environmental impacts.

Product design issues are coordinated across all product lines by a technical review committee chaired by the group vice president of the division. Within that committee is a product safety task force chaired by the product safety manager. This committee ensures that product and environmental design considerations are identified and uniformly implemented throughout the product line.

The Facilities Department is responsible for installing appropriate environmental abatement equipment to ensure that our facilities will meet the regulatory requirements and that continuous progress is made in reducing the amount of emissions from our facilities. Since the environmental engineers are responsible for establishing requirements, monitoring the progress, and reporting to the regulatory agencies, the Facilities Department and the corporate Environmental, Safety, and Health Department are located adjacent to each other and regular review meetings are held to ensure good communication and inclusion of environmental requirements in all facility modifications or new designs. Safety engineers review all facilities plans.

Design for Environment Perspective

Applied Materials focuses on environmentally friendly design in two areas, equipment design and facility/factory design. We supply the "front-end" process equipment needed to produce semiconductor devices on silicon wafers. Applied Materials' equipment is used for deposition of materials onto semiconductor wafers, patterning of wafers by dry chemical etching, and embedding ions of dopant materials into the wafers to vary the properties of the materials. (See Figs. 15.1 and 15.2.) Our customers are the manufacturers of semiconduc-

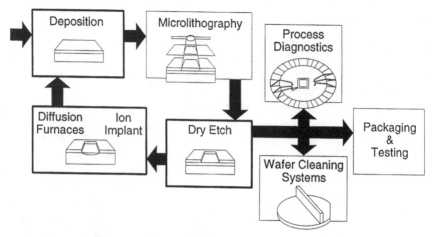

Figure 15.1 Semiconductor wafer processing.

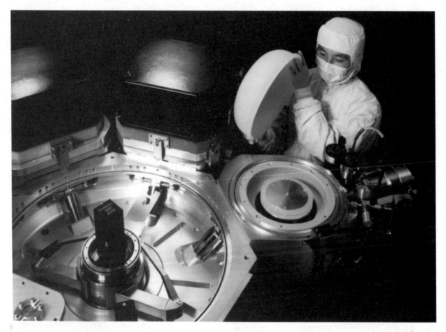

Figure 15.2 Provision 2000.

tor devices—for example, Intel, IBM, Motorola. Our customers manufacture the semiconductor devices ("chips," microprocessors, etc.) in a factory referred to as a "fab," where the devices are fabricated by passing the wafers through a series of process steps (as many as 300), using equipment like Applied Materials' to produce the semiconductor device on the wafer.

The design and building of a fab in a desirable location is a complex and expensive process involving the purchase of many pieces of process equipment and obtaining the permits and plan approvals to operate them. A fab typically costs up to $1.5 billion to construct. The time required to obtain the necessary permits may be as long as two years due to the nature of the toxic materials needed to produce the product and the potential human and environmental damage that could result from uncontrolled release of these materials or their by-products and waste materials. It is essential to the survival of our customers that the environmentally related costs associated with the installation of process equipment be minimized.

Applied Materials' primary value to our customers is in *the processes* we develop for their use in manufacturing semiconductor devices. The design of equipment to deliver the process to the customer is the second step, not the primary one. This places us in a position of being able to influence the environmental exposures of our customers. The nature of our business is to first develop a process to meet the specific wafer-processing needs of our customer. For example, the customer may want a process to deposit a layer of silicon dioxide on a wafer that has very specific physical and chemical properties; in addition, the process must be accomplished within the time and cost parameters established. Once the process is developed, then the equipment needed to do the process on the customer's wafer under production conditions must be designed and built. During the process development step, we are in an ideal position to work with the customer to select process materials and processing steps (physics and chemistry) that will result in an environmentally friendly piece of equipment.

Applied Materials' customers are currently addressing environmental issues by focusing on (1) zero-emissions performance of their factory and (2) driving down the cost of ownership for process equipment. Applied Materials is taking steps to support our customers in each of these areas.

Zero-emissions performance. The semiconductor industry is sensitive to public perception and recognizes its responsibility as a good citizen to reduce environmental emissions to the minimum. Some semiconductor device manufacturers have therefore established long-term goals for zero emissions from their factories. Cooperation from the equipment manufacturers is essential if they are to meet that goal in a cost-effective way. Current abatement technology utilizing "end-of-pipe" treatment systems to remove contaminants from effluent prior to discharge to the environment is expensive to purchase (capital cost), expensive to operate, and does not reach the zero-emissions goal.

Cost of ownership. *Cost of ownership* is defined as the total life-cycle cost of owning the equipment, including all of the support costs in addition to the costs of initial acquisition and installation. The cost of ownership for a semiconductor process tool system is impacted by the following elements that are related to the design of the equipment:

- Permitting by regulatory agencies
- Electric power consumption
- Storing, handling, and dispensing hazardous process materials
- Selection of process materials
- Efficiency of use of process materials
- Exhaust air needed to carry away and dilute the gaseous wastes
- Water and chemical treatment systems to neutralize liquid wastes
- Abatement systems for gaseous wastes

Permitting. Each potential factory location is controlled by federal, state, and local regulations. Permission to build a factory is contingent on obtaining permits for the type of operation intended in the factory. Permitting agencies may include the city building department and fire department, the county Department of Toxic Substances Control, the Regional Air Quality Control Board, and the Regional Water Quality Control Board, just to name a few. Permitting for a semiconductor fabrication plant requires a thorough understanding of the process materials required, and the air, water, and hazardous waste effluents from the plant and its individual sources (a process tool is considered "a source"). This information is needed for the design and installation of suitable safety and environmental abatement equipment required to meet the local regulatory requirements. In many cases customers have had to wait for the delivery of their process tools before they could determine what kind of abatement equipment was needed and how effective it was, and then gather data for the permit application. This is a time-consuming process, and in the fast-paced electronics industry the customer can ill afford to lose the time.

Regulations in California are becoming particularly difficult to meet. In addition to meeting the air, water, and waste requirements, a facility may be required to have a risk management plan that defines the risks to the community and the specific plans and equipment that are in place to prevent exposure to the community. Minimization of the use of toxics makes it easier for the customer to obtain approval of such plans.

There have been situations where it has taken two years to complete all of the studies and obtain all of the permits needed to start up a new fab in California. This is one of the reasons semiconductor manufacturers have increasingly considered other locations for their factories. As an equipment manufacturer, we can make the customer's life easier by characterizing our equipment in advance of the sale, thereby enabling the customer to plan its permitting strategy and abatement equipment purchases well in advance.

Hazardous materials handling and storage. A significant part of the installation and operating expense associated with a process tool is related to the proper storing, handling, and dispensing of hazardous production materials such as hydrogen gas (explosive), silane (pyrophoric gas), arsine (poison gas), and chlorine (poison and corrosive gas). Codes and regulations developed to ensure the safety of the workers in the fab and the surrounding community require such safeguards as double-walled gas piping, special storage areas for bulk gas cylinders, sensing and monitoring equipment, and automatic shutoff devices that are activated in case of a leak or an earthquake.

Selection of process materials that require fewer safeguards would result in large cost savings to the customer. For example, the industry has been trying to find alternative materials to replace silane for many years, and is making progress in some areas. Applied Materials markets a process using TEOS (tetraethlyoxysilicate) which has successfully eliminated silane in one application. TEOS is a low-vapor-pressure, high-flashpoint, flammable liquid which has low toxicity and is not easily ignited. It does not require monitoring, double-wall piping, or the specialized storage arrangements that are required for silane. In general, Applied Materials tries to use the process material which represents the lowest possible risk when designing the process provided the other customer-specified parameters are met. Unfortunately, there is insufficient research data available on many of the potential process materials and the pressure of time during process development does not allow for consideration of all possibilities. This is an area that is currently being addressed by SEMATECH, the semiconductor industry research consortium; they will be studying possible alternative materials for implementation by tool suppliers and their customers.

Efficiency of use of process materials. Process materials are supplied to the process tool and are reacted in a chamber with the wafer being processed in an environment of high temperatures, outer space vacuums, and gas plasmas. The key to success in the past has always been the achievement of the desired results on the wafer, with little consideration for conservation of the process materials. As a result, there are many process tools that have unreacted process materials coming out of the chamber exhaust. It is estimated that the average efficiency of process material use is less than 5%. The chamber exhaust containing the unused process materials and the by-products of the reacted portion of the materials must be diluted (if flammable) by suitable quantities of nitrogen and abated at point of use and/or by the main scrubber system in the fab. The sizing and therefore the cost of the abatement equipment is directly related to the quantity of the material processed. In addition, the cost of the process materials supplied to the tool in many cases is a significant cost also.

Exhaust air. One of the key factors to successful yields of semiconductor devices in a fab is control of microcontamination. When the feature size of the devices being built on the wafer is less than a micron (one millionth of a meter) contamination of the device by a single airborne particle of dust, for example, is like dropping a basketball-size chunk of contamination onto your computer's printed circuit board. The result is a piece of scrap instead of a completed device. One of the necessary ingredients to control microcontamination is very clean air, such that less than one particle of half-micron size is present in each cubic meter of air. The filtering process to provide this ultraclean air is expensive, and conservation of the clean air is of concern to the cost-conscious fab manager. Regulations require that sufficient exhaust air be passed through areas of the tool and supply gas piping that could leak so that the largest potential leak would be reduced to harmless concentrations by the dilution effect of the air. As a result, large quantities of expensive cleanroom air are exhausted through the systems. Substitution of nontoxic process materials would eliminate the need for the supply of exhaust air to the tool and the supply systems.

Waste treatment systems. Point-of-use abatement systems and main fab scrubbers typically will use water and some chemical treatment as part of the process to remove and/or convert exhaust gases to acceptable levels of contamination prior to discharge to the environment. The waste from the abatement system must then be treated prior to discharge, typically to the sanitary water disposal system operated by the city. Once again, the necessity for, and the size of, these waste treatment systems is driven by the toxicity and quantity of process materials.

DFE Accomplishments and Challenges

Applied Materials is in the early stages of integrating DFE into the processes of operating the company. However, the commitment to these principles has produced significant accomplishments.

In 1989, Applied Materials announced that it would totally eliminate CFCs from all manufacturing processes and from our process equipment design by the end of 1993. This was done in response to the growing worldwide awareness of the ozone depletion potential of CFCs. AMAT was the first process tool company to make this commitment. Changes had to be made to our own internal manufacturing processes. Substitute cleaning methods had to be investigated, tested, and evaluated for cost effectiveness. One of the outcomes was the standardization of an aqueous, biodegradable soap-based cleaning process that was less expensive to perform than the old CFC process and produced cleanliness as good or better than the old process. Thus, the company achieved a net cost savings while realizing the environmental goal.

Applied Materials' process tools were selected by some customers because initially the company was the only tool manufacturer offering a process that did not require the use of CFC process gases. Again, this illustrates a financial gain as a result of environmental consciousness. The degree to which this company attitude influenced the customer base's opinion of Applied Materials as a preferred supplier is unknown, but it certainly has had a positive effect. We are often consulted by our customers regarding the environmental effects of our tools and they claim that we are more responsive than our competitors.

One way Applied Materials assists customers is in the characterization of tool effluents. The accurate characterization of effluents is an expensive and time-consuming problem that involves first determining *what* is there and then *how much* is there. With the potential for literally hundreds of chemical compounds being formed from the recombination of the process chemicals, a means was needed of narrowing the possibilities to a reasonable number for which to test. Applied Materials was able to find a consultant that could predict the qualitative and quantitative aspects of the effluent using a computer-modeling technique. A program has now been established to verify the model data with real test data which can be given to our customers. This has significantly enhanced the customer's ability to plan cost-effective abatement procedures and equipment.

Early evaluation of potential process chemicals is a key to cost-effective control of process chemical selection. Applied Materials has developed and implemented a chemical authorization policy that prevents use of unauthorized chemicals in its facilities. Any time a new chemical is being considered for purchase, or a new use for a previously authorized chemical is proposed, the requester is required to obtain approval from the corporate ESH organization. When the request is received by ESH, it is evaluated to determine where it will be used, what the hazards of use are, what regulations apply to its use, and what controls must be in place to use it safely. We consider our own use of the material and also the use in a customer's facility and/or tool if the intended use is a process chemical in one of our tools. As an example, a highly explosive, reactive, unstable chemical was once proposed because it had the right chemical makeup for good process results on the wafer. When the hazards and the costs associated with its use were made clear, it was eliminated from consideration.

Applied Materials' Superfund site has been an example of proactive compliance and cooperation with regulatory agencies. In the early 1980s, groundwater contamination from leaking underground tanks became an issue in California. Applied Materials aggressively took independent action to check on its tanks. The groundwater contamination was discovered in advance of any regulatory action and steps were taken to abate the problem. Applied Materials was ready to take action before the regulators could complete their process, ironically resulting in delays caused by the regulatory environment.

On a smaller scale, Applied Materials has implemented many environmental programs to conserve resources and reduce waste, such as:

- Recycling of fluorescent light tubes
- Recycling of waste cardboard and paper
- Energy conservation by use of control systems on lighting and heating
- Hazardous waste recycling instead of disposal

Even when there is a commitment to improve in environmental stewardship, there are practical challenges that must be addressed in the process. First, given the state of technology development in some areas, the cost of "doing it right" may be excessive at this time. For example, to do the best possible job of cleaning up a groundwater contamination problem in saturated soils, all of the soil would have to be excavated and incinerated because there is no in situ treatment that has been developed for that kind of application. Another example, this one related to process design, is that materials technology may not exist or be difficult to identify. For example, there is no database for the selection of alternative process materials that makes it easy and efficient for a process engineer to evaluate options that may be more environmentally friendly than the most obvious ones.

Every company has some limits on what it can spend for any activity, and DFE activities are no different. The practical limitations of budget constraints cause companies to make choices; the money will be spent in areas where the perceived benefit is greatest for the money spent. Because regulators are not willing and/or able to apply a risk-benefit approach and instead rely on mandated activities in a regulatory framework, a company's available money may be spent on regulatory compliance activity with little payoff instead of nonrequired DFE activities that have large long-term payoffs. For example, there is a case of known groundwater contamination where the EPA mandated a multimillion-dollar cleanup effort in spite of the fact that a "no action" alternative had the least risk to health and the environment. This money would have been much more productive had it been invested in a search for less toxic process materials, for example.

Examples of Related Business Practices

Concurrent (simultaneous) engineering

Another key program at Applied Materials that promotes the active consideration of DFE issues is the concurrent engineering program, which was developed with the direct involvement of the ESH staff. This program follows the usual model for concurrent engineering—all requirements are identified at the beginning of the project including input by the specialty groups; the project team includes representatives from each of the specialty groups; there are specific "gates" identified where all requirements must be reviewed and progress held up until all requirements are met or agreements reached regarding changes in requirements. In the Applied Materials concurrent engineering program, the corporate ESH staff is represented by a product safety engineer that is part of the project team. ESH requirements are integrated into the project requirements and sign-off by safety is required prior to passing from one development phase to another and prior to release.

Requirements related to ESH are derived from a number of sources. Customers typically have detailed requirements as part of their purchase specification, regulatory requirements must be considered, best available practices from Applied's experience are considered, and industry standards are also consulted.

Semiconductor Equipment and Materials International (SEMI), an industry association, has published a number of safety guidelines intended to standardize the safety requirements for industry. One of these is SEMI S2, "Safety Guidelines for Semiconductor Manufacturing Equipment." Part of the S2 requirements are related to DFE (Section 20, "Environmental"). Applied Materials has included these requirements internally for all new development since the first draft publication of the S2 requirements.

Environmental quality management

The CEO of Applied Materials recently said, "We will measure everything we do" (as part of our process of continuous improvement).

Environmental measurements are becoming a part of the Applied Materials total-quality management system. The key measurements are related to minimization of the waste streams of hazardous waste. As an overall measure, the ratio of waste tonnage to revenue is calculated. This is a measure used by other industries and also allows for normalization of the data adjusted for growth of the business (see Fig. 15.3).

One of the methods used to drive down the hazardous waste rate is to charge the operating units for the hazardous waste costs associated with their operations. Hazardous waste costs are allocated based on the number of square feet of waste-generating activities occupied by each organization. This is an incentive to reduce the amount of waste-generating activity (and thereby their specific charges) and to reduce the amount of waste generated so the overall total cost is lowered.

Enterprise integration

The corporate Environmental, Safety and Health Department is the central policy and standards organization for the company and the central data collector and auditor. Corporate ESH maintains files on a local-area network (LAN) in the Corporate offices in Santa Clara, California. The files include all measurements of ESH activities, regulatory requirements, Material Safety Data Sheets, and will soon include on-line access to corporate standards, policies, and procedures.

Other company locations have a responsibility to meet corporate standards and/or local regulations, whichever are more stringent. They are also required to measure their activities and report to corporate ESH on the results of their activities. The corporate LAN is linked with all other locations by a worldwide wide-area network. Safety data can be exchanged with all locations in the company.

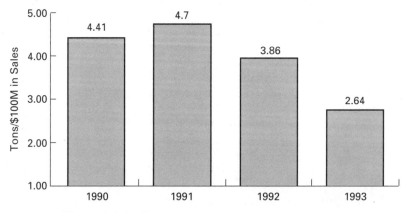

Figure 15.3 Waste minimization.

Partnerships and Alliances

The semiconductor industry is a closely connected group of companies that range from component and material suppliers, through equipment manufacturers, specialized construction companies, semiconductor device manufacturers, and ultimately the manufacturer of the final product such as a computer or stereo system. Also in close alliance with these companies is a group of industry associations, consultants, and consortiums. Any action by a member of this "food chain" can affect every other member downstream and also the final product. This is also true where environmental impacts are concerned.

A good example of how this can work is the mandate to eliminate the use of CFCs because of the ozone depletion problems associated with them. The federal government had encouraged companies to take steps for CFC elimination since the Helsinki Accord in 1978, when 80 industrialized nations agreed to gradually eliminate CFC usage. Some companies, including Applied Materials, took voluntary steps to eliminate CFCs. However, the establishment by the EPA in 1993 of a labeling requirement for any product that included CFCs in the manufacturing process, or that included components that had CFCs in their manufacturing process, was the catalyst that caused real progress in the industry to implement controls on this issue. Manufacturers of the final products were feeling public pressure and did not want to market a product that had been labeled. When the end-product manufacturers stated to their suppliers that they would not purchase components which would require them to label their products, the suppliers all the way up the food chain made the necessary changes to avoid being left out of the picture.

The above example shows how the industry can react to an involuntary, market-driven requirement in a quite efficient manner. The same sort of progress can be made when members of the industry food chain voluntarily form partnerships and/or alliances to capitalize on market opportunities in the environmental area. In one example, Applied Materials agreed to work with a key customer, an abatement device manufacturer, and with SEMATECH to develop and test a new approach to point-of-use abatement of process tool effluents. If successful, the customer will have cost-effective abatement that meets regulatory requirements, the industry will have a qualified supplier of a new abatement device, and Applied Materials will have in-depth knowledge of an abatement device that is proven successful with one of its process tools.

Applied Materials is aggressively pursuing cooperative agreements with SEMATECH that will allow the company to leverage the knowledge base at SEMATECH, the government-funded research being conducted there, and the practical business application experience that is represented there by the member companies.

Contributions to Profitability and Business Development

Applied Materials' customers have made it known that they want equipment suppliers like Applied Materials to address their needs for low-cost, low-effort environmental compliance. There is no question that the first process tool supplier that satisfies the customers' needs in the area of environmental compliance will receive preferential treatment when new tools are ordered. Applied Materials is approaching the DFE issue as a market opportunity, determining what the best way is to meet the customers' needs in a cost-effective way as has always been done in the past. Determining what should be done, and finding ways to support and implement such programs, is the main challenge in a company where extremely fast growth consumes available resources and the setting of priorities is difficult.

Future Issues and Needs

Organizational development

Applied Materials is a very competitive company, internally as well as externally. The company's compensation systems are set up to reward achievement against objectives that are established for all employees. For the DFE programs to become successful throughout the company at the same level as other programs, objectives will be established that are appropriate to drive the responsible organizations to achieve the desired results. Audit systems will be used to measure performance and the results will be made visible to the senior management. This visibility gives executives the ability to drive the issues. In the current state, the program is not well enough defined to establish the objectives except in some obvious areas like waste management.

Legislative and regulatory changes

Applied Materials is a customer-driven enterprise. When the customers' needs are stated loud and clear, Applied Materials will respond. This does not work well, though, for long-term planning on environmental issues that do not have current-day impact on the customer. For example, progress on CFC elimination was slow until the market impact of selling a labeled product caused the manufacturers to push for a solution.

A better method is needed to motivate industry to make the investment in people and dollars necessary to take the long view and work for solutions that will have long-term payoff but no short-term profit. Tax incentives or other incentives from the regulatory agencies for providing environmentally friendly systems would assist in motivating companies like Applied Materials to address environmental issues. A good example of that kind of regulation is the pollution credit system established for regulation of air emissions: if a company does a good job of eliminating emissions, the pollution credits can be sold to companies that are less successful at implementing controls. Those that do a good job have the benefit of good public relations, and a source of income from the sale of their pollution credits.

Government funding of R&D projects that have joint benefit to industry and to the government is beginning to occur since the downsizing of the defense industry. Applied Materials sees this as a major opportunity for itself and others in the industry to focus on the long-term environmental needs of the industry and obtain funding to support the necessary research and development.

Enabling technologies

Cycle time for development, test, and shipment of a new product in the process tool industry must be 18 months or less for a successful business. Design and development engineers do not have the time to do research into environmental requirements or to investigate obscure, low-probability process alternatives. On-line environmental requirements and environmental impact data would assist in getting design engineering cooperation and speed up the integration process. The ideal may be an artificial intelligence–type system that could be queried about the effects of using a specific combination of process chemicals or what potential chemical compounds, in order of environmental friendliness, could meet the specified parameters. Included would be the availability of abatement technologies, energy consumption requirements, undesirable by-product reactions, effects on tool life and maintenance, and other critical decision factors with some algorithm to assist in evaluating alternatives.

Until there is some framework to support industrywide cooperation in the development of solutions that are far-reaching up and down the industry food chain, we expect that we will continue to see companies addressing those issues which they can optimize locally, and only when they are pressured by the customer. The Clinton administration's support of environmental issues and the cuts in defense spending have caused programs to be started and money to become available for environmental research and development. Industry consortia and associations would seem to be the best avenue for coordination of an effort to effectively use the resources that are becoming available.

16

DFE at
Pacific Gas & Electric

Peter Melhus

Director, Corporate Environmental Quality
Pacific Gas & Electric Company
San Francisco, California

Claude G. Poncelet, Ph.d.

Manager, Corporate Environmental Quality
Pacific Gas & Electric Company
San Francisco, California

Introduction

As a society, we can no longer continue to view economic growth and the environment separately; they are part of the same equation. Similarly, the business of producing, distributing, and using electricity and natural gas and the business of protecting the environment cannot be viewed separately. As a result, in the last few years, Pacific Gas & Electric Company (PG&E), based in San Francisco, has been integrating its environmental and energy strategies, recognizing that the long-term economic health of its service territory, and therefore the long-term economic health of the company, depend on the quality of the environment. PG&E also recognizes that environmental excellence is an important element of success in an increasingly competitive marketplace.

In May 1990, PG&E added a new corporate environmental goal to the five existing in its mission statement. PG&E's environmental goal is to *improve* the quality of the environment by leading efforts to increase energy efficiency, develop environmentally preferred technologies, and expand the use of clean fuels, and by conducting all aspects of our business in an environmentally sensitive manner." Environmental improvement has therefore become a fundamental corporate direction for the company, along with other corporate goals relating to customer services, earnings, human resources, operation of the Diablo Canyon Nuclear Power Plant, and PG&E's unregulated business. It has become an integral part of PG&E's core business. Key to this corporate commitment to environmental quality are an increased awareness of the role of government, the business community in general, and the utility industry in particular, in providing leadership in protecting the environment; the need to incorporate environmental and economic factors in the context of sustainable economic development; and the search for collaborative interactions with environmental organizations, government, and other organizations that aim at creating win-win situations.

When adopting its corporate environmental goal, PG&E's strategy included ensuring that employees and other constituents knew why the company was pursuing environmental excellence. Essentially there are two reasons: Environmental problems exist, and it's good business.

The list of environmental problems is long, and includes such things as local air quality, global climate change, species extinction, and water quality. As a utility, PG&E contributes to some of these problems, particularly air quality. As an environmentally responsible utility, PG&E needs to be part of the solution. PG&E is convinced that a sound corporate environmental policy and sound business practice go hand in hand.

For example, PG&E's past energy-efficiency programs have enhanced its competitiveness and the competitiveness of its service territory, while simultaneously contributing to environmental enhancement. For the period from the mid-1970s through the 1980s, PG&E spent $1.5 billion on conservation and energy efficiency and estimates the resulting customer savings at $3.5 billion.

From a business perspective, PG&E's financial success depends on sound environmental policy. A long-accepted axiom in the utility industry is that the financial success of the utility is dependent on the financial success of its service territory. It is now becoming clear that the financial success of a utility's service territory is very much a function of the quality of the environment in the area. Environmental values are becoming a priority of society, and environmental costs are beginning to be internalized in the economy. By assuming an environmental leadership position, PG&E can more effectively help shape future changes in utility economics and regulations. There are also new business opportunities that have the potential to enhance PG&E shareholder value while helping solve environmental problems. And environmental excellence can reduce environmental liabilities and the costs of environmental compliance.

Process for Developing Environmental Policy

In 1989, PG&E conducted an assessment of its responsibilities and role in environmental protection. As a result, an environmental initiative was one of a number of high-priority programs of company-wide significance, or corporate initiatives, adopted by company management as part of the 1990–1994 corporate business plan.

Later that year, PG&E conducted a comprehensive survey of 1500 shareholders, customers, and employees concerning the environment and PG&E's role in environmental protection. They listed environmental issues as being of greatest concern more than twice as often as any other specific problem. PG&E's employees associated themselves with environmental causes even more strongly than its customers. Among the survey respondents, 64% of the PG&E customers, 74% of shareholders, and 84% of employees also felt that PG&E was well suited to help solve environmental problems.

Based on PG&E's past experience, it was clear that full "ownership" of the environmental policy on the part of employees and management at all levels was critical. A cross-sectional working group of employees was created to make recommendations on the company's environmental policy and programs. Many of the employees involved were volunteers who asked to participate. Yet PG&E did not wait for an environmental policy to be fully sorted out to launch specific initiatives, such as the expanded energy-efficiency programs and alternate-fuel vehicles program.

In the spring of 1990, PG&E's senior management annual strategic meeting focused exclusively on the environment. The result was the adoption of the corporate environmental goal and a comprehensive corporate environmental policy which PG&E calls its Commitment to Environmental Quality[1] and which establishes specific objectives to achieve the goal. The environmental policy was approved by the Board of Directors in the summer of 1990. A detailed statement of the Commitment to Environmental Quality, including the specific objectives, was sent to each employee by PG&E's chairman and CEO in July 1990.

PG&E's Environmental Policy

In developing its environmental policy, PG&E attempted to abide by several principles:

- The objectives should be substantive and deal with PG&E's basic business as an electric and gas utility.
- The commitment should be for the long term.
- The company should build on its strong environmental record to establish a leadership position on the environment.

Seven key areas or elements to achieve PG&E's goal on the environment were identified. These elements are in the areas of customer energy efficiency, electric resources planning, clean fuels, clean-air vehicles, natural resources stewardship, employee involvement, and environmental management.

Customer energy efficiency

PG&E has put in place a major expansion of its customer energy efficiency programs, which constitute its largest electric resource option for the 1990s. The objective for the decade is to achieve savings equivalent to 2500 MW of generating capacity, or about 75% of the projected load growth for the decade. Customer energy efficiency is a prime pollution prevention approach and the most environmentally acceptable way to meet energy needs. PG&E expects to spend almost $2 billion during the 1990s for customer energy efficiency.

The blueprint for the expanded programs was developed as a result of an innovative collaborative process which included PG&E, other California utilities, the California Public Utilities Commission (CPUC) Division of Ratepayer Advocates, the Natural Resources Defense Council, and local consumer groups. Under the new regulatory rules jointly developed through this collaborative process, and approved by the CPUC, PG&E has, for the first time, an opportunity to earn a profit for its shareholders on energy-efficiency programs.

From the introduction of the expanded program in mid-1990 through the end of 1993, over 1.5 billion kWh were saved, equivalent to the annual usage of about 296,000 PG&E area households; 97 million therms of natural gas have been saved, equivalent to the annual space-heating needs of about 169,000 PG&E area households, and construction of more than 1000 MW of new electric generation capacity has been avoided, enough to serve a city of 1 million people (Table 16.1). The air emissions avoided due to this increase in efficiency include almost 2 million tons of carbon dioxide and almost 3000 tons of nitrogen oxides (Table 16.2). The pollution savings since the

TABLE 16.1   Goals and Results,
1990–2000
(Millions of Kilowatthours Saved)

Year	Projected	Actual
1990	186	278
1991	273	525
1992	484	486
1993	628	491
1994	606	
1995	606	
1996	747	
1997	747	
1998	747	
1999	746	
2000	746	

TABLE 16.2   Emissions to Be Avoided Due to
Customer Energy-Efficiency Programs, 1990–2000

	Cumulative emissions avoided (tons)*		
Year	CO_2	NO_x	SO_x
1990	143,555	211	57
1991	512,263	752	205
1992	1,055,252	1,550	422
1993	1,797,202	2,639	719
1994	2,788,947	4,096	1,116
1995	4,030,990	5,919	1,612
1996	5,581,570	8,196	2,233
1997	7,440,687	10,926	2,976
1998	9,608,339	14,110	3,843
1999	12,084,116	17,745	4,834
2000	14,868,015	21,833	5,947

*Figures for 1990–1993 are actual; others are projections.

expanded CEE programs began in 1990 are the equivalent of taking
200,000 cars off California highways. Shareholders have earned
almost $120 million in the same time frame (Table 16.3).

As part of its energy-efficiency programs, PG&E offers product-specific rebates for homes and businesses, customized rebates for large
commercial and industrial customer projects, cost incentives to
builders of new homes and nonresidential facilities and to equipment
manufacturers to exceed state energy-efficiency standards, energy
management and information services, direct assistance to low-income
customers, as well as showcase homes and other model projects.

While many of PG&E's energy-efficiency programs are implementa-
tion-focused, that is, directed at helping customers use energy more
efficiently, PG&E is also focusing R&D on improving energy-efficiency

TABLE 16.3   Shareholder Earnings Due to Customer Energy-Efficiency Programs, 1990–1993

(In Millions of Dollars)

Year	Shareholder earnings
1990	15.4
1991	45.1
1992	41.4
1993	16.9

Figure 16.1   PG&E Energy Center in San Francisco.

technologies across a wide range of applications. Included is the construction of the 25,000 ft², $7.5 million PG&E Energy Center in San Francisco, which opened in late 1991. (See Fig. 16.1.) This showcase and laboratory gives those who design and build homes, offices, stores, and factories convenient access to the latest energy-efficiency information and a chance to experiment with new technology and techniques. The PG&E Energy Center is located at 851 Howard Street in San Francisco.

PG&E also embarked on a multiyear, multi-million-dollar energy-efficiency research project, jointly with the Rocky Mountain Institute,

Lawrence Berkeley Laboratory, and the Natural Resources Defense Council, to conduct research and demonstration projects on the most advanced lighting, building design, electric motor, and other technologies, in order to test the hypothesis that integrating energy-efficiency technologies can result in energy savings of up to 75%, at or below the cost of new supplies. Retrofit design of the first commercial building is complete and monitoring equipment is in place. The design indicates that electric use can be reduced 65% and gas use reduced 17%. The project includes four commercial facilities, four residences, and an agricultural pumping plant.

Energy efficiency is a cornerstone of PG&E's environmental policy and is clearly a win-win proposition. The environment wins because of the emissions reductions attributable to energy efficiency. PG&E's ratepayers win in two ways. First, those that have participated are using less energy than they would otherwise. Therefore, their bills are lower than they would otherwise be. Those that have not yet participated also win because it costs PG&E less to invest in energy efficiency than to invest in new power generation. Therefore the rate per unit of energy has not and will not increase to the extent it would if PG&E were building power plants. The economy wins as savings are reinvested, local businesses become more competitive than they would otherwise be, and jobs are created to manufacture and install the energy-efficient technologies. And, PG&E's shareholders win due to the incentive regulatory structure now in place in California.

Electric resources planning

PG&E has one of the most diverse electric power resource mixes in the world, including hydroelectric, geothermal, biomass, nuclear, and steam plants that burn primarily natural gas (see Table 16.4). It is also one of the world's largest purchasers of wind generation. During an average hydro year, almost 70% of PG&E's energy comes from nonfossil resources.

TABLE 16.4   PG&E's Electric Resource Mix*

Source	Percent of mix
Fossil fuels	31
Hydro (California)	25
Nuclear	15
Wind, solar, biomass	9
Geothermal	10
Northwest imports (primarily hydro)	10
Total	100

*Percentages given are for a year with average hydro generation.

PG&E has adopted an electric resource plan which places primary reliance on energy efficiency and which avoids the need for major new power plants in the 1990s. Electric load is projected to grow by 3300 MW in the 1990s; 2500 of this PG&E expects to meet with customer energy efficiency, with the remainder coming from independent power producers under contract and some hydro upgrade.

PG&E's electric resource strategy is one of bridging the decade of the nineties with efficiency to the turn of the century, when it is expected that environmentally favorable technologies, such as renewables, will be financially viable. In the 1990 through 1992 time frame PG&E spent an average of $10 million for an R&D program on solar, wind, and fuel cell technology. This R&D has been directed primarily at wind and photovoltaic development, such as the Photovoltaics for Utility Scale Applications project being done in conjunction with the U.S. Department of Energy and others. Other key elements of this R&D program have included the development of the new, variable-speed, third-generation wind turbines (Fig. 16.2). A wind turbine demonstration project by a consortium including PG&E showed that the cost of wind generation at the best sites in PG&E's service territory is now competitive with the best fossil fuel technologies for the PG&E system. The new machines are capable of generating electricity at 5.3 cents/kWh. The first two units were installed at Altamont Pass, east of San Francisco, in 1993 and commercial systems are targeted for 1994. Others in the consortium are U.S. Windpower, the Electric Power Research Institute (EPRI), and Niagara Mohawk.

Figure 16.2   Wind turbines at the Altamont Pass, near San Francisco.

A likely future scenario for the electric utility industry is movement away from the traditional large, central station power-generating facilities that have been the hallmark of the industry for decades. The economies of scale which led to the proliferation of these large power plants is being offset by long lead times necessary to design, permit, and build them, and the inherent risk of major long-term investments in an era of increasing competition and deregulation in the electric power industry. Economies of mass production will likely make smaller, decentralized, modular generation units competitive with the larger systems. Because of shorter lead times to build these modular units and the inherently smaller investment, the financial risk to the utility is reduced. These smaller systems are generally environmentally more compatible than larger, centralized units built away from the load centers. PG&E expects that these smaller systems will be either highly efficient natural gas–fired plants, renewables, or most likely a combination of both.

The decreasing likelihood that PG&E as a utility will be building and owning any power plants in the future has resulted in PG&E substantially reducing its own investment in renewable energy R&D. The company is now working to support national energy policies that place a priority on the timely commercialization of renewable—and in particular, solar—energy technologies.

Clean fuels

From an environmental perspective, natural gas is the premium transition fuel between other fossil fuels and renewable resources. PG&E is committed to develop and promote the use of natural gas, and to support the development of new clean-fuel technologies. In November 1993 operation of a major expansion of the PG&E/Pacific Gas Transmission Co. natural gas pipeline began. The pipeline will bring 755 million cubic feet per day of additional natural gas supplies to the California market. PG&E is pursuing market opportunities for natural gas sales both in power generation and in direct end use. About 95% of the $1.7 billion, 900-mi PG&E/PGT natural gas pipeline expansion was built on existing rights of way, thereby minimizing environmental impact.

Clean-air vehicles

Air quality improvements in California depend to a large extent on reductions in vehicle emissions. Depending on location, the transportation sector contributes up to 60% of the air emissions in the state. As part of PG&E's environmental initiative, we have entered the clean-air vehicles market with programs in natural gas vehicles (NGVs) and electric vehicles.

Figure 16.3 PG&E's NGV program encourages use of natural gas by vehicle fleets.

PG&E's NGV program encourages the use of natural gas by vehicle fleets (Fig. 16.3). At the end of 1993, there were 1900 fleet vehicles in PG&E's service territory (including almost 700 PG&E vehicles) operating on natural gas. The objective for the year 2000 is 125,000 natural gas and electric fleet vehicles (Table 16.5).

Natural gas as a vehicle fuel is environmentally preferable to gasoline, and presents economic advantages. The lack of a fueling infrastructure makes this a "chicken or the egg" problem, and PG&E's program is aimed at jump-starting the market by laying the foundation for such an infrastructure. From 1990 to 1993, 42 new natural gas stations were opened in PG&E's service territory, including 30 owned and operated by PG&E. By 1995, 150 fueling stations are expected to be operating throughout the service territory (Table 16.6).

The four areas described above deal with much of what PG&E's basic business is, i.e., the generation and provision of electric and gas services. The remaining three areas in PG&E's environmental policy—natural resource stewardship, employee involvement, and environmental management—deal with daily operations and business practices.

TABLE 16.5   Natural Gas and Electric Vehicles to Operate in PG&E Service Territory

	Number of vehicles	
Year	Actual	Projected
1990	255	
1991	461	
1992	1,032	
1993	1,900	
1994		5,100
1995		9,400
1996		16,400
1997		27,000
1998		52,000
1999		85,000
2000		122,000

TABLE 16.6   Number of Natural Gas Fueling Stations Projected for PG&E Service Territory, 1990–2000.

	Number of locations	
Year	Actual	Projected
1990	7	
1991	14	
1992	24	
1993	42	
1994		80
1995		120
1996		160
1997		240
1998		500
1999		800
2000		1200

Natural resources stewardship

PG&E is one of the largest landowners and managers in California, with over 250,000 acres of land containing 160 lakes, and providing habitat for over 150 rare, threatened, or endangered species (Fig. 16.4). With over 60 campgrounds and recreation facilities, PG&E is the state's fourth-largest public recreation provider. Typically, 150,000 to 200,000 visitors use PG&E facilities each year. PG&E has, for decades, responsibly managed its land and has protected wildlife. Regulators view many of PG&E's natural resource programs as models for others to emulate. PG&E currently employs about 100 full-time land, wildlife, water, and timber specialists.

PG&E is committed to being a good steward of the natural resources under its management, including the protection of land, water, wildlife, and timber resources under its care, to provide opportunities for responsible recreational use of those natural resources, and to work cooperatively with environmental, conservation, and governmental organizations to further resource protection goals.

Natural resources stewardship is a broad area which comprises many smaller efforts and projects. They include, among others, funding for habitat protection and species restoration programs, restoring and maintaining wetlands, revegetation and tree planting, and protection of old-growth forests. While a number of these projects fall under federal and state regulatory requirements, PG&E has carried out, and will continue to carry out, voluntary projects. Recent examples of such voluntary projects include funding for and employee involvement in major reforestation projects, and an erosion control

Figure 16.4 PG&E owns or manages 250,000 acres of land containing 160 lakes and providing habitat for over 150 rare, treatened, or endangered species.

project to demonstrate new structural and nonstructural methods and technologies for stream bank restoration toward reducing the rate of sedimentation in the Feather River Watershed. In the City of Mountain View, 45 miles south of San Francisco, PG&E joined the local Shoreline Wildlife and Recreation Area, the Audubon Society, the Humane Society, and others to create the Burrowing Owl Alliance. The burrowing owl is a species being threatened due to development in the South Bay area. The owl creates nests on the ground. The Alliance is creating habitat in areas such as landfill and utility rights of way to offset the habitat losses due to development.

Another voluntary project provided recognition to PG&E's employees for their efforts which led to PG&E receiving presidential recognition in 1991. PG&E received one of only nine gold medals in the inaugural President's Environment and Conservation Challenge Awards. To recognize its employees for this honor, PG&E entered into a partnership with the World Wildlife Fund and the Hoopa Valley Tribe, a native American tribe located in northwestern California. As part of the agreement, PG&E planted more than 27,000 (one for each employee) Douglas fir, Port Orford cedar, and coastal redwood seedlings on 52 acres in the Hoopa Valley Reservation, helping restore this portion of the reservation to its natural micro-ecology (Fig. 16.5).

Employee involvement

PG&E has about 25,000 employees, working in hundreds of large and small offices and facilities: 96% of PG&E employees report they have a personal commitment to improve the quality of the environment. Managing the company's own house in an environmentally sensitive manner, with the daily involvement of all employees, is an important part of PG&E's commitment to improve the environment. In this area, the company is focusing on recycling efforts, from office paper to used motor oil; the reduction of energy consumption at company facilities; the use of environmentally preferred materials; and the reduction of employee commute impacts through greater use of car and van pools and public transportation.

The results are impressive. In 1993, PG&E employees in the corporate office alone recycled 1000 tons of office paper, which translates into savings of almost 17,000 trees and 7 million gal of water. Perhaps most importantly, recycling the paper saved 3000 yd^3 of landfill space. In total, in 1993, PG&E employees recycled some 15,000 tons of metal, paper, plastic, and miscellaneous products, which in addition to saving hundreds of cubic yards of landfill space, generated more than $3.2 million in revenues.

PG&E is also focusing on purchasing environmentally preferred products, including but not limited to recycled paper. In 1993, PG&E

Figure 16.5 More than 27,000 seedlings were planted on 52 acres in the Hoopa Valley Reservation.

centrally purchased about 5.3 million lb of paper products, more than 85% of which contained at least 10% postconsumer waste. The intent is to continue to increase the percentage of postconsumer waste in the paper products purchased. PG&E was a founding member of the Recycled Paper Coalition, a voluntary organization hoping to stimulate demand for recycled paper products and to encourage corporate paper recycling. At the end of 1993, the Coalition had grown from its original seven members to 93. The telephone hotline number for the Coalition is (415) 985-5568.

To help the buyers in PG&E's outlying offices find environmentally preferred products, PG&E has developed a "Green Catalog" which includes recycled and recyclable products as well as waste minimization products. At year-end, 1993, the catalog contained more than 800 products.

Environmental management

The last element of PG&E's environmental policy is environmental management, which broadly addresses PG&E's commitment to pursue business practices that protect and improve the quality of the environment. PG&E's goal is to make environmental consideration as much a part of its corporate culture as safety is.

It is a company objective to comply fully with the letter and spirit of environmental laws and regulations in conducting its business and managing its 1500 facilities, which include power plants, electric substations, natural gas compressor stations, and service centers. In addition, it is PG&E's objective to make consideration of environmental factors an integral part of planning and operation and to clearly identify accountability. Fundamental in integrating environmental responsibility into day-to-day operations is waste minimization and pollution prevention. After peaking in 1984 and 1985 at about 95,000 tons per year, PG&E reduced its total hazardous waste by about 78% to less than 20,000 tons in 1993 (Table 16.7). Of the 20,000 tons generated in 1993, 16% was recycled.

In 1991, PG&E and the U.S. Environmental Protection Agency (EPA), Region IX, entered into a precedential agreement to jointly pursue pollution prevention projects. Through this partnership, 12 projects have been completed or are under way, including increasing energy efficiency in federal buildings, providing pollution prevention education materials for elementary school children, and providing household environmental tips for residential customers.

In the early 1900s, gas was manufactured from coal and oil at various sites throughout California. Following the practice of the day, wastes were disposed of on-site. PG&E and the industry now recog-

TABLE 16.7   Annual Hazardous Waste
Generation by PG&E, 1984–1993

Year	Waste generated (tons)
1984	95,581
1986	50,210
1987	29,538
1988	24,815
1989	21,579
1990	13,712
1991	61,237
1992	20,719
1993	20,641

nize that many of those wastes are hazardous. In 1991, PG&E completed a major soils cleanup at a former manufactured-gas plant site in Sacramento. About 43,000 yd^3 of soil, or more than 2700 truckloads, were removed from the site. When possible, the residues were recycled into an asphalt roadbase material, reducing by more than 20% the amount requiring disposal in a secured landfill site.

Organization and Implementation of PG&E's Environmental Policy

PG&E's vice president and general counsel (VP&GC) is the lead officer for the company's environmental goal, reporting to the chairman and CEO. Reporting to the VP&GC, in addition to the Law Department, are the Corporate Environmental Quality, Environmental Services, and Safety, Health, and Claims Departments.

The Environmental Services Department has responsibilities in environmental compliance and planning, including the investigation and remediation of hazardous waste sites, regulatory interface and regulation interpretation, environmental auditing, and environmental staff support for line organizations.

The Corporate Environmental Quality Department has responsibility for ensuring continued environmental excellence by developing environmental policy and goals; fostering ownership of those goals among those company units and management responsible for the goals; raising outstanding issues that may impact on the achievement of the company's environmental goal and seeking timely resolution of these issues; acting as a facilitator and conduit to support those units and management responsible for implementation of the policy goals; and maintaining mutually beneficial relations with external constituencies such as environmental groups and business and government, as related to environmental policy.

Lessons Learned and Conclusions

Environmental leadership has benefited PG&E as a business. It has provided PG&E the opportunity to participate in the development of environmental and energy policies at both state and national levels. It has led to development of substantive relations with key environmental groups that have resulted in support that prior to PG&E's environmental leadership would have been virtually unimaginable. It has resulted in direct cost savings and increased shareholder earnings, and provides potential future earnings. And, it provides an added value for PG&E customers—a value customers have indicated they want.

PG&E understood from the start the difficult and time-consuming task of changing the company's culture to one that completely integrates environmental responsibility into all decisions and actions. It was understood that success in implementing the environmental goal depended on the implementation happening on a decentralized basis. Much of the cultural change has occurred. Yet much remains to be done, particularly in an industry that is undergoing rapid and fundamental change as a result of deregulation and competition.

PG&E also believes strongly that partnerships work. Based on its experience in creating and participating in partnerships, we recommend a few basic tenets for a successful collaborative process:

- There should be a reasonable likelihood of consensus.

- Participating parties need to focus on win-win outcomes.

- All major stakeholders' interests should be represented.

- Participants understand and accept that the parties will have areas of disagreement but focus on areas of commonality: i.e., all participants must be willing to agree to disagree.

- Discussions need to be open and candid.

- Each participant must be willing to state his or her point of view.

- Each participant must be willing to listen to other positions nonjudgmentally.

- There must be no surprises between participants, especially in areas of disagreement.

Since 1990, PG&E has produced an annual report to its Board of Directors on the progress towards achieving the objectives in its Commitment to Environmental Quality.[2] This report is also made available to the public. Initially, there was doubt expressed internally as to the wisdom of publicly reporting on compliance performance (e.g., notices of violation, fines). Since 1992, compliance performance has been included in the report. In hindsight, the company believes that including these data is critical from two perspectives. First, it adds a substantial measure of credibility to a report that could otherwise be perceived as "puffery." Second, it provides another motivational force to those responsible for the infractions identified. Since adding this data in 1992, external reactions have been exclusively positive.

PG&E's environmental record has brought a fair amount of recognition. However, as this recognition is discussed with employees and others, PG&E stresses that the recognition is not the driver in the company's environmental efforts. The substantive results are the driver. PG&E is encouraged by its environmental record but recognizes it has traveled only a short distance on a long road. In the mid-1990s, PG&E is just beginning to integrate environmental responsibility into all its management systems, including compensation systems. It is still in the process of formalizing a comprehensive set of measures for reporting. These and other tasks must be taken on in a time of rapid change for the electric utility industry and industry in general. PG&E is convinced that environmental excellence will be an even greater competitive edge in the future than it has been in the past. The message that management is sending is that the company must improve earnings, it must improve customer service, it must improve the environment while simultaneously reducing costs. These are the ingredients of a successful company in a changing and increasingly competitive marketplace.

References

1. Pacific Gas & Electric Company, "Commitment to Environmental Quality," San Francisco, 1990.
2. Pacific Gas & Electric Company, "1993 Environmental Report of PG&E," San Francisco, 1993.

17

Environmental Management for the 1990s at ARCO

ARCO ✦

Kenneth R. Dickerson

Senior Vice President, External Affairs
Atlantic Richfield Company
Los Angeles, California

Introduction

Since 1969, when an oil spill blackened California's beaches near Santa Barbara, the environment has been a hot topic. At the extreme, laissez faire boosters and no-growth advocates have used near apocalyptic predictions to make their cases. But now, more than two decades later, it seems time to put away the extremes. The public favors a clean environment and supports regulation to achieve it. In many cases, the costs of compliance are huge, but the cost of noncompliance is even higher. Finding creative ways to meet environmental goals while reducing bottom-line costs is the challenge for business today.

ARCO has accepted this challenge with a top-down commitment that permeates the company, shaping organizational structure and programs to achieve environmental excellence without doing unnecessary harm to the company's bottom line. This includes a program of regular environment, health, and safety audits; responsive and innovative remediation of Superfund sites; and creative environmental stewardship that extends to exploration, production, and remediation, as well as a clean fuels program to meet future challenges.

Leadership: The Essential Foundation

About 25 years ago, ARCO hired its first environmental scientist. Today, approximately 300 employees staff the combined corporate and operating companies' Environment, Health, and Safety departments (EH&S), under the aegis of a corporate vice president and a board-level committee whose membership includes a former president of the Nature Conservancy.

This legion of people exists for only one purpose: to ensure that ARCO fulfills its health, safety, and environmental responsibilities to the public and to its employees. It's neither easy nor cheap, but it is far less costly than damage to our reputation, regulatory fines, litigation expenses, remediation for environmental damage, or, worst, injury and loss of life.

As serious as ARCO and other responsible companies are about the environment, the company and its environmental experts are not motivated wholly by altruism. Government regulations, public pressure, litigation expense, and a desire to be a socially responsible corporation have all contributed.

Several years ago, ARCO put its environmental commitment in writing and distributed it to employees, shareholders, and a variety of others. ARCO pledged to make good environmental stewardship standard operating procedure in every department of the company and backed its commitment with adequate financial resources. To achieve that, all ARCO EH&S managers are empowered to be innovative and—where appropriate—proactive, and are given the resources to implement needed improvements.

Preparation and Prevention

The best environmental management is prevention, and that priority governs waste minimization programs and audits of all ARCO facilities, including those of subsidiaries. It is our policy to meet the intent of all U.S. health, safety, and environmental standards, even in countries with lesser requirements. But the measure of good environmental or safety practices isn't standards, but results: a safe workplace and a clean environment. That requires integration of safety and environmental awareness into every aspect of a business, and every employee must become a practitioner—a big challenge in a company as diverse as ARCO. The corporate structure supports several decentralized operations—from domestic and international oil and gas exploration and production, refining, storage, marketing and transportation, to coal and chemicals production and marketing. Circumstances vary widely from site to site, necessitating various responses to environmental and safety challenges.

Safety—A Priority

For any safety effort to be effective, safety must become a conscious priority for each employee. That's one reason we do not just talk about *safety programs*. A safety program is someone else's responsibility. At ARCO, *safety* is everyone's responsibility. That requires individual initiative and good communication.

ARCO also believes that any effective safety effort must include contractor safety, and this receives very close attention at ARCO. For example, all ARCO contractors are required to have the resources and equipment for safe operations. In addition, ARCO's contracts require quality performance and injury reports, which are tracked back through operations to accountable facility management. And we enforce our contractual agreements. At the completion of operations, contractors are evaluated, and poor performers are removed from ARCO's bid list.

Safety, like quality or success in any aspect of business operations, is not the result of any one factor, but the sum of all factors: high-quality engineering, instruction, maintenance, operations, and training. None of these is defined specifically as a "safety activity," but all are determinants of a safe environment.

Finally, ARCO sets high standards for itself and measures performance with an aggressive EH&S auditing plan. Although we have not yet met our goals, we want to do more than exceed the industry average. We want to lead, and we want to be accident- and illness-free.

Environmental Stewardship

Environmental stewardship certainly includes prevention, but its scope is wider. At ARCO, it's not enough to prevent damage; it is also a goal to sustain—and, where possible, improve—the land, air, and water where we operate.

Clearly, avoiding all environmental impact is not an option for the oil industry. Oil and gas production, coal mining, and other "earth" industries inherently disturb natural resources. Transportation and refining of petroleum products—even the end products themselves—affect air quality or other aspects of the environment. This close relationship with nature keeps us ever aware that environmental stewardship must be part of every decision we make if we are to operate responsibly and maintain public trust.

As discoverer, developer, and co-operator of the Prudhoe Bay oil field on Alaska's North Slope, ARCO has become expert in environmentally friendly exploration and production. In 1968, when the Prudhoe Bay field was discovered, little was known about major industrial operations in Arctic environments. It fell to ARCO to sponsor scientific studies and gather information on its own.

As part of this effort, ARCO retained naturalist Angus Gavin to monitor Arctic wildlife and assess the effects of drilling and production. For more than 12 years, Gavin was on site, providing consultation and conducting studies. ARCO published and disseminated Gavin's findings about Alaska's wildlife, increasing public knowledge and providing a basis for safe development in Arctic areas. In addition, ARCO conducted its own studies of fisheries and shoreline vegetation.

Today, a plethora of laws and regulations have codified environmental protection, but ARCO continues its own efforts to obtain scientifically accurate information about fragile environments. On the North Slope, beneath the sea, in the rain forest, in the discontinued mining operations of Montana, or in Bakersfield, California, good environmental management requires continuing scientific study and monitoring.

In Alaska, the results of these efforts are most apparent in the Trans Alaska Pipeline System (TAPS), which was engineered and constructed with an eye to avoiding harm to migrating caribou herds, air quality, and the delicate Arctic tundra. The results can be seen in the thriving herds that frequent the area, crossing over and under the pipeline, finding shelter from wind and insects in its shadow (see Figs. 17.1 and 17.2).

In wilderness areas, we know we are only guests, and we operate with that in mind. Someday, when the oil is gone, the pads, gravel

Figure 17.1 Summertime in Prudhoe Bay: Grazing caribou dot the landscape around ARCO's Prudhoe Bay production facilities. Herds have doubled in size since operations began, a testament to the high priority placed on environmental protection.

Figure 17.2 Brief daylight illuminates ARCO's facilities on the North Slope. Prolonged darkness and harsh weather contribute to the Arctic's fragile ecosystems.

roads, and pipelines will be removed. The land will be remediated and, in time, reclaimed by the harsh Arctic conditions. Then, as before and during our operations, Arctic ecosystems will remain intact and functioning.

Exploring for a Safe Environment

Working in the fragile Arctic environment has prepared ARCO well for the nineties and beyond. With depletion of overall U.S. oil reserves, and the closure of many promising but environmentally sensitive domestic areas, exploration and production activities are moving to the Middle East, Asia, Europe, South America, and other overseas locations. Techniques developed by ARCO for North Slope and offshore operations are being applied in sensitive areas to minimize environmental impact. A good example of this effect is ARCO's current operations in the Orient basin of Ecuador, a fragile rain forest.

Environmentalists are rightly concerned about the preservation of rain forests. They support greater numbers of plant and animal species than any other terrestrial habitat. In addition, rain forest soils depend on degrading leaf litter and fallen trees to supply nutrients, which are quickly depleted by the abundant flora and leaching of minerals by frequent rains. Disturbing the soil and vegetative cover disrupts this cycle and soon threatens vegetation and wildlife.

Rain forests may also be rich in exploitable resources: gold, silver, precious stones, timber, and hydrocarbons. Many operations designed to harvest these resources are destructive to rain forests, destroying approximately 1 to 2% each year by some estimates. Logging may be the most destructive of all activities in these regions, but colonization, agriculture, some types of tree farming, livestock grazing, land speculation, and wood-based fuel gathering may be the major threats.

Although oil and gas exploration and production do not rank as significant rain forest destroyers, they are still an intrusion, and early operations conducted without the environmental awareness that prevails today have contributed to water contamination and other environmental degradation. In addition, roads and pipelines constructed to move equipment and liquids provide access to others, and new land opened to colonization by citizens of the host country pushes the forest back a little further. Indigenous people may be displaced, or find their way of life threatened.

Given the risks, many argue that intruders do not belong in the rain forest at all. But many of these areas are located in emerging nations anxious to develop resources and share in the benefits industrial society has to offer. By working closely with national governments and local communities, ARCO plans to meet these challenges by developing procedures that respect the land and its indigenous people. (See Figs. 17.3 and 17.4.) We believe that environmentally conscious companies can ensure safe development in fragile environments. Indeed, if environmentally responsible companies do not take the lead in sensitive environments, others will develop the resources without worrying about such safeguards.

ARCO's approach is simple: to protect the environment, animals, and plants and to work with indigenous peoples. In the rain forest, that encompasses some very specific guidelines. So far, ARCO has conducted all operations without constructing any new roads, but as standard policy, the company limits road construction and minimizes land and tree removal. All wastes are treated before release into the environment and nonbiodegradable wastes are handled in an environmentally sound manner. We preserve and replace topsoil, reclaim disturbed sites, and prohibit hunting by anyone associated with the project, with the exception of local forest dwellers hunting on their own behalf.

As on the North Slope, airlifting equipment to exploration sites eliminates the need for roads and prevents subsequent access by others. And the same platform technology that enabled us to drill beneath the sea confines development to a small area. These lessons of a quarter century of environmentally sensitive industrial development will continue to serve ARCO well. Together, advanced

Figure 17.3 Rain forest reforestation: Salvaged lumber is recycled into pallets that provide essential shade for new growth in a reforestation project at an ARCO drilling site in Ecuador.

Figure 17.4 ARCO environmentalists study new vegetation sprouting along construction camp path separating housing from the drill site. Within months, reforestation and biodegradation will reclaim the boards.

technology and responsible management will enable us to work in the rain forest with minimal impact and restore the land to its natural state when operations are completed.

Unfortunately, it wasn't always that way, and both industry and the environment continue to pay a high price. Remediation is always more costly than prevention, but new approaches are enabling us to clean up old sites—many of them long closed—in timely and economical ways.

Hazardous Waste Sites: Legacy of the Past

In 1990, frustrated by delays and high legal costs, ARCO set a new goal for handling historic waste sites: to locate, remediate, and close every hazardous waste site we had *before* it became the subject of litigation or regulatory gridlock. We believed that reaching a consensus on cleanup standards and methods at the negotiating table rather than in the courtroom would expedite cleanup, reduce costs, and directly add to ARCO's bottom line.

To test this thesis, a few comparisons were made. For example, in 1990, costs of remediating one 100,000-yd^3 site that was involved in litigation and regulatory oversight were estimated at $72 million over a 12-year period. The company located a similar unburdened site, applied our best science to it, and cleaned 72,000 yd^2 in 22 months at a cost of $6 million.

The key to this kind of effectiveness is people. ARCO assigned some of its best—highly skilled and technically savvy project managers, able to work with local communities and regulators to negotiate solutions agreeable to everyone. Most were not scientists and were surprised to find themselves tapped for an assignment in remediation, but they have found that creative management of some of the company's most intractable problems provides very satisfying results.

Good research is essential to ARCO's prompt and aggressive site remediation. Problems are identified by running potential sites through an assessment model we have built to prioritize ARCO's sites. Knowing exactly what we are facing has enabled ARCO to plan for remediation before public concern has arisen.

Once identified, methods of remediation and levels of cleanliness are negotiated with current owners and other stakeholders in the community. These are critical decisions. Too often regulators have demanded pristine cleanliness and driven costs unnecessarily high. The emerging standard—and one that ARCO supports—is a low-risk environment. That is a standard measured against planned use of each site. Sites to be used for industrial or commercial purposes need not be cleaned to playground standards. ARCO supports "planned use" as the best guideline in determining site cleanup methods. And methods must be grounded in good science.

Unfortunately, remediation guidelines of the U.S. Environmental Protection Agency (EPA) and those of other regulatory agencies, have often evolved from incomplete or inaccurate information rather than from valid scientific studies. In many cases, this has resulted in costly, unnecessary, and even ineffective action. This scenario threatens to repeat itself at two old Montana mining sites, where the results of scientific studies of lead and arsenic levels are in conflict with EPA mandates for soil removal and remediation.

One site, in Butte, Montana, includes a large residential area containing various levels of lead in the soil. EPA cleanup standards are based on a computer model of assumed "worst-case" information which has fostered predictions of high blood lead levels in children and could require massive soil removal. This may be the worst possible action to take.

In an effort to determine the best course of action, ARCO funded several independent, peer-reviewed scientific studies to determine the actual risks in Butte and other similar mining sites. A three-year study conducted by Dr. Robert Bornschein of the University of Cincinnati revealed that blood lead levels in Butte were well below the average for children throughout the United States. Tracking studies indicate that this level has fallen, and will continue to fall as lead is removed from water, gasoline, and food products—factors totally unrelated to the EPA's proposed action. In addition, the results from these studies show that lead from mining wastes does not impact blood lead levels. The EPA has confirmed this in a $15 million, four-year study which produced similar results. The clear indication is that removing massive amounts of soil in order to reduce blood lead levels in children would not only be unnecessary, but disruptive of community life with no resulting benefit. Absent the aggressive scientific research led by ARCO, the community would have been disrupted by unnecessary remediation mandated by a regulating agency relying upon flawed scientific efforts.

ARCO applied the same kind of rigorous scientific study to the effects of arsenic residues at an old copper smelter in Anaconda, Montana. The research results revealed that arsenic levels in local children and adults were no higher than in residents of areas without smelters, again casting grave doubt on the value of the EPA's proposal to remove and remediate soil.

A safe, healthy, and pleasant environment can only be achieved with *effective* remediation actions. Basing environmental decisionmaking on solid science can save us expensive and futile efforts and free valuable resources for methods that do work. Good science, properly applied, will also reduce the impact of remediation on local citizens.

In addition to levels and methods of remediation, the issue of joint and several responsibility is a huge contributor to cleanup costs at hazardous waste sites. The changes in Superfund legislation recently proposed by EPA Administrator Carol Browner are very positive, and ARCO is cautiously optimistic that they will resolve some of the problems that have made hazardous waste cleanup such a slow and costly process.

New Technological Solutions

Unfortunately, businesses tend to be defensive about hazardous waste cleanup, and that has hindered development of problem-solving technology. But ARCO is looking to its areas of strength for technologies that can be used to benefit the environment. We are, for example, experts in moving liquids—and in some cases, substances that facilitate fluid flow in pipelines such as polymers and anaerobic bacteria can be used to clean contaminated aquifers.

Deep-well treatment and injection (DWTI) is an innovation that applies ARCO's expertise in drilling, production, and seismic technology to solid waste disposal. In this process, solid waste, such as sludge, contaminated soils, or even naturally occurring radioactive material (NORM), would be pumped down a new or existing well deep into the earth—thousands of feet below drinking-water levels—where it is hydraulically injected into a fracture. Geophones placed at varying levels continuously monitor the process and transfer the information to a computer, where it is instantly accessible. This makes the fracture activity visible at all times and allows accurate and immediate control of the pumping process. When pumping stops, the fracture closes, forming a permanent tomb. The well is then cut off below the surface and sealed with cement, leaving no surface evidence of the procedure (Fig. 17.5).

DWTI offers great promise for hazardous waste disposal because it is a permanent, cost-effective method that eliminates the difficulties often associated with surface landfills, such as long-term monitoring and transportation. The development of DWTI is an outstanding example of an innovative cross-disciplinary effort to transfer oil field technology to environmental problems. Because it offers benefits to so many difficult disposal problems, ARCO has involved the EPA and other regulatory agencies, as well as potential DWTI users such as the U.S. Departments of Energy and Defense, in the evaluation and testing processes. Much of the technology is proprietary to ARCO and protected by patents. With regulatory approval, DWTI could be a widely used, safe, and effective alternative for solid waste disposal.

ARCO is also looking for new uses for old oil. In the early days of the industry, oil was refined in batches for very specific uses. The

Figure 17.5 Platforms limit environmental contact with oil production to a small area. Originally designed for offshore operations, platform technology is now being converted for use in other fragile environments, such as rain forests.

residues were simply discarded in pits. Over the years, hundreds of different products have been refined for nearly every fraction contained in crude oil. ARCO's goal is to recycle the old oil residues into useful products. In one area, oil residue may be transformed into paving asphalt in the plant that currently occupies the site.

Of course, not all of the problems are technical. People play an important role in environmental remediation. Hazardous waste frightens residents. It threatens their families, neighborhoods, and economic well-being. A plant producing fuel for nuclear submarines in Parks, Pennsylvania, has elicited such fears. Although it operated under ARCO ownership for only four years in the late 1960s and early 1970s, ARCO has joined with current owners and local community leaders to find solutions to nuclear waste disposal that satisfy everyone. Emotions have run high, and it is only by responding to concerns of residents, participating in community affairs, and sharing costs with the present owners that we will find workable solutions.

Blueprint for the Future

Even the most creative remediation must be regarded as retroactive environmental policy—the price of past mistakes, abuses, and ignorance—and it is costly in human and financial resources. Over the past quarter century, environmental understanding has mushroomed, and today the combination of knowledge, technology, and regulation makes it possible for industry and the environment to flourish in tandem. But many people are reluctant to embrace this truth, and fear of the past threatens to hobble our future. A good example can be found in the sad state of domestic oil and gas exploration and development.

In the United States, the "oil patch" areas that fueled the nation for a century are nearly depleted. The massive Prudhoe Bay field in Alaska, ARCO's chief resource, is in decline, and new domestic discoveries have been few and far between. The most promising sites for new petroleum discoveries are environmentally sensitive and therefore legally out of bounds. Alaska's Arctic National Wildlife Reserve and the country's outer continental shelf, particularly offshore California, are effectively closed to our industry. More than half a million jobs have disappeared in the past decade as the major companies increasingly move overseas.

More and more, the trend toward international development is fueled by simple economics: each barrel of oil produced in the United States costs several times as much as a barrel from the Middle East. Indeed, economics alone may make reliance on international oil sources inevitable, but it is our company's position that to allow environmental fears to accelerate the process is a grievous error. The environment and the oil industry are not incompatible.

Over and over again, the oil industry has proven that it can operate in harmony with sensitive environments. Every day, offshore operations safely pump oil from the ocean floor to refineries miles away, and more than three decades of Alaskan oil and gas operations have been carried on without major damage to wildlife or landscape. There have been problems, of course, as a major industry established itself in rugged yet fragile terrain. The 1989 spill from the *Exxon Valdez* is an obvious case in point. But in many ways, it is the exception that proves the rule. The Alaskan oil industry is by and large a clean one.

As the largest operator in Alaska, ARCO's record is, in this author's view, representative—and virtually unnoticed. Each year, ARCO Marine, Inc., safely transports 200 million barrels of oil from Valdez, Alaska, to West Coast ports in the lower 48. That's approximately 200 separate trips annually, excluding the frequent transit of refined product from ARCO's Cherry Point refinery in Washington's Puget Sound to points south including San Francisco, Long Beach, and Los Angeles. This outstanding record is the result of ARCO's training, policies, and systems that focus on prevention.

For example, all ARCO vessels loaded with crude oil stay a minimum of 85 miles from land. Product-carrying ships maintain a dis-

Figure 17.6 Tanker: The 70,000 dead-weight-ton *ARCO Sag River* has a 500,000-barrel carrying capacity. Formerly a crude oil carrier, the *Sag River* is now assigned to product transport. All ARCO tankers carrying crude oil maintain a distance of 85 miles from shore to ensure safety. Product carriers maintain a 50-mile distance.

tance of 50 miles from shore (Fig. 17.6). This policy increases our costs, but it also adds an important margin of safety. ARCO's safety policy also demands strict ship maintenance schedules, and we enforce a policy of zero tolerance for alcohol and drugs. As a result, it is the company's belief that its crews are among the best seafarers in the business.

In addition, ARCO has a spill-response team in place, kept at a high level of efficiency by frequent training and regular exercises. The members are trained and equipped for containment, recovery, and removal of oil and participate annually in a major drill in the Gulf of Mexico or along the West Coast. Everybody—spill team members, regulatory agencies, and local representatives—works together as a coordinated team. ARCO is also a member of regional spill-response cooperatives wherever the company has operations (see Fig. 17.7).

"Teamwork" pretty well sums up ARCO Marine's training and culture. Aboard ship, everyone on the bridge participates in team management. In an innovative new program, ship's officers and deck and engine team leaders are brought ashore to attend a rigorous program in teamwork, which is then integrated throughout the ship. The navi-

Figure 17.7 Oil spill response: Spill response teams like the Ship Escort/ Response Vessel System (SERVS) are equipped with TRANSREC skimmers and other state of the art equipment for rapid cleanup.

gational bridge crew, including officers, unlicensed staff, and even the harbor pilot, participate in a separate shore-based simulator program that also focuses on team effectiveness. In addition, the company provides extensive technical and behavioral training to ensure good decisionmaking.

Finally, ARCO applies the best available expertise and technology to marine safety. In harbor waters, ARCO uses tug escorts and local pilots. The company is also investing in high-tech, on-board radar plotting devices and recently launched a partnership with Foss Towing to design and build an 8500-hp tractor tug to guide ships to port in Puget Sound, Washington.

ARCO applies the same attention to safety and environmental stewardship on land as it does offshore. A little more than a year ago, ARCO entered a unique private-public partnership with California's Department of Fish and Game that preserves more than 6000 acres of natural habitat in the San Joaquin Valley—home to more endangered species than any other area in the continental United States—and also facilitates the permitting process for oil and gas operations. The project was initiated in response to requirements of the Federal Endangered Species Act.

Under the agreement, ARCO deeded acreage in its Coles Levee oil field to California's Department of Fish and Game. In return, Fish and Game designated ARCO as manager of the preserve—a responsibility that will run concurrently with oil and gas operations on the property. Eventually, when petroleum activities are ended, the Coles Levee Ecosystem Preserve will be permanently set aside by the state of California. Meanwhile, ARCO's "environmental credit" will shorten the permitting process for oil and gas operations from 14 months to 4 to 6 weeks and reduce accompanying costs (see Fig. 17.8). The Coles Levee agreement marks the first time that a private landowner has been allowed to manage a conservation easement and ushers in a model for future public-private partnerships that will benefit the environment and simultaneously encourage economic development.

Fuels of the Future

ARCO's policy is more than prevention and stewardship—it is a philosophy that looks to the future and seeks to find a better way. This proactive approach underlies successful programs like the Coles

Figure 17.8 Coles Levee Ecosystem Preserve: Oil production and endangered plant and animal species exist in harmony in the Coles Levee Ecosystem Preserve—a 6000-acre easement in California's San Joaquin Valley deeded to the state by ARCO in 1992 as a permanent reserve.

Levee Preserve, as well as ARCO's pioneering efforts in developing cleaner-burning, reformulated gasoline.

As a company headquartered in Southern California, ARCO has had a strong motivation to help improve air quality. The area's infamous smog has generated increasingly restrictive and costly regulations on both stationary and mobile emissions sources. By the late 1980s, the South Coast Air Quality Management District (SCAQMD) developed a plan that would replace gasoline as the primary motor vehicle fuel—first with methanol, then, a few years later, with electricity—all within 20 years. With more than 24 million vehicles on California's roads, the SCAQMD plan would have caused serious economic dislocation throughout the state.

ARCO's position was that the SCAQMD plan would not work. New plants would have to be constructed to produce the vast quantities of methanol needed for California's fleet of cars and trucks. Supplies of natural gas feedstock would have to be imported, or the methanol itself made abroad and shipped to this country. Distribution systems and vehicles capable of handling methanol would have to be designed, and cars and trucks already on the road would require costly retooling. As proposed, the plan would have been a costly and disruptive effort to utilize a fuel that has many drawbacks of its own, including reduced energy compared to gasoline and its own problem emissions, primarily formaldehyde, a toxic.

In September 1989, ARCO responded to the methanol challenge by introducing the world's first reformulated gasoline (RFG). It was called EC-1, for "emission control," and targeted to the dirtiest cars on the road, those built before the advent of catalytic converters. From conception, ARCO's EC gasolines were an effort to improve air quality, not just another marketing program, and the company worked hard to establish the distinction (Fig. 17.9).

But the development of ARCO's reformulated gasoline was really a public-private partnership. ARCO worked closely with SCAQMD and the California Air Resources Board (CARB). We used independent labs for all our testing and shared the results with the two regulatory agencies every step of the way. At EC-1's introductory press conference, the executive directors of SCAQMD and CARB joined with state and local elected officials, and community and environmental leaders, in testifying to the importance of this new advance in clean-fuel technology.

A year later, in September 1990, ARCO introduced EC-Premium for high-performance cars to the same enthusiastic response (Fig. 17.10). Since their introduction, ARCO estimates that these two gasolines have reduced mobile emissions in Southern California by more than 400 million lb. The air today in the Los Angeles Basin is cleaner than it's been since measurements were first taken 40 years ago, and

Figure 17.9 Los Angeles refinery: ARCO's "emission control" gasolines are blended at its Los Angeles refinery. The refinery is currently undergoing a $450,000 retrofitting to enable production of CARB Phase II gasoline, ARCO EC-X, by 1996.

ARCO is proud to have contributed to this improvement. ARCO's efforts also led the EPA to approve reformulated gas as an acceptable clean fuel for the nine metropolitan areas in the United States with the highest ozone levels. These regulations went into effect on January 1, 1995.

Next, on March 1, 1996, California drivers will begin filling up with a remarkable new fuel designated CARB Phase II reformulated gasoline. CARB Phase II, which goes beyond EPA regulations, will be the cleanest-burning gasoline ever made. And it is closely modeled on ARCO's latest and most sophisticated RFG formula: EC-X.

Manufacturing Phase II gasoline will require more than $500 million to retrofit ARCO's Los Angeles refinery. In 1992, CARB approved the formula as the standard for 1996, and ARCO moved ahead. ARCO estimates that if all California's cars and trucks used the new fuel, pollution from vehicles would drop by 3.8 million pounds per day. That's equivalent to removing 8 million cars—nearly one-third of California's vehicles—from the road.

The development of reformulated EC gasolines provides an excellent example of the creative solutions that can develop when government sets the standard and lets industry find the means to fulfill it. That is the most effective public-private partnership.

Figure 17.10 ARCO service station and A.M./P.M. minimarket: ARCO offers its EC gasolines at its minimarkets located throughout the five western states. On average, ARCO stations pump twice as much gasoline each month as their competitors.

ARCO developed EC gasolines because of its belief that available alternatives would be less efficient and far more costly, and costs simply cannot be ignored in working for environmental improvement. No business can operate for long at a loss. And, however desirable the change or improvement, people will not purchase a product that is uncompetitive in price or performance. These two criteria are the factors that make reformulated gasoline the fuel of choice for the future.

Although reformulated gasoline costs more to manufacture than conventional gasoline, it is far cheaper than alternatives. CARB estimates that Phase II gasoline will cost about 15 cents a gallon more than conventional gasoline, and ARCO estimates for EC-X fall within that range. Methanol, by way of comparison, would be 40 or 50 cents higher than conventional unleaded gasoline. Natural gas and electricity and the vehicles that can use these fuels are also more costly than either conventional gasoline or RFG.

Other Air Quality Issues

Mobile sources aren't the only challenge in the effort to clean the air. Stationary sources were among the first to be targeted by regulators.

In California, the filters, scrubbers, and reformulating requirements for the larger stationary polluters—refiners and furniture paint and coating manufacturers—have raised the operating costs of large and small businesses alike. Many have left the state or are considering doing so. Until recently, these defections were not particularly noticed, but the decline of California's defense industry, coupled with the recession, has forced the economics of environmentalism to the forefront.

In 1992, SCAQMD adopted a new program designed to reduce emissions from stationary sources, primarily large polluters like refineries. The Regional Clean Air Incentives Market plan (RECLAIM) is based on marketplace principles that assign individual facilities a certain number of pollution credits, which can be traded. Cleaner facilities can sell their credits to others with greater emissions. Cleaner facilities thus save money and dirty ones are motivated to reduce costs by reducing pollution.

ARCO supports the idea of trading pollution "rights," using market forces to help solve environmental problems. But in this case, the original RECLAIM plan proposed an unrealistic standard of emission reduction by industry. ARCO, for example, whose refinery emissions had already been reduced 85% by existing control measures, would be held to the same future reductions as those who had made none at all.

Even if technologically possible, the expense entailed in effecting such drastic stationary source reductions could have blocked the investment needed to make CARB Phase II reformulated gasoline, which will reduce emissions statewide. Had the original RECLAIM plan prevailed, we would have reduced some stationary emissions a little but precluded the reduction of major mobile source emissions. In SCAQMD's zeal to fix small problems, we almost lost sight of our primary goal: cleaning up the air.

The original RECLAIM program sought to reduce air pollution from stationary sources by an additional 85%. ARCO believed 70% to be a much more reasonable goal. Since RECLAIM's most difficult requirements would not take effect until the year 2000, many companies were willing to acquiesce in the plan, assuming that extensions would be granted when the deadline loomed. We thought that was very risky, and worked with a coalition of other companies to find a more workable plan. The aim was clean air *and* economic health, and the RECLAIM plan finally adopted in 1993 included such cost factors and technical feasibility in its compliance requirements.

Southern California's topography—a basin framed by mountains and sea—has built-in environmental barriers to achieving clean air. In fact, computer modeling has shown that the South Coast basin might never achieve Clean Air Act ozone attainment goals, even if all cars, industry, and people were removed. That's neither desirable nor realistic, but it illustrates the difficulty of our task: improving our environment without destroying the economic and social setting that also enriches our lives. We can only do this by forming creative partnerships between industry and government to ensure a quality of life that is both environmentally clean and economically strong. ARCO believes these goals can be balanced to the satisfaction of the public, government, and business located here, and this belief forms the rationale for all that we do and hope to accomplish in the years to come

18

Caring for the Environment at Baxter Healthcare

Baxter

Nicholas Fotis

Manager, Packaging Development
Rexam Medical Packaging
Mundelin, Illinois

Lisa Petrilli

Senior Product Manager
Baxter Healthcare Corporation
Deerfield, Illinois

Pat Bartholomew

Director of Environmental Affairs
Baxter Healthcare Corporation
Deerfield, Illinois

"Consider the Iroquois Indians. They opened each tribal meeting with this invocation: 'In our every deliberation we must consider the impact of our decisions on the next seven generations.' Whenever important matters were to be decided, a vote would be cast on behalf of those future generations. I would like to think our environmental commitment is a vote on behalf of our future generations."

VERN LOUCKS
Chairman and CEO, Baxter Healthcare

Introduction

At Baxter Healthcare, caring for the environment is considered a logical extension of caring for health. Baxter is a $9 billion international company which supplies over 200,000 products to hospitals, clinics, and alternate site facilities in 100 countries. Described as the leading healthcare supplier in the world, Baxter has extended its environmental commitment unilaterally from Europe, where environmental concern is high, to developing countries where public and governmental pressure to protect the environment is sometimes nonexistent.

Baxter's environmental stewardship does not result from recent media coverage and public pressure for more "green" products, but rather reflects the way the company has been doing business since its founding in 1931. In early 1977, Baxter established a formal Environmental Review Board, composed mainly of members of the Board of Directors and key Baxter executives, to be the main voice for the environment within the company. The Board has established an aggressive policy for ensuring that decisions made at Baxter are in the best interest of the environment. Additionally, it oversees the publication of the Annual Environmental Report, which is available to the public. In 1990 the Board reinvigorated the company's philosophy by publishing Baxter's Worldwide Environmental Policy (Fig. 18.1). Among the eight points in the document are:

- The role and scope of the Environmental Review Board
- Legal compliance and risk control
- Waste minimization
- Environmental leadership
- Establishment of division and facility environmental managers
- Training and audit policies
- Responsibilities of unit managers

Of special interest are the concrete goals for waste minimization—an 80% reduction in air emissions by 1996—and the commitment to environmental leadership. The U.S. Environmental Protection Agency (EPA) recently recognized Baxter Healthcare for its corporate commitment to the EPA Administrator's 33/50 program, a voluntary initiative to reduce toxic emissions nationally and foster pollution prevention as the preferred approach to environmental improvement.

Goal number 5 of Baxter's environmental policy, the commitment to leadership, states specifically that "Baxter will establish and maintain an environmental program to be considered state-of-the-art among the *Fortune* 500 companies." To this end, the company spon-

Baxter's Environmental Policy was adopted in 1990. The policy is applicable to Baxter's operations worldwide.

1. *Environmental Review Board.*   An Environmental Review Board (ERB) appointed by the Public Policy Committee of the Board of Directors of Baxter is responsible for overseeing implementation of the environmental policy. The ERB will review and decide matters of environmental importance and will make an annual report to the Board of Directors.

2. *Legal Compliance.*   Baxter will comply with all applicable environmental laws.

3. *Risk Control.*   Baxter will not create unacceptable risks to the environment and will minimize risk to the company from previous, existing, and potential environmental conditions.

4. *Waste Minimization.*   Baxter will aggressively pursue opportunities to minimize the quantity and degree of hazard of the waste that results from its operations. It will reduce toxic and chlorofluorocarbon air emissions 60 percent by 1992 and 80 percent by 1996, from 1988 levels based on equivalent production.

5. *Environmental Leadership.*   Baxter will work to become a leader in respect for the environment. It will establish and maintain an environmental program to be considered state-of-the-art among the Fortune 500 companies. Baxter will accomplish this goal by 1993 in the United States, Puerto Rico, and Canada, and by 1996 worldwide.

6. *Environmental Coordinators and Managers.*   The manager of each manufacturing and distribution facility, and other division group managers where appropriate, will appoint a qualified environmental representative to coordinate and manage the unit's environmental program. However, compliance with this Policy is not just the responsibility of these representatives; it is the responsibility of every employee and particularly every manager.

7. *Training and Audit.*   Corporate environmental personnel, divisions, and facilities will provide coordinated, effective environmental training, awareness and audit programs as appropriate.

8. *Unit Manager Responsibility.*   The manager of each unit of the company will assure that the following are accomplished by the unit wherever relevant:
   8-1 Determine the facts regarding generation and release of pollutants from its facilities and responsibly manage its affairs to minimize any adverse environmental impact.
   8-2 Develop and implement its own environmental management program to comply with this Policy.
   8-3 Select, design, build, and operate products, processes, and facilities in order to minimize the generation and discharge of waste and other adverse impacts on the environment.
   8-4 Utilize control and recycling technology wherever scientifically and economically feasible to minimize the adverse impact on the environment.

Figure 18.1 Baxter's Worldwide Environmental Policy.

sored a study to establish a baseline for "state of the art" and has been continuing to draw near to the goal. By 1992, the program was 85% of the way there. It is interesting to note that in 1991 the program was 90% of the way to the goal, but was adjusted back in 1992—not because of a diminished effort, but because the state of the art goal is constantly being readjusted and the comparison is made to real, present-day technology.

To understand the organization of Baxter's environmental effort, one must understand the interaction between nine independent operating divisions and the Corporate Environmental Law group. Each division has its own division environmental manager (DEM), who is responsible for ensuring the division's conformance to the corporate policy. The Corporate Environmental Law group facilitates communication and provides a platform for recognition and awards for division programs. Environmental goals are routinely incorporated into executive, middle-manager, engineer, and hourly PMO (performance management objectives) documents. In fact, over 300 managers have specific environmental goals in their annual PMOs. This has had a pronounced effect in improving the involvement of management in the program. The PMO goals range from emissions and waste disposal to product and package design for the environment.

Since Baxter Healthcare sells its products in a regulated industry, the company cooperates with government regulatory agencies in the approval and distribution of its products. Each new drug application filed with the U.S. Food and Drug Administration (FDA) has a section which assesses the environmental impact of the new product. Additionally, Baxter has volunteered for participation in other government voluntary programs, among which is the EPA's Green Lights program. Currently the company is 60% of the way to achieving the 1996 target for installing energy-conserving lighting systems. The company also encourages employees to save energy and reduce air pollution through ride-sharing programs at over 30 sites.

Perhaps one of the most visible signs of the commitment to the environment made by Baxter in recent years involves the company's acceptance of the CONEG challenge (see Chap. 3). Baxter was one of only 29 original companies to accept the challenge and, as of its most recent report, was 76% of the way toward its goal of a 29-million-lb decrease in packaging. By year-end 1993 the company had reduced packaging by over 22 million lb. The dollar savings resulting from this reduction in packaging was approximately $16.7 million. Division action teams have identified 210 separate projects to reduce packaging waste.

In 1990 the Company Wide Environmental Packaging Task Force was established (see Fig. 18.2). The task force, a group of 62 people,

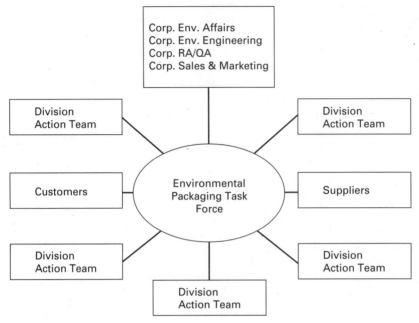

Corp. Env. Affairs
Corp. Env. Engineering
Corp. RA/QA
Corp. Sales & Marketing

Division
Action Team

Division
Action Team

Customers

Environmental
Packaging Task
Force

Suppliers

Division
Action Team

Division
Action Team

Division
Action Team

Figure 18.2 Environmental Packaging Task Force.

meets quarterly to review national and international environmental legislation, share success stories, exchange ideas for improvement and keep track of progress toward the CONEG commitment. In 1991, the task force issued the Baxter Environmental Goals for Packaging (see Fig. 18.3). Each year an assessment of conformance to these goals is made and results are submitted to the CONEG group.

The Corporate Environmental Packaging Team has also undertaken various subprojects, among which are the preparation of a template for the analysis of returnable/reusable container systems, a review of medical marketing forces in the environmental movement, and an environmental packaging manual for use by new and existing packaging engineers to facilitate efforts to make sound business and environmental decisions regarding future packaging.

General Business Practices

When considering the broad area of design for the environment (DFE), Baxter's approach is to look at the products it designs, manufactures, and distributes with the *leased-product concept* in mind. Under this concept, the product is designed in such a way that no design feature would be dependent upon the customer to have ultimate responsibility

1. Reduce by 1995 the average per-unit weight of packaging by 15 percent from 1990 levels.

2. Use the maximum feasible amount of recycled fiber in corrugated shipping containers.

3. Assure that no heavy metals are intentionally added to inks, dyes, adhesives or other packaging components.

4. Eliminate the use of foam packaging made with chlorofluorocarbons.

5. Facilitate recycling of packaging by:
   a. Applying the American Paper Institute recycled/recyclable symbol to all appropriate packaging;
   b. Applying the Society of Plastics Industry identification codes to all rigid plastic containers of capacity greater than 8 oz.

6. Reduce packaging waste by promoting the sale of single-package, multi-product medical kits and the use of reusable shipping containers and pallets.

7. Evaluate recycling of I.V. containers through pilot programs in hospitals in 1992.

8. Utilize the Preferred Packaging Guidelines of the Coalition of Northeastern Governors in the design of new packaging.

9. Initiate educational programs with customers and suppliers to expedite packaging source reduction and recycling.

10. Minimize the use of chlorine-bleached paper and paperboard in packaging.

11. Encourage suppliers and vendors to follow the above practices.

12. Each division will develop plans and goals specific to its type of products, packages and distribution systems to reduce environmental impacts.

Figure 18.3   Baxter Environmental Goals for Packaging.

for the recycling/reuse or disposal of the product. Thus, the design engineer takes responsibility for the "cradle-to-grave" fate of the product whether the final consumer disposes of the product or returns the product to Baxter for disposal. Disposal may take the form of reuse, recycling, composting, incineration, or landfill. This design concept is a logical extension of current business practices, since many of the company's divisions do indeed lease products like infusion pumps to customers and must be concerned not only with their functionality and safety, but with ultimate disposal when the product returns.

The leased-product concept is motivated by three distinct factors:

1. *Changing environmental and medical device regulations.* For example, freon was used in the past for cleaning some medical devices, but is no longer a viable option. The definition of hazardous waste material is also in constant flux. Products must be designed initially in a robust manner to survive not only the rigors

of use, distribution, and time, but also the rigors of the changing regulatory climate.

2. *Scarcity of resources.* Along with new "right-to-know" legislation and community awareness comes increased corporate responsibility to communicate environmental efforts and to design products in a way that maximizes the utilization of scarce resources, both natural and human. The average Baxter employee of the 1990s is an environmentally aware person, and will generally not tolerate the wasted resources and the resulting needless cost increases associated with poor design.

3. *Corporate goals.* As mentioned above, Baxter is striving to be an environmental leader and has set some aggressive goals in the areas of air toxics, reduced waste, and energy conservation.

The DFE philosophy is incorporated into training for new and existing engineers as part of divisional product development process (PDP) training programs. This training emphasizes the importance of elimination or reduction of toxicity, cost, and energy usage through the four-point EPA hierarchy of waste minimization: *eliminate, reduce, reuse, recycle.* Engineers are instructed on using recycled materials, exploring the options for reusable systems, and increasing the use of postconsumer materials in an effort to foster the growth of the recycled-materials market.

Although designers are provided with example checklists of DFE criteria, the preferred approach is not to put a check in the right box, but rather to provide appropriate guidelines and philosophy and leave the engineers free to apply the principles to their specific case in a way that will meet both product and environmental requirements. As Pat Bartholomew, the I.V. Systems Division Environmental Manager states: "These engineers are the creative ones. They come up with the new products. If given the opportunity and the understanding of the leased-product concept philosophy, they will be in the best position to use this information to provide the most environmentally responsible products."

Engineers are encouraged to think of their products as part of a total system and to create a process flow diagram to identify all of the materials, chemicals, equipment, and energy required. They then attempt to minimize material usage; adopt single-component construction; design for reuse, disassembly, or recycling; incorporate recycled materials; determine if the final product (if not recyclable) is suitable for landfill or incineration; consider ink and label contamination; and determine trade-offs between using less material and producing longer product life. Designers are also referred to the EPA publications *Life Cycle Assessment: Inventory Guidelines and Principles* and *Life Cycle*

Design Manual: Environmental Requirements and the Product System as excellent resources. As they are shown the basics of life-cycle assessment methods and past Baxter success stories, they are then asked to take the leased-product concept and make it their own.

The positive results of this philosophy are evident in the division-specific efforts outlined below. These efforts attempt to conform hundreds of different products and thousands of different requirements to the goal of minimal environmental impact.

Divisional DFE Efforts

The following are examples of division-specific initiatives that may serve as a template for DFE efforts of other corporations.

EnVision™ Recycling Program. Baxter Healthcare is the market leader in supplying I.V. solution bags (see Fig. 18.4a). As opposed to coextruded materials made of layers of differing plastics, these bags are made from a single homogeneous plastic and so are candidates for recycling. The I.V. Systems Division has devoted significant energy since 1990 to creating a closed-loop recycling system for these products. Through an initial pilot study, it was shown that these contain-

Figure 18.4a   Baxter Healthcare I.V. solution bags.

ers, their high-density-polyethylene (HDPE) overpouches, and polypropylene plastic pour bottles can be collected from hospitals, separated, and reprocessed to produce products for sale back into the hospital market. The reclaimed I.V. solution bags have been made into fatigue mats, the plastic pour bottles have been made into sharps containers, and plans are under way to produce red bags from the HDPE. Rather than just printing a material identification code, or a "Please recycle" logo, Baxter has closed the recycling circle by providing both a material and a market for the reclaimed product.

Vernacare.   This is a full line of products made from 100% recycled paper and pulp. These products are molded-pulp bedpans, emesis basins, large bowls, and urinals which, after being used, are masticated in a special machine. The resulting material is disposed of directly into the municipal sewer system and produces no materials for incineration or landfill. Besides providing a "waste-less" system, the product line also provides a market for recycled paper and pulp. Although not available in all areas, Baxter worked together with Claude Rounds at the Albany Medical Center to collect phone books from the local community which were then manufactured into Vernacare products to be used at the local hospital.

Homogeneous materials efforts.   Increasingly important is the effort to use homogeneous materials whenever possible to promote recyclablility and to maintain the value of the postconsumer waste stream. There are several programs to convert paper labels to plastic in order to assist waste haulers and reprocessors in retrieving usable materials.

Jacksonville, Texas, facility goals.   The Jacksonville, Texas, facility has established an extremely lofty goal of disposing of zero waste. They have dramatically cut their manufacturing waste by concentrating on source reduction projects in purchasing, increasing the use of recycled materials in their processes, and finding brokers for recyclable waste materials. After three years of conducting their "We Cycle" program, the plant had reduced its nonhazardous solid waste by 97.5% (see Fig. 18.4b). The reason for this reduction is the commitment of the facility's 600 employees to environmental action. Bill Raven, the facility's health, safety, and environmental assurance manager, notes that "employee commitment is the key. The employees know that the landfill is right in town, it is a small town, and as the largest employer in the town, Baxter has to take a leadership role in the reduction of solid waste."

Custom sterile kits.   Baxter has an entire division which specializes in reducing waste while increasing convenience for the customer. Custom kits are produced for various medical procedures and opera-

Figure 18.4b   "We Cycle" program, Jacksonville, Texas, facility.

tions which contain only those materials and drugs ordered by the hospital based an a physician's request. Not only does this reduce the amount of material which must be disposed of by the hospital; it also has the added advantage of the packaging never having to be produced at all. Since Baxter buys in bulk, intermediate packaging is done away with, thereby reducing both waste and cost.

Premixed drugs—Galaxy®   In 1985, Baxter introduced the next-generation plastic container for its frozen and nonfrozen premixed drugs. An olefin-based plastic bag, this container is lighter in weight than the previous bag and is less fragile and so required less packaging materials. Total reduction in waste is estimated at nearly 1 million pounds per year. In addition, since this product is a premixed drug, the hospital pharmacists do not have to mix the drug themselves, saving the waste of drug vial, carton, shipping carton, syringe, syringe blister package, and shipping carton, as well as swabs and labels.

Radiation sterilization. As new materials have become available, more and more Baxter facilities and products have converted to radiation sterilization as opposed to ethylene oxide sterilization. This results in a net decrease of air emissions from Baxter facilities. Some people have the mistaken impression that radiation sterilization is bad for the environment, but actually radiation enables significant improvement in air emissions from Baxter facilities as well as improved safety. Conversions of this type may involve analyzing many competing plastic materials candidates, testing thousands of product samples, and conducting detailed materials tests.

Disappearing corrugated box. The shipping carton used to ship various Baxter products has been reevaluated. Through a process known internally as "challengineering," various requirements of the package are systematically challenged and where possible reduced. A recent change in the way Baxter warehouses its containers allowed for a 3.5-million-lb reduction of fiber in I.V. solution bag corrugated shipping cartons. Together with previous reductions of 5 and 10-million-lbs when the I.V. Systems Division went from regular slotted container (RSC) style to bliss-style boxes and from standard corrugated board to high-performance materials, the amount of material has been reduced by 18.5 million lbs per year. (Figure 18.5 shows the five-year progress in total source reduction by this division.) The box has begun to be known as the "disappearing corrugated box" within the company.

Supplier environmental commitments. A significant effort to cooperate with Baxter suppliers and to encourage them in their environmental initiatives has been ongoing since 1991. In order to achieve "preferred-supplier status" a supplier must demonstrate a concrete environmental commitment. This is especially true of suppliers who utilize sol-

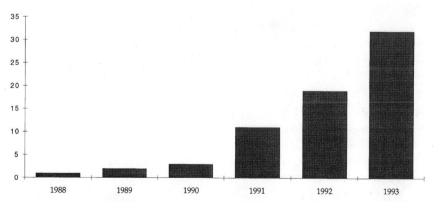

Figure 18.5 Cumulative material savings for I.V. Systems Division source reduction projects (millions of pounds).

vents, inks, and adhesives as part of their processes. Communication from Baxter to major suppliers has asked them to provide information on their commitment to the environment, action plans for improvement, and examples of results, with the goal of having all of Baxter's suppliers harmonizing with the company's corporate initiatives.

Disposables vs. reusables. The Convertors/Custom Sterile Division and the Hospitex Division supply both disposable and reusable materials to hospitals and other customers. Many conflicting studies have been done which support the environmental superiority of one system over the other. Baxter works in partnership with its customers to determine which product line is most appropriate in meeting clinical requirements as well as minimizing overall environmental impact.

Waste Management, Inc., partnership. Through the ACCESS™ program, Baxter's corporate customers have the opportunity to establish their own effective waste management initiatives. Under this program, Waste Management, Inc., will come into a hospital and conduct a waste audit and customer education campaign to help the hospital reduce it's total medical and nonmedical waste cost. Especially significant is the educational program designed to encourage hospital workers to segregate regulated infectious medical waste from nonmedical waste, as the cost for disposing of the regulated waste is often 10 to 20 times that of nonregulated.

One of those customers receiving free consulting services from Waste Management, the 288-bed Children's Memorial Medical Center in Chicago, saved over $500,000 in waste disposal costs over three years.

The EnVision™ Recycling Program

One of the above-mentioned programs deserves a more detailed analysis, providing insight into how environmental programs develop within large companies. This program is the EnVision™ recycling program, which began within the I.V. Systems Division.

Program inception

The EnVision™ recycling program, as described earlier, is an effort to create a closed-loop recycling system which would sell medical products into the hospital, collect the residual containers and packaging after the product is used, and utilize these materials to produce new (usually lower level) products which would then be sold back into the healthcare institution.

In March of 1991, the I.V. Systems Division president reviewed the group's annual report and was impressed with the significant amount of environmental activity taking place in its manufacturing facilities. This activity involved not only complying with national and local government regulations, but actions beyond those required by regulators. Included were efforts to reduce the use of supply materials and prevent landfill consumption by recycling.

However, the division president, Lester B. Knight, was adamant that a new focus was needed at the division level. He insisted that the focus be on customers who had similar problems with escalating landfill and incineration costs. "We need to help our customers with the success stories that our manufacturing plants have already learned. Our customers are facing increasing regulations just as we are. We need to make sure we are helping and not causing problems," Knight has said. This directive led to the formation of an environmental team at the division level, which was challenged with ensuring that the division's environmental programs were not just internally focused, but customer focused as well. Once this team was developed, it became clear that a special subgroup was needed to concentrate solely on developing a hospital recycling program. Thus, the Plastics Recycling Task Force was born.

Fortunately, a marketing manager, Lisa Petrilli, was available to take on the responsibility of leading this task force. In accepting this responsibility, Lisa quickly joined a team of Baxter professionals from a wide range of disciplines as they began to plan out their strategy. Among those involved in the initial formulation of the recycling task force were the following:

- Pat Bartholomew, division environmental director, responsible for overall division environmental compliance and leadership
- Mike Scharf, group manager of new-product development, responsible for the design and development of the product line and bringing technical and engineering skills to the team
- Steve Giovanetto, financial manager of new-product development, with specific skills in strategic planning and cost accounting
- Mike Cycyota, member of the I.V. Systems Environmental Affairs Team, with abilities to make contacts within the emerging recycling industry network, communicate his knowledge of environmental laws and regulations, and generally "make things happen"
- Michelle Moran from the divisional purchasing group, who could identify and help to qualify potential suppliers and users of recycled materials

The team was later expanded to include sales representatives and finance personnel.

Task force initiatives

The mission of the task force was to determine whether it was logistically and economically feasible for hospitals to recycle their plastic waste from medical products. To achieve this, the team first reviewed the types of waste generated from hospitals. In the United States, approximately 23 pounds of waste per bed per day are currently generated. The team examined product changes that had recently occurred, or could occur in the future, to minimize hospital waste. It was determined that product modifications that had been made in preceding years had several positive results. These results included not only improved labor efficiencies and process design improvements, but also a reduction in the amount of materials used and, ultimately, the ability to meet changing customer needs. The team discovered that, in 1991 alone, the savings had amounted to over a million pounds of material source reduced or eliminated, thus preventing the landfill or incineration of this material.

Next, the team examined the division's plastic and glass containers used to hold I.V. solutions and irrigating solutions as a potential source for material reductions. In the United States, Baxter contains these I.V. solutions in vinyl flexible bags, polypropylene plastic pour bottles, and glass containers. None of these containers are reused for the original purpose due to FDA regulations. What the task force realized, and had been hearing from its customers, was that a significant percentage of these containers never become biohazardous as defined in the United States. Further, if these containers could be gathered and sent to a reclaimer to be refabricated into other, non-clinical products, it was realized that the energy value of the petro-carbons could be salvaged and reused instead of discarded. Upon further review, these selected plastics were demonstrated to be ideally suited for reclamation.

The overpouches for the I.V. solution bags are plastic protective bags composed of HDPE. Overpouches had been redesigned about five years previously and were now being made of one homogeneous material. This allows for easy recyclability. Also, due to the manner in which these overpouches are used, there is rarely a pathogenic issue.

The flexible I.V. solution container sold by Baxter as the VIAFLEX® container is also made of a homogeneous material. This is a single layer of polyvinyl chloride, which was selected as the material of construction due to many of its characteristics. Since there is no need to bond layers of different materials together when manufacturing it, this container is ideally suited for recycling. The plastic pour bottle is also a homogeneous material and capable of being recycled.

The task of setting up a recycling protocol, creating an infrastructure to support the recycling of these three plastics, identifying potential reclaimers, and determining feasibility and logistics of wet and flexible regrinding was a huge challenge. The various members of the team contributed in a variety of different ways: The marketing manager chaired the task force and focused on hospital selection and customer requirements and needs. The new-product development manager sought out and located a reclaimer who was able to work through the technical issues on wet and flexible shredding and regrinding the plastic. The purchasing liaison was utilized to expedite suppliers required for the pilot program. The financial manager performed process flow analysis of the wastes as they currently were generated at the pilot program hospitals. He assessed the needs for the implementation logistics. The environmental engineers provided technical expertise for the programs and addressed the hospitals' waste regulations and recycle transport issues.

Once five hospitals were selected for implementation of the recycling pilot program, the team began to educate hospital senior management on the specifics of the program and the anticipated benefits they would receive. Effort was also given to training the employees who would be directly participating in the program, as well as housekeeping and building services employees, on the proper disposal procedures.

Recycled-product design

Once materials began to flow from the hospital to the reprocessor and accumulate as a separated, clean source of raw material, the most critical decision point of the program was encountered: the selection of products to be manufactured from the recycled plastics. The team was not satisfied with generating recycled and reprocessed materials, but was now turning the corner and attempting the close the loop in the recycling system by identifying products and markets. Four criteria were used to identify a product area for further development:

1. Look for an established, existing market.
2. Choose an item which will be forgiving of the imperfections inherent in recycled plastics.
3. Choose darker colors.
4. Choose a manufacturer's process which would be forgiving of the material's quality.

Several products are currently under development for sale into the hospital, but one has already joined the division product catalog, namely, sharps containers used for the safe disposal of used needles and other sharp objects.

Program benefits

Since the program's inception in 1991 several significant benefits have been realized:

1. The pilot program has proven that, if this program is adopted nationwide, 10 to 50 tons of plastic can be diverted from the waste stream per year for every hospital that participates in the program.

2. The existence of the EnVision™ recycling program is evidence to hospital employees that products usually thought of as not recyclable can, in fact, be recycled, and that solutions can be found to difficult environmental problems.

3. Hospitals can avoid, on average, 25 to 30 cents per pound in costs for waste that would have been incinerated. This is especially important in an age of health care restructuring and redeployment.

4. Hospitals can receive a significant amount of favorable public relations in their communities as a direct result of the program and can contribute to the environmental awareness needed within their locale.

5. Hospitals are able to strengthen their employee morale through participation in the program. Most employees who have provided feedback after the commencement of the recycling effort—including doctors, nurses, and anesthesiologists—feel that efforts like this are well worth their time in implementing. They express pride in their hospital for the willingness of their management to make such a visible commitment to the environment.

6. Perhaps one of the greatest areas of contribution is summed up by Claude Rounds, vice president of plant management at the Albany Medical Center, when he states that "Baxter's program helps us demonstrate to the state and to the public that these products can be safely handled, recycled, and reused in a way that protects the public. It's the perfect link between our product management and waste management efforts."

Important Achievements and Lessons Learned

There is little doubt about the benefits of the DFE efforts at Baxter. The business benefits have been measured in the millions of dollars, but perhaps greater still are the environmental and human benefits of these actions. Working on programs for the environment has given designers and engineers, marketing and sales people an additional opportunity to fulfill their calling of benefiting the healthcare community.

As Baxter Chairman and CEO Vern Loucks said to the INOVA Health Systems conference on "Our Environment: A Healthcare Commitment:"

> So there are good business reasons to invest in the environment. There are ethical reasons, as well. Environmental protection lies at the very core of our social duty. Our industry is dedicated to preserving and improving the health of mankind. We serve the sick and the injured, help bring new life, and comfort the old. Those we serve place their lives in our hands. Indeed, our industry has a special bond of public trust, a special connection to life that no other industry shares. But we cannot preserve that trust and uphold that bond if we ignore the environmental consequences of our actions. We cannot fight for life at one moment and destroy it the next. We cannot help those at our front door and harm them by the wastes we send out the back. Caring for health and caring for our environment are closely intertwined.

Publications and Trade Associations

Useful publications

Among useful publications in the field consulted by Baxter staff are the Office of Technology Assessment's *Green Products Design*; several EPA publications, including *Pollution Prevention Guidelines, Life Cycle Assessment: Inventory Guidelines and Principles,* and *Life Cycle Design Manual: Environmental Requirements and the Product System*; *Education for an Environmentally Sustainable Future,* Environmental Science and Technology ST 26(c) 1108; and *Design for Environment,* by D. Mackenzie, Rizzoli, 1991.

Contacts—Industry and trade associations

- Health Industry Manufacturer's Association (HIMA)
- Society of Plastics Engineers (SPE)
- Institute of Packaging Professionals (IoPP)

Coors' Ten Ways to Prevent Pollution by Design*

Sandra Woods

Vice President, Chief Environmental Officer
Coors Brewing Company
Golden, Colorado

"Truly exceptional environmental performance is a dependable path to profitability. Find pollution or waste, and you've found something you paid for but can't sell."

PETER COORS
CEO, Coors Brewing Company

Coors Brewing Company is known for taking its own path, and its environmental programs are no exception. Instead of following the standard corporate pattern—first control pollution at the back end, then reduce it up front—the company's approach has long been to explore ways to eliminate the creation of waste, with end-of-pipe controls and disposal applied as last resorts.

In the process, over the past generation Coors has learned something about how to develop a corporate environmental program with front-end strengths—cost effectiveness, high impact, innovation, continuous improvement—but without sacrificing back-end compliance.

---

*The author gratefully acknowledges the aid of California Futures and Global Futures, which prepared research materials for this chapter.

Now, after the spinning off of nonbrewery operations in 1992, a new generation of employees is exploring new ways to apply the lessons the company has learned, this time in an era when positive corporate environmental performance is expected in a competitive consumer marketplace.

Cultural Evolution: Moving from Front-End to Back-End

Like most corporations, Coors has spent hundreds of millions of dollars on environmental programs, including $23 million in 1992 alone. Much of that went to control air and water pollution after the fact, through the installation of end-of-the-pipeline equipment.

But Coors' real proficiency has been at the front end: identifying and reducing pollution and waste before it is generated, through source reduction and recycling. A thoroughgoing corporate aversion to waste, stretching back more than a generation, has helped cultivate a myriad of initiatives at Coors, all aimed at designing waste out of operations, either by reducing it, recycling it, or eradicating it altogether.

As a result, while Coors' compliance record is average, its pollution prevention history is very strong. The company has been strikingly effective at systematically driving waste out of its operations. The corporate culture at Coors, with its emphasis on technology, ingenuity, and self-reliance, has fostered a series of innovations that have turned one-time waste into profitable products, divisions, and spin-off companies going by a host of different names: The Zeagen spin-off uses Coors' spent grains to make feed, fertilizer, and nutrition products. Graphics Packaging produces a patented folding carton which provides superior graphic and barrier qualities that competitors cannot achieve without costly and environmentally unfriendly alternatives. Golden Aluminum buys back between 90 and 100% as many cans as Coors sells, and operates the most efficient aluminum can sheet plants in the world, capable of recycled content up to 95%. Coors Ceramics is aggressively pursuing new applications for ceramics that can replace metal and other conventional materials. It expects to be a significant player in several growing markets such as the fluid-handling, power distribution, and telecommunications markets. Golden Technologies developed Bio-T, a citrus-based solvent that substitutes for petroleum solvents. Figure 19.1 illustrates how the drive to prevent pollution has led to a diversification of Coors' ecosystem over the years.

The focus on waste reduction has not abated. Since 1987, solid waste volume from the Golden, Colorado, brewery has declined another 50%, largely through a program to turn wood wastes and organics

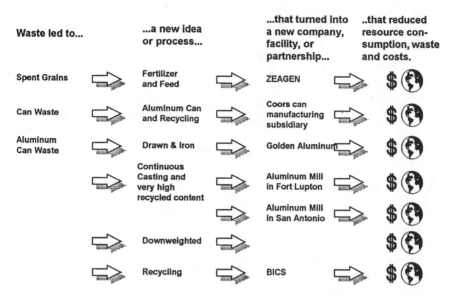

Figure 19.1 Coors' industrial ecology: How waste reductions trigger new products, companies, and profits.

into compost. In addition, Coors' emissions of chemicals under the federal Toxic Release Inventory (TRI) reporting requirements fell by 26% in 1992, continuing a trend that brought a 55% reduction from 1989 to 1992 (see Figs. 19.2 and 19.3).

But as successful as our front-end efforts have been, the back end has historically been a tougher challenge. While our compliance record is consistent with others in the brewing industry, we are striving for a record well ahead of the pack. The problem is that front-end accomplishments are a world apart from back-end ones, at least as much of the corporate community has approached them so far. They call for a different management approach, different tools, and much different expectations. Coors has had difficulty integrating into our operations the command-and-control approach implicit in regulatory compliance, because of our traditionally more decentralized management style.

Ecology transfer: Applying a front-end approach to back-end controls

Until a few years ago, Coors' source reduction and pollution prevention accomplishments resulted mainly from the ad hoc pursuit of resource efficiencies. But by 1988, the benefits of our successes, and the costs of our shortcomings, had grown significantly. To fully comply with a myriad of new environmental requirements at every level of

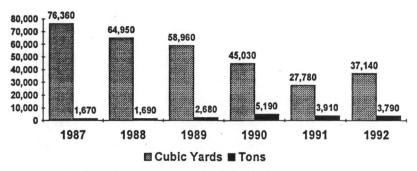

Figure 19.2   Nonhazardous waste sent to landfills (Golden facilities).

government, it became clear that a more systematic approach was needed.

In 1988, Coors set out to develop such an approach, one that would assure compliance while strengthening rather than sacrificing its pollution prevention aptitude. Today, Coors is implementing a company-wide system of principles, goals, objectives, and incentives designed to continuously improve both the environmental and economic performance of the company. Some of the tools we have begun to put to work:

- Corporate environmental principles that establish *zero-based resource budgeting*—i.e., principles that presume pollution and waste can be driven toward zero, at a net cost savings

- *Environmental audits* that isolate waste, identify options to eliminate it, and show the potential improved efficiency

- *Decentralized management systems* that give every division and every employee both the responsibility and the authority to reduce waste under their control

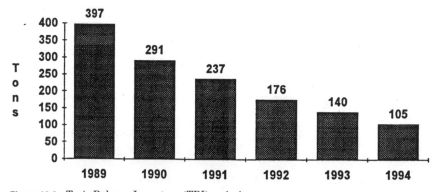

Figure 19.3   Toxic Release Inventory (TRI) emissions.

- Two *environmental accounting methods*—the Environmental Management System (EMS) and Coors Business Information System (CBIS)—that track the purchase, use, and waste of materials, and assign the costs of waste to the responsible profit centers, to motivate reductions

The change comes in concert with a thorough corporate restructuring which began at Coors in 1992, and which included the spin-off of its highly successful technology companies into a separate holding company, ACX Technologies. With a new president, downsized management, and more tightly defined corporate objectives, that left Coors Brewing Company free to focus on its core brewing operations, and on the positive role environmental programs might have in overall corporate performance.

In this context, we reviewed all our past environmental programs. We asked what worked, what hadn't worked, and what new strategic and management approaches were suggested by our experience. What we found has confirmed a long-time predisposition within Coors: that the most effective programs paid off at both bottom lines, the economic and environmental. The lesson was simple: When profitability is clearly tied to waste prevention in advance, we improve. When it's not, we risk performing below our expectations—and paying the price later.

Lessons from "The Tragedy of the Commons"

There is a natural analogy for the above insight, that is explicitly set forth in a classic essay on ecology. Corporate environmental managers, not to mention CEOs and governmental affairs directors, could gain much by applying the core lessons of this article. In this 1968 essay, "The Tragedy of the Commons," University of California ecologist Garrett Hardin described how, in an unmanaged pasture, herders would tend to overgraze the pasture past the point of sustainable yield. In his story, each new head of cattle added to the field reduced the take of all the others. Nevertheless, each individual herder gained more by expanding his herd than by reducing it, since he gained the marginal benefits, but the marginal costs were shared by all the other herders. The inevitable result of this pursuit of individual self-interest was the depletion of the field's capacity to support any cattle at all. "Freedom in a commons brings ruin to all," wrote Hardin.

Simply put, Hardin's lesson in economics is that, when someone impacts the environment, he or she needs to be held responsible for both the costs and the benefits. So long as the costs of waste are spread among everyone—"the commons"—but the benefits are focused on one, then waste will continue to increase.

Hardin's essay offers two methods for assuring responsibility. If "freedom in a commons brings ruin," then there are only two ways to prevent ruin: restrict freedom, or restrict the commons. The problem with some traditional environmental regulations, and the corporate programs they spawn, is that they often don't do either very well. They attempt to use Hardin's first approach, restricting one's freedom to pollute—to "overgraze the commons"—by drawing up rules of behavior that control pollution using end-of-the-tailpipe technologies. But often those regulations don't solve the problem. They just move it around, transferring pollution from one medium to another.

For example, under the Federal Clean Air Act and Clean Water Act, air pollution controls and industrial wastewater treatment help prevent wastes from going to air or water. But they do so in part by concentrating them into solid waste, ash, and sludge that require land disposal. Landfills, landfarms, and deep wells may slow the pace at which the materials reach air or water, but they don't always prevent it. In addition, water pollution controls often reach large industrial sources of emissions, but they cannot address the more than 50% of water pollution that comes from nonpoint sources, like agricultural runoff.

The EPA's own single-media offices, often created sequentially as individual environmental problems were identified, have resulted in regulations that until recently mostly discouraged a multimedia approach. The lesson for both business and government is this: In any organization, if the benefits of a wasteful practice accrue to one person or division, but the costs are externalized to another division, to the community, or to the future, then pollution will increase. It is only natural.

Elements of two federal laws suggest that perhaps government is beginning to heed that lesson. Section 313 of the Superfund Amendments and Reauthorization Act (SARA) required manufacturers to report emissions of 337 chemicals across media: air, water, and land. And the Pollution Prevention Act of 1990 established a Pollution Prevention Hierarchy that prioritized source reduction first, then recycling, treatment, and disposal.

Those two portions of federal law take Hardin's second approach to saving the commons. Rather than trying to merely control the polluter—i.e., eliminating freedom—they eliminate the commons, identifying by name and quantity exactly who is responsible for every pound of pollution emitted.

That creates legal, economic, and personal incentives for corporations to reduce their emissions to the environment. In addition, it suggests that the corporations create similar incentives internally. Rather than restricting freedom—imposing top-down controls within corporations—they encourage corporations to assign internal "ownership" for pollution that is later dispensed to the environment. In practical terms, that means isolating the point of creation of pollution and waste, assigning responsibility for it, and rewarding those responsible when they clean up the problem.

All forms of effective environmental management must take at least one of two approaches. They can mimic the old regulatory approach, imposing top-down restrictions that take away individual responsibility and opportunity. Or they can mimic the newer approach, empowering individuals to reduce waste by assigning them the responsibility, authority, and opportunity to do so. The most effective management approach would probably integrate the two, creating an overall framework of incentives within which people are free and incentivized to reduce pollution at every opportunity. The greatest challenge I face as the principal environmental officer at Coors is to reconcile and thereby take full advantage of these two distinctly different approaches.

We have just begun. What follows are ten ideas that have contributed to the process.

How to Incentivize Superior Environmental Performance: 10 Tips

Tip 1—Corporate philosophy: *Recognize that all pollution and waste is lost profit*

Not all corporate environmental philosophies are the same, nor should they be. In order to be most effectively implemented, a corporate environmental philosophy needs to reflect deeply held corporate values and practices. In the case of Coors, one of the enterprise's longstanding corporate beliefs forms an effective foundation for most of the company's environmental principles and programs.

When I first joined Coors, it became quickly obvious that this company wasted very little. It seemed every waste product, and every underutilized technology, was destined to become a new subsidiary. Chairman Bill Coors has written that "all pollution and all waste is lost profit." By using waste as a red flag for inefficiency and insufficient technology, Coors Brewing has put that idea to very effective use, from both an economic and an environmental perspective. This waste-reducing orientation is planted very deep within the Coors culture, even for the new generation now moving to the fore.

The power of an idea to substitute for raw materials has long been a part of this company's history. The development and introduction of the aluminum can reduced by half the tonnage of metal required to deliver the company's product. The development of drawn-and-iron technology cut its use of aluminum by another 50% per can. Finally, Coors' development of continuous-casting technology for can making eliminated an entire stage in the manufacturing process, and made it possible to use up to 95% recycled content in our cans. All of the reduced costs and enhanced profits from these innovations were produced not through the consumption of more materials, but through the "consumption" of better ideas—an abundant and renewable resource.

Today, through the pursuit of waste prevention strategies, Coors' core brewery has spawned a host of subsidiaries, spin-offs, and partnerships that often feed off of what we or others once threw away. For example:

- To capture the energy embedded in billions of Coors cans, Coors introduced the first aluminum cans in 1959, then opened the first network of buyback recycling centers.

- To drive markets for recyclable materials, Coors' Golden Aluminum spin-off buys back between 90 and 100% as many cans as Coors sells. As a result of technology developed by Golden Aluminum, Coors has the highest aluminum recycled content in the industry: over 70%. In addition, 34% of its glass bottles, up to 20% of its secondary packages, and as much as 94% of its corrugated has been made from recycled materials.

- To eliminate much of the company's wood waste—wooden pallets comprised half the waste at our brewery in 1991—Coors switched to more durable pallets. When they can no longer be used, they are combined with spent grains from the brewery to make a compost product. Overall, that cut the brewery's waste 30%.

- To make full use of its spent grains, Coors formed and later spun off an innovative company called ZeaGen, which uses the grains and other raw materials to manufacture everything from animal feed and fertilizer to food supplements and health foods.

- To replace petroleum-based solvents, Coors developed Bio-T, a citrus alternative, now marketed through another spin-off, Golden Technologies.

- To capture the full value of the highly resource efficient advanced ceramics we developed for brewing, Coors Ceramics was formed; now as a division of ACX Technologies, Coors Ceramics is developing super-lightweight, fuel-efficient engine parts, and ceramic filters for cleaning air and water.

Not every company will have the same underlying philosophy. But by discovering the specific beliefs and strengths of a corporation—in our case the ability to reduce, recycle, or divert pollution and waste—companies may be better able to mobilize more fully behind their environmental initiatives, and maximize their environmental performance.

Tip 2—Principles: *Formalize the waste reduction philosophy; establish a corporate principle to minimize and strive to eliminate pollution and waste*

It may seem unrealistic to establish "zero pollution" as a goal for any corporation. Yet the quality movement has popularized the notion that "zero defects" is a valuable objective, not because it will ever be 100% achieved, but because it can be continually approached.

It is a similar article of faith at Coors, supported to a great extent by the company's experience, that the potential for reducing waste and maximizing resource efficiency has hardly been tapped. Through new ideas and innovative technology, it is possible to continually drive waste toward zero. As Bill Coors has said, "A central purpose of any business that seeks profits should be to maximize efficiency, and thereby reduce, and ultimately eliminate, pollution and waste."

Consistent with this belief, the original environmental principles of the Adolph Coors Company state:

> We will minimize and strive to eliminate the creation of wastes and the release of pollutants.
>
> We will minimize and strive to eliminate environmental, health, and safety risks to our employees and the communities in which we operate.
>
> We will seek innovative technologies and use prudent selection, reuse, and/or recycling of materials to conserve resources and eliminate wastes.
>
> We will hold ourselves totally accountable by conducting our businesses as though everything we do will be scrutinized by the public. We will conduct periodic self-assessments of our progress.

As the only remaining subsidiary of Adolph Coors Company after the 1992 restructuring, Coors Brewing Company established its own environmental principles in 1992, drawn from the ACC principles, but providing more tangible, short-term specifics. These included:

Tip 3—Integrated goals: *Establish integrated goals, so that economic and environmental performance are positively correlated*

Just as a corporation's environmental principles need to reflect its philosophy, so its environmental programs need to serve its economic imperatives, and vice-versa. If a corporation's overall goals are established without an understanding of the importance of environmental programs to its overall success, then when times are tough the environment may be sacrificed.

To help assure that economic and environmental goals are pursued in a mutually supportive manner, Coors has established four principal corporate goals which serve the overall success of the corporation: to improve (1) service, (2) environmental health and safety, (3) quality, and (4) productivity. Each of these is continuously tracked to assess overall progress. These four corporate goals "cascade" through the company: they lead to the establishment of appropriate subgoals and objectives for every division, manager, and employee.

For example, within Environmental Health and Safety, we used the corporate goals to establish four subgoals: accountability, functional integration, risk reduction, and compliance. The number one subgoal, *accountability,* means designing incentives, disincentives, position descriptions, and performance appraisals which support the corporate and EH&S goals. *Functional integration* means integrating environmental concerns into all company operations. It is exemplified by Coors' cross-functional approach to environmental compliance, described below. *Risk reduction* can be achieved through pollution prevention activities—for example, source reduction, energy efficiency, or using the TRI listing and other sources as a guide to materials *not* to use. The final subgoal, *compliance,* requires that we conduct assessments and audits of our operations, and train all employees so they have the tools to meet their environmental expectations. Our objective is to measure, maintain, and continually improve compliance throughout the company.

Tip 4—Quantitative targets: Establish quantitative environmental targets, to provide achievable near-term goals

In addition to the integrated goals above, quantitative environmental performance targets provide close-range goals that help focus the activities of individual divisions, managers, and employees.

For example, Coors has long employed a three-pronged approach to reducing its packaging waste: downweighting, increasing recycled content, and increasing recyclability. The approach has proven highly cost effective. Recent improvements now save about $1.3 million each year. To further reduce packaging, Coors accepted the CONEG Challenge, issued by the Coalition of Northeastern Governors in 1992, which asks companies to reduce packaging by 50% overall by 2000 (see Fig. 19.4). To meet and exceed that medium-term goal, Coors established specific 1994 goals for reducing packaging waste. Those goals are shown in Fig. 19.5.

Activities 1992:			
Aluminum		25,886	Tons
Keg Boards		1,944	Tons
Claycoated Secondary Packaging		3,284	Tons
Recycled Content (Post Consumer)			
Glass	30%	106,100	Tons
Corrugated	60%	25,389	Tons
Aluminum	68%	69,615	Tons
Reuse			
Glass		84,318	Tons
Stainless Steel Kegs		71,799	Tons
Keg Boards		2,964	Tons
Pull Sheets*		7,351	Tons
*(Reprocessed pallet replacement)			
Recover Recycle			
Corrugated		4,797	Tons
Office Waste Paper		126	Tons
Plastic Film		300	Tons
Composting (scrap wood)		1,474	Tons

Figure 19.4   Coors recycling data, 1992.

Although quantitative goals can produce significant positive results, they should be utilized with care. The establishment of specific quantitative goals and objectives can have both positive and negative effects. On the one hand, they encourage progress in bite-size pieces. Since zero waste cannot be achieved in a single stroke, short-term quantitative objectives focus on and reward incremental progress. But if objectives are not established within a bold framework that anticipates continuous improvement *beyond* short-term goals, then breakthroughs that can dramatically reduce waste may be overlooked.

For example, in 1955, if our engineers had tried to set a reasonable goal for increasing the efficiency of the steel can, they might have settled on an annual downweighting of perhaps a percent or two. But would they have stretched their thinking beyond that? Or would they have overlooked the huge, 50%-plus weight reduction from developing and improving the aluminum can? Similarly today, if we are limited to seeking incremental improvements in, say, aluminum efficiency, perhaps we will overlook an outside-the-box opportunity that far exceeds our expectations.

Coors has a multi faceted plan to reduce municipal solid waste which includes package elimination, reuse, source reduction, recycling, improved recyclability, and composting. Specific goals for 1994 are:

Increase glass post consumer recycle content to over 35%.

Increase aluminum post consumer recycled content to 75%.

Increase corrugated post consumer recycled content to 90%.

Have a 20% post consumer recycle content for claycoated secondary packaging.

Have 15% post consumer recycled content for composite can packages.

Continue to compost scrap wood.

Source reduce all packaging where functionally feasible.

Expand internal paper, plastic, glass, and aluminum recycling programs.

Maintain 90%+ recycle content of point of sales material.

Figure 19.5   Coors 1994 recycling goals.

Setting short-term goals too low may lead to missed opportunities. Setting them too high may dampen enthusiasm and lead to failure. Establishing realistic short-term goals within a framework that drives toward absolute efficiency may foster both incremental gains and conceptual leaps.

Tip 5—Priorities: *Use the Pollution Prevention Hierarchy as a guide to prioritizing action*

Once overall goals have been established, how can people in corporations establish priorities to reach the goals? One way is to identify those that will have the greatest combined environmental and economic benefits. If environmental successes lead to increased profits, then the expenditure is easier to justify, and goals are easier to reach.

A tool that can help identify the options with the greatest environmental and economic payback is the Pollution Prevention Hierarchy, established for hazardous materials at the federal level in the Pollution Prevention Act. The Pollution Prevention Hierarchy contains four elements: source reduction, recycling, treatment, and disposal. By emphasizing source reduction first, the hierarchy tends to encourage activities which reduce both economic and environmental costs, by reducing the front-end use of materials that cost money, create safety hazards, and require environmental controls.

Conceptually, the hierarchy makes logical sense: reducing the use of materials should save money; reducing the need to throw them away should save even more. But to make the hierarchy more useful in identifying options for a specific facility, it may be useful to break it down to create a more complete range of subcategories. For example, the hierarchy (shown in Fig. 19.6) may be better at identifying options within Coors' brewery and container operations.

Finally, when it comes time to brainstorm specific options within each element of the hierarchy, a useful process may be to break each into a greater number of functional elements, as Fig. 19.7 illustrates. Categorizing types of source reduction options can help trigger more complete creative thinking, and identify options that might have been overlooked otherwise. The Pollution Prevention Hierarchy, both in its simple and more sophisticated forms, can provide corporations with a rough road map to the most affordable and effective waste reduction programs.

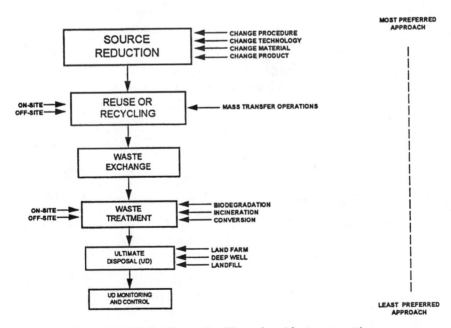

Figure 19.6 Expanded Pollution Prevention Hierarchy with program options.

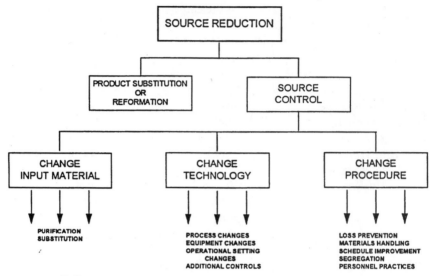

Figure 19.7   Pollution Prevention Hierarchy: source reduction options.

Tip 6—Environmental audits: *Audit and monitor your program and operations regularly*

Another tool for developing goals, priorities, and targets is an environmental audit. There are many types of environmental audits from which we have selected. These include:

- Compliance audits, to determine whether all appropriate environmental requirements are being met. For example, Coors conducted Phase I monitoring for lead and copper in 1992, as a part of its compliance with the Safe Drinking Water Act.

- Energy audits, which measure the amount of energy consumed in a process, product, or facility, and identify possible ways to save.

- Materials flow analysis, which tracks the flow of materials from point of entry to point of use and exit from an organization, to determine the uses it serves and the point at which it becomes waste. Beginning in 1993, Coors initiated the first stages of a continuous materials flow analysis through the EMS and CBIS systems described under "Tip 8."

- Life-cycle analysis, which attempts to measure the full environmental impacts of a product from cradle to grave. For example, life-cycle analyses of beverage containers, first conducted in the 1970s by the Midwest Research Group and others, have helped Coors to estimate how much energy, water, air pollution, water pollution, and even employment is associated with different types of beverage containers in different circumstances. Life-cycle analysis has its limits, but it can be useful for comparing the impacts of products in specific applications. It can also be useful in product design and innovation. For example, our knowledge of where the most energy use occurred in the life cycle of aluminum justified the development of the recyclable aluminum can.

In 1990, Coors formalized an environmental audit process, first implemented in 1991 and 1992, with comprehensive assessments of all Coors facilities carried out by independent outside consultants. Using the results of these audits, Coors first addressed any issues with potential to pose immediate threats to the environment or safety, then established programs to evaluate, prioritize, and resolve all other problems, and began developing systems to help prevent any recurrences.

At Coors, a primary objective of our environmental audits is to help reduce and eliminate accidental spills and releases. In 1992, Coors recorded 18 spills and releases that required reporting to the U.S. Environmental Protection Agency (EPA) or state regulators. None of the spills were dramatic or costly, but they represent a continuing barrier to improved environmental performance.

One limitation of audits: they do not substitute for aware and involved employees. Outside experts and reengineering professionals are never going to know the operational intricacies that one's own people know. Any company can hire auditors to periodically check on how it is performing. The real challenge is to hire and train technical people internally, and credit and reward them when they find ways to reduce waste. That will help enable the use of audits in a more profitable manner: to help move well beyond compliance, toward continuous improvements in overall efficiency. That way, audits can help tell not how badly a company is failing, but how much better it could succeed.

Another potential limitation of audits: they can unfortunately be used to unfairly penalize a company trying to do the right thing. An example is our experience with volatile organic compounds, when our self-audit led to a much criticized fine. The example is described below.

Why corporate lawyers don't always like audits: A case study. For any corporation that wants continuous improvement in its environmental performance, environmental audits are a must. But they can set a corporate attorney's nerves on edge. Here is an example. In September 1991, Coors launched the most comprehensive inventory of emissions from brewery operations ever conducted. We did so because we questioned the validity of EPA assumptions about the volume of volatile organic compounds (VOCs) emitted by breweries. We thought the EPA's estimates were *too low.*

By law, Coors could have simply used EPA's data to file its own estimate of VOC emissions, as every other brewer presumably did. Instead, we spent nearly $1 million to investigate every possible source of emissions from our brewery and related facilities in Golden, through extensive stack testing, computer modeling, and data analysis. We submitted thousands of pages of data to the Colorado Department of Health, concluding that breweries were significant sources of VOCs. Golden emitted 750 tons of VOCs per year, we determined. That amount, although less than 1% of the total in the Denver region, was not insignificant.

What reward did Coors receive for going "beyond compliance" and identifying a flaw in EPA data? The state initiated an enforcement action that diverted attention for a full year of negotiations, and imposed a $237,000 fine.

Tip 7—Overall management: *Decentralize power so that every employee is responsible for reducing pollution and waste*

To achieve continuous improvement in environmental health and safety, it is important to have continuous employee commitment. That is why decentralized management and cross-functional integration are so important. They help assure that environmental performance is not regarded as someone else's sideline, but as an integral part of the success of every element of the business.

Like many companies, Coors has had to evolve its system of environmental management, first to formalize its response to increasing environmental concerns in the 1970s, and then to move beyond control-directed activities in the 1980s. In the early 1970s, when Coors was a private company focused primarily on brewing, environmental affairs were managed by an eight-member environmental control committee. By 1979, a new centralized department, Regulatory Affairs, was created to manage compliance and permitting issues. But as environmental regulations became more pervasive and complicated, having the regulatory experts removed from the operations made it impossible to identify and address compliance challenges.

To accommodate those trends, in 1988 Coors decentralized its environmental management organization, implementing a more strategic, focused, grassroots system. Under that system, each unit of the company, and ultimately each employee, is held accountable for adhering to the company's environmental principles (see under "Tip 2"). To oversee the system, a new position was created, Principal Environmental Officer, to which I was appointed. In addition, an Executive Environmental Committee (EEC) was established, comprised of top executives from each operating area and chaired by the principal environmental officer.

Decentralizing environmental management meant pushing compliance reporting and management activities out to the grassroots level of the company, where the greatest knowledge of our actual procedures and performance resides. We wanted the people closest to operations to be watching out for environmental compliance and opportunities. Therefore, more than 50 environmental staff who work within various Coors divisions were named to watchdog, manage, and report on our environmental activities. Twice each month, Coors' environmental managers meet together as the Environmental Working Group. A total of about 90 people participate; 20 are full-time environmental coordinators, 13 are full-time health and safety people, and 40 or 50 others have part-time EH&S responsibilities. Under the facilitative leadership of Jerry Fasso, Environmental Control Director, the EEC provides an interdisciplinary, cross-functional opportunity to review compliance activities, explore innovative solutions, recognize accomplishments, and share new technologies that reinforce and improve corporate environmental performance.

The rule at EEC meetings is that any idea is okay. The only bad idea is an unstated one. We hear some of the craziest notions, and some of the most brilliant, and often they are the same.

Fasso's team is organized around compliance. But it is not hierarchical. Fasso does not dictate the means by which team members achieve compliance. Instead, team members retain their positions within the operations-driven sectors of the company, but are individually responsible for compliance as one part of their operations-related duties. None has top-down authority to tell the others what to do. Fasso brings together the team to share ideas, brainstorm options, and keep track of the overall environmental performance of the company.

In many cases, EEC serves as a catalyst. Our main philosophy is to bring together a diverse array of people who can brainstorm operations, implement change, demonstrate the potential for improvement and cost savings, and provide recognition and rewards. The emphasis on diversity and creativity allows the status quo to challenge itself in a gentle manner.

By making every division and every employee responsible for the environmental impacts of their operations, managers and employees realize they will have accountability and an opportunity for reward. When responsibilities are shared, accountability is uncertain. But when you are one-deep, you know you are responsible.

Holding people accountable for environmental performance may sound imposing at first. Overall, however, it can be positive and motivating, so long as the emphasis is on clearly defined responsibility, authority, effective training, and rewards. It is important not to assign accountability to an employee without also empowering him or her to take action. That requires training. Since 1989, more than 1000 Coors employees have completed elective training in environmental management; the company's objective is to have baseline environmental training in place for every employee.

With compliance assumed through this process, the balance of the EHS group is free to focus on moving the company beyond compliance. Within EH&S, for example, we are able to focus on legislative and regulatory advocacy; developing integrated EH&S processes, systems, and programs; and targeted outreach in environmental areas of highest priority to the company.

Tip 8—Environmental accounting: *Assign the costs of pollution and waste to the divisions responsible, to create incentives for continual reductions*

Within a decentralized management structure, enforcing environmental compliance can be difficult, unless incentives and communications processes are well developed. In order to retain the advantages of decentralization with no sacrifice in terms of compliance, it is important to assure that every manager and every employee has a positive incentive to meet and exceed environmental regulatory standards.

One way that Coors is seeking to assure this is through the implementation of better environmental accounting. To further document chemical use and waste generation, Coors is implementing an Environmental Management System (EMS) that will track chemicals and raw materials purchased, used, or discarded anywhere in the company. One application of the system is to enable the company to drive down waste so significantly by 1995 that we achieve small-quantity generator status, the status assigned to facilities that produce minimal volumes of hazardous waste.

The five-year-old software development project provides internal information needed to reduce waste, using a hazardous material index to deliver information on chemical toxicity, risk, regulating status, and inventories, so that every manager and employee benefits from the available information. The system will also help enable automated or semi-automated compliance with a complicated maze of state and federal laws that require manufacturers to report toxic materials they use or discard. The company's Material Safety Data

Sheets (MSDS) and Toxic Release Inventory (TRI), for example, will both be driven by the system, with the data available on-line to any employee.

For the longer term, EMS will share information with a new corporate management accounting and information process, the Coors Business Information System (CBIS). CBIS is an integrated business system including inventory systems, based on accurate material tracking: assuring that the quantity of materials purchased by the company matches the quantity used, recycled, or disposed, to assure there is no waste along the way.

Coors expects EMS and CBIS to pay off at both bottom lines, economic and environmental. Past source reduction programs often produced returns on investment in the 230% range, a record which suggests CBIS may make an effective tool to enhance productivity. In fact, the greatest cost-cutting and environmental feature of CBIS may not be lower disposal costs, but more efficient operations overall. The system suggests processes that are superfluous and wasteful, allowing Coors to transfer people and capital to more productive operations.

Tip 9—Stakeholder communication: *Speak with environmental stakeholders, to share ideas and clarify expectations*

Perhaps as important as accounting for environmental successes internally is gaining external input. To determine how well we might be adhering to the environmental mandates imposed by law, as well as the expectations of the groups that passed many of those laws, Coors has carried out a unique environmental stakeholder survey. Both internal and external stakeholders were represented in this survey. Although there was, as expected, a wide diversity of opinions, stakeholders generally agreed that corporations must play a positive role in protecting the environment, and that one of their first priorities is compliance.

In late 1992, to add greater depth to the stakeholder process, Coors began the first of a series of face-to-face meetings with leaders in the environmental community and a wide array of all Coors stakeholders. Our primary purpose was to listen. We heard many different ideas. We clarified objectives and expectations, and laid the groundwork for potential future partnerships. But perhaps the most important benefit was a recurring theme of the meetings: the need for more communication between Coors and our stakeholder communities.

To begin to meet a part of that need, Coors initiated a series of letters and mailings to environmental leaders, academics, and activists throughout the United States. Our objective was to approximate on a larger scale the personal interplay that our one-on-one meetings produced. The first of those letters was mailed in November 1993. It included a cover letter from CEO Peter Coors, a copy of our 1992 Environmental Progress Report, and a comment form to encourage replies. Follow-up mailers are to address recycling, water, pollution prevention, and any other topics which prove of mutual interest with our environmental stakeholders.

Coors looks upon the stakeholder process as a continuing commitment. It is not a one-shot project. Our objective is that it result in a continuing dialogue. To help that happen, we are considering the development of an informal advisory group—an ad hoc committee of outside experts that allows us to quickly tap a wide range of environmental expertise when issues arise.

We want to be networking with people in the environmental movement and business to find the best environmental practices. We don't want to be benchmarking just to come in third.

Tip 10—Indicators: *Establish indicators of corporate environmental stewardship, to show how well the corporation is designing out pollution*

The environmental stakeholder process helps Coors track its success from the vantage point of our stakeholders. Another tool is what might be called an *indicator of corporate environmental sustainability.* Such an indicator shows whether a corporation is becoming more or less efficient in its use of resources. As resource efficiency rises, so does the degree to which the corporation is using resources in a sustainable fashion.

One way ecologists assess sustainability is to measure whether resources are being utilized in a way that maintains sustainable yield. That is, are they being consumed at a rate equal to or less than their replacement rate. For a company, or an economy, the equivalent question is as follows: "Is the efficiency with which we are using resources increasing faster than the resources are being depleted?" So long as efficiency increases faster, then the effective supply of the resource is sustained. Unfortunately, recent studies by organizations such as California Futures indicate that most resources are still being consumed at nonsustainable rates.

To assess whether Coors is utilizing resources in a sustainable manner, we have begun to measure the materials and energy efficiency of our operations. Interestingly enough, measures of corporate sustainability are exactly the same as measures of corporate productivity. In other words, as our environmental performance improves, so does our potential profitability.

Figures 19.8, 19.9, and 19.10 represent our first indicators of Coors' corporate sustainability. They show that at the Golden brewery, we have successfully improved our energy and materials efficiency, and reduced our wastes. On a per unit basis, solid waste volume declined

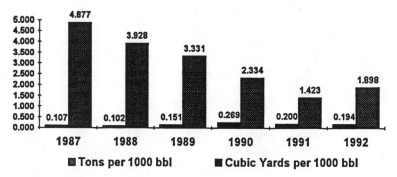

Figure 19.8   Solid waste index.

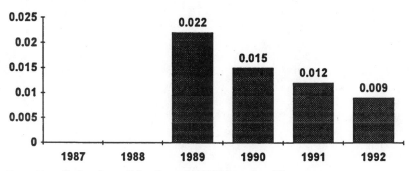

Figure 19.9   Toxic release index (tons per 1000 barrels sold).

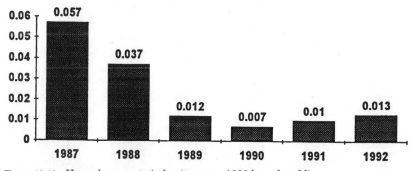

Figure 19.10   Hazardous waste index (tons per 1000 barrels sold).

51%, TRI wastes more than 59%, and total hazardous wastes 77%, between 1987 and 1992.

Corporate Cultural Evolution: From Prevention to Control to Both

One of the major challenges at Coors Brewing has been to somehow reconcile two very different corporate cultures: the one that constrains people to adhere to strict regulatory standards to assure against back-end pollution, and the one that frees them to be creative and resourceful in developing efficiencies that reduce waste before it starts. At Coors Brewing, we have begun to do so, learning from past generations whose emphasis on decentralization, innovation, thrift, efficiency, and personal responsibility continuously drove down waste through source reduction, recycling, and pollution prevention. Now, as a new generation takes up position at the new Coors Brewing Company, the lessons learned from past successes and shortcomings can be utilized to further improve our environmental performance, not just by controlling pollution and waste, but by preventing it in the first place.

20

Environmental Practice at WMX Technologies

WMX

Leah V. Haygood

Director, Environmental Planning and Programs
WMX Technologies, Inc.
Washington, D.C.

Michael Gershowitz

Research Analyst
WMX Technologies, Inc.
Washington, D.C.

Introduction

WMX Technologies, Inc. (WMX) is a global environmental services company providing comprehensive solid and hazardous waste management programs, energy recovery, and environmental technologies and engineering resources. The company provides environmental services through more than 900 operating divisions throughout North America and in a growing number of countries overseas. WMX and the environmental services industry in general are in a unique position among companies seeking to integrate environmental concerns into their core business. In a sense, the environment *is* our business. Public concern for the environment created the market for environmental services and fueled its explosive growth in the 1970s and 1980s. In the 1990s, environmental service companies must continue to think strategically about how public policy, public opinion, and, increasingly, the environmental agendas of other companies offer opportunities for new environmental services or make existing ones obsolete. In addition, the laws and regulations that created the environmental services industry create narrow confines in which suppliers of services must work. To stray outside is to risk the business. As a result, effective environmental management is as important as effective strategic analysis and planning.

This chapter discusses how public opinion and public policy have created opportunities for environmental service companies and how the company has responded to them, how several programs at WMX have been the drivers for integration of environmental concerns into day-to-day operations, and how WMX companies have approached specific design for environment projects.

Environmental Policy and Principles

In 1990, WMX—then Waste Management, Inc. (WMI)—adopted a comprehensive set of 14 environmental principles. The preamble to the Environmental Policy and Principles states:

> WMX Technologies, Inc. is committed to protecting and enhancing the environment and to updating its practices in light of advances in technology and new understanding in health and environmental science.
>
> Prevention of pollution and enhancement of the environment are the fundamental premises of the Company's business. We believe that all corporations have a responsibility to conduct their business as responsible stewards of the environment and to seek profits only through activities that leave the Earth healthy and safe. We believe that the Company has a responsibility not to compromise the ability of future generations to sustain their needs.
>
> The principles of this policy are applicable to the Company throughout the world. The Company will take demonstrable actions in a continuing basis in furtherance of the principles." (See Fig. 20.1.)

The company emerged as a public entity in 1971 to manage municipal solid waste—trash—which, at the time, was a primary environmental concern. As the scope of environmental concerns and issues has expanded over the last two decades, so has the range of services offered by WMX. The WMX environmental policy and its 14 principles apply to all aspects of the company's business, but they should not be considered exclusive to an environmental services company. They address the basic elements of conducting business—any business—in a manner beneficial to the environment.

The 14 principles provide clear direction on areas for focus in fully integrating environmental principles into all aspects of this company's operations. Because the principles represent WMX's commitment

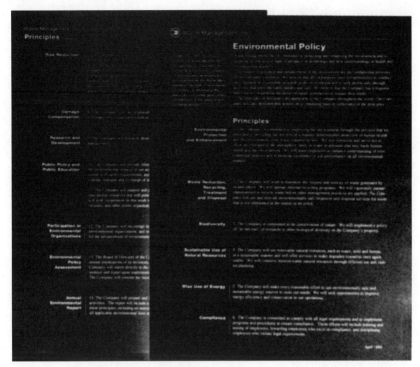

Figure 20.1 WMX Environmental Policy.

to this process of integration and offer specific insight into how environmentalism has been entwined with how we conduct business, we include them here:

1. *Environmental protection and enhancement.* The Company is committed to improving the environment through the services that we offer and to providing our services in a manner demonstrably protective of human health and the environment, even if not required by the law. We will minimize and strive not to allow any release to the atmosphere, land, or water in amounts that may harm human health and the environment. We will train employees to enhance understanding of environmental policies and to promote excellence in job performance on all environmental matters.

2. *Waste reduction, recycling, treatment and disposal.* The Company will work to minimize the volume and toxicity of waste generated by us and others. We will operate internal recycling programs. We will vigorously pursue opportunities to recycle waste before other management practices are applied. The Company will use and provide environmentally safe treatment and disposal services for waste that is not eliminated at the source or recycled.

3. *Biodiversity.* The Company is committed to the conservation of nature. We will implement a policy of "no net loss" of wetlands or other biological diversity on company properties.

4. *Sustainable use of natural resources.* The Company will use renewable natural resources, such as water, soils and forests, in a sustainable manner and will offer services to make degraded resources once again usable. We will conserve nonrenewable natural resources through efficient use and careful planning.

5. *Wise use of energy.* The Company will make every reasonable effort to use environmentally safe and sustainable energy sources to meet our needs. We will seek opportunities to improve energy efficiency and conservation in our operations.

6. *Compliance.* The Company is committed to comply with all legal requirements and to implement programs and procedures to ensure compliance. These efforts will include training and testing of employees, rewarding employees who excel in compliance, and disciplining employees who violate legal requirements.

7. *Risk reduction.* The Company will operate in a manner designed to minimize environmental, health, or safety hazards. We will minimize risk and protect our employees and others in the vicinity of our operations by employing safe technologies and operating procedures and by being prepared for emergencies. The Company will make available to our employees and to the public, information related to any of our operations that we believe cause environmental harm or pose health or safety hazards. The Company will encourage employees to report any condition that creates a danger to the environment or poses health or safety hazards, and will provide confidential means for them to do so.

8. *Damage compensation.* The Company will take responsibility for any harm we cause to the environment and will make every reasonable effort to remedy the damage caused to people or ecosystems.

9. *Research and development.* The Company will research, develop and implement technologies for integrated waste management.

10. *Public education.* The Company will provide information to and will assist the public in understanding the environmental impacts of our activities. We will conduct public tours of facilities, consistent with safety requirements, and will work with communities near our facilities to encourage dialogue and exchange of information on facility activities.

11. *Public policy.* The Company will support and participate in development of public policy and in educational initiatives that will protect human health and the environment. We will seek cooperation on this work with government, environmental groups, schools, universities, and other public organizations.

12. *Participation in environmental organizations.* The Company will encourage its employees to participate in and to support the work of environmental organizations, and we will provide support to en-

vironmental organizations for the advancement of environmental protection.

13. *Environmental policy assessment.* The Board of Directors of the Company will evaluate and will address the environmental implications of its decisions. The Executive Environmental Committee of the Company will report directly to the Chief Executive Officer of the Company and will monitor and report upon implementation of this policy and other environmental matters. The Company will commit the resources needed to implement these principles.

14. *Annual environmental report.* The Company will prepare and make public an annual report on its environmental activities. The report will include a self-evaluation of the Company's implementation of these principles, including an assessment of the Company's performance in complying with all applicable environmental laws and regulations throughout its worldwide operations.

Development of the Waste Management Industry and WMX

To best understand the role of environmental concerns in shaping WMX, it is helpful to examine the background and development of both the waste management industry and WMX specifically. Particularly instructive is an analysis of environmentalism in two areas: public perception and public policy.

Public perception

While there is no single perfect indicator of public perception, opinion polls provide a way to identify issues that have been seen as important and to trace the shifting focus of environmental concerns. A very telling pair of polls illuminates the emergence of environmentalism as a significant public issue in the late 1960s. A 1965 Gallup poll asked participants to name three categories which should get the most attention from government.[1] Only 17% of the respondents said "reducing pollution of air and water."[2] Five years later, after the first Earth Day, 53% of those polled selected pollution control as a top governmental priority.[3] Polls conducted since 1970 have continued to demonstrate a growing concern for the environment. A 1989 poll indicated that 90% of Americans rated stronger action by the government to protect the environment as a top priority.[4]

Public policy

Governmental actions—laws, regulation, and voluntary programs— like public perception, also provide an important touchstone in viewing the progress and development of the environmental services industry. The nation's first solid waste management law, the Solid Waste Disposal Act, was signed into existence in 1965. The word "environment" does not appear at all in its text, nor was there a federal agency specifically responsible for the environment at the time of its passage.* Treating solid waste disposal as little more than a logistical matter, it authorized the Department of Health, Education, and Welfare (HEW) and the Department of the Interior to provide grants to develop waste management practices. Several years still lay ahead before issues of disposal would become a lightning rod for environmental activity and environmentalism would become a significant public and political issue.

A good example of the canon of environmental legislation that dominated the 1970s and 1980s is the Resource Conservation and Recovery Act (RCRA). The name of the law indicates the growing interest in wastes as a resource. First signed into law in 1976 and reauthorized several times since, RCRA represents the traditional "stick" approach to federal environmental legislation. Relying on penalties to punish noncompliance, and with a strict regimen of standards and regulations, RCRA outlined what behavior and standards were permissible for business and individuals dealing with solid and hazardous waste. At a time when the waste management industry was beginning to boom and the country was demanding that more attention be paid to pollution in general, establishing a basic set of rules, protective of the environment, under which to operate was the most logical and, perhaps, the most efficient course to follow. As the range of environmental concerns has expanded, however, approaches to environmental protection have necessarily begun a shift to a "carrot"-oriented approach to increase pollution prevention and spur innovation in environmental technologies. These methods include disclosure of environmental information such as toxic releases; market-based incentives, including the sulfur dioxide emission cap under the Clean Air Act (CAA) Amendments of 1990; and voluntary programs such as Green Lights.

As an example of the most recent policy approach, consider this statement from the overview of the Climate Change Action Plan (CCAP) presented by President Bill Clinton and Vice-President Al Gore in October, 1993: "This plan harnesses economic forces to meet the challenges posed by the threat of global warming. It calls for limited, and focused, government action and innovative public/private

---

*Prior to the creation of the U.S. Environmental Protection Agency (EPA), environmental concerns were dealt with secondarily in departments such as Agriculture, HEW, and Interior. The EPA was not created until 1970, when Congress approved President Nixon's Reorganization Plan No. 3 of 1970.

partnerships. It relies on the ingenuity, creativity, and sense of responsibility of the American people." Instead of trying to regulate all of the diverse activities of industry, the CCAP attempts to encourage innovation in order to find the solutions to environmental problems.

The business

It is more than coincidence that WMX Technologies' evolution has paralleled public opinion and public policy. As the 1970s began, an industry that had once been classified as scavengers and haulers, mainly responsible for getting waste out of the way, began to assume responsibility for more than just hauling waste. The National Solid Wastes Management Association (NSWMA) was formed over the same period of time that public opinion shifted to identify pollution control as a national priority and the government realized the necessity of designating a specific agency to deal with environmental issues. Names *are* important for companies and groups, and names like Waste Management and the industry's NSWMA signaled the need not only to haul and dump waste, but also to *manage* it, which included added precautions to minimize the impact of waste in the environment and to prevent pollution. As public perception shifted and environmentalism became more independently rooted in government, the function and responsibilities of the industry became "greener" as well. In Waste Management's first annual report as a public company, the environment played an important role. The company's founders believed that the environmental movement of the 1960s provided the impetus to warrant the development of the modern waste management company. They also anticipated that the environment would be the engine for the company's growth.

The company indeed grew. From 1970 to 1994, WMX grew from hundreds of employees working primarily in the Midwest and Florida to more than 70,000 offering services in 18 countries. The company's operations have expanded from hauling waste to include services ranging from waste reduction and recycling to environmental engineering and water and wastewater treatment. When, in the late 1960s and early 1970s, environmental and governmental conceptions of waste management focused on finding safe places to store society's waste, the company aimed to be the foremost provider of safe, efficient disposal services. As environmental concerns broadened, WMX expanded its operations to include a diverse range of services which would manage, among other things, hazardous and low-level radioactive waste. The focus of environmentalism has continued to shift and expand. As the public and government have called for increased recycling, pollution prevention, and design processes that result in less and less waste, WMX has become the nation's largest provider of recycling services and developed partnerships in the public and private sectors to help reduce the amount of waste we, as a society, produce.

The environment as a strategic issue

The traditional influence of the environment on business is represented in the potential of regulations to create business. While stringent regulations hammer nails into the coffins of companies which cannot comply, they drive business to those which can.

Perhaps the best example representing regulatory influence on business is seen in the hazardous waste provisions of RCRA. RCRA was nothing less than a regulatory catalyst which helped transform the waste management industry from one of nominal governmental oversight to one of the most highly regulated in existence. Prior to RCRA, there was no federal legislation prohibiting the operation of open dumps. Subtitle D of the legislation provided a regulatory focus on protecting ground and surface water and air quality in the disposal of nonhazardous solid wastes. Subtitle C of RCRA directed the EPA to develop standards for the siting, design, construction, operation, and closure of hazardous waste facilities. Subtitle C also defined what a hazardous waste was and provided criteria for identifying hazardous wastes in the future.

Responding to the opportunity, WMI invested hundreds of millions of dollars in acquiring hazardous waste facilities which would meet the future regulatory requirements. The company was betting on reasonably swift action by the EPA in producing final permitting regulations which would have the teeth necessary to punish noncompliant operators. Companies which had operated in ignorance of environmental protection, and which did not have the capital necessary to upgrade their facilities and operations, were simply not in a position to make the transition to the post-RCRA world. Waste Management, on the other hand, thrived as investments in permittable facilities and safe disposal methods, protective of human health and the environment, paid off. By the time the regulations took effect, the company was the sole provider of hazardous waste services that could claim a nationwide network of facilities.

In the late 1980s, public enthusiasm for recycling inspired local and state programs to increase collection and processing of materials for recycling. WMI judged the public commitment to recycling to be lasting and began offering recycling services. Its recycling customers now number more than 6.5 million (see Fig. 20.2).

The effect of regulation on today's environmental services industry is still significant, but regulatory stimuli are necessarily limited in

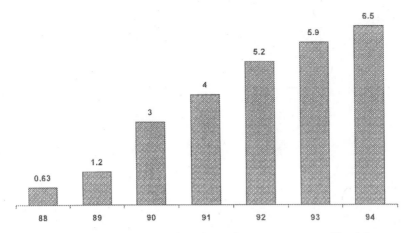

Figure 20.2   North America: Number of recycling customers—residential, commercial, and industrial.

their scope and duration. Michael Porter, a professor at the Harvard Business School, points out that companies respond to environmental regulation dynamically through innovation. Companies innovate to minimize the cost of compliance (for example, by reducing wastes) and in some cases are able to more than offset the costs of compliance (for example, by changing products or processes to eliminate waste and increase productivity).[5] While RCRA provides for safe handling and disposal of waste, voluntary initiatives and competitive pressures are helping generators produce less of it in the first place. WMX is responding to the call for environmental innovation within industry by seeking out and developing partnerships with other companies in an effort to help them meet internal corporate goals which provide environmental benefits outside the scope of the existing regulatory scheme. To support its recycling services, for example, in 1990 WMI formed two partnerships to help assure stable markets for materials recovered from municipal solid waste. The Container Recycling Alliance, a partnership with American National Can, now operates three glass-processing plants, and markets steel and aluminum cans. Paper Recycling International, a partnership with Stone Container, marketed nearly 4 million tons of paper in 1994 (see Fig. 20.3).

Cemtech, a limited partnership between CWM and Holnam Cement, was developed in an effort to market waste products as fuel substitutes to cement kilns and other major industrial energy users. Waste reduction goals of the paper industry have provided an opportunity for Cemtech. While paper is a commonly recycled material, the de-inking process typically results in about twice as many pounds of

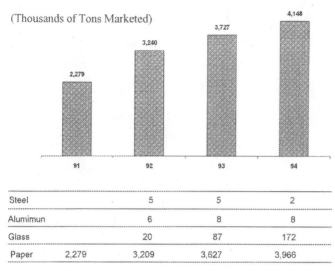

(Thousands of Tons Marketed)

	91	92	93	94
Steel		5	5	2
Alumimun		6	8	8
Glass		20	87	172
Paper	2,279	3,209	3,627	3,966

Figure 20.3 WMI recycling marketing partnerships.

solid waste per ton of product as the virgin production process. The wastewater treatment sludge generated by paper mills presents an interesting dilemma according to Amy Schaffer, director of industrial waste programs at the American Forest and Paper Association. "We are recycling more recovered paper because it is the right thing to do: yet, the more we recycle the more [sludge] we generate."[6] Cemtech produces fuel pellets using new technology that can handle materials ranging from paper mill sludge to wet-manufacturing rejects and non-marketable coated and treated wastepapers.

Cemtech's pelletization process also addresses a number of other environmental concerns. Sam Garre III, president of Cemtech Fiber Fuels Group, points out the benefits of the process: "It removes nonrecyclable paper and plastics from solid waste landfills; it recovers the resource value of sludges in an environmentally sound way; and it provides a renewable fuel product that, when used to augment coal, burns cleaner."[7]

WMX companies have also developed waste reduction services. Since 1990, WMX companies have conducted more than 500 waste reduction studies for businesses and institutions ranging from hospitals to automobile manufacturers (see Fig. 20.4). In addition to offering waste reduction services in the United States, WMX has carried out studies in Australia, New Zealand, Argentina, Germany, Italy, and the United Kingdom. Waste audits provide both economic and environmental benefits for the company's customers. The studies

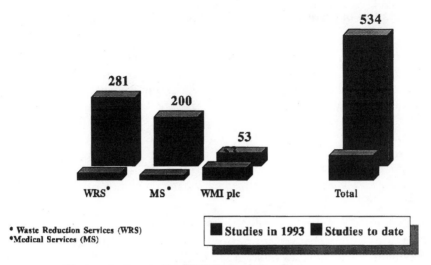

Figure 20.4   Waste reduction studies, WMX Technologies, Inc.

have identified practical recommendations for reducing waste directed to landfills by 10 to more than 80% and have identified opportunities to save millions of dollars.

WMX created its Medical Services (MS) in order to address the
unique environmental needs of hospitals. Hospitals generate about 23
pounds of waste per inpatient bed per day—compared to 4.3 pounds
per person per day for municipal solid waste. Hospital wastes include
infectious, radioactive, and hazardous waste as well as ordinary trash
and recyclable materials. In partnership with Baxter Healthcare
Corporation, WMX has helped more than 200 hospitals reduce and
better manage their wastes (see also Chap. 18). The partnership has
enabled hospitals to minimize waste, improve safety, and reduce
costs.

WMX's partnership projects embody several aspects of the growing
potential of the environment to affect business. First, because of environmental awareness and the need of companies to meet environmental goals that typically were not established a decade ago, new
avenues are opened and opportunities presented for business partnerships. Cemtech, for example, exists primarily because other companies are interested in finding beneficial uses for their waste. Second,
innovation and new technologies are encouraged as industry addresses the broadening range of corporate environmental goals. Finally,
new partnerships and technologies lead to results and environmental
gains that might not have occurred when the environment's impact
on business was limited to regulation.

Integration of Environmental Principles

Integrating an ambitious environmental policy into all facets of a business is challenging, even for a company whose core business is environmental. For WMX, as for many businesses, functions such as environmental compliance management and legislative and regulatory analysis have not always meshed with strategic planning and operations management. Several programs—the WMX quality program, preparation of its annual environmental reports, and third-party review of its environmental management systems—have been the major drivers of integration at WMX. Compensation and bonus reviews and a "measurement project" have been among the vehicles.

Total-quality environmental management

WMX first embarked on a quality management program, called the Expanded Management System (EMS), in the early 1990s. CWM has been the laboratory within the WMX family of companies for total quality environmental management (TQEM) approaches, demonstrating the use of tools such as surveying, benchmarking, setting goals, and measuring.

EMS addresses four "pillars"—customers, environment, people, and shareholders. CWM quickly identified environmental compliance as a survival issue for the company. Despite sophisticated programs for environmental management and compliance, including a well-established corporate environmental audit program, CWM's first survey of all of its employees revealed a lower than expected rating of the company's commitment to environmental protection and compliance. Though disturbing, the finding illustrated the value of the survey as a quality tool. Top management had placed considerable emphasis on environmental compliance, but employees sent the message that the importance of the company's environmental principles was not yet fully integrated into day-to-day operations and consciousness. CWM set an objective of being recognized as an environmentally excellent company, with corresponding goals to reduce compliance incidents and improve survey results on environmental commitment. Among the programs developed to meet these goals were:

Environmental criteria and award program. Drawing upon the model of the Global Environmental Management Initiative's Environmental Self-Assessment Program, CWM broke the WMX Policy and Principles into 25 elements and each element into levels of achievement relevant to CWM facilities. "Basic achievement" requires compliance with legal requirements. Higher ratings of "satisfactory" and "excellent" require efforts that go beyond current regulatory requirements. The elements are weighted according to their importance and each level of achievement is assigned a numerical score, yielding a score for the facility.

CWM has asked each facility to rate itself. The ratings are used as the basis for the CWM President's Award for Environmental Achievement. The first awards were announced in April of 1994. The program allows each facility to track its own progress over time. It also allows management to track progress for the company as a whole and compare different facilities.

Environmental excellence councils and process improvement teams. Another important element of CWM's TQEM approach is the establishment of an Environmental Excellence Council at each of its facilities. The councils involve representatives of all affected employees—not just environmental managers—in identifying and addressing environmental issues that need attention and developing programs for recognizing employee efforts in environmental protection.

For example, CWM's Trade Waste Incineration facility in Sauget, Illinois, established an Environmental Excellence Leadership Group (EELG) composed of first-line supervisors. Designated workers conduct inspections on each shift and identify and try to resolve any environmental issues immediately. The resolution of issues is reviewed by the EELG. Issues that cannot be readily resolved are forwarded to an Issue Resolution Council, a subset of the EELG composed of first-line supervisors and representatives of the Environmental Management Department (EMD). EMD representatives provide information on the permit requirements and regulatory framework relating to the issue. Supervisors are responsible for developing a solution, which becomes a standard for operating the site.

The simple, though often overlooked, strategy of involving those who must implement the solution has raised the awareness of all employees at the site about environmental compliance and improved performance. During 1993, for example, facility employees and management reduced reportable spills at the facility by 63%. The site also conducts continuous audits of 16 environmental compliance activities or systems. The results are summed and posted weekly to reinforce awareness of environmental issues. These audit results improved 49% during 1993.

The Environmental Excellence Councils at various CWM sites have spun off process improvement teams to address particular issues. CWM's Model City, New York, Environmental Excellence Council, for example, appointed a process improvement team to reduce site-generated waste. The cross-functional team identified and characterized the wastes and ways to reduce them. Carrying out their recommendations reduced site-generated wastes by 40%, saving $143,000 per year.

Through these and other measures, CWM has made progress in integrating the environmental principles into day-to-day operations and raising employee consciousness of the environmental goals of the company. Despite a very difficult business year (1993) in which the work force was reduced by 20%, the employee rating of the company's environmental commitment increased 7% overall and 24% among environmental professionals. Agency notices of violation, another—though lagging—indicator of environmental compliance performance tracked by CWM, declined by 13% in 1993.

Annual environmental reports

Principle 14 of the WMX Environmental Policy commits the company to issuing an annual environmental report evaluating progress in carrying out the policy and principles. WMX's 1990 Annual Environmental Report was one of the first such corporate reports. The WMX report is prepared by its Executive Environmental Committee, whose members include the chairman and CEO of WMI (who is also president and chief operating officer of WMX), the presidents of Rust International and WTI, the executive vice president of WMI plc, and the environmental vice president of CWM. The committee also includes five WMX corporate officers, including the WMX chief environmental officer, who chairs the committee. The Board of Directors reviews and approves the report.

WMX's corporate environmental reports have differed from most in their scope and comprehensiveness. Many environmental reports serve primarily to present and discuss environmental data such as Toxic Release Inventory (TRI) emissions and hazardous waste generation and management. The WMX reports, in contrast, have been structured around the 14 principles and so address everything from WMX biodiversity programs to cooperation with environmental groups. The first three reports were 150 to 170 pages long, with a 20- to 50-page summary prepared and distributed widely. The 1993 report was intermediate in length, at 75 pages. Following a process improvement effort, WMX published a 24-page 1994 report, made it available on the Internet (at WWW.WMX.COM) and provided a more detailed report on computer disk. The 1994 report includes Consumer Report-style "progress report" that summarize the status of key programs in each of the operating groups. The reporting process has not been driven by quantitative data; rather, the reporting has served to drive the process of gathering and standardizing data.

Because issuance of the first report followed closely the adoption of the policy, preparing the report required an examination of existing goals and data at the corporate level and in the operating groups. Not surprisingly, some areas, such as environmental compliance and health and safety, had well-developed goals, programs, and quantitative indicators. Other areas, such as environmental education, had no particular quantitative goals defined and thus were addressed descriptively in the report. There were also areas where quantitative information was collected at facilities but not rolled up and tracked as a performance indicator. Information tracked by different WMX groups was not consistent. This lack of standard performance indicators under the policy was one impetus to the "measurement project" discussed below.

The process of preparing and approving the reports has focused the attention of top management and the Board of Directors on progress in implementing the Environmental Policy and Principles. It has also served as an important internal communication tool and exposed areas where more quantitative data is needed.

Third-party review of environmental management systems. Beginning in 1990, WMX has engaged Arthur D. Little, Inc., to conduct an independent annual assessment of its environmental management systems. The assessment is part of the process of self-evaluation for the Annual Environmental Report. It also guides management in making changes to improve the systems. Each Annual Environmental Report has published ADL's opinion of WMX's environmental management systems. ADL has given the WMX Environmental Policy and Principles high marks as a leading corporate environmental policy. Their reports to management have recommended ways to improve integration of the policy with business operations, including development of additional guidance on the policy by operating groups and development of quantitative performance indicators under each principle.

Management of the operating groups each year has prepared a response to the ADL recommendations. This response is reviewed by the Board of Directors, further serving to elevate the visibility of environmental management issues.

Measurement project

In 1992, WMX began a process of developing "measurables" under the environmental policy. Although quantitative performance indicators existed at the corporate level and within operating groups, this was the first attempt to define facility-level measurables that would be reported by all groups and tracked by group and corporate management. The project began with facility-level pilots to learn what kind of information is already tracked and what indicators are meaningful to both site and upper management. The Executive Environmental Committee then appointed a task force of individuals from each of the operating groups to recommend a short list of measurables to be collected companywide.

Developing such a list is a daunting task. The need for the measurables to be few, simple, verifiable, and not too burdensome often conflicted with the desire for more and better information. To take one example, spills are a logical indicator to use for principles 1 (environmental protection and enhancement) and 8 (responsibility for damage to the environment). Reporting the total number of spills is a reasonable indicator of the success of efforts to prevent spills. Reporting the amount spilled, however, may be a better indicator of environmental impact, though one would also want to know whether the spill was contained, how promptly it was cleaned up, whether any hazardous materials escaped into the environment, and the sensitivity of that environment. Either the number of spills or amount of materials spilled could also be indexed by using a unit of business activity (e.g., tons of waste managed, dollars of revenue) to account for changes in the number of opportunities to spill materials. A physical unit such as tons of waste probably correlates better to opportunities. However, dollars of revenue translate better across diverse businesses.

The list of measurables approved by the Executive Environmental Committee in early 1994 includes about a dozen items. Operating groups carried out the measurement plan for the first time in 1994. Examples include:

- Amount of hazardous waste generated per ton of waste managed
- Percent of facility operating employees receiving environmental training
- Ratio of the acres of wetlands restored or created to wetlands filled
- Total amount of energy generated from managing waste

Simply reporting quantitative performance indicators under the policy, of course, is not the end of the process. It is important for management to incorporate the measurables into reviews of division and group performance and set goals for improvement. The measurables fit well with CWM's system for reviewing and rewarding progress in implementing the policy, as discussed above. WMI plc has developed a plan to begin tracking measurables immediately and phase in more demanding goals under the principles over time. The phase-in approach recognizes the diversity of WMI plc's acquisitions and the regulatory frameworks in which they operate.

Compensation and bonus reviews

A policy is only a policy until someone's pay depends upon it. WMX groups base some or all of the compensation of key operational and environmental managers on their success in implementing the environmental policy. At the highest levels of the organization, for example, as a prequalifier for any bonus, the chief executive officer and chief operating officer of WMX and the presidents of each of the principal operating groups are required to have established programs and systems that are adequate to further the implementation of each of the 14 environmental principles. Employee performance reviews throughout the company were based on what they did to advance the "four pillars"—including the environment.

Are we there yet?

The process of making an environmental policy an operational rather than aspirational credo may seem never-ending. At WMX, we certainly are not all the way there. But with several forces converging, we have made considerable progress in the years since adoption of the policy.

Design for Responsibility and Competitiveness

As other companies go through similar processes to truly integrate environmental concerns into product and process design, they will also find many opportunities for innovation, and may, in fact, find ways to innovate away the need for waste management services. Opportunities still exist in some regulation-driven markets, for example, in air pollution control, where WMX is well positioned to meet industry's needs. In other areas, such as municipal wastewater treatment, it is hard to imagine how source reduction could eliminate the need for the service. But many of the cutting-edge opportunities for WMX's future lie in projects undertaken in partnership with other businesses and government that address multiple environmental issues and involve rethinking traditional approaches and designing systems from the ground up. These design for environment projects often occur internationally and may provide opportunities for several members of the WMX family of companies.

Process and project design

The best opportunities for preventing pollution and dealing efficiently with residuals from industrial processes occur during the design of a production process. Rust International's engineering division has worked in partnership with several major companies to change their industrial processes and reduce the use of toxic substances, use energy and materials efficiently, and minimize emissions. Rust engineers working in teams with customer companies and outside experts have developed creative approaches to bringing about greener production processes. In mid-1991, Rust formed an alliance with the Hoechst

Celanese Film and Fiber Group to significantly reduce chemical emissions by 1996. The first project undertaken by the alliance involved engineering and construction of a new process for manufacturing acetic anhydride, a chemical intermediate used in processing wood pulp into cellulose acetate fiber. With environmental goals in mind, the redesigned process eliminates the use of benzene. The alliance extends to hundreds of environmental projects, using expertise from various WMX groups.

A Rust partnership with Union Camp represents another innovative design project. The two companies have teamed up to design the world's first large paper mill to make printing and writing papers from up to 100% postconsumer mixed office paper. When no existing single system could be found to support Union Camp's 0quality and environmental goals, Rust and Union Camp engineers used elements of North American, European, and Japanese technologies to develop a unique design for the plant which would meet multiple product quality and environmental objectives. The $90 million facility will use wastewater from an existing paper mill to wash pulp. The process will also use waste heat from the existing mill and require no steam source of its own. In addition, the facility will employ only nonchlorine bleaching procedures. Union Camp broke ground on the plant in June 1993 and completed in 1994. The plant reached full production in the first quarter of 1995.

In another Rust project, the company is helping Roslyn Farm Corporation build its 298-acre Ruffin Mill Industrial Park in an ecologically sensitive area near Richmond, Virginia. The creek that serves as the site's eastern boundary ultimately empties into the Chesapeake Bay, making stormwater runoff from the site a major consideration in the proposed development. Rather than design the project and then attempt to mitigate its environmental impacts, at Rust's recommendation, Roslyn Farm conducted all environmental and ecological work up front and then performed the engineering design according to the findings. When completed, the industrial park is designed to reduce pollutants leaving the site by 40% from current levels. Through its efforts, Roslyn Farm hopes to not only meet but exceed the stormwater management requirements of Virginia's Chesapeake Bay Preservation Act, as well as other state and federal requirements, while creating new wetlands and restoring farmed wetlands.

Innovation abroad

In November 1990, the Hong Kong Government Environmental Protection Department (EPD) awarded a contract to build and operate a Chemical Waste Treatment Center (CWTC) to Enviropace Limited, a joint venture of a unit of Waste Management International (WMI plc). For decades prior to the opening of the CWTC in 1993, untreated hazardous chemical wastes had been discharged into Hong Kong's sewers and rivers, ultimately winding up in Victoria Harbor. The vast majority (90%) of Hong Kong's 10,000 chemical waste producers are small factories in multitenant industrial buildings without the resources or space to treat their hazardous waste in-house. Considering that Hong Kong's industrial sector produces over 100,000 tons of hazardous waste annually, the effects on the environment of unrestrained dumping were enormous.

In the early 1980s, the Hong Kong government began addressing what, by then, had become a serious environmental crisis. At the time, there were few established regulatory guidelines and little environmental infrastructure. Thus, the challenge went beyond design of a facility to handle hazardous waste. What was needed was an entire system of incentives, regulations, infrastructure, and waste-tracking procedures appropriate for the needs of Hong Kong industry. The government developed cradle-to-grave legislation which would oversee storage, transportation, treatment, and disposal of all of its chemical waste. Part of its chemical waste control strategy included the creation of a central, all-purpose collection and treatment facility.

Hong Kong's particular industrial situation posed a number of challenges for an environmentally responsible management system. First, a single CWTC had to employ technology capable of treating virtually every type of liquid chemical waste. In addition, the center would have to provide the flexibility to address any future changes in Hong Kong's waste stream. Finally, the facility would need to provide waste collection and tracking systems to process a variety of wastes from diverse industries. These challenges were enhanced by EPD's schedule to complete the plant within 680 days with just another 90 days to performance-test all processes to ensure it met stringent standards and regulations before operation. The project drew on resources from throughout the WMX family of companies. CWM designed the facility and its treatment processes, and trained the employees. Rust International provided project management, cost control, contract administration, and worldwide just-in-time procurement. WMI provided financial control, business and administrative expertise, and set up the transportation system. Wheelabrator furnished the air pollution control systems.

Enviropace completed the plant three months ahead of schedule. The charge to design a state of the art facility from the ground up presented some interesting opportunities for the integration of treatment processes. In its first commercial application, the plant uses the

PO*WW*ER™ system* to treat wastewaters and recover water pure enough to use in plant processes. Heat is recovered from the incinerator and valuable metals and chemicals are recovered from waste streams as well. Treatment processes include:

- Separation of oils from water and biological treatment of organically contaminated wastewaters
- Physical-chemical treatment of inorganic aqueous wastes, including oxidation-reduction, neutralization of acids and bases, and precipitation of toxic metals
- Fine treatment of various wastewaters by evaporation and catalytic oxidation
- Recovery of metal from the waste by-products of electronics
- High-temperature incineration
- Stabilization of sludges and CWTC process residues

Early in the design process, WMX carried out a detailed risk analysis on the design specified in the contract. The analysis revealed that changing some of the processes could reduce risks substantially. These changes were incorporated into the final design.

The CWTC completed its first full year of operation in mid-1994. The facility has reached its boilerplate capacity and is now processing 100,000 tons of hazardous waste. Wastes from generators are collected in specially designed containers. To assure proper treatment, wastes from each generator are "fingerprinted" and a bar code for the generator assigned. At the plant, technicians scan the bar codes and analyze a sample of the waste to ensure that it matches the fingerprint.

It is interesting to note that, although the CWTC and its associated collection systems are without question the most modern and sophisticated in the world, they do not follow a pollution prevention approach. This was the choice of the Hong Kong government and probably reflects the desire to make rapid progress in eliminating a major source of environmental pollution. Nor could the government be sure of results from a program addressing the manufacturing processes of 10,000 waste generators. As it stands, Enviropace and

---

*The PO*WW*ER system uses evaporation to produce solid-free steam from contaminated waters. Pollutants in the steam are destroyed or detoxified through catalytic oxidation. The steam is then condensed in a heat recovery system and the pure condensate is reused in the plant. The system produces pure water from wastes containing such diverse contaminants as PCBs, lead, phenol, amines, mercaptans, trichloroethylene, and many others.

the EPD cooperated to end Hong Kong's days of virtually unrestricted chemical waste dumping and establish a program that can adapt to the environmental needs of the future.

Protecting nature

Conservation of biological diversity has received considerable attention in recent years because human activities have dramatically increased ecosystem loss and extinction rates. Loss of biodiversity can be irreversible and has enormous implications for the planet as a whole. Species that could be useful to humanity (undiscovered medicines or potential food sources, for example) are being lost. In spite of increasing and sincere efforts of government and business to account for environmental concerns in their activities, many of their efforts are directed at specific problems or environmental media and do not necessarily consider the impact of human activities on nature as a whole. WMX's environmental policy specifically calls for "no net loss" of biological diversity on its own properties. The company has also developed tools that may help others in their attempts to account for their impacts on biodiversity.

WMX's willingness to consider a groundbreaking commitment to conserve biodiversity was based in part on its experience at one of its facilities in central California. In the mid-1980s, the company proposed to build a new landfill at Kirby Canyon near San Jose, California. In the course of studying the site, a population of Bay Checkerspot butterflies was discovered. Although the species was not listed as threatened, WMX recognized its rarity and began a dialogue with state and federal agencies and the Stanford Center for Conservation Biology over measures to protect the butterfly population.

In 1986 the Company agreed to a habitat conservation plan for the Bay Checkerspot butterfly at the landfill site. The plan provides for the management of the inactive portion of the site to enhance its capacity to support butterfly populations. The Stanford Center for Conservation Biology has monitored butterfly populations at the site for eight years, commencing before landfill construction. Monitoring data shows that fluctuations in the butterfly populations have closely tracked climatic conditions. The presence of the landfill at the site has not adversely affected the butterfly; in fact, the monitoring data has shown that active management for butterfly habitat has improved the carrying capacity of the site.

Although protection measures for the butterfly added significantly to the cost of the project, the agreement allowed development of the site to proceed. It also demonstrated to the agencies and nonprofit groups involved the company's commitment to go beyond the letter of the law to protect the environment and the biological resources of the site.

WMX laid groundwork for a systematic biodiversity program in several steps. It made $100,000 in grants to the World Wildlife Fund to underwrite a report on model corporate policies for protecting biological diversity, and to sponsor a conference on the topic. With this information in development, WMX retained a consultant who prepared initial guidance on biological diversity conservation and prepared pilot conservation plans for three sites: two in the United States and one in New Zealand. The guidance developed seven "commandments" of biological diversity conservation:

- Look at the big picture.
- Promote native species and natural succession.
- Protect unique species and environments.
- Protect the sensitive.
- Give species space.
- Emphasize natural management.
- Avoid unnecessary harm and mitigate wisely.

In February 1993, Rust's Environment and Infrastructure subsidiary finalized a detailed guidance manual for biological diversity planning at sites (see Table 20.1 for a summary of the fundamental elements of the guidance). The system outlined in Rust's guidance manual represents the first comprehensive approach to conservation of nature that is geared toward assessing biological diversity on private lands in a rigorous, quantitative way. The Rust method essentially analyzes plant and animal communities at a particular location and uses a "similarity index" to compare the current biological richness of the site to the site's richness in a natural state. Based on inventory results, a conservation plan can be prepared and results tracked.

Plans have been completed at four WMI recycling and disposal facilities; another five are in the process. In addition, Rust's system can be marketed to companies or organizations that desire to enhance nature and protect the habitats of their properties.

WMX's experience developing a comprehensive biodiversity program is important for several reasons. First, the program suggests the potential of companies to undertake successful internal programs and develop them for circulation in the environmental services marketplace. Second, it illustrates that companies need not limit activities on behalf of the environment to those mandated by law. Corporate decisionmakers will inevitably find themselves in situations which fall outside the scope of any existing legislation where their decisions will either help or harm the environment. Wide-reaching, long-lasting gains in environmental protection will only come as

TABLE 20.1   Rust International's Biodiversity Management Guidelines

Inventory

Map plant communities by air.
List plant species in community layers.
Determine relative frequency, coverage, and density for each plant species in a community layer.
Determine relative abundance of species by community.

Characterization and Status

Establish geographic information system database from aerial mapping and other field inventory data.
For each plant community, calculate:
   Total area, edge, and ratio of area to edge
   Number, size, and separation of patches
   Relative abundance of plant, mammal, and bird species (and reptiles, amphibians, and benthic macroinvertebrates where regionally important)
   Percentage and importance of native versus nonnative species
   Similarity index comparing the 10 plant species currently most important with the 10 species most important before modern land use

Management Objectives

Maintain or increase similarity indices in communities.
Maintain or increase the percentage and importance of native species in communities.
Maintain or increase area: edge ratio.
Maintain or increase patch size; decrease patch number and separation.
Follow "seven commandments" of biological diversity conservation.

companies internalize environmental principles, and act on behalf of the environment out of genuine interest, not regulatory necessity.

Conclusion

Due to the constant advance of technology, the environmental services marketplace is an ever changing one, and management methods practiced today may indeed be primitive in twenty years. As companies integrate environmentalism into their businesses, they bear a twofold responsibility. First, they must be environmentally responsible in their current everyday operation. In addition, companies should develop long-term goals to sustain environmental quality and protect nature.

The development and pursuit of environmental principles has helped WMX address these responsibilities. That the company has embraced environmentalism as a basic element of business is seen at both internal and external levels. Progress integrating the principles has established that environmentalism is and will remain a key part of both corporate policy and business practice. The scope of the company's commitment to the environment is further broadened by the diversification of services offered and the development of environmentally based partnerships with other companies and organizations. In designing entirely new systems (such as production processes and biodiversity programs) which are motivated primarily by environmental goals, WMX begins a new chapter in its history as a provider of environmentally sound services.

The demand for new partnerships and services highlights the limits of existing technologies, but it also encourages development of methods to address the environmental needs of the future. For most of WMX's twenty-five years as a publicly held company, environmentalism has focused primarily on the need to minimize society's impacts on the land on which we live, the water we drink, and the air we breathe. Accordingly, the company has aimed to operate its business and offer services which utilized the best technology and methodology available. While such a focus is well directed and fairly effective, it possesses one significant shortcoming: it necessarily separates society from the environment. One must be protected from the other.

Considering the traditional goals of government and industry, a scheme in which society is an entity separate from the environment is natural; however, it is also natural—and necessary—that that scheme evolve. The environmentalism of the last several decades stems from a time when, in relationship to the vastness of nature, civilization was a relatively isolated phenomenon. Today, however, lands untouched by human development have dwindled and we must realize that the footprints of society and industrialization are almost as pervasive as nature itself. Together, environmentalists, government, and industry must begin to look for ways to allow society to coexist with nature.

References

1. Jo Kwong Echard, "Protecting the Environment: Old Rhetoric, New Imperatives," Capital Research Center, Washington, DC, 1990, p. 18.
2. Ibid.
3. Ibid.
4. *Washington Post*/ABC News Survey, April 1989.
5. Michael E. Porter, "Towards a New Conception of the Environment-Competitiveness Relationship," presentation to Global Environmental Management Initiative Conference, March 16, 1994.
6. "Minimum Waste, Maximum Benefit: The Pulp and Paper Industry Explores Sludge Disposal Options," *Views on Responsible Environmental Management*, vol. 1, no. 4, Autumn 1993, p. 8.
7. Ibid., p. 9.

Chapter

21

Building a Sustainable
Future at Dow Chemical*

Frank P. Popoff

Chairman and Chief Executive Officer
The Dow Chemical Company
Midland, Michigan

Introduction

In 1992, Dow Chemical Company developed its first global Environment, Health and Safety Report. This was no small task for a company that manufactures in 30 countries and sells products in nearly 200 countries around the world. Over the past eight years, worldwide capital spending for environment, health, and safety increased significantly. About 2000 Dow employees work directly with Dow's environment, health, and safety efforts.

The company has increased dialogue with its key stakeholders through Community Advisory Panels and a Corporate Environmental Advisory Council. The Waste Reduction Always Pays (WRAP) program has made significant progress in reducing emissions since it began in 1986. We will continue our emphasis on pollution prevention, which is the only logical alternative to today's end-of-pipe command-and-control regulations.

In 1992, Dow's Environmental Care Award was established to recognize employees who have demonstrated environmental excellence. Fifteen global awards, representing the efforts of 109 employees, were

*The material in this chapter is based on the "1993 Environment, Health and Safety Report" published by the Dow Chemical Company.

given to individuals and teams who improved the environment. More than 300 projects were nominated for the award.

In other areas, there is still much work to do. Dow is tracking its spills, and while the vast majority are captured by secondary containment and have no effect on the environment, the company is setting aggressive goals for reduction. We also need to improve our environmental compliance systems in each of our plants so that we can meet complex regulations all of the time. Implementation of the Responsible Care initiative continues.

The company continues to set more goals and measurements for environmental, health, and safety performance. One of the key priorities is to better integrate environmental, health, and safety performance issues into our business plans.

Besides the work inside the company, Dow is also helping to set some overall environmental reporting standards. Dow is one of the 10 charter companies that established the Public Environmental Reporting Initiative, which sets guidelines for environmental reporting.

Global Principles of Sustainable Development

In 1992, Dow announced a commitment to become a premier company in the practice of sustainable development, defined by the Brundtland Commission as "development that meets the needs of the present without compromising the ability of future generations to meet their own needs." Ten principles of sustainable development were articulated:

> The following 10 principles will guide the company toward sustainability. We recognize that the public's understanding of the concept continues to evolve; so, too, will these principles as Dow strives to meet and exceed society's expectations. In doing so, we will periodically report our progress.

- We will integrate environmental considerations into all business decisions, including the strategic planning of new and existing products, processes, and business opportunities.

- We will design or modify our products to minimize their environmental impact by encouraging their prudent use so as to reduce the amount of material requiring ultimate disposal; and prolonging their useful life through reuse, recycle and recovery.

- We will continuously improve the efficiencies of our current and future manufacturing processes to better conserve energy and natural resources.

- We will emphasize pollution prevention in our processes and use a hierarchical approach to waste management, with source reduction as the preferred option, following by recycling, treatment and destruction, and secure landfills to be used only as a last resort.

- We will transfer and utilize the best available technology throughout the Dow world so as to build the most environmentally sound facilities.
- We will adhere to the Responsible Care® guiding principles and codes of management practice through our global operations.
- We will work closely with our customers and distributors to ensure they use and dispose of our products in a safe and environmentally responsible manner.
- We will be open and responsive to the public concerns through thoughtful listening and meaningful action, and assume a leadership role in promoting partnerships between industry, government, the environmental community and other key stakeholders in an effort to develop solutions to common problems.
- We will participate in conservation projects on and near our properties so as to leave the land and its ecosystem as we found it—if not better.
- We will use our resources and expertise to support education initiatives at all levels to help improve the public's scientific and environmental literacy.

Pollution Prevention

As Dow develops technology to improve environmental, health, and safety performance, it disseminates that technology to its operations around the world. New plants, regardless of location, incorporate advanced technology, and an existing facility may pass on improvements to a similar plant in a different country. By sharing this information to continually reduce waste, Dow sometimes achieves cost savings as well as environmental, health, and safety benefits. Here are several examples:

Latex plant waste reduction

In 1989, Dow's latex plant in Midland, Michigan, was one of the biggest contributors to Dow's landfill, sending more than 1000 yd³ of material each month. The plant also sent more than three dozen tank trucks of organic wastes to Dow's incinerator each year and accounted for some of the location's air emissions.

Plant workers looked at the volume of waste their plant generated and saw an opportunity to reduce it—one step at a time. Employee teams evaluated each aspect of latex production—every piece of equipment and every procedural step. Figure 21.1 shows 2 of the 91 employees who contributed to this effort.

The improvements that they introduced ranged from complex chemical engineering changes, such as improving the performance of raw materials to simple, commonsense measures, like building a roof over the solid waste collection area to keep rain out and reduce the material required to solidify the waste. Some ideas came from indi-

Figure 21.1   Employees involved in latex plant waste reduction.

viduals and some from teams; none involved major capital investments, and several actually decreased the plant's operating costs.

Together, these "small" steps resulted in an 80% reduction in the
latex plant's waste to the landfill, a 50% reduction in waste to the
incinerator, and a 78% reduction in air emissions. The changes also
save $700,000 each year in environmental costs and improved yield.

These achievements did not result from a detailed plan imposed by
management; they evolved from agreement among plant staff that
the waste was much too high. And within the framework of the
WRAP program, plant workers were encouraged to do something
about it.

The impact of these waste reduction efforts extends far beyond the
latex plant in Midland. In fact, the lessons have been applied to a new
latex plant in Thailand. Dow's Latex Technology Center compiled
information and technology from Dow's worldwide latex operations
and shared it with the Thailand plant.

Hundreds of similar waste reduction projects have been initiated at
Dow since the WRAP program began in 1986, and the company has
reduced its wastes and emissions to the environment by an estimated
120 million pounds per year. At the same time, it has made plants
more efficient and saved Dow millions of dollars each year.

Biological wastewater treatment

Dow Europe is introducing state of the art biological treatment technology at its two largest facilities, located in Stade, Germany, and

Terneuzen, The Netherlands. Treatment towers in Stade were started between 1987 and 1992 and have contributed to a 20% reduction in the site's COD (chemical oxygen demand) load to the Elbe River. (COD shows how much oxygen is required to oxidize, or chemically break down, a compound when it is discharged into water. It indicates how much the natural cleansing capability of the receiving water is reduced. The lower the COD, the lower the pollution impact on the water.)

Wastewater from production at the Stade site is sent to the treatment towers, where microbes consume the contaminants and produce a nontoxic biomass known as "filter cake." The filter cake is fed into the site's rotary kiln incinerator, producing energy for the site. The cleaned water is then discharged into the Elbe River.

Scheduled to begin operations in 1995, the Terneuzen facility is expected to virtually eliminate waste to the Scheldt River.

Advanced VOC removal technology

The Sorbathene® solvent vapor recovery unit, a unique application of pressure swing adsorption, allows Dow plants to meet strict air emission regulations while recovering raw materials. The unit removes volatile organic compounds (VOCs) from vent streams with more than 99.9% recovery of the organics. Conventional systems achieve 95 to 98% recovery.

The technology is used when vapor is displaced from transportation equipment or in process streams where volatile compounds exist in the vent stream. In 1988, the first Sorbathene unit was started at a trichloroethylene plant in Texas. Currently, 20 units are operational at plants in Canada and the United States. More than 20 additional units are under development throughout the world. The team developing this technology was one of 15 winners of Dow's Environmental Care Award.

Closed-loop wastewater recycling

Dow's new fractionator and ethylene plants, part of a $600 million expansion at its manufacturing site in Fort Saskatchewan, Alberta, do not discharge process water to the nearby North Saskatchewan River. To accomplish this, Dow has incorporated unique design technology for the closed-loop recycle and reuse of wastewater.

A large evaporator (much like a tea kettle) boils the wastewater to separate the impurities. The water is recycled and reused within the plants. The impurities are nontoxic mineral solids and are sent to an underground disposal cavern. This technology is a first for Dow, and quite possibly for ethylene manufacturers worldwide.

Clean production plants in Asia

Clean technologies, developed by Dow, have been introduced at state of the art manufacturing plants in Map-Ta-Phut, Thailand, and Merak, Indonesia. Working with joint venture partners, the innovative plants include developments such as a ventless polyol reactor to eliminate air emissions and zero process water discharge for polyol and latex plants.

These plants, which opened in 1993, illustrate how Dow is building in industrializing countries using the latest environmental, health, and safety technology. The plants also set an example in helping to raise industry performance in these key Asian countries.

Innovative sealless pump

The San Lorenzo plant in Argentina began a waste elimination project in 1988 to achieve zero "white water" discharge at the site. (When latex disperses in water, the water turns white, hence the name "white water.") Since the plant's start-up in 1970, pump seals were the largest source of yield loss and waste buildup at the site holding ponds. Employee commitment to solve the problem led to development of a sealless pump that eliminated emission at the source, while cutting other losses by improving operating practices. The pump is being adopted at other plants.

Designing for Sustainability

It is increasingly important to integrate environmental, health, and safety considerations into business decisions. This approach is reflected in product designs that minimize environmental impact and in pollution prevention efforts in manufacturing processes. Several examples follow.

Environmentally sensitive herbicide

Discovering new products or redesigning existing ones to make them more sensitive to the environment is a major focus for research and development at Dow. Customer demand and market trends have played an important role in stimulating this investment.

An example of this ongoing research effort is DowElanco's new herbicide, Broadstrike®, which received registration by the U.S. Environmental Protection Agency (EPA) in October 1993. Highly effective and essentially nontoxic, Broadstrike is applied at ounces instead of pounds per acre. In addition, the compound can be used on both corn and soybeans, which allows increased flexibility in crop

Figure 21.2 Broadstrike® herbicide is highly effective and nontoxic.

rotation (see Fig. 21.2). Broadstrike also offers less risk to people and animals because it works against weeds by affecting amino acids found only in plants.

Registering a new compound in the United States takes five to seven years and from $35 to $50 million to complete the safety tests required by the EPA. Registrations have been obtained in Austrailia and Argentina, where the compound is sold as Preside®, and in Brazil, where it is sold under the trademark Scorpion®.

With both favorable environmental and toxicology profiles, Broadstrike herbicide is the first major product introduced by DowElanco, a joint venture formed in 1989 between Dow's Agricultural Products Division and Eli Lilly's Elanco Crop Protection business.

Alternative cleaning methods

Dow's Advanced Cleaning Systems, a new business established in 1992, offers efficient transitions to optimum alternative cleaning processes for customers involved in parts cleaning. For example, Therm-O-Disc, a Dow customer based in Mansfield, Ohio, relied on vapor degreasing with chlorinated solvents to clean soils and processing oils from its metal components. Growing awareness of environmental trends and increased government regulations prompted Therm-O-Disc to look at alternative surface-cleaning methods. Dow's Advanced Cleaning Systems helped the customer convert two of its surface-cleaning locations from vapor degreasing to ultrasonic aqueous (water-based) cleaning.

Clean-coal power generation

A clean-coal generating project is being developed at a PSI Energy station in Indiana with support from PSI Energy, the U.S. Department of Energy, and Destec Energy, a Dow subsidiary. Because the process removes nearly all of the coal's sulfur before it is burned, the plant will significantly outperform U.S. Clean Air Act standards established for the year 2000. The plant is scheduled for completion in mid-1995.

Dow began developing clean-coal technology during the energy crisis in the 1970s. When Dow turned to coal as a fuel alternative, its major research and development project became developing clean-coal power generation. The technology is today marketed by Destec Energy.

Water purification membranes

During the 1994 floods in the U.S. Midwest, the municipal water supply in Des Moines, Iowa, was contaminated when the Rocky River overflowed into the city's water treatment facility, forcing it to shut down for several days. To cope with the emergency water shortage, the National Guard was called in with reverse-osmosis water purification units. These mobile water purification plants feature Filmtec® membranes at the heart of the purification units. The elements are connected in series and mounted on trailers that can be moved anywhere fresh water is needed. A typical system can produce up to 3000 gal/h of purified water.

Similar water purification systems with Filmtec membranes also have been used by U.S. forces for Operation Restore Hope and Operation Desert Storm. The membranes were developed and are manufactured by FilmTec, a wholly owned Dow subsidiary.

Consumer product packaging

DowBrands, Dow's consumer product subsidiary, focuses its packaging development efforts on source reduction and waste minimization.

In Canada, DowBrands has developed the capability to incorporate 50% postconsumer recycled (PCR) resin in its product packaging. This packaging development eliminates about 500,000 lb of high-density polyethylene waste from the municipal waste stream. This is one of many projects enabling the company to exceed the timetable set by the Canadian federal government for significant packaging reductions.

Two product line extensions that incorporate environmental improvements were introduced in Canada in 1992. Fantastik® all-purpose cleaner introduced the first reclosable pouch package, which allows easy pouring and storage. It also reduces packaging by 68% and contains 20% PCR resin. Additionally, Handi-Wrap® brand plastic film introduced a refill roll that effectively reduces packaging by 50%.

In the United States, DowBrands has developed production capabilities to incorporate at least 25% PCR resin in its bottles, which contain familiar products such as Dow Bathroom Cleaner with Scrubbing Bubbles® and Fantastik all-purpose cleaner. The goal is to achieve the same standard in all major cleaning-product containers by 1998.

Life-cycle analysis framework

Dow is developing a life-cycle analysis approach to evaluate the environmental, health, and safety impact of its products. Each stage of a product's life cycle is reviewed—from development through recycling or disposal—against key environmental issues for vulnerability, opportunity, and current resources. Vulnerability is determined by the impact an issue may have on a product. Opportunity is the potential for new or improved business, and resources are the people, time, and money currently allotted. The completed matrix for a product will identify priorities for attention. For example, if a product is identified as being especially vulnerable to an issue like global warming, and this is not being addressed, additional resources will be allocated to the business.

Two pilot programs have been completed in the chemicals and plastics businesses, and several projects have been initiated to address their findings. Full implementation of this process is planned by 1995.

External Relationships

The environmental movement has matured beyond confrontation. Today, the expertise and resources of each organization—whether they be industry, environmental advocates, regulatory agencies, or the local community—can be more effective by working together rather than apart. Dow believes harnessing collective energies and setting priorities through partnerships will bring the greatest progress in protecting and enhancing the environment. Here are several examples:

Community Advisory Panels

Rheinmuenster, Germany, home to one of Dow's specialty chemical sites, is a small, rural community of 6000 residents. Located in the southwestern corner of the country, it's not the type of place where a chemical manufacturing facility blends into the surroundings unnoticed. When residents think of Dow, they may picture the site with its stacks of blue-wrapped Styrofoam® brand plastic foam, a complex collection of pipes, tall steel tanks, and office buildings. But the workings of the site itself—its products and processes—are often a mystery to neighbors.

In 1992, the site launched Dow Europe's first Community Advisory Panel (CAP) as part of its Responsible Care commitment to become a more approachable neighbor. The 16-member panel is a cross section of the community, including a homemaker and a retiree as well as business, community, and educational leaders. The group is led by the director of a high school. Panel goals include increasing discussion, communicating Dow and chemical industry activities, establishing direct contact with neighbors, and alleviating fear caused by lack of understanding.

Figure 21.3 shows CAP members visiting the plant. Input from the CAP has already been used to develop new programs and refocus some existing ones. For example, Dow learned that transportation safety is a major concern for the citizens of Rheinmuenster and nearby Lichtenau. Dow has since initiated an emergency response training program with nine local fire brigades. The program ensures better knowledge and improved cooperation.

Eighteen Dow CAPs are operating throughout the world. These CAPs also include environmentalists, students, and local firefighters. These volunteer advisory groups meet regularly to discuss plant oper-

Figure 21.3 Community Advisory Panel members visiting a plant.

ations, community involvement, emergency preparedness, environmental issues, and a variety of other subjects related to the site.

Recycling at national parks

Working with the U.S. National Park Service, Dow has helped to launch a program to recycle plastic, glass, and aluminum at seven of the country's most popular national parks. In 1990, recycling began at Acadia (Maine), the Grand Canyon (Arizona), and the Great Smoky Mountains (Tennessee and North Carolina). Yosemite (California) and Mount Rainier (Washington) National Parks were added in 1991; the Everglades (Florida) and the National Mall (Washington, D.C.) joined the program in 1992.

More than 2000 tons of recyclables were collected in the first three years of the program, 1990–1992. In 1993, more than 30 million visitors collected over 944 tons of recyclables.

Improved employee safety

Four Dow U.S. sites have achieved Star status in the Occupational Safety and Health Administration (OSHA) Voluntary Protection Program, which was begun in 1982 to recognize and promote effective safety and health management. In an effort to encourage government, labor, and management to work together, plant sites voluntarily submit to OSHA documentation on their safety performance. OSHA conducts on-site verification, including employee interviews. If the site achieves Star status, reverification occurs every three years. Of the 6 million work sites in the United States, OSHA has recognized just 121 Star sites.

As a result of Dow's participation, OSHA has sent teams to Dow sites to learn about several of its safety programs, such as steel erection safety, scaffolding safety, and process safety management. They have also shared Dow practices with other companies who are working on ways to improve their own safety programs.

Responsible Care

Responsible Care is a public commitment by the chemical industry to continuously improve its environmental, health, and safety performance. It has been launched in nearly 30 countries around the world and represents industry's response to increasing public concern about the impact of chemicals on the environment and human health.

As a Responsible Care company, Dow is publicly accountable for continuous environmental, health, and safety improvements. Many of the activities included in the Responsible Care initiative have been in place at Dow for years. Responsible Care now serves as a framework, and Dow is committed to implementing the initiative in all countries where it does business. Dow pledges to operate according to the Guiding Principles and to communicate its performance to the public. The Codes of Management Practices formalize procedures for the development, manufacture, distribution, storage, handling, and use of chemicals. They also address the importance of open dialogue with plant communities on day-to-day operations and in planning for future developments and potential emergency response situations.

Codes of management practices

At the heart of Responsible Care are the specific Codes of Management Practices—listed below—which are designed to improve the manufacturing, transportation, and handling of chemicals:

- Community Awareness and Emergency Response: Aimed at assuring emergency preparedness and fostering better communications with residents of plant communities.

- Pollution Prevention and Waste Reduction: Designed to achieve ongoing reductions in wastes and emissions as well as manage all waste products in an environmentally sound manner.

- Process Safety: Aimed at preventing fires, explosions, and accidental chemical releases. It covers process design, plant operation, routine maintenance, and employee training.

- Distribution and Transportation: Designed to reduce risk to the general public, carrier, distributor, contractor, chemical industry employees, and the environment posed by the transportation and storage of chemicals.

- Health and Safety: Intended to protect and promote the health and safety of people working at or visiting company work sites.

- Product Stewardship: Considers possible health, safety, and environmental effects of new and existing products and promotes the safe and environmentally sound development, manufacture, transport, use, and disposal of products.

Product stewardship: The umbrella code

The Product Stewardship Code is the most comprehensive of the Codes of Management Practices. It promotes the safe handling of chemicals at all stages—from design to final disposition—encompassing pollution prevention and waste reduction, process safety, distribution and transportation, health and safety, and community awareness and emergency response.

Under this code, Dow must give customers and distributors information on the proper handling, use, and disposal of products. Through Product Stewardship programs, Dow informs customers and distributors about known use limitations and instructs them to use products in accordance with label information and regulatory requirements. Depending on the product and the expertise of the customer, Dow visits customer facilities to review product characteristics and any special considerations.

Emissions and Waste Reduction

Emissions reduction programs for Dow are based on government regulations as well as self-established priority compound lists.

33/50 program

The EPA introduced a voluntary emissions reduction program in 1991 called the 33/50 program. It challenged companies to reduce emissions of 17 priority compounds by 33% by 1992 and by 50% by 1995. Dow has adapted and expanded this into a global emissions reduction program. Aggregate emissions of the 17 compounds are shown in Fig. 21.4, and a list of the compounds and their 1988 and 1993 emissions are displayed in Fig. 21.5.

Baseline measurements were taken in 1988, and comprehensive corporate data were not available until 1991. The goal is to reduce

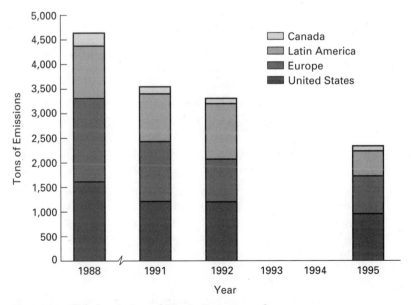

Figure 21.4 Global emissions of 17 priority compounds.

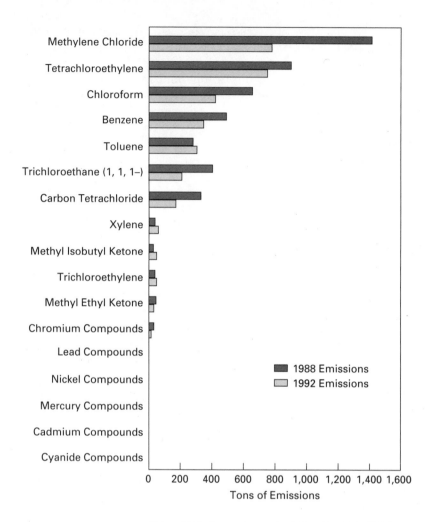

*List of Priority compounds defined by U.S. EPA in 1991

Figure 21.5   Global emissions by compound.

aggregate emissions of these compounds by 50% of the baseline by 1995. Almost all of the emissions associated with the 17 priority compounds are to the air.

Each Dow geographical area has expanded the 33/50 list to include priority compounds specific to its needs, priorities, and regulations. Each area has set a goal to reduce emissions of these compounds by 50% by the end of 1995 using 1988 as the baseline (1989 for Canada). Reduction efforts had resulted in the elimination of about 44,200 tons of emissions annually by 1993.

For example, the priority list in Europe includes the chemicals listed as priorities by the national governments in the countries where

Dow operates as well as all wastes designated as hazardous. The U.S. goal includes all SARA-listed chemicals, and the Canadian program includes both hydrocarbons and nitrogen oxides. All lists include the 33/50 program's 17 priority compounds.

SARA Title III

Title III of the Superfund Amendments and Reauthorization Act (SARA) was passed by the U.S. Congress in 1986 and established requirements for emergency planning and community right-to-know reporting on hazardous and toxic chemicals. Dow has also tracked these emissions globally, as shown in Fig. 21.6.

In the United States, Dow bases its emissions reduction program on the SARA Title III list of chemicals. The goal is to reduce emissions of all SARA Title III substances to air, water, and land by 50% of the 1988 baseline level by the end of 1995. The 1993 emissions show a 45% reduction from 1988. Although chloroflurocarbon (CFC) emissions were measured in 1991 and 1992, they are not included in the 1995 goal. Of the companies reporting SARA emissions, Dow ranked 28th in 1989 and 42nd in 1990.

Pollution Prevention Act

In 1992, the Pollution Prevention Act in the United States required additional chemical-specific information on recycling, energy recovery, and treatment activities for SARA-listed compounds.

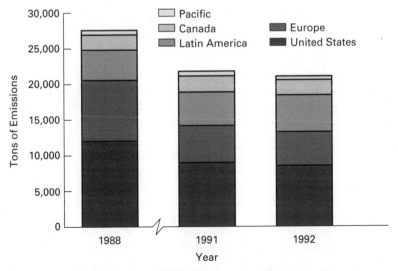

Figure 21.6   Global emissions of SARA-listed compounds.

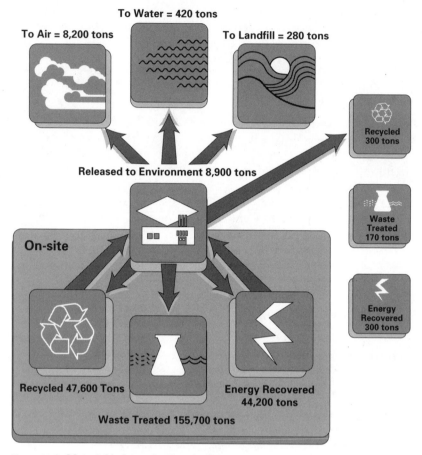

Figure 21.7   Material balance for Dow facilities.

Dow adheres to a waste management hierarchy that minimizes the impact of wastes on the environment. First, Dow works to eliminate or minimize the generation of waste at the source through research, process design, plant operations, and maintenance. Second, the company finds ways to reuse and recycle materials.

Unusable or nonrecyclable hazardous waste is treated before disposal to eliminate or reduce the hazardous nature and volume of the waste. Treatment may include destruction by chemical, physical, biological, or thermal (incineration) means. Disposal of waste materials in landfill is considered only after all other options have been thoroughly evaluated (see Fig. 2.17).

Dow has specific requirements for materials that are transferred to non-Dow facilities. Materials that are recycled, treated, or recovered for energy off-site represent less than 1% of the total amount of materials reported as part of the Pollution Prevention Act. Dow plans to collect waste-to-treatment and energy recovery data for all of its facilities on a global basis.

Chemical categories of concern

Dow's total emission numbers are comprehensive and include the range of materials emitted through our manufacturing operations. However, the company's progress on specific chemical categories is highlighted here because of public interest.

Global-warming materials.   Carbon dioxide (CO_2) equivalents are used to determine the global-warming potential of other materials. Of the weighted direct global-warming materials, CFCs made up 69% of Dow's global-warming emissions in 1988. Since the phase-out of CFCs began in 1989, emissions have dropped significantly. In 1992, CFCs made up only 20% of the CO_2 equivalent emissions. Most CO_2 comes from power generation.

Combustion gas emissions.   Emissions of sulfur dioxide (SO_2), nitrogen oxides (NO_x), and carbon monoxide (CO) contribute to smog formation. SO_2 is produced by the combustion of fuels containing sulfur. Wherever possible, Dow purchases fuels that have a low sulfur content. NO_x is generated whenever fuel is burned in air. Dow reduces NO_x emissions by improving burner technology, reducing energy use, and using fuels like natural gas that produce less NO_x. CO formation is minimized by process controls and burner management.

Volatile organic compounds.   In general, volatile organic compounds (VOCs) are organic compounds that contribute to ground-level ozone formation. *Volatile organic compound* refers to any organic compound released including emissions of hydrocarbons such as propane, butane, and HCFCs. Emissions of methane, ethane, methylene chloride, and CFCs are not included because they have been shown to have negligible light-activated chemical reactivity. Many of the compounds included in the area priority emissions lists are VOCs and targeted for reduction.

CFC emissions.   Dow does not produce CFCs, but has used them as blowing agents in the manufacture of foamed plastics and as refrigerants and heat-transfer fluids in operations. Use of CFCs is being phased out worldwide. CFC emissions in 1992 had decreased 85% from 1988 baseline levels. Of the weighted ozone-depleting materials, CFCs still represented 72% of Dow's ozone-depleting emissions in 1992. These emissions are targeted for elimination in accordance with the Montreal Protocol schedule.

Energy Efficiency

Many of Dow's production processes are energy intensive, and the company takes energy reduction very seriously. Over the years, Dow has employed cogeneration, energy recycling, and waste-to-energy methods.

The majority of energy produced by Dow comes from cogeneration. Cogeneration is a particularly efficient process that uses the heat content of exhaust gases to produce steam and results in efficiency yields of 80% compared to less than 40% for power produced by a conventional utility.

Recycling energy also adds considerably to Dow's energy efficiency. Wherever possible, energy generated during one chemical production process is fed or recycled into another process, and, in many cases, flammable gases from processes can provide fuel for furnaces.

Figure 21.8 illustrates Dow energy-efficiency improvements for U.S. plants. Total energy efficiency improved 24% from 1982 to 1992 as a result of installing gas turbines, individual plant efforts, and replacement of obsolete plants with modern facilities.

Audit Programs

Environmental, health, and safety audits are used by management to continually measure and report Dow's progress against environmental, health, and safety expectations. These audits are systematic, documented, and objective processes intended to verify the accuracy of data as well as statements or reports made by the audited facility. Dow is committed to act on discrepancies.

Dow conducts many different kinds of audits and assessments globally to determine overall conformance with company standards, gov-

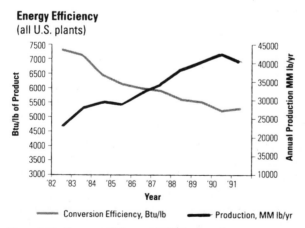

Figure 21.8   Energy efficiency (all U.S. plants).

ernment regulations, and industry initiatives like Responsible Care. Audits are useful and necessary management tools and help identify opportunities for continuous improvement. The audits range from daily employee self-assessments to detailed audits involving independent third parties. The specific components and timing vary depending on location and the type of facility.

Individuals are responsible for environmental, health, and safety activities in their daily jobs. Equipment inspections, job procedure checklists, compliance confirmations, and other routine practices are completed on a daily basis. Site management often conducts similar reviews for the entire work group.

Many inspections and equipment checks are performed on a weekly, monthly, quarterly, or annual basis. Maintenance and capital project reviews are conducted as required during various phases of the project. Plants are periodically audited by Dow technical experts from other locations to provide independent perspective and to insure consistency between operations.

Every three years, Dow facilities undergo formal, detailed audits of their manufacturing, maintenance, distribution, and research functions. The audits may last from several days to a week. As of 1992, 80% of Dow facilities worldwide had undergone these detailed audits.

Dow also routinely participates in various forms of independent third-party audits. Third-party reviews bring a different perspective and added assurance that Dow's internal evaluations are consistent with external expectations. Dow has participated in government agency audits, insurance audits, and International Organization for Standardization certification. In addition, other third parties may be invited to review Dow's practices because of their unique expertise.

Conclusions

Protecting, preserving, and promoting the health of people and the environment are essential to Dow's success. Around the world, our ability to produce and sell products, enter new markets, and continue to attract the best employees all depend on our environmental, health, and safety performance. Recognizing this imperative, we are working to emphasize pollution prevention, reduce and eliminate waste, and make our products safer to produce and use. But we also understand that environmental improvement and economic growth are interdependent. Our investments in environment, health and safety can—and must—create value for Dow. We must practice sustainable development.

This chapter has described how we are working toward sustainable development around the globe. Our efforts include Responsible Care—an industrywide commitment to performance improvements, dialogue, and outreach that is now a part of business in nearly 30 countries.

A genuine concern for the environment, health, and safety is part of Dow's culture. Rather than being isolated in a separate function, these issues are increasingly integrated into our business decision processes. At every level, teams of people are focusing on business opportunities and practices that sustain our economic and environmental performance. We believe, as we have for many years, that the factor likely to have the greatest impact on Dow's future will be our environmental, health, and safety performance.

22

The U.S. EPA's DfE Program*

EPA

Deborah L. Boger

Office of Pollution Prevention and Toxics
U.S. Environmental Protection Agency
Washington, D.C.

Claudia M. O'Brien

Office of Pollution Prevention and Toxics
U.S. Environmental Protection Agency
Washington, D.C.

Introduction

This book describes a major shift in the way many organizations think about their environmental programs. Companies today are not only assuring that they can safely contain and control toxic or hazardous substances and wastes, but they also are increasingly trying to think ahead so that they do not produce wastes or undesirable releases in the first place. This type of thinking needs to occur at the design stage, where decisions are made that will largely determine the environmental attributes of a product or process, including materials used, by-products and wastes produced, energy requirements, and recyclability.

*The authors would like to thank the EPA staff who helped them prepare this chapter.

The goal of the U.S. Environmental Protection Agency's (EPA's) Design for the Environment (DfE) program is to promote the design of products and processes that are safer for public health and the environment. DfE addresses several areas in which improvement is needed to accomplish this goal. First, DfE provides information to industry decisionmakers to promote environmentally responsible changes in business practices. DfE also seeks to reshape management decision processes in order to create incentives for cost-effective pollution prevention. In addition, the DfE program acknowledges that chemical manufacturing is the base upon which other manufacturing processes are built, and it seeks to promote chemical design and manufacturing that reduces both the quantity of wastes generated and the associated degree of hazard.

The DfE program was created in September of 1992 and is located in EPA's Office of Pollution Prevention and Toxics (OPPT). It is a multifaceted program working on a wide range of projects. Because of the originality and flexibility with which it approaches these projects, DfE is a rapidly changing and expanding program. A description of its current projects is provided below.

Cleaner Technology Substitutes Assessment

Too often, companies find themselves employing a chemical, process, or technology that either has been regulated, will soon be regulated, or is suspected to have adverse environmental effects. As a result, these companies adopt alternative technologies without an attempt to assess the environmental impact associated with the changes. Similarly, the EPA often assesses the potential hazards of specific chemicals and neglects to evaluate the potential hazards of possible substitutes until late in the risk assessment process. Thus, organizations may switch processes or chemicals in order to comply with regulations and discover later that the alternative is equally harmful or more so. Companies cite numerous examples in which they have switched from a regulated chemical only to find the alternative is regulated a few years later. By assessing alternative options *a priori*, such problems may be avoided, anticipated, or at least minimized. In addition, this approach is more efficient than the EPA's traditional regulatory approach because the risk analysis of the substitutes is done along with the risk analysis of the original chemical. The Cleaner Technology Substitutes Assessment (CTSA) provides an analytic tool whereby such analyses may be made (see Fig. 22.1).

The CTSA is currently being applied in several of DfE's cooperative industry projects (described below) to compare the trade-offs associated with substitute chemicals, processes, and technologies. It produces a document which includes cost, performance, and environmental risk information on possible alternatives. It provides businesses with

Cleaner Technology Substitutes Assessment

Modify Process	Substitute Solvents	Substitute Technologies	Improve O&M	Recycle/ Reuse	Do Nothing

Toluene Substitute 1	Ethylenediamine Substitute 2	Isopropanol Substitute 3	Aqueous Ammonia Substitute 4

Multi-Media Risk	Performance	International Trade Issues
Hazard Chemical mfg Release Product mfg Exposure Use Disposal	P2 Opportunities & Environmental Technologies	Cost

Releases	Resource Conservation	Energy Impacts

Figure 22.1 Cleaner Technology Substitutes Assessment. Line 1 represents different options open to a DfE project in looking at alternatives for a chemical, process, or technology of environmental concern. These options are developed after identifying a use cluster on which to concentrate. A CTSA seeks to address all or most of these options. Line 2 shows examples of alternative solvents that could be evaluated in a CTSA. The remaining boxes delineate the categories in which the alternatives are evaluated.

guidance on which options have fewer environmental impacts, are technologically feasible, and are financially sound at the same time.

The development of a CTSA first necessitates an identification of the relevant *use clusters* in an industry process. A *use cluster* is a set of chemicals, processes, and technologies that can substitute for one another to perform a specific function (e.g., paint stripping). Each one of these products, processes, or technologies, plus the alternatives that may substitute for it, would be a use cluster. For example, if the aircraft industry decided that the chemicals used to strip paint off airplanes were of environmental concern, it would develop a "paint stripping use cluster." The cluster would include the current chemicals used in the process plus all of the alternatives (i.e., other potential chemicals, water blasting, sand blasting, scraping, using wall surfaces that don't require paint, etc.).

Next, all of the industry use clusters are ranked using an EPA scoring system that incorporates factors such as human health, ecological hazards, exposure, regulatory interest, and pollution prevention opportunities. The ranking system helps to prioritize and direct research to those use clusters that show the greatest need and potential for improvement. Based on the results of the ranking system and on industry's experience, EPA and its industry partners identify use clusters for which industry would like to seek substitutes.

Once industry has decided on a use cluster which merits some effort, EPA jointly with industry collects information on all existing alternatives in the use cluster and searches for other promising options. This phase is conducted with considerable industry input and also with the assistance of EPA scientists. The DfE program lists all of these alternatives in a "use cluster tree" for chemicals, processes, and technologies that can substitute for one another in performing a particular function.

Sometimes, alternatives are not at all similar. In the paint-stripping example, the paint-stripping function in maintenance applications can be accomplished through the use of chemical solvents such as methylene chloride and N-methyl pyrrolidone (NMP), or through alternative practices such as sandblasting and plastic pellet blasting. It can even be avoided altogether by using a nonpainted surface finish. Compiling all these options into a substitutes tree provides the foundation for the CTSA.

The information in the substitutes tree is combined with risk, cost, and performance information on all of the alternatives in the use cluster and put into a CTSA document. With the help of the CTSA, a business person can examine the environmental impacts of each process option alongside the performance characteristics and the cost information, and thus make informed business decisions.

Substitutes that are clearly the most preferable option are rare. For example, a process which uses fewer chemicals may use more water or be much more expensive. For this reason, the CTSA presents information in a flexible format that allows systematic comparisons of the trade-offs associated with different alternatives. Traditional trade-offs such as cost and performance are brought together with environmental trade-offs including comparative human health and ecological risk, energy impact, and resource conservation for each alternative. A completed CTSA should provide all the information that a designer, engineer, or business person needs to decide among alternatives.

A CTSA enables companies to make rational choices according to specific circumstances. A shop undertaking paint stripping in the eastern part of the United States may decide water conservation is not as high a priority as it is for a similar operation in the western United States, where water is more scarce. Therefore, the eastern paint stripper may choose an option which requires more water. The aim of the CTSA is not to influence everyone to make the same decisions; rather, it is to allow everyone to make informed decisions.

Cooperative Industry Projects

The premise of DfE's cooperative industry projects is that companies do not want to pollute the environment unnecessarily, but that they often lack the multimedia environmental information required to make informed choices about materials and chemicals. Many companies simply do not have the resources to explore the environmental impacts or consequences of the different business options open to them. In some cases, information on different options does not even exist. As a result, firms that change their business practices to help the environment or to comply with regulations often switch from one product or process to another with equally serious, or more serious, consequences to the environment. This situation has been a problem in a number of industries where environmental risk and impact information is not readily available to members of the industry.

The EPA's DfE program was created to help solve this type of problem. The program's efforts are directed largely at providing businesses with the accurate, current information they need to practice DfE. The information deals with environmental risk, cost, and performance trade-offs associated with the choice of materials, products, or processes in manufacturing.

EPA's DfE program is engaged in a number of cooperative industry projects; each one is organized around a specific industry with a specific need. Through the DfE program, the agency forms voluntary partnerships with industry, professional organizations, state and local governments, other federal agencies, environmental organizations, and the public to evaluate possible solutions to some of the environmental issues that the industry would like to address. These issues span the spectrum from current or future regulation of a widely used industry chemical to specific emissions problems. The partners compile information to inform and facilitate pollution prevention efforts within the targeted area. This type of information enables industry to be environmentally informed when making business choices. Whatever change the industry wishes to make, the EPA will work with them to evaluate their options and to develop creative solutions. The resulting partnership is completely voluntary, although it may arise from the need to respond to regulatory pressures.

The DfE industry projects come about in different ways. In some cases, industry members approach the EPA with a request for assistance in evaluating options for change. In other cases, EPA approaches industry with an offer to assist during the industry's period of transition.

Regardless of how the projects start, all industry projects have essentially the same components, as illustrated in Fig. 22.2: (1) technical, (2) outreach, and (3) implementation. The technical component consists largely of the development of the CTSA document described earlier. This document compiles information on the environmental risk, cost, and performance of each alternative. The information is collected in three ways: (1) by gathering information from industry

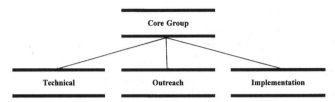

Figure 22.2 Structure of a typical DfE industry project. DfE projects are typically organized into four groups: the Core Group, and the Technical, Outreach, and Implementation Workgroups. Membership on the workgroups is open to any individual or organization. Chairpeople of the different workgroups sit on the Core Group; in addition, the project may invite additional people to sit on the Core Group if it feels that certain interests or groups are not adequately represented.

members about their products and processes, (2) by analyzing assessments and studies of the various alternatives, and (3) by actually testing or demonstrating the products or processes. The outreach phase of the project starts at the outset of the partnership. In the beginning stages, most outreach is devoted to making industry contacts and to making industry members and the public aware that the project exists. The goal of this initial outreach effort is to get people interested in participating in the project. Some initial outreach also focuses on informing companies of successful pollution prevention efforts by others in their industry. Most of the outreach occurs, however, once the CTSA is completed. At this point, international, federal, state, county, and local networks, both public and private, will be used to disseminate the information in the CTSA to individual businesses, government programs, and the general public. Finally, in the implementation phase, the EPA helps industry actually begin to implement the information they have received.

The DfE government-industry relationship is extremely valuable to both industry and the government. For industry, the benefits include guaranteed input into any evaluations made of the current situation. Industry works closely with the government to gather, coordinate, and analyze information in a more effective and efficient use of resources than if each company conducted analyses itself. More importantly, some of the options laid out in the CTSA may enable industry to adopt cleaner, more environmentally sound technologies that save money and attract customers, making the industry more competitive. A unique characteristic of the DfE program, much appreciated by industry, is that it concerns itself not only with the environmental safety of a business, but also with its financial health.

For example, a firm can reduce its waste by changing or reducing the amount of input materials; this in turn may lower production costs. Generally, if a company reduces its environmental releases, it may enjoy cost reductions in the following areas: (1) need for end-of-pipe treatment (e.g., waste treatment); (2) regulatory compliance costs (e.g., record keeping, reporting, penalties for noncompliance); (3) potential Superfund liability; (4) worker health and safety costs (lost days at work due to sickness from exposure or accidents); (5) potential insurance premium reductions (e.g., a company that practices DfE may be less likely to have an industrial accident with toxics).

The Design for the Environment program is also extremely valuable to the EPA. It deals with sectors of industry that are environmentally important, but that may not have been covered by EPA regulations, such as small and midsized businesses. In this way, EPA gets a chance to find out exactly what the needs of industry are and how they can best be met. On both sides, a good working relationship is developed. Thus the DfE program stimulates environmental improvements that might otherwise not occur.

The DfE program is different from traditional programs under existing EPA environmental statutes, which normally focus on a single medium (e.g., air, water, land) and generally do not address the transfer of pollutants from one medium to another. DfE, however, considers multimedia concerns; it acknowledges trade-offs and does not favor one medium over another. It accomplishes this by involving industry voluntarily, providing them with information, letting them decide how to best integrate pollution prevention into their processes, and then helping them do it.

Dry-Cleaning Project

The DfE Dry Cleaning Project is a cooperative industry project partnership between the EPA and the dry-cleaning industry. The purpose of this project is to reduce exposure to chemicals used to dry-clean clothes.

With more than 34,000 commercial shops in neighborhoods and malls across the country, dry cleaners are one of the largest groups of chemical users that come into direct contact with the public. Some dry cleaners use petroleum-based chemicals, some use CFC-based chemicals, but most dry cleaners use perchloroethylene (PCE or "perc") to clean clothes. PCE is a chlorinated organic solvent, and it is designated as a hazardous air pollutant under Section 112 of the Clean Air Act and under many state air toxics regulations. Numerous studies show that PCE is potentially carcinogenic.[1] According to a study conducted on Staten Island and in New Jersey, PCE is among the toxic air pollutants found at the highest concentrations in urban air.[2] Because of the potential health and environmental concerns associated with the use of PCE, the EPA, through its DfE program, is now working in partnership with the dry-cleaning industry to reduce exposures and to evaluate alternatives to PCE.

The Dry Cleaning Project came into existence through efforts by both the EPA and the industry. In May 1992, EPA convened the International Roundtable on Pollution Prevention and Control in the Dry Cleaning Industry in response to a number of general concerns about dry-cleaning chemicals. Researchers, industry representatives, and government officials met to exchange information on a number of issues related to dry-cleaning, including exposure reduction, regulation, risk communication, financing options, and pollution control. The participants also listed issues that needed to be addressed through research initiatives and future discussion forums.

As a result of this roundtable, the EPA and industry leaders decided that unresolved issues from the roundtable could be addressed most effectively using the DfE program's nonregulatory, voluntary, and proactive approach. Therefore, they agreed to apply the design for the environment methodology to work cooperatively and to evaluate options for reducing exposure to dry-cleaning chemicals.

As in the other DfE industry projects, the Dry Cleaning Project consists of three components: technical, outreach, and implementation.

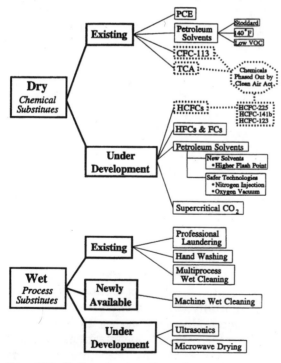

Figure 22.3 Clothes-cleaning alternatives.

The technical work being done on the project is included in a dry-cleaning CTSA that systematically evaluates a number of alternative cleaning technologies, substitute solvents, and methods to limit chemical exposure from dry cleaning. Figure 22.3 shows the use clusters that were developed through this CTSA.

The evaluation considers factors such as worker exposure, environmental releases, energy impacts, resource conservation, and human health and environmental risk. Information on cost and performance of the current processes compared to the alternatives is also presented. The CTSA weighs the trade-offs, or the pros and cons of competing environmental objectives, in order to help dry cleaners make informed business choices. The EPA will produce informational documents for industry and the public that will communicate these trade-offs in a flexible format enabling these groups to understand the results of the public-private partnership.

In the dry-cleaning CTSA, DfE evaluates a number of different solvents, processes, and technologies. The CTSA includes three sections on solvents; the first is a section on PCE. This section evaluates the currently available processes using PCE as a solvent. First, transfer technology is evaluated. Transfer technology is a process where the clothes are washed in PCE in one machine, then transferred to a separate machine to be dried. In this process, clothes are cleaned in a similar manner to home washing, except PCE is used instead of water.

Second, dry-to-dry technology is evaluated. In this process, clothes are both washed and dried in one machine. This one-machine technology eliminates the step where the clothes, still wet with PCE, must be pulled out of the washer and transferred to the dryer, exposing the worker. Both dry-to-dry and transfer technologies use certain control mechanisms on the dryer vents to limit releases of PCE. The major control options are carbon adsorbers (CAs) and refrigerated condensers (RCs). Both capture escaping PCE vapors and return them to the machine. The CTSA will evaluate the effectiveness of both of the cleaning-process technologies and these and other control options in terms of cost, performance, and environmental impact.

The CTSA also evaluates petroleum dry-cleaning solvent processes. Many cities' fire codes do not allow petroleum solvent clothes cleaning due to its potential fire hazard, so it is not widely used in small dry-cleaning establishments. However, petroleum solvents are still in use in some larger operations outside residential areas, so DfE includes these alternatives in its CTSA. Stoddard and 140 F are examples of petroleum solvents currently being used. Petroleum processes can be carried out with uncontrolled venting as well as with CA controls. Also, a selection of new processes using petroleum solvents lowering the explosion potential may allow these technologies back into the smaller city shops.

A section on CFC solvent substitutes is also included in the CTSA. CFCs have been classified as ozone depleters and will be banned at the end of 1995. The section includes evaluations of solvent substitutes for the current CFC machines. The substitutes include HFC (hydrofluorocarbon) 134a, HCFC (hydrochlorofluorocarbon) 141b, HCFC 225, and HCFC 123, all of which have been used as CFC substitutes. HCFCs will be banned in 2001 because they are also ozone depleters. CFCs are currently used as the only method to clean some delicate garments such as leather products.

In addition to solvents, the CTSA evaluates alternative processes and technologies. One alternative technology that was discovered and evaluated in the CTSA is a cleaning technique called "multiprocess wet cleaning." DfE staff became aware of this alternative clothes-cleaning technique as a result of the International Roundtable. This process relies on the controlled application of heat, steam, pressing, and soaps to clean clothes that are typically dry-cleaned with PCE. In order to determine if multiprocess wet cleaning is a viable alternative to dry cleaning, the EPA conducted preliminary tests on this process at a Florida dry-cleaning plant. For these tests, a comparative cost analysis of dry-cleaning and wet-cleaning techniques was completed. These low-volume tests suggested that the multiprocess cleaning method had merit. However, it was determined that a larger, higher-volume test for economic feasibility and performance was required.

For four weeks in November and December of 1992, the EPA and members of the clothes-cleaning industry conducted a short-term, high-volume test to compare the costs and performance of multiprocess wet cleaning and conventional PCE dry cleaning. In this test, over 1500 garments were collected from consumers employed in government agencies in Washington, D.C., and New York City and shipped to the New York School of Dry Cleaning in Manhattan. There, an economic feasibility study and a performance test were carried out on the alternative process. In the economic feasibility study, a comparison of raw capital, operating, and labor costs unique to each cleaning process was made. Based on these figures, a theoretical model plant analysis was developed. Models were developed for a variety of mixed-mode* facilities ranging from a 100% dry-cleaning facility to a 100% wet-cleaning facility. The performance test was carried out by soliciting customer satisfaction information.

The cost and performance studies indicate that, under certain situations, multiprocess wet cleaning is technically feasible and economi-

---

*A mixed-mode facility is one in which both dry-cleaning and wet-cleaning processes are used to clean clothes.

cally competitive with PCE dry cleaning. The results show that, when opening a new facility, the highest profit margin is achieved with multiprocess wet cleaning. When building a new mixed-mode facility, the profit margin remains essentially the same up to 50% wet cleaning. If more than 50% of the garments are wet-cleaned, dry-cleaning equipment is underutilized and the profit margin begins to go down. If an existing facility converts to a higher percentage of wet cleaning, the already purchased dry-cleaning machinery becomes less utilized. Because of this underutilization, the profit margin decreases as an existing facility moves to more wet cleaning.

Both cleaning methods generated positive and negative responses in the performance study, with a statistically significant preference shown for the multiprocess wet-cleaning method, particularly with regard to odor. A test garment wear study showed limited results when comparing the shrinkage, stretching, and color change caused by either cleaning method. In this respect, no appreciable difference was found between the two processes.

A second technology that is evaluated in the CTSA is machine wet cleaning. This process involves special detergents and controlled washing and drying cycles depending on fabric type.

The CTSA also evaluates a cleaning process using supercritical CO_2 (CO_2 between liquid and gaseous states). In this process, CO_2 is put under very high pressure, and it becomes a supercritical fluid. In this form, it has the ability to pull dirt out of clothes. This process is currently under development and is not yet available.

Ultrasonic washing is another technology that is assessed. In this process, sound waves are used to dislodge dirt from garments. The garments must be immersed in water or some other solvent, but the sound waves do not agitate the clothes while cleaning. This may be a gentler option than machine wet cleaning and more suitable for some clothes.

Finally, microwave drying is evaluated, in which clothes are dried using microwaves. Because this process can dry clothes at lower temperatures, it may make other nonsolvent cleaning alternatives more viable.

Once the technical work is completed, the project will concentrate on its outreach and implementation steps. The outreach component of the project will involve a number of different information products developed from data included in the CTSA. These products are intended to make dry cleaners aware of the project and its issues and to give them the information they need to make changes in their business practices. This technical information dissemination will be carried out through industry, federal, state, and local networks.

The outreach effort will also be geared toward the public. One important piece of the project is to make consumers aware of alternatives to traditional dry-cleaning chemicals. Informed consumers will have the choice of patronizing environmentally safer establishments, and thereby they can create incentives for businesses to practice DfE in their workplaces.

As a part of the outreach phase of the project, DfE program staff will conduct consumer research to determine clothes-cleaning preferences, perception of dry-cleaning risk, and effective communication channels. This type of activity will assist in any future outreach efforts.

Finally, the project will enter the implementation phase. In this component, DfE staff will help dry cleaners actually begin to implement some of the pollution prevention steps described in the CTSA. This phase will consist of setting up alternative dry-cleaning demonstration sites for dry cleaners to learn new, environmentally preferable technologies. Staff will also conduct training workshops for dry cleaners and develop pollution prevention training manuals to be used by technical transfer professionals in "train the trainer" workshops.

Printing Project

There are over 62,000 printing establishments located in the United States. They perform functions as diverse as printing labels for cans of soup, publishing daily newspapers, printing pictures on candy wrappers, printing decals on T-shirts, and publishing books. In the course of providing their services, printers select and mix chemicals for applications from hundreds of printing inks, cleaning solvents, and other chemical products.

The purpose of the DfE Printing Project is to encourage pollution prevention and environmental risk reduction within the American printing industry. Eighty percent of printing establishments employ fewer than 20 people; therefore, very few of these small businesses have the time or resources to learn how to choose chemicals, work practices, and technologies that are safer for the environment. The project focuses on improving the access of small and medium-sized printers to pollution prevention and environmental information about printing processes.

The Printing Project can be thought of in terms of the same three steps as the other cooperative industry projects: technical, outreach, and implementation. The technical work, however, focuses primarily on three different sectors of the printing industry. There are six different methods used by printers: screen printing, lithography, flexography, letterpress, gravure, and plateless technologies. Each of these printing methods has different chemical and technological alternatives. Industry representatives identified areas of environmental concern in three of these printing sectors, based on regulatory requirements and information from the EPA about the risks associated with various products and processes. These three industries are lithography, screen printing, and flexography. These processes and the identified areas of concern are considerably different, and each warrants its own CTSA. Table 22.1 summarizes the corresponding use clusters.

In the *screen-printing industry,* screen reclamation, or screen cleaning, was chosen as the main area of concern. Screen printing involves applying ink to a substrate through the use of a porous screen mesh (see Figs. 22.4 and 22.5). The screen mesh is stenciled to define the desired image. Screen printers clean (reclaim) their screens for further reimaging and printing by using ink remover, such as solvents or water-soluble ink degradants. An emulsion remover is applied to remove the stencil or emulsion; often the use of a high-pressure water blaster assists in stencil removal. From time to time, ghost images caused by ink residue in the mesh must be removed with ghost/haze removers, which are typically strong caustics.

The screen-printing CTSA evaluates a number of alternative methods that are currently practiced by screen printers. One alternative is simply to discard the screen after use. This eliminates the use of chemicals to clean screens, but it creates a disposal issue. Most printers do currently reclaim their screens; however, some printers who use very small screens may dispose of them after use.

There are four similar methods of chemical-based screen reclamation that the CTSA evaluates; although they are similar, the slight

TABLE 22.1   Printing Project Use Clusters

| | Printing processes investigated | | |
	Lithography	Screen printing	Flexography
Potential use clusters	Blanket washes Dampening systems Inks Prepress operations	Inks Platen adhesives Screen reclamation	Inks Cleanup solvents Adhesives
Use of cluster chosen	Blanket washes	Screen reclamation	Inks
Traditional products	High-VOC, solvent-based	Volatile solvents and caustics	Solvent-based inks
Alternatives under investigation	Vegetable oil/solvent mixtures Water/solvent emulsions Water/surfactant mixtures Automatic systems Work practice changes	Nonvolatile solvents Low-toxicity chemicals Surfactants Enclosed systems Work practice changes	Water-based inks UV-curable inks Work practice changes

Figure 22.4 Using chemicals and a high-pressure spray gun, a worker removes ink and emulsion from a screen. This process, known as screen reclamation, allows the screen to be reused.

Figure 22.5 Small amounts of solvent are used on press to remove excess ink. The screen may then be reclaimed, or stored for further printing. This is the first step of the screen reclamation process.

variations in products and equipment make a difference in the quantity of chemicals necessary. Also, two of the methods do not include a haze remover, and this eliminates the use of some caustics and solvents.

Another option for screen reclamation is automatic screen washers, enclosed systems that are available for ink removal only or for total removal (ink/emulsion/haze removal). This system reduces occupational exposure but is very expensive.

The CTSA also characterizes the risk trade-offs between a number of technologies that are as yet undemonstrated (not used commercially). These methods are all being used for paint stripping, so it is possible that they will be useful in ink removal. The first options are blasting methods. Dry abrasives—e.g., plastic beads, wheat starch, carbon dioxide—or wet abrasives such as sodium bicarbonate could be used to blast the screen. Crystalline ice blasting and carbon dioxide ice pellet blasting are also options, although carbon dioxide ice pellet blasting is likely to damage the screen. Using stripping methods such as dry or wet mechanical sanding, using heat guns to burn off ink, or using liquid nitrogen (cryogenic) spray with dry blast media are other options. Technology is evaluated in which the use of water-soluble stencils and emulsions allows emulsion removal with water only. Further options include using pulse light energy in laser stripping or in a Xenon flashlamp, where the high frequency of the lamp takes the paint off the screen.

In *lithography,* or more specifically, sheetfed offset printing, the blanket-washing process was identified as the priority area of concern. In this process, an elastomeric rubber-covered blanket is mounted on a blanket cylinder in the press machine. This blanket receives the inked images and passes them onto the substrates. The ink must be washed off the blanket between printing jobs, and various chemical solvents are used to perform this function. The chemical solvents used to do this are called "blanket washes." Blanket washes are necessary to remove the old image; prevent buildup of paper dust, starch, and clay; and maintain image quality. Part of the concern about blanket washes is that many of them still have a high content of volatile organic compounds (VOCs).

The DfE program seeks to identify and evaluate alternatives that may limit occupational exposure to blanket washes. The lithography CTSA evaluates currently used solvent-based blanket washes. These blanket washes range from fast-drying to medium-dry (100 to 110°F flashpoint) to slow-dry (more than 140°F flashpoint). There is also a UV/EB-cured ink solvent presently used as a blanket wash that is evaluated.

The CTSA also evaluates a number of washes intended for use on different parts of the printing machine, but that are currently used incorrectly by many printers as blanket washes. The first of these types of products is a press wash, needed to clean the metal parts of a press. This is a low-VOC blend with the ability to cut ink quickly. A second type of product, a roller wash, is also evaluated. Roller washes are slowly evaporating chemicals that clean the ink rollers in the inking system. The third type of product is a type wash; while this type of solvent is very effective at removing inks, it has a high VOC content.

In addition, the CTSA evaluates alternatives currently in limited use or that demonstrate future potential. One example is water. Typically, water is not capable of effectively removing the hydrophobic ("water-hating") inks on the blankets. However, the Deluxe Corporation has developed a new vegetable oil–based hydrophilic ("water-loving") ink that can be washed off the blanket with water. Therefore, water (used only with this new type of ink) is an alternative blanket wash, and is included in the CTSA. Additional alternatives being considered include low-VOC washes such as water and surfactant washes, water and solvent emulsions, water and vegetable oil emulsions, vegetable oil and solvent mixtures, and other nonvolatile materials.

The lithographic CTSA also evaluates several technologies that limit exposure. These technologies include automatic blanket washes, in which the blanket-washing step is enclosed so that exposure to the worker is reduced. Sometimes the blanket washes can be recycled; however, this technology is expensive and not economically feasible for most smaller businesses. Another technology examined is one in which the entire press is enclosed within a box and no blanket wash is needed, so fewer fumes are emitted.

Playing a large role in the technical and outreach parts of the project is the series of case studies that illustrate the DfE theme in the printing industry. The first two studies provide examples of printers that were able to achieve significant environmental results in a cost-effective way. The first case study illustrates how a successful pollution reduction program was implemented at Romo Incorporated, a screen-printing operation in De Pere, Wisconsin. Over the forty years of its operation, Romo has experienced increasingly stringent environmental and health regulations, many of which have required expensive changes or threatened high fines for noncompliance. A change in ownership in 1983 led company management to make a conscious decision to stay ahead of the regulations. In 1987, Romo began to look for pollution prevention opportunities, particularly in the screen reclamation process. They decided to concentrate on three processes in screen reclamation: ink removal (screen cleaning), emulsion removal, and haze or "ghost image" removal. To reduce chemical risk,

Romo pursued three strategies: (1) reducing the volume of all products used, (2) testing alternative application techniques, and (3) experimenting with alternative formulations of traditional products. To improve the ink removal process, Romo began to recycle their inks. They installed a distillation unit at a one-time cost of $2900, and saved the company $20,750 per year. In addition, Romo fit the screen-cleaning spray nozzle with a device that controls the amount of solvent needed for each screen. Finally, Romo was able to reduce its use of chemicals listed by the EPA as ingredients of environmental concern by 70% by switching to screen cleaners with alternative product formulations.[3]

Romo cut down on the amount of emulsion remover it used by buying a high-pressure water blaster, diluting the emulsion remover with water before blasting, and creating a new applicator for emulsion remover. The plant engineer estimates that the combination of these changes has resulted in a 75% reduction in emulsion remover use, and it has saved the company $3800 per year. The next step for the company is to find ways to reduce it haze remover use.

The second case study illustrates how the John Roberts Company in Minneapolis, Minnesota, switched to using environmentally safer solvents and reduced its use of solvents altogether while saving money. The John Roberts Company, a commercial printer of annual reports, brochures, catalogs, forms, limited-edition fine art prints, and direct mail pieces, used leased towels as wipers for press cleanup. The company sent the towels to an industrial laundry for cleaning, and the laundry was approached by the local regulatory agency because too much solvent was being washed out of the towels, causing the vapors from the laundry's effluent to exceed the lower explosive limit (LEL). The John Roberts company decided to concentrate on two main objectives to address this issue: (1) to change the nature of the solvent that was left in the towels from cleaning presses, and (2) to reduce the volume of solvent left in the towels. Upon examining the nature of the solvent currently being used, the company discovered that a highly volatile solvent was being used incorrectly to clean its presses. The company then developed a list of criteria that a blanket wash would need to meet in order to fill the company's needs. The company tried a series of new solvent blends, found one that did the job, and trained its workers to use it efficiently. In addition, the company began to centrifuge rags before sending them to the laundry in order to wring more solvent out of them. After implementing these changes, the company found that they were recovering and reusing much more solvent than before, resulting in a savings of more than $34,000 in the first year alone, quickly paying for the $15,000 centrifuge.[4]

Although these two companies performed their analyses and implemented changes prior to joining the DfE project, their success provides real-world examples to printers that pollution prevention solves problems and can pay for itself. As such, these cases show printers how they can make use of the results of the technical work developed by the DfE project.

Another part of the DfE printing project is ensuring that the case studies and other information get distributed to the printing industry and to the public. In order to do that, DfE uses existing communication networks among printing organizations; it also uses a variety of networks associated with technical assistance programs, such as the State Technical Assistance programs, the Department of Commerce Manufacturing Extension program, and the Small Business Administration programs. In one pilot project, EPA is working with the Great Printers Project (organized by the Environmental Defense Fund, the Council of Great Lakes Governors, and the Printing Industries of America) to distribute pollution prevention information developed in the DfE Printing Project through state-organized "one-stop shops" for printers. These information clearinghouses will give out information as well as refer small business to state technical assistance programs and federal technology centers for further assistance.

Along with getting technical information out to people, the DfE program is taking steps to provide incentives for printers to begin using cleaner, safer products and processes. One step in creating incentives is the development of a total-cost accounting manual which demonstrates how lower-risk pollution prevention alternatives identified in the technical analysis can save printers money. This manual will be distributed through the Small Business Administration and other technical assistance program workshops.

A second step toward implementing improvements is technical training. In focus groups with screen printers, it was discovered that one of the most effective mechanisms for communicating environmental information to printers would be to incorporate that information into training videos which a printer could show new employees. The DfE program, in cooperation with the Screen Printers Association International, is planning to develop a training video of this type.

EPA-GSA Cleaning Products Project

The General Services Administration (GSA) provides cleaning products both for use in federal government buildings maintained by its Public Buildings Service (PBS) and for sale to the rest of the federal government through the Federal Supply Service (FSS). In January 1993, the GSA approached the EPA for assistance in selecting cleaning products based on their safety to custodial workers and the environment. As a result, GSA and EPA launched a joint project to examine different techniques for this selection process, which would be a part of an integrated assessment approach. This approach includes evaluations of product efficacy by GSA.

The techniques include "traditional" risk assessments of products, risk- and hazard-based criteria for environmentally preferable products, and eventual consensus standards. In addition, testing of several general-purpose cleaning products (see Fig. 22.6) was conducted at a federal courthouse building in Philadelphia, Pennsylvania. At this site, the GSA tested three general-purpose cleaning systems, claimed to be environmentally preferable, to see how well they work. The test was done through a survey that the EPA developed and administered to employees who use these products in the buildings. The survey asked workers about product effectiveness and indications of any possible health problems resulting from exposure. The products tested in this study are the candidates for the "traditional" risk assessment, which will rank the products by relative risk.

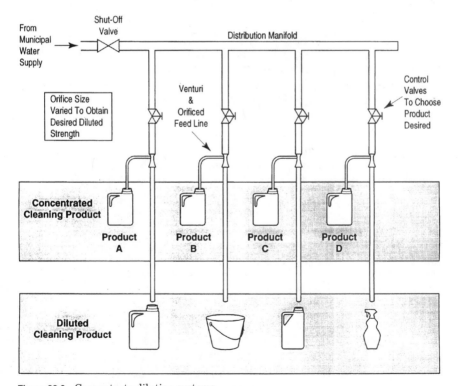

Figure 22.6 Concentrate-dilution systems.

As a part of the effort to develop risk- and hazard-based criteria for environmentally preferable products, the EPA is communicating with industry, labor, public interest, and environmental groups. Criteria being considered in this effort include chronic human health risk, irritation, aquatic toxicity, biodegradability, VOC content, ozone depletion chemicals, packaging/recycling, flammability, energy use, and unnecessary additives.

The EPA and GSA are coordinating with other government agencies who may also be interested in procuring environmentally preferable products in order to avoid duplication of effort. However, once product criteria and guidance have been established for a given category, EPA involvement will be minimal. This project will eventually extend to include other products, such as snow removal compounds, floor care products, sweeping compounds, and carpet care products.

Institutional Projects

Environmental Accounting Project

Every business decision is affected by financial and economic considerations, and, in general, businesses try to undertake investments which will be profitable or cost effective. A common misconception throughout the business community is that all business investments, expenditures, or policies dealing with environmental issues are financial losers, detracting from the profitability of the business. A growing body of evidence suggests that, on the contrary, by considering environmental costs up front in decisions, businesses can reduce must-do regulatory compliance costs, increase overall profitability, and at the same time, do the right thing for the environment.

Information collected in a business's management accounting system is the foundation for many business decisions. The information is used for supporting decisions, such as product pricing and investment decisions; directing management attention to problem areas, such as higher than anticipated production costs; and controlling operations, motivating behavior, and evaluating line and management performance. Cost information is crucial in all of these core business activities, and environmental cost information is a frequently overlooked element in these important activities.

The DfE Environmental Accounting Project addresses these deficiencies by encouraging and motivating businesses to understand the full spectrum of environmental costs they face and to integrate these costs into their decisions. Although there are a number of ways to advance this objective, the EPA's effort will do so by promoting the development and use of improved accounting and capital budgeting.

One of the principal goals of the EPA's project is to encourage businesses to separate environmental costs from routine overhead costs, giving the business manager a more accurate idea of environmental management and pollution costs associated with a particular process or product. This information will help managers identify opportunities for savings that could accrue from investments in cleaner technologies. Lack of information creates additional disincentives. For example, managers who undertake environmental cost reduction projects will not be rewarded during their performance appraisals or through their compensation if senior management does not have any way of assessing the achieved savings.

One of the more significant reasons that managers do not have this important information is because environmental costs are often pooled (and thereby hidden) in an overhead account. Traditionally, part or all of the costs for waste treatment, disposal, and administration have been allocated to overhead pools which mask the true environmental costs of a particular process or product. In addition, other costs are more difficult to estimate, such as wasted raw materials and future liabilities, and the cost of poor quality is often not accounted for at all.

For example, suppose a company produces product A and product B, and both products require the same amount of labor for production. Also assume that only product A has associated environmental costs such as waste treatment or disposal. In the traditional accounting system that allocates overhead based on labor hours, environmental costs would be inappropriately linked to product B. In turn, product costing and pricing decisions would be skewed in favor of product A. In essence, the cost of production of product B subsidizes the cost of product A. Sound decisionmaking requires managers to understand how such subsidies work. Product A is certainly less profitable than management originally thought, and may in fact be unprofitable. In addition to being inefficient, the subsidy obscures opportunities for management and design engineers to find cheaper and more environmentally sound processes to manufacture product A.

There is no guarantee that all, or even most, pollution-prevention-oriented projects will succeed if more accurate cost accounting procedures are adopted. At the very least, however, the EPA's project works toward breaking down some of the institutional barriers that stand in the way of pollution prevention activities. It encourages companies to identify how much they spend on environmental management practices and to allocate those costs to the processes or products responsible for them. In addition, the EPA is encouraging business to recognize the varied streams of benefits and longer time horizon often necessary to level the playing field between investments in end-of-pipe technologies and pollution prevention technologies.

Suppose, for example, a business faces a regulatory requirement with which it could comply by using end-of-pipe controls (such as a scrubber on a smokestack) with a moderate up-front cost, or by changing its manufacturing process (by eliminating the hazardous material that contaminates the smoke) and paying a higher up-front cost. Based on a first-cost analysis, the end-of-pipe solution is cheaper and therefore more cost effective. If, however, the analysis also includes "hidden" costs such as compliance and environmental permitting costs, waste disposal and raw material losses in the waste stream, and the cost of penalties, fines, and possible future liabilities, the process change option may be more economically viable.[5] The process change may not only meet regulatory requirements but also reduce costs, risks of environmental accidents, and future liabilities.

The EPA's DfE efforts are based on several key assumptions which have been developed by stakeholders outside the agency. First, cost accounting and capital budgeting processes can be improved to more fully incorporate environmental costs. Second, better information can help managers evaluate the full spectrum of choices and the costs and benefits of business actions that prevent pollution. Third, and finally, because much work is currently under way to improve accounting and capital budgeting, there is an unprecedented opportunity to gather this expertise to stimulate an interdisciplinary dialogue. In order to promote the project's objectives and build on existing expertise, the Environmental Accounting Project takes a four-pronged approach: (1) developing, piloting, and testing new analytical accounting and capital-budgeting tools, (2) sponsoring research, (3) promoting curriculum development, and (4) facilitating dialogue among key stakeholders. These four elements are discussed below.

Tools.   Although the EPA does not require any particular method for conducting a financial analysis of pollution prevention projects, the agency's research has identified several criteria for evaluating such tools and a number of important elements that should be found in any adequate method. Specifically, a useful financial analysis tool should first encourage and help users identify a complete set of environmental costs and savings and allocate them to a product or process. Second, the simpler the method, and the less time it takes to use, the better. Third, availability of both paper worksheets and software is desirable.[5]

The EPA has identified several interesting total cost assessment techniques that meet some or all of these criteria. The agency anticipates publicizing additional methods late in 1995. The first of the methods is the General Electric (GE) method. This method allows the user to quantify direct cost (out-of-pocket cash costs routinely associated with waste management and disposal) and future liability costs (including potential environmental liabilities for remedial action costs, and related costs for personal injury and property damage) of the waste management method they are currently using versus an alternative waste minimization option.[5]

In this method, users are provided with a workbook and a financial software package that allow them to identify and estimate the direct capital and operating costs associated with their waste management practices. Based on this and other information, the software will calculate streams of after-tax incremental cash flow of the investment, the net present value (NPV) for the current and alternative practice, the break-even point, the return on investment (ROI), and discounted cash flow rate of return. Finally, the workbook offers recommendations for using the financial indices to identify and rank waste minimization projects.

One limitation of this method is that it does not encourage comprehensive pollution prevention approaches like materials substitution and process change; it focuses primarily on waste minimization for the purpose of reducing disposal costs and long-term liability.[5]

The second method, developed by the EPA in the late 1980s and often referred to as the "Benefits Manual," is designed to assist in the cost comparison of a number of different pollution prevention alternatives. The method sets up a hierarchy of costs, which progress from the most conventional and certain costs in Tier 0 to the most difficult to estimate and least certain costs in Tier 3. The hierarchy is set up as follows:

Tier 0:   Usual costs—e.g., equipment, labor, and materials
Tier 1:   Hidden costs:—e.g., compliance and permits
Tier 2:   Liability costs—e.g., penalties/fines and future liabilities
Tier 3:   Less tangible costs—e.g., consumer responses and employee relations

The method relies on worksheets to assist users in calculating costs associated with their practices at each tier. The manual provides a summary of relevant regulatory programs to assist users in calculating Tier 1 regulatory costs, and cost equations to assist users in determining potential future liabilities. The multitiered structure of this system allows users to start their step-by-step analysis with the most certain and defensible usual costs and progress to less certain, more subtle costs only if necessary. The EPA believes this approach is a key element to simplifying any analysis. One limitation of this method is that the program has no software; this may make it difficult for some people to carry out the calculations.[5]

Another method the DfE program has set forth is known as PRE-COSIS. Somewhat like the GE method, the method was designed for use in the financial analysis of waste reduction projects. With this method, users can enter information about their current waste management system and information about an alternative system (or systems) on the software and come up with a financial comparison of the options. The software will compute NPV, estimated payback years, internal ROI, and other financial indicators. For these calculations, the program will consider labor resources, materials, facilities, revenues, and waste management.

This program is valuable if a company needs to assess (1) the economic feasibility of waste minimization projects or (2) the financial differences among waste minimization alternatives. Its drawbacks are that it is not similar to standard project financial analyses and that it takes a long time to learn how to use the software.[5]

After reviewing the previous three methods, the EPA has developed software for a fourth method, P2/FINANCE. This user-friendly spreadsheet program is designed to guide companies in the data collection and analysis essential to a clearer financial evaluation of pollution prevention projects. P2/FINANCE is designed to complement a company's existing project evaluation practices while ensuring that prevention investments receive balanced and comprehensive treatment during the capital-budgeting process. For companies or projects where no formal budgeting guidelines are in place, P2/FINANCE offers a valuable starting point for introducing a total cost assessment (TCA) approach. The TCA approach differs from conventional practices in four key ways: a broader inventory of costs and savings, allocation of all costs and savings to specific process and product lines rather than to overhead accounts, expanded time horizons for the capture of long-term benefits, and the use of profitability indicators which incorporate the time value of money.

Users input their capital and operating costs for a current product or process and an alternative product or process, and the program outputs a fifteen-year cash flow analysis and a profitability analysis summary. The profitability analysis summary uses three financial indicators: NPV, internal rate of return (IRR), and simple payback. The time horizons used are five, ten, and fifteen years, as well as an additional period defined by the user. A manual comes with the software and an in-depth example of one company's use of the program.[6]

Distinct from promoting improved capital budgeting tools, the EPA is promoting innovative managerial accounting techniques. For example, the agency has cofunded a study by the World Resources Institute (WRI) to examine existing accounting practices in a small number of *Fortune* 100 companies. The report, the first of its kind, provides in-depth case studies of their internal corporate accounting practices.[7]

Curriculum development. The second element in the project's approach is curriculum development. The National Pollution Prevention Center for Higher Education at the University of Michigan has developed a curriculum module on environmental accounting to which the EPA is contributing. The module provides an introduction to the application of pollution prevention in business accounting. It is a continuously evolving resource list of educational materials.

In addition to developing university curricula, the EPA recognizes the need for curricula to train professionals in business and government. Therefore, the agency has begun to develop cooperative efforts with the major accounting associations in the United States, the American Institute of Certified Public Accountants and the Institute of Management Accountants, that are expected to lead to industry-sponsored continuing professional education courses. While the EPA will continue to explore the development and dissemination of information on curricula for business, some materials are already available through State Technical Assistance Programs and Small Business Development Centers.

Research. Research is the third element in the project's efforts to achieve its goals. Most people realize that pollution prevention can reduce future liabilities. There is growing anecdotal evidence, however, that lawyers and accountants often advise their clients not to estimate or document any information on potential liabilities because if they do, the businesses will be more likely to incur the cost of those liabilities or be required to report them to the Securities and Exchange Commission, to potential investors, and to others. This situation creates disincentives for businesses to practice pollution prevention. The result may leave businesses caught in a "Catch 22"; liability drives pollution prevention, but may also discourage it. To explore this issue and develop a framework for addressing it, the EPA is funding a research effort, to explore the connection between various environmental liabilities (CERCLA, criminal, tort, etc.) and managerial decisions to prevent pollution. A managerial accounting framework is the filter for how managers consider liabilities in their decisionmaking. The framework continues to be developed. In addition, the EPA is funding the Tellus Institute, another nonprofit research institute, to conduct a survey of corporate accounting practices which incorporate total cost assessment concepts.

Facilitating dialogue. The fourth and perhaps most important element of the Environmental Accounting Project is facilitating dialogue. The EPA has held focus group meetings and a national workshop to develop a National Action Agenda to promote improvements in managerial accounting and capital budgeting practices. The agenda, developed by approximately 100 key stakeholders, recommends issues and action items for all of the stakeholder groups. The EPA is inviting all interested parties to help implement some aspects of the agenda by themselves or in cooperation with other stakeholders, including the agency. The agency is also interested in cohosting future conferences for the purpose of promoting interdisciplinary dialogue on environmental management accounting and capital budgeting issues. Key stakeholders include representatives from the accounting community, management consultants, business, government, academia, and other trade and professional groups.

In addition, EPA maintains a network of hundreds of financial and environmental professionals interested and active in accounting and capital budgeting issues. The network has built momentum around these issues and is facilitating the exchange of ideas and information.

Insurance/Risk Management Project

The financial DfE program seeks to effect voluntary changes in corporate decisionmaking that facilitate investment in and diffusion of pollution prevention practices and technologies by translating pollution prevention into terms that make sense for professions, such as insurance, accounting, and financing. Through the DfE Insurance/Risk Management Project, the EPA hopes to integrate pollution prevention principles into the day-to-day practices of insurance underwriters, brokers, and corporate risk managers.

Risk management is a proactive decisionmaking process for planning, organizing, and controlling the resources and activities of an organization to *prevent, minimize,* and *finance* the adverse effects of accidental losses—including those associated with the environment—of an organization, while still fulfilling the organization's mission. Risk managers seek to accomplish the dual goal of minimizing both the chance that a loss will occur and the financial impact of losses that cannot be prevented.

Pollution prevention fits into the risk management process both as a "risk control" and a "risk financing" technique. It can serve as a risk control technique because implementation of source reduction measures can prevent or reduce environmental risks borne by organizations. As a risk-financing tool, implementation of various pollution prevention practices may make it easier for a company to obtain pollution insurance or lead to lower insurance premiums.

As a first step in developing and utilizing external partnerships to effect voluntary change in the risk management profession, the EPA has entered into a cooperative effort with the American Institute of

Chartered Property Casualty Underwriters (AICPCU), an independent nonprofit organization offering educational programs and professional certification for people in the risk management and insurance industry. As a short-term objective, the EPA is assisting AICPCU to incorporate pollution prevention into the course materials used in one of its professional certification programs. In the longer term, the EPA and AICPCU hope to build on the success of this initial effort and more comprehensively integrate pollution prevention into the institute's certification curriculum.

In a separate effort, the EPA is analyzing the current state of the pollution insurance market and the corporate risk management process to investigate a range of opportunities for integrating pollution prevention into this profession. The EPA will seek partnership with key stakeholders to identify options for further investment by the EPA in the risk management/ insurance profession.

Financing for Pollution Prevention Project

The goal of the DfE Financing for Pollution Prevention Project is to break down barriers to pollution prevention practices. There are a number of constraints that often prevent businesses, especially small and medium-sized businesses, from adopting pollution prevention technologies. With limited possibilities for self-financing or for raising funds through the capital markets, these firms generally depend on commercial banks for their credit needs. A common problem is that they cannot obtain the necessary financing or credit from local financial institutions to implement pollution prevention projects. One reason for this is that the financial community is unfamiliar with pollution prevention. At the same time, stricter controls on commercial lending in recent years, together with an uncertain legal landscape regarding lender liability, have served to constrain bank lending in general, and in the environmental arena in particular. Banks tend to view investments in the environmental realm more as a potential liability than as an opportunity. In addition, small businesses often lack the resources to prepare convincing loan application packages. As a result, small businesses find it difficult to obtain funding for their pollution prevention initiatives.

The EPA is pursuing three objectives in the Financing for Pollution Prevention Project. First, it will work to enhance the ability of small to medium-sized businesses to obtain financing (primarily from commercial banks) for pollution prevention projects. This objective includes helping them to present their financing needs for pollution prevention more effectively. Second, it will seek to harness the financial community's inherent influence over business to promote prevention-oriented behavior. Finally, in conjunction with the EPA's

Environmental Technology Initiative, put forth by President Clinton in 1993 to encourage research into environmentally friendly technology, the financing project will elevate the profile of prevention in capital markets in order to increase the supply of investment capital for the development of pollution-prevention-oriented technologies.

To investigate and address the obstacles that face small and mid-sized businesses in obtaining credit for implementing pollution prevention measures, the Maryland Department of the Environment (MDE), EPA's DfE program, and EPA Region III's Pollution Prevention program are conducting a pilot project. This pilot project is the first step in the financing project and will help to address the first objective of presenting financing needs for pollution prevention more effectively.

Through this pilot project, the EPA has enlisted the support of key stakeholders. Stakeholders include small and mid-sized businesses that have experienced difficulty acquiring credit for pollution prevention projects or that are about to seek financing; banks and other lending institutions involved in the loan process for the types of businesses that would be likely to implement pollution prevention projects; and local, state, and federal agencies and trade associations that can help identify problems and develop solutions. Focus group discussions have been conducted with representatives of the key stakeholders to examine specific reasons and circumstances under which credit was denied for pollution prevention projects.

After the problems have been characterized, the project will identify potential solutions by coordinating with existing institutions that have expertise in assisting businesses in obtaining credit, and it will develop outreach materials for businesses and lending institutions as needed. The MDE and EPA anticipate that this pilot will be an important first step in institutionalizing a working relationship between environmental regulatory agencies and the financial community.

Chemical Design Project

The purpose of the DfE program's Chemical Design Project is to change the way organic chemists approach the design of synthetic pathways for chemical production. The production of synthetic organic chemicals is a major industry in the United States. Chemicals are designed for purposes ranging from making antifreeze for cars to developing synthetic animal hormones to aid in medicine and animal research. The incredibly large number of uses for synthetic organic chemicals translates into an equally large amount of chemicals being produced and designed yearly.

There is not just one way to produce these chemicals; instead, there are literally hundreds of different chemical reactions that can be utilized to construct a desired organic chemical. Chemists can design their own pathways from these reactions. The moment that a chemist puts pencil to paper to design how a chemical product will be made, he or she also intrinsically makes the following decisions:

- What hazardous wastes will be generated
- What toxic substances will need to be handled by the workers making the product
- What toxic contaminants might be in the product
- What regulatory compliance issues will be faced in making this product
- What liability concerns there are from the manufacture of this product
- What waste treatment costs will be incurred

Traditionally, the decision as to what synthetic sequence to use ultimately is based on yield. *Yield* can be defined roughly as what percentage of the starting material becomes the final product. Chemists use the pathway that will give them the largest yield; this often results in the production of large amounts of toxic chemicals. But at a time when costs of regulatory compliance, waste handling, treatment and disposal, and liability insurance may well outweigh the price of starting materials, sacrificing some yield in order to address other concerns may be beneficial.

In its efforts to promote pollution prevention, the EPA recognizes the fundamental role of the chemist in designing ways of making chemicals that don't involve the use or generation of toxic substances. The DfE program has started several initiatives which are designed to support the role of chemists in pollution prevention in industry, academia, and government. In the academic world, the agency is funding six research projects that will seek to minimize or eliminate hazardous feedstocks, catalysts, solvents, or by-products in the synthesis of organic chemicals. Following is a description of these grants.

Replacing heavy metal catalysts.   Catalysts are of the utmost importance to the industrial production of chemicals, yet they often have toxic components, including silver and mercury, that contribute to hazardous waste disposal problems when the catalysts are discarded. One research project considers the effectiveness of a more environmentally benign alternative: molecules that can be activated by inexpensive artificial light sources. This research is developing a large-scale methodology for the light-induced cleavage of dithianes and benzyl ethers, reactions commonly used in the dye industry.[8]

New synthesis of styrene.   Styrene is a high-volume chemical that has hundreds of applications in everyday products. This research project seeks to develop an alternative synthetic method for the manufacture of styrene. The proposed method uses less toxic chemicals as substitutes for problem environmental chemicals including the known carcinogen benzene, which presently serves as a basic feedstock of styrene.[8]

Visible light to replace the Friedel-Crafts reaction.   This project researches an innovative photochemical alternative to the Friedel-Crafts reaction, one of the top 10 most used chemical reactions. (See Fig. 22.7.) The use of visible light as a mechanism for initiating the reaction could provide an economic incentive for replacing a well-known reaction step that uses toxic pollutants.[8]

Elimination of tin-based catalysts.   This project seeks to reduce the hazard posed by radical cyclization reactions which use highly toxic tin-based catalysts by substituting a recyclable catalyst that will not accumulate in waste effluents. The improved synthetic selectivity of this approach should result in greater yields of the target compound and fewer impurities that enter the waste stream.[8]

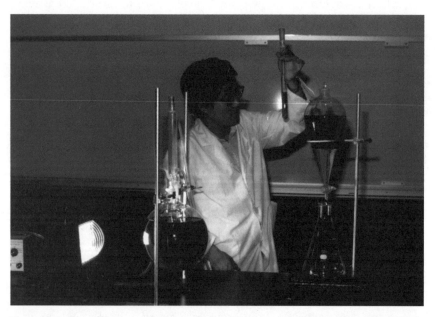

Figure 22.7 Qingi Wang, graduate student in the research laboratories of Prof. Gary Epling at the University of Connecticut, examines the progress of chemical transformations promoted by visible light. The Epling group seeks to develop environmentally benign alternatives to oxidation reactions that involve toxic or hazardous compounds.

Replacing benzene with simple sugars.   Benzene is a basic ingredient in many commercially important industrial chemicals including hydroquinone and benzoquinone. Although benzene is an extremely useful petrochemical, it is a known carcinogen and problem pollutant. This project seeks a new, environmentally benign method of producing hydroquinone and benzoquinone that replaces the use of benzene. This method utilizes a genetically engineered bacterium that produces quinic acid from D-glucose. The quinic acid is converted into hydroquinone and benzoquinone under more environmentally safe conditions.[8]

Alternatives for toxic solvents.   This project evaluates the utility of supercritical carbon dioxide (carbon dioxide between liquid and gaseous states) as the solvent for certain free-radical chemical reactions. This approach may provide an economic incentive for industry to make the transition away from currently used problem solvents such as chlorofluorocarbons, carbon tetrachloride, and benzene.[8]

The EPA is also working closely with the National Science Foundation (NSF) to fund research, education, and outreach in chemical design, and it is working on a number of different research projects with the New Jersey Institute of Technology.

In the industrial arena, the project is providing suggestions to industry for alternative chemical synthetic designs to consider in voluntary pollution prevention programs. It is also developing guidance to industry on methods to assess the pollution prevention potential of different synthetic pathways. One example of how the project is doing this is with alternative synthetic design software. This software is able to show the user several possible synthetic routes to arrive at a specified chemical, and it will alert the user to any synthetic alternative that produces toxic feedstocks or by-products. The project is also in the process of developing a database that will contain summaries of published chemical reactions that qualify as "benign" processes or as viable alternatives to procedures that are of environmental concern.

In addition, the EPA is funding projects to research the possible uses for supercritical CO_2 as part of the Environmental Technology Initiative. Potential uses for supercritical CO_2 include the following: (1) as an alternative to solvents for degreasing; (2) as a reaction solvent for the synthesis of polymers; (3) to conduct free radical reactions; (4) to conduct nucleophilic aromatic substitution reactions. Supercritical CO_2 may prove to be a less toxic catalyst and reaction medium, so it would effectively cut down on pollution as a result of chemical syntheses.

The DfE program encourages industry-university collaboration in the development of innovative approaches to pollution prevention and cleaner production technology. These creative and nontraditional efforts include DfE's participation in the NSF Industry University Cooperative Research Center (IUCRC) at the University of Washington's Center for Process Analytical Chemistry (CPAC).

CPAC is supported by some 50 industrial and governmental sponsors to develop real-time process chemistry sensors, analyzers, chemometric software, and information-processing systems to optimize production while minimizing pollution. A spin-off of the CPAC program has been the advent of new relationships between industrial sponsors at the Center. Dow Chemical and Perkin Elmer have established a Strategic Alliance for Advanced Analytical Technology. The Alliance focuses on the development and implementation of real-time industrial and environmental sampling and analysis systems tailored to particular industrial requirements. The DfE program has played an integral role in fostering this collaborative environment amongst academic, industrial, and governmental scientists to adopt a pollution prevention perspective in the design of analytical systems for the marketplace.

Additional examples of the DfE program's efforts include the development of a curriculum module for the University of Michigan's National Pollution Prevention Center. This will allow the so-called "Benign-by-Design" ethic to be incorporated into the basic training of the synthetic chemist. The Chemical Design Project staff is also sponsoring symposia in conjunction with the American Chemical Society. These large national meetings are invaluable in spreading the word about pollution prevention to synthetic chemists throughout the country.

Curriculum Development Project

While pollution prevention concepts are being incorporated into many businesses and even entire industries, recent surveys of universities nationwide show that they are not being taught or incorporated in the classroom. Discussion about pollution prevention in higher education institutions is extremely valuable. These institutions create forums for creative and progressive discussion, and they play a large role in influencing a student's views. Moreover, businesses are beginning to recognize the need for graduates with knowledge about pollution prevention. For these reasons, it is important that pollution prevention information be incorporated into curricula, and available to students.

The EPA selected the University of Michigan to serve as the base for the National Pollution Prevention Center for Higher Education (NPPC). The NPPC is a collaborative effort between business, industry, government, nonprofits, and academia to facilitate the teaching of pollution prevention in the classroom. The mission of the NPPC is fourfold:

1. Educate students, faculty, and professionals about pollution prevention concepts. Emphasis will be put on encouraging them to evaluate the full range of environmental effects associated with a product from raw materials acquisition and manufacturing to use and disposal. This life-cycle framework provides the greatest opportunity for minimizing human and ecological impacts.

2. Create educational materials that reflect multisector perspectives on pollution prevention. Successful pollution prevention initiatives should address and balance environmental, technical, economic, social, and legal issues.

3. Provide students, faculty, and professionals with tools and strategies for addressing relevant environmental problems.

4. Establish a national network for the collection and exchange of pollution prevention educational materials.

To accomplish its mission, the NPPC is developing a number of curriculum modules to incorporate pollution prevention into a variety of disciplines. These modules consist of some or all of the following components:

- Annotated bibliographies
- Case studies
- Original papers on the topic plus other key articles
- Engineering design problems
- Quantitative problem sets
- Videos
- Computer software
- Syllabi of courses currently being taught around the country
- List of key personnel around the country

The modules are developed by NPPC by gathering educational materials and developing new resources. Once the modules are developed, they are made available to faculty and the public, who are encouraged to provide feedback and any additional materials they feel would enrich the module. There are currently existing modules in accounting, business law, chemical engineering, corporate strategy, and industrial engineering and operations research. Architecture, chemistry, environmental engineering, industrial design, marketing, material science, and operations management are modules under development.

In addition to facilitating the development of curriculum modules, the NPPC provides internships to undergraduate and graduate students. These students get practical experience by working with corporate sponsors on pollution prevention projects and with faculty mentors to develop educational materials. Finally, the NPPC holds periodic conferences and workshops. These gatherings are intended to facilitate thought-provoking discussion and original ideas on critical pollution prevention issues.

Conclusions

The Office of Technology Assessment finds that the federal government is uniquely responsible for the following four areas of environmental need: (1) research, because there are no incentives for private companies to conduct this research, and not enough is known about which problems pose the greatest risk; (2) credible information for consumers, because consumers do not know which products are environmentally preferable or what criteria to use to select products; (3) market distortions and environmental externalities, because failure to consider environmental costs in design and production decisions can make environmentally sound choices seem economically unattractive; and (4) coordination and harmonization, because there is little coordination between the several projects relating to green design that are being sponsored by the federal government.[9]

The EPA's DfE program addresses all of these four issues. First, the EPA and its partners conduct much of the research that private companies have no incentive to conduct. Second, one of the main goals of the DfE program is to provide information to businesses that would like to make changes in their business practices to help the environment. Through the DfE program, the EPA wants to make informed consumers out of industry. Also, DfE's outreach efforts may make the public more informed about environmental options. Third, the Environmental Accounting Project addresses the market distortion issue. Fourth, the program is working to coordinate efforts between the EPA and the GSA to procure environmentally safer products for use in cleaning federal buildings.

By helping industry think about the environmental consequences of the way products are produced, the DfE program attempts to ensure that environmental protection is incorporated into all aspects of company decisionmaking, rather than being the sole domain of environment, health, and safety personnel. This integration of the environmental philosophy will help ensure that products are manufactured with fewer and fewer environmental impacts, thus protecting the environment and helping to put U.S. industry on the road to sustainability.

References

1. U.S. Environmental Protection Agency, "Health Assessment Document for Tetrachloroethylene (Perc)," EPA600-8-82-005F, prepared by the Office of Health and Environmental Assessment, Washington, DC, 1985.
2. U.S. Environmental Protection Agency, "Multiprocess Wet Cleaning: A Cost and Performance Comparison of Dry Cleaning and an Alternative Process," EPA744-R-93-004, prepared by the Office of Pollution Prevention and Toxics, Washington, DC, 1993.
3. U.S. Environmental Protection Agency, "Design for the Environment Printing Project Case Study #2," EPA744-F-93-015, prepared by the Office of Pollution Prevention and Toxics, Washington, DC, 1993.
4. U.S. Environmental Protection Agency, "Design for the Environment Printing Project Case Study #1," EPA744-K-93-001, prepared by the Office of Pollution Prevention and Toxics, Washington, DC, 1993.
5. U.S. Environmental Protection Agency, "Total Cost Assessment: Accelerating Industrial Pollution Prevention through Innovative Project Financial Analysis, with Applications to the Pulp and Paper Industry," EPA741-R-92-002, prepared by the Office of Pollution Prevention and Toxics, Washington, DC, 1992.
6. U.S. Environmental Protection Agency, "Fact Sheet on Pollution Prevention Financial Analysis Software," EPA742-F-94-003, prepared by the Office of Pollution Prevention and Toxics, Washington, DC, 1994.
7. U.S. Environmental Protection Agency, "Design for the Environment: Environmental Accounting and Capital Budgeting Project Update #1," EPA742-F-93-007, prepared by the Office of Pollution Prevention and Toxics, Washington, DC, 1993.
8. U.S. Environmental Protection Agency, "Design for the Environment Chemical Design Project," EPA744-F-93-005, prepared by the Office of Pollution Prevention and Toxics, Washington, DC, 1993.
9. U.S. Congress Office of Technology Assessment, "Green Products by Design: Choices for a Cleaner Environment," E-541, Washington, DC, 1992.

Charting the Course:
The Road Ahead

Chapter

23

Organizational Issues in DFE

Robert Shelton

Director
Environmental, Health & Safety
Management
Arthur D. Little, Inc.
San Francisco, California

"...where in the waste is the wisdom."

JAMES JOYCE
Finnegan's Wake

Design for the environment (DFE) appears to be one of the few elements of environmental, health, and safety (EH&S) management that has found a comfortable organizational home in corporations. Traditional EH&S management organizations have historically had difficulty finding an effective positioning in the business enterprise because they require corporate autonomy and objectivity combined with detailed involvement in the operating unit's manufacturing and service activities. Appearing to be neither fish nor fowl, EH&S activities have often had difficulty becoming sufficiently integrated with the business units to be effective, and sufficiently "corporate" and autonomous to provide the essential, independent perspectives that are critical for environmental quality assurance and enforcement. The tensions that this dual role of EH&S creates within the overall organization have never been fully resolved.

DFE, on the other hand, has found integration with business units and line operations easier. DFE organizations have successfully been organized either close to or inside the organizations that claim primary responsibility for the design function without compromising those organizations' need for independence. Among the many companies that have established successful DFE operations are Xerox, Hewlett-Packard (HP), AT&T, Levi Strauss, Syntex, IBM, and DEC. The importance of organizational considerations to the effective introduction of DFE is evident in many of the company-specific chapters in Part 3 of this book.

The purpose of this chapter is to present some general principles of DFE organizational design, based on lessons learned from working with leading companies.

Start with Organizing Principles

DFE is a technology management issue

At its roots, DFE is a *technology management* activity whose goal is to align product development activities in order to capture external and internal environmental considerations. That means, in practice, that DFE has a big "D" and a little "e." Technology management typically addresses the strategy, organization, and operations of R&D, product development, technology transfer, and engineering support within a company. In day-to-day activities, technology management provides the essential linkage between the company's technical capabilities, business functions, and markets. Because organization should follow strategy, the DFE organization of a company must reflect the essential features of technology management (i.e., product management and development) and the overall business strategy of the company.

The first issue to address is, "What are you going to do with DFE inside your company?" Stated differently, "What technology issues are you trying to manage?" Clarification of this issue is important because DFE is a broad concept that covers a wide range of activities. Selecting the appropriate organization—or more likely, modifying the current organization—thus depends in part on the specific goals that you establish for the DFE program. Creating an organization that is tailored to your specific needs at that time—and not trying to create an organization that can do everything for everybody at all times—is the first organizing principle for DFE.

Table 23.1 describes five DFE goals and their related activities and issues. Depending on the current state of development of the DFE program in a company, one would expect different mixes of DFE goals over time. Companies often shift back and forth among the goals or bundle together several to be sought at the same time.

For example, the first stage of DFE introduction requires a broad "big picture" assessment to determine the potential threats and opportunities that a company may face. This type of DFE analysis should

TABLE 23.1 Characteristic DFE Goals and Related Issues

Goal	Key activities	DFE issues	Organization issues
View the big picture	Infrequent activity Identify key threats/opportunities	Formative Little detail	Cross-functional teams Cross-business teams
Devise corporate guidelines	Infrequent activity Overview Develop operating principles Identify organizational options	Policy development focus Companywide applicability	Key role for EH&S Cross-functional teams
Protect mature products	Limited frequency of activity Identify/assess emerging issues Identify low-cost mitigation	Static product/process Constrained options Incremental change Limited growth potential constrains investment/change Specific/detailed DFE	Product/process focus Product team locus
Rejuvenate existing products	Ongoing activity Seize growth potential	Wide range of options Flexible products/processes Specific/detailed DFE	Multifunctional focus
Commercialize new products	Continuous activity Create competitive advantage	"Unlimited" options Precommercial product Malleable product/processes Specific/detailed DFE	Multifunctional focus

involve a cross-functional team that includes all the relevant business lines. The focus is on prioritizing the most important issues, and only on rare occasions does the analysis delve into the details of specific products. One company used the "big picture" to establish the appropriate role for DFE within its industry and to help some of its key players to become comfortable with the concept and its role. Such a broad DFE perspective can be crucial to subsequent stages of development, but it is not necessary to conduct such an exercise on a regular basis, and the DFE team devoted to this goal thus meets infrequently.

Similarly, developing corporate DFE guidelines requires infrequent team meetings. Here, the focus is on developing policy and organizational options that can serve companywide—that is a slightly narrower scope, but the focus still encompasses the entire company. In this instance, the EH&S organization may play a more visible role because the guidelines entail compliance issues. However, the guidelines will also require implementation at the operating levels, and as a result the multifunctional team is still critical.

DFE for product development requires different activities and is much more narrowly focused than the previous corporate DFE initiatives. Recent experience demonstrates that there are three types of product development DFE: (1) protecting mature products, (2) enhancing current products with high growth potential, and (3) commercializing new products.

The protection of existing products in a company's portfolio is often overlooked in DFE organizational design because DFE is usually thought to apply exclusively to precommercial activities. However, when a company undertakes a DFE program, after it has developed the big picture and defined corporate guidelines, it will face the reality of dealing with a large number of existing products that were developed and commercialized without much, if any, DFE input. Many of these existing products will face increasing environmental demands (e.g., disposal, recycling) and require post hoc DFE.

A mature product has little room for alteration or modification—either of the product itself or of its manufacturing process—due to financial, logistical, and market constraints. Unless the threat to the product is enormous, the potential payback from DFE-induced modifications will be small, and management will balk at making the investment because of the low return. For example, commercial airframe manufacturers face this situation. Their products have a very long lifetime, and they introduce new products only every ten to twenty years. Similarly, returns on DFE-related investments can be low in any industry, especially in cases in which the potential for improving market share or profit margins is low or negligible. For well-established, mature products, it is likely that there will be only small, incremental growth in market demand for DFE-related changes because the franchise for the product is firmly established in the context of long-standing brand and performance characteristics.

Therefore, the DFE goal for mature products is to introduce low-cost mitigation efforts to protect market share. Because of the financial and logistical constraints on potential modifications, little room exists for major modifications, and companies must do the best they can with minor "tweaks" to the product specifications, bill of materials, manufacturing process, and packaging. In addition, some companies have found that education of the customer regarding their products' environmentally beneficial attributes (or lack of adverse attributes) is a valuable activity. Because of the constraints on investment, the DFE team or individual must work closely with the product management team for incremental improvements (e.g., packaging), and DFE has little need for heavy input from R&D. However, successfully introducing DFE into mature products generally requires a great deal of ingenuity, given the constraints on investment and the established customer expectations. Several companies have found that additional information on customer expectations and innovative brainstorming sessions were required in order to integrate the relatively new environmental constraints into the existing mature product.

Existing products with high growth potential face a different situation, and the degree of freedom to make modifications is greater. The potential for growth clears the way for investments in the product or process (or both) and liberates the DFE team from the demand that all changes be incremental. In this instance, the DFE team typically includes members from a wide range of disciplines because of the variety of options for change that are available.

Finally, commercializing new products requires an active DFE team that is immersed in the details concerning the product, process, customers, and competitors. In the precommercial phases of development, latitude for change and innovation is at its maximum. However, the environmental requirements are just one of the crucial boundary conditions in the design equation, and trade-offs between customer, technical, strategic, and environmental constraints are part of the overall process.

In summary, each type of DFE is different and has different organizational issues. At the heart of the DFE concept is the goal of technology management—the effective delivery of technology to the marketplace. DFE is one module in the larger technology management function, and its organization and execution are dependent on the company's specific goals.

Companywide DFE initiatives belong
(briefly) to corporate management

The development of a formative "big picture" and of corporate guidelines requires a DFE organization that has three framing concepts:

- It is organized and run by the corporate level.
- It is staffed from all operating divisions and all functional groups.
- The team goes out of business after it meets a specific goal.

This type of short-lived DFE organization is essential in the early phases of development within a company. Leading-edge companies in many industries have used the same up-front corporate involvement to develop concepts and set general criteria. Getting started requires facilitation and contributions from all relevant parts of the organization. The initializing DFE team is thus multifunctional and multibusiness.

Although this type of organization is crucial at the nascent stage, it is sure death for product-related activities. It is too big and too remote of a topic to be of any use to operations in the commercialization of competitive products (see the following discussion). One company found that maintaining the DFE initiative at the corporate level (after its initial creation there) effectively halted implementation across the boundaries between operating units. The operating groups felt that if "corporate" wanted DFE it could have it, but they weren't willing to be involved if they weren't in charge.

Product-oriented DFE belongs to the
product development group

Product-development-oriented DFE includes protection of existing mature products, rejuvenation of existing products, and enhancement of precommercial products (see above). These are different from DFE used for big-picture and design criteria assessments in that they focus on a selected product or set of products and must deal with technical and market specifics. For these product-related activities, DFE should be organized as a component of the Product Development Group. Doing so ensures adequate DFE input and prevents disruption of the product development schedule.

For DFE to succeed, it must mimic the activities and speed of the product development organization. One clear lesson is that, with increased emphasis on time to market, there is no tolerance for DFE that significantly lengthens the product commercialization cycle. If the DFE organization is not seamlessly interwoven into product commercialization and significant disruptions to the process occur, "organizational antibodies" will appear and attempt to undercut the DFE organization. The appearance of an outside EH&S staffer will not be a welcome sight in the product development process. It smacks of the "I'm from Corporate and I'm here to help you" phenomenon that most operations folks have learned to be wary of.

One major oil and chemical company places responsibility for DFE ("product stewardship" in the company lexicon) firmly in the hands of the operating companies. The DFE team, which consists of engineering, R&D, and EH&S staff, reports to the chairperson of the product stewardship committee, who in turn reports to the president.

Different industries have slightly different approaches and names for DFE that reflect their history and characteristics. For example, the oil and chemical industry focuses on "product stewardship," which balances the traditionally heavy focus on environmental management in the processing stage by placing equal emphasis on the product and its complete life cycle. This shift reflects the lessons learned from remediation of past market mistakes and product-related liabilities. It is still DFE, but an emphasis on "product stewardship" complements the industry's historical process-oriented approach. The utility industry has some of the same characteristics, and some leading utilities also use the term *product stewardship* for DFE-related activities.

The electronics industry approaches DFE in a different light. In contrast to the oil and chemical industry and utilities, the electronics industry has never had many environmental management concerns. The recently introduced DFE-related management efforts start with a fairly clean sheet of paper. Therefore, the electronics industry has aggressively pursued DFE and associated analytic methods generally known as "life-cycle assessment" (LCA). Leading companies in the electronics industry have simultaneously focused on product and process aspects and have organized DFE teams to include all aspects of both.

DFE in the product development process

DFE is one of the critical components in the product development process. Typically, the product development process has six stages, as shown in Fig. 23.1, and different teams organize and convene for each stage. A core team usually participates all the way through the process, but many additional players from inside and outside the product group join the team as necessary. Thus, although DFE should be organized and located in the product development organization, DFE will have a constantly changing configuration, it will interact with different players inside and outside the product development organization, and it will generally conform to the overall development process, as discussed below.

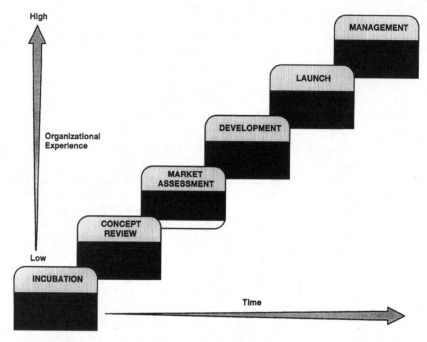

Figure 23.1   Six stages of product development.

1. *Incubation* is a continuous process that occurs in the technology/market arena and does not have a formal organizational design. DFE threats and opportunities should be included in the review of each possible new product or process, and market demand and technology capabilities should be assessed to stimulate innovation and breakthrough ideas. Each member of the product development team should take responsibility for DFE at this stage. This approach helps make DFE an integral part of the overall process and a concern of every product development team member.

2. *Concept review* occurs when a new-product idea is introduced into the product development pipeline. The objective is to review the concept and assess its fit with the strategic requirements of the business unit. The concept review team typically forms in response to the introduction of the concept into the pipeline and includes:

- A product manager
- A business manager
- A manufacturing manager
- A quality manager
- A DFE contributor
- A marketing manager
- Other specialists as required

The DFE contributor may be an individual, or the role may be assumed by one of the other participants. The key is to infuse the team with the appropriate DFE considerations at this formative stage.

3. *Market assessment* is aimed at defining specific market demand and customer requirements for the proposed product. In addition, the profit potential of the product (estimated costs, risks, competitive strengths, and technology issues) is assessed. The team includes the same components as the concept review team, but the individual members may change to reflect the greater level of detail and increased technical economic analyses. DFE participation in the product development team becomes most important in this stage.

DFE should be customer-driven. The DFE team—which may be one individual or numerous participants in the product development function—must gather, assess, and introduce customers' DFE considerations in a manner that integrates DFE goals into the overall development plan. Consideration and integration of internal DFE issues are important, but they may not contribute significantly to the competitiveness and profitability of the commercial product. However, understanding and meeting customers' DFE needs can significantly contribute to the product's commercial success. Being driven by the *customers'* EH&S needs makes the DFE process and organization a real-life business activity, in contrast with traditional EH&S compliance activities.

4. *Development* is the stage for the actual construction and testing of precommercial products. This stage focuses on product performance and specifications, manufacturability, and DFE considerations. Of necessity, technical details are numerous, and the DFE contributor must be closely aligned with the technical specialists or be one of them.

5. *Product launch* requires a myriad of activities and numerous actors. At this point, the DFE organization should be involved only in checking and supporting the overall team. In addition, immediately after the launch, DFE should play a part in the crucial postcommercialization modifications aimed at getting the product on target.

6. *Product management* is an ongoing activity throughout the life of the commercial product. The DFE organization plays different roles in the product management phase. For young products with growth potential, the DFE organization may be very active and may contribute in a significant manner to the continued competitiveness and growth of the product.

DFE programs start small, expand incrementally

One of the crucial lessons from successful DFE users is that critical mass is a red herring. A large, centralized DFE organization is not necessary for effective implementation and integration of DFE into the product development process. The DFE teams should be located in the product development organization in each of the operating units. As one experienced corporate staff member said of DFE, "It's a good subject for staffers to kick around, but ultimately it belongs with the engineers."

The more you centralize the product-related DFE organization, the more you will have to mediate tussles between central and operating units. This type of tension occurred at Xerox when the operating division presidents questioned the value of corporate-mandated DFE. Only after the divisions internalized the function did it begin to take hold and grow. A small, central DFE function located in EH&S can be valuable for maintaining and improving the DFE program and for cross-fertilization between operating units. But in the end, product-related DFE must be located in and owned by the operations side of the house.

Getting DFE to fit the company culture and the organization requires a phased approach. A leading materials company realized that early in its DFE development program and made plans to expand the DFE approach incrementally to fit its culture. Forcing DFE into the organization rapidly is a risky undertaking; that approach usually generates formidable opposition from line management and releases all of the "organizational antibodies." These forces can significantly delay development and implementation, and damage the effectiveness of the DFE organization.

Problems usually arise because:

- Line managers are often skeptical of the value of DFE.

- DFE does not fit easily into the product development "culture" of the business unit.

- DFE requires the participation of multifunctional teams, which can pose problems for traditional organizations.

- DFE is usually seen as a cost rather than as a mix of costs and benefits.

- The DFE organizing principles cited here are violated.

The best way to avoid these problems is to start small and to use a specific operation and product line as a pilot project. This builds momentum and generates critical learning about what works and what does not work in the organization. Xerox used the Departmental Copiers Program as its guinea pig. Other division managers saw that it worked and began to wrestle with how to implement DFE effectively in their own organizations.

One major electronics firm used a similar approach, described as consisting of the following steps:

- Introduce the DFE ethic with a small pilot project.
- Generate experience, including breakthroughs in design that will demonstrate the effectiveness of DFE.
- Proliferate throughout the organization.

After successful demonstration of the pilot project, it is possible to expand to other parts of the organization. However, expansion must be handled with care and an awareness that neither immediate nor uniform adoption is likely. In particular, companies should

- *Expect resistance:*   One company's managers asked, "Why do we need this if it isn't the law?" They wanted to know how DFE was going to help *their* business, and they required some reasonable proof that tinkering with the product development process was worth the effort and risk. Each point of resistance requires some additional communication and education, and the emerging DFE organization must provide them.

- *Expect uneven adoption among divisions:*   DFE is not crucial for all types of business, and some managers will remain inherently skeptical about it. Even today, some managers at one of the leading DFE practitioners, a large consumer goods company with many DFE initiatives, are not stalwart champions of DFE.

A successful DFE program is not related to a large central organization or uniform DFE organizations at the operating level. Small, nonuniform DFE organizations embedded in product development organizations are the key.

Move Beyond Organization

Early success with a DFE organization is not a guarantee of ultimate success or uninterrupted progress. Communications between the principal participants and stakeholders are required. One major computer company recently experienced a notable setback that illustrates that an integrated organizational design is not by itself a guarantee of success.

The company's engineering group housed the company's leading-edge environmental management activities, including its DFE. Thus, DFE was embedded in engineering and was close to the product designers and to the pulse of the business activities. In contrast, the company's traditional EH&S was organized in the financial sector and, in keeping with its corporate oversight role, operated as part of the corporate environmental assurance program. The leading-edge, nontraditional environmental group experienced early successes and was generally believed to be well integrated into the fabric of the engineering group in which it was housed.

However, during the business downturn of 1993, the company was forced to reduce staff. Most observers were flabbergasted when the computing company eliminated the entire leading-edge environmental group, and with it the DFE function. No one could understand why such a vital and proven set of environmental management activities was purposefully discarded.

Apparently, the company's engineering management and environmental management had not reached common agreement regarding the benefits of the embedded environmental function. No clear measure of its benefits, including those from DFE, was available for engineering management to use in assessing its effectiveness. The environmental group assumed that the benefits of its nontraditional activities, including DFE, were evident and fully appreciated by engineering management. Engineering, on the other hand, had no clear picture because no specific measurement system had been established and agreed upon, despite the excellent working relationship that had been developed.

The lesson here is applicable to every DFE and EH&S activity in the corporate environmental management arena: "You can't manage what you can't measure." This has been said many times, but the computer company's recent experience demonstrates that its analogue, "You can't sustain what you don't measure," is equally true. Measurement provides crucial signals and metrics to the stakeholders about the need for and robustness of the DFE program, as well as about its bottom-line contributions. These are crucial to long-term success and survival in the turbulence of corporate organizations.

In addition, this lesson illustrates what could be called the fifth organizing principle: *It is critically important to rotate members through the DFE organization.* These special tours of duty can help outsiders to learn about the value of DFE and assist with the transfer of DFE principles to other groups. In addition, they give the DFE organization a fresh stream of ideas and innovations related to methodology and its application to real world business situations. Very few companies are formally embarking on rotation, but traditional transfers and personnel changes have provided examples of the value of rotation within the DFE organization.

Conclusion

Design for environment is one of the success stories in the emerging arena of EH&S management. Companies such as Xerox, IBM, PG&E, and others have demonstrated that DFE, carefully embedded within product development and expanded in stages, can significantly contribute to competitive advantage and the bottom line.

A key factor DFE's success is proper organizational design. Organized as part of product development and tied tightly to the technology management organization, the DFE group produces timely, usable, and credible inputs to the product development process.

Chapter

24

DFE: Corporate Planning and Compliance Opportunities

Edward L. Quevedo, Esq.

Wise & Shepard
Counsellors at Law
Palo Alto, California

Introduction

Environmental regulation in the United States began in earnest in the early 1970s, with passage of the National Environmental Policy Act, the Clean Water Act, and the Endangered Species Act. Although significant environmental statutes existed before, and have been passed since, the period between 1970 and 1979 saw the dawn of emission-based regulation that characterized the first generation of industrial environmental regulation.

Regulation of industry has evolved significantly since that time, and environmental regulation has expanded around the globe. In this chapter, we will briefly explore the evolution of industrial environmental regulation, tracking the progress of regulators from emission regulation, to process regulation, and ultimately to product regulation.*

By making the commitment to regulate products, as we will see, regulators have given industry a significant opportunity to advance

---

*The phases of environmental regulation to be considered here are not strictly linear. Rather than proceeding historically one after the other, the four models of environmental regulation considered entail some overlap.

its own interests and agenda while making a substantial dent in environmental problems. Finally, we will examine the next generation of environmental regulation, management regulation, and consider its implications for industry and the environment.

Regulatory Origins of DFE

Design for environment (DFE) is the label applied to a variety of current environmental regulatory initiatives, from environmental product design, to life-cycle analysis, to environmental performance. To understand the significance of DFE, we need to understand how we got here and where we have been.

Emissions regulation

As noted above, U.S. environmental regulation began with emissions regulation. Whatever the medium (air, water, soil), emissions regulation focuses on the emissions outputs to that medium and aims to reduce the volume of effluent. Emissions regulation is a crude and largely ineffective tool.

First, emissions regulation is derivative: its relevance is limited to the kind and type of effluent flow. Second, emissions regulation is reactive. It responds to effluent or contaminants that have already been generated. Third, emissions regulation is narrow. It is unconcerned about, and largely blind to, preemissions inputs and impacts. Emissions regulation, for example, does not take account of or even consider workplace safety, raw materials selection, or product disposal options.

Process regulation

Recognizing the limitations of emissions regulation, government advanced to process regulation. In this second generation of environmental regulation, the focus shifted from effluent flows to effluent control processes. Government began to specify the methods and technologies to be applied to treating effluent to minimize residual contamination of soil, air, and water.

Process regulation constituted an improvement over emissions regulation. By regulating industrial processes, government began to force industry to *improve* and *enhance* pollution control technology. Process regulation also began to take account of workplace safety and worker exposure. And because it focused on activities somewhat (if only marginally) upstream of actual effluent flows, process regulation led to some advanced planning by industry. In this way, process regulation moved environmental protection away from a purely reactive model.

At the same time, process regulation has its limitations. It is still narrowly focused and does not take account of raw materials selection, energy consumption, or product disposal. Further, process regulation is derivative of the process or function in question—its principles do not translate easily from one industry or even one operation to another.

Product regulation and DFE

The limitations of process regulation, and the continuing degradation of the environment by industry, have led regulators to forge ahead into the third phase of environmental regulation: *product regulation.* DFE falls squarely within this model.

As described in Part 2 of this book, DFE, whether as a regulatory goal or a corporate program, is a methodology for systematic identification and reduction of environmental impacts and risks due to products and their associated processes. DFE represents an integrative response to the piecemeal and reactive regulatory approach that is typical of earlier emissions and process regulation.

Of course, DFE reflects certain existing regulatory imperatives. Under current law, the following statutory regimes impose DFE-related requirements on industry:

- *Clean Air Act:* Requires waste reduction and product review to achieve air emissions control objectives.
- *Clean Water Act:* Requires waste minimization and control.
- *Resource Conservation and Recovery Act:* Mandates use of alternative disposal technology and reduction in waste streams.
- *Occupational Safety and Health Act:* Requires product review as part of injury and illness prevention programs.
- *Toxic Substances Control Act:* Mandates chemical manufacturing product review.
- *Consumer Product Safety Act:* Requires product design to ensure safe use by consumers.
- *Pollution Prevention Act:* Mandates broad waste reduction and waste stream management planning (see the discussion in Chap. 3).

As noted, DFE is systematic. This characteristic is predicated upon a key assumption of DFE: all environmental and workplace safety risks and harms result directly or indirectly from *products*. This is an unassailable proposition.

The making of products, or things, is responsible for all adverse environmental and worker safety problems which we face. Therefore, decisions about product design, configuration, operation, use, etc., drive and create (or can identify and help to eliminate) all ecological and workplace harms.

Thus, DFE proceeds from a fundamental improvement in the perspective of environmental regulation. By acknowledging that products are the ultimate culprits and can be the ultimate solution, DFE catapults industry and regulators forward into a greatly more efficacious model.

Implementing DFE Programs

The application of DFE to industrial product development depends upon two kinds of systematic analyses: (1) integration of various corporate functions and (2) breakdown of the product development, use, and disposal life cycle into its component parts. These are interdependent exercises. By looking first at the product development element, we can better understand both the corporate integration element and the true long-term value of DFE.

Product development process elements

The systematic product analysis entailed in DFE can be divided into several substantive elements. Implementing this analysis requires that corporate functions previously divided by time and operation can begin to work together.

Whether in its form as a pilot program of the U.S. Environmental Protection Agency, as a component of the European Union's Eco-Management and Auditing Regulation, or as the driving force behind the British Standard Institute's BS 7750 Standard, DFE takes as its point of departure the process of materials selection. The substantive DFE process elements include:

1. Raw materials selection
2. Preliminary structural and presentation design
3. Process inputs (energy, water, labor hours)
4. Modularization and assembly design
5. Health and safety inputs and application of labor
6. Vendor selection and due diligence
7. Packaging and labeling design and manufacture
8. Preparation and final assembly
9. Hazardous materials application and management
10. Hazardous waste generation and management

11. Customer use and disposal documentation

12. Transport and delivery options and impacts

13. Life-cycle and useful life analyses

14. Disassembly, recycling, reuse, and reclamation options

15. Product return and stewardship options

16. Disposal options and analysis

As each of these elements is implemented, the corporate finance and corporate legal departments can and should be consulted in order to ensure that the DFE process comports with legal requirements or expectations of the company. Corporations should also not underestimate the importance of committing significant financial resources to the DFE process. If corporate spending is keyed to DFE via infrastructure investment (e.g., process area redesign or R&D of product modularization to increase recyclability and reuse potential of components), both employee and public response to the program is likely to be more favorable. Of course, this kind of commitment to investment will help to ensure the ultimate success of the DFE program, as well.

Internal communication

Apart from the attributes identified above, DFE carries with it substantial potential for other positive corporate benefits. Not the least of these is improved corporate communication. A successful DFE program demands the participation and cooperation of numerous corporate divisions which historically either have been isolated or have worked at cross purposes.

For example, the marketing function is keenly attuned to customer desires and preferences, and is driven chiefly by the need to respond to these factors. The design function, on the other hand, is often indifferent to customer preferences and focuses instead upon elegance and durability of product layout and function. Meanwhile, engineering is less concerned with customer appetites than with whether a particular design will work. Finance, of course, cares primarily about the cost of product development.

And, notably, the environmental function has traditionally been anathema to marketing, design, engineering, *and* finance. Health and safety has been at least as remote from these other divisions, and often as unwelcome, as the environmental function. However, as described in Chap. 6, DFE has begun to break down these barriers. DFE throws marketing, R&D, engineering, finance, environment, and health and safety together and gives them each a reason to collaborate and find common ground. Often, of course, the result is a better product.

Marketing will remain the primary point of interface between customers and the corporation. Marketing is acutely aware (or should be) of the appeal of environmentally friendly or responsible products. EH&S can help marketing achieve this goal. Design and engineering can make practical recommendations for waste minimization, pollution prevention, product modularization, and energy consumption. All of these suggestions will improve the product's environmental performance. And they will usually result in substantial savings for the company.

The potential profit contribution of DFE has been illustrated in Chap. 1. For example, corresponding to each pound or ounce of reduction in hazardous virgin stock used in products, the company realizes direct savings in storage, training, disposal, and risk management costs. As each hazardous feedstock is further reduced or eliminated, these savings increase.

Increased energy efficiency and reduced water consumption, of course, will also result in corporate savings. Most importantly, application of DFE to product development, design, manufacture, distribution, and disposal (including reuse, reclamation, recycling, and waste stewardship) will result in an environmentally more friendly product. No consumer today will overlook this attribute.

Compliance Reengineering

Perhaps the most significant attribute of DFE is the opportunity it presents for industry to reengineer, and improve the efficiency of, its corporate EH&S compliance matrix. To date, of course, EH&S compliance has tracked the media-specific regulatory scheme predominant in the process regulation era. This scheme, in addition to focusing on separate compliance elements for air, water, and soil issues, has been further truncated by distribution of regulatory authority among federal, state, and local agencies, and by separation of environmental compliance (through the EPA as the chief federal agency) from health and safety compliance (through OSHA and various mirror state agencies).

DFE, because of its systematic nature, allows a corporation to realign responsibility for EH&S compliance. Instead of dividing compliance into the random categories specified by existing environmental regulations, a corporation can redefine compliance duties based on the "design cycle" created by DFE. For example, corporate managers responsible for selecting raw materials requiring special reporting, handling, or training can make compliance judgments as a part of the product design process, and key their compliance efforts to those judgments. Similarly, production and manufacturing staff responsible for hazardous materials use and hazardous waste management can key their compliance efforts to product design decisions, making more accurate and efficient judgments about quantities, qualities, and fates of hazardous waste.

These efficiencies can continue throughout the corporate matrix as the various corporate functions become more acclimated to working with each other and making informed, systematic EH&S decisions, rather than reactive, post hoc determinations.

Future Directions

In light of the progression of environmental regulation from emissions to product regulation, it is fair to ask where we will go from here. The answer is that environmental regulators in Europe, the Pacific Rim, and North America are making clear their intention to follow product regulation with management regulation.

Typical of this new trend in EH&S compliance are the EU Eco-Management and Auditing Regulation ("the Regulation") and BS 7750. These mechanisms require corporations to establish complex management structures to identify, track, and reduce *all manner of environmental impacts*. The Regulation and BS 7750, for example, require adoption of a corporate environmental registry, which catalogues a very wide array of environmental impacts, from raw materials selection to noise and dust generation to energy and water consumption and efficiency.

Once listed in the registry, the company must set specific goals to reduce environmental impacts. These reductions are measured in terms of the company's *environmental performance*. Environmental performance figures are then required to be released to the public. Communities in which companies operate can thereby track improvements or degradation in environmental performance. In this way, the public is invited into the process of corporate performance and EH&S compliance. This represents, particularly for U.S. companies, a substantial new development.

The Regulation proceeds from two focal points: the environmental audit and the environmental management system. Objective, activity-oriented environmental audits are becoming the norm and the international standard for evaluating a company's environmental performance. For example, whereas audit teams might at one time have asked "Do we have a training program?" and "How much hazardous waste do we generate?" they must now ask more sophisticated questions such as "How *effective* is our training program?" and "*Why* do we generate so much hazardous waste?"

Other subjects covered by the Regulation and BS 7750 in the audit cycle include the following:

- Increased energy efficiency and reduction of energy use
- Process water recycling, efficiency, and reduction
- Noise reduction and control
- Product planning, including design, packaging, transportation, use, and disposal
- Environmental performance of vendors and suppliers

The state of the art environmental audit, unlike traditional compliance-oriented reviews, is driven by the need to collect baseline data and therefore must be undertaken with a view to maximize data collection. In addition, since external bodies will increasingly be involved in verifying the audit results, accuracy and candor (at a level sometimes beyond the level of comfort of U.S. corporate executives) must define the audit report.

This new audit format also takes account of new categories of information, including site history (including past activities which may have caused contamination) and the environmental setting of the corporation's facilities (including regional land use, regional geology, sensitive natural habitats, etc.).

As the International Organization for Standardization (ISO) continues the process of adopting its 14000 series of standards for environmental management, the transnational importance of management regulation will continue to increase. Prudent corporate officials and counsel will continue to implement environmental product design, DFE, and related programs to keep ahead of the regulatory agenda and to realize the collateral benefits outlined above. Both industry and, in the long term, the physical environment, will benefit from these efforts.

Benefits of DFE

Dividends paid by DFE programs are many. One of the primary motivating factors for such programs is customer inquiry or requirements for DFE activities by their suppliers. Thus, a successful DFE program can create increased customer loyalty. Typically, DFE initiatives will also result in risk management savings as companies inform their insurers that new products have reduced environmental impact and therefore will be less likely to lead to Superfund or RCRA liability when the products are disposed of.

DFE also reorients the traditional compliance functions. Historically, EH&S managers reacted to regulatory and statutory changes by cobbling new paperwork and implementation goals to meet the changes. However, once a company adopts DFE, environmental impacts (from energy consumption to product disposal) are effectively catalogued. From that catalogue, an EHS director can derive a *systematic* environmental performance program which goes beyond mere compliance. Unifying and organizing environmental impacts, as DFE does, provides an invaluable tool to increase the efficiency and ultimately the performance of EH&S systems.

Finally, DFE overcomes the nettlesome problem of divergent regulation. Transnational firms must monitor environmental compliance in myriad jurisdictions. The task of achieving compliance in 5 or 10 or 50 countries can be daunting indeed. However, a DFE program will result in companywide environmental performance systems which will translate effectively from country to country. Ultimately, the same DFE performance matrix can be used to structure compliance in, for example, the United States, the United Kingdom, Vietnam, and Germany.

Conclusion

The future of environmental regulation will be defined by incentive-based programs such as DFE. Today, customer demands and industry standards are the primary forces behind DFE. However, as product take-back and life-cycle analysis programs move from a voluntary to a mandated status, corporations will be required to undertake DFE and environmental product design programs just to stay in business.

The leading standard for environmental performance in the early years of the new millennium is expected to be the emerging ISO 14000 series on quality environmental management. The ISO group working on the new standards, Technical Committee 207, has released preliminary drafts of its work. The eco-auditing and eco-management drafts directly incorporate product planning and design concepts. The impact of the ISO standards, when published in 1996 or 1997, will be to unify DFE principles and set a new benchmark for environmental performance which will likely apply in most industrialized (and many emerging) economies.

25

Industrial Ecology: A Context for Design and Decision

Ernest Lowe

Managing Partner
Indigo Development
Oakland, California

"In the short term, Design for Environment is the means by which the still vague precepts of industrial ecology can in fact begin to be implemented in the real world today. DFE requires that environmental objectives and constraints be driven into process and product design, and materials and technology choices."

BRADEN ALLENBY
Circuits and Devices[1]

Introduction

Design is a resonant word. It suggests the innovation of artistic conception merged with the rigor of engineering design. Some managers speak of "designing" their organizations. A new breed of politicians seek to lead us in the "design" of solutions rather than the solving of problems. The power of this word suggests that *design for environment* may be seen as a response to a nested set of challenges from individual product development to global policies. As suggested in

Fig. 25.1, sustainable environmental performance requires design at the level of:

- Products
- Services
- Processes
- Materials and energy flows
- Facilities
- Business organizations/missions/strategies
- Intercompany relations
- Community and regional infrastructure
- Societal institutions and policies

With this broad design context the basic questions become: "How can we act with creativity and rigor to design effective environmental solutions at all of these levels?" "How can we best evaluate alternative solutions?" "How do we know the right level of design for approaching a particular issue?" "How do we resolve conflicts across levels of design?" "How do we maintain a coherent view of the whole system in order to manage design decisions well at any level?"

Industrial ecology (IE) is emerging in response to this set of questions. It is a broad, holistic framework for guiding the transformation of the industrial system. This will be a profound shift from a linear model (mine pit to producer to consumer to dump) to a closed-loop model more closely resembling the cyclical flows of ecosystems. Industrial ecology offers a whole-systems context for effectively using the tools and methods of DFE, pollution prevention, total-quality environmental management, and other valuable environmental management approaches.

Ultimately all of these buzzwords will fall away as we abandon the fantasy that our industrial world is somehow independent of natural constraints. We will arrive at a normal way of doing business that recognizes our plants, offices, and shops as organisms existing in cooperation with local ecosystems and the global biosphere.

This integrative function may be the central contribution of industrial ecology to environmental management. Its proponents suggest that managers of the industrial system must treat it, at every level, as a set of organisms, subject to ecological constraints, like any other member of an ecosystem. Most other approaches fall short of this perhaps radical position. They define constraints in regulatory, economic, and engineering terms. These are necessary but not sufficient conditions for effective environmental management.

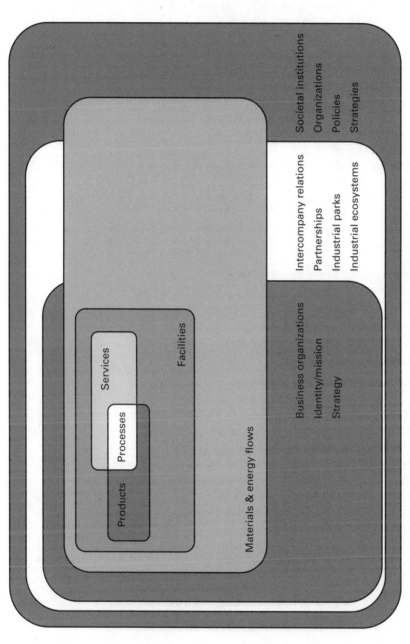

Figure 25.1 Realms of design. Industrial ecology is a framework for coordinating environmental design strategies across nested levels, from specific product and process design up to the design of societal institutions and policies. (*Copyright 1994 Indigo Development.*)

Products

Processes

Services

Facilities

Materials & energy flows

Business organizations
Identity/mission
Strategy

Intercompany relations
Partnerships
Industrial parks
Industrial ecosystems

Societal institutions
Organizations
Policies
Strategies

In discussions of industrial ecology critics often say, "But this is just good common sense. There's nothing new here!" Indeed, there's nothing new in seeing human activities as integral to their natural settings. Traditional cultures around the planet thought this way. But as industrial culture spawned disciplines to manage its operations, this common sense was forgotten. Economics and accounting drove the natural world off the balance sheet for companies and societies, except as an apparently infinite source of materials and bottomless dump for wastes. We can now see that this convenient fiction of environmental costs being "externalities" turns out to be a radical departure from common sense.

In this chapter we will introduce central industrial ecology themes; discuss several distinctive IE tools; review cases that suggest how IE is now expressed and what full application of IE might mean for industry; and expand on the potential role of industrial ecology as an organizing framework for the necessary transformation of industry.

Levels of design in transportation: Three cases

Incremental improvement in the design of automobiles, the Supercar concept, and an integrated rail-based transportation system illustrate the broad spectrum of design necessary for sustainability. Each case is at a different level of system and in a different time frame.

Automobile redesign within the current product concept. *The automobile and its infrastructure, as now designed, constitute a major environmental threat. The production of cars and their fuel generates pollution to land, sea, and air. Autos are a major contributor to atmospheric ozone pollution, generate 18% of global carbon dioxide emissions, and are a significant source of water pollution. Autos use nonrenewable petroleum at an ever increasing rate. Roads, freeways, and parking garages typically use between one-third and one-half of urban space and a major share of transportation dollars. Interstate highways cover valuable agricultural land while air pollution damages crops and forests.[2]*

In the area of process design, the automobile industry has already made serious efforts to prevent pollution in manufacturing processes, decrease materials wastes, and practice internal and external recycling of metals and plastics. Product design seeks improved fuel efficiencies and lower emissions, usually through redesign of the internal combustion engine and specific innovations such as the earlier catalytic converter, electronic fuel injection, and composite materials.

Designers are also seeking to greatly enhance recyclability of automobile components. Anticipated European take-back legislation is prompting automakers there to begin design for disassembly and to team together in setting up an infrastructure for realizing value from cars returned to them.³

Change in design in the United States is largely driven by Clean Air Act revisions, CAFE mileage standards, zero-emissions vehicle legislation in California and the Northeast, and Germany's proposed take-back legislation (placing responsibility on manufacturers for recycling at the end of a car's life). But the targets are still generally modest given the magnitude of the automobile's burden on the environment. The redesign is incremental change in the basic familiar product. Even "Big Three" electric car designs to meet California's 1998 zero-emissions deadline are retrofitting of existing internal combustion models. (The mandated standards call for 2% of fleet sales in the state to be zero-emissions vehicles.)

This incremental level of DFE is necessary to develop improved but still inadequate products in a time of transition. Business constraints on more fundamental innovation include the large investment in traditional production facilities, lack of strong demand for change from markets (in North America as well as those opening in Asia), and relatively modest performance standards set in public policy. Continuing to apply DFE at this level may give very wise decisions about very wrong long-term choices. Most solutions are likely to be short-lived.

The Rocky Mountain Institute Supercar. *Amory and Hunter Lovins have challenged the automobile industry to stretch to another level of design with the Rocky Mountain Institute (RMI) Supercar proposal. The Lovins assigned a team at RMI to go to the basic physics and engineering of small-vehicle design. Forget the common wisdom of the industry. The result is a design with radical implications for fuel and materials efficiency, emissions, manufacturing processes, and the nature of the business itself.*

The Supercar is projected as an ultralight, highly aerodynamic vehicle powered by a small electricity-generating engine (gasoline, liquid gas, or hydrogen cell). The engine transmits current to drive mechanisms in the wheels, which also recapture energy from braking (~70% of braking energy). Highly energy efficient accessories (lights, heating, air conditioning, radio) also reduce energy demand. Body and frame design with strong composite materials provide passenger safety higher than in traditional vehicles at almost one-third the weight. Selective use of superstrong carbon fiber and other composites will reduce number of body parts and simplify production and assembly.

The RMI performance models indicate Supercars will be 100 times cleaner than present cars (or pure electrics) and operate at 150 mpg in the near-term design. (GM's Ultralite concept car has demonstrated only 62 mpg.) Potential fuel efficiencies could double and triple that high level with more advanced designs. The total energy draw will equal that used for accessories in present autos.

RMI indicates the Supercar design concept will enable an equally radical transformation of automobile production. "Molded composite cars need much less and vastly cheaper tooling. The tooling's short life and very quick fabrication supports fast cycles, short time-to-market, continuous improvement, small production runs, and strong product differentiation—a striking strategic advantage." Conceivably the U.S. Big Three and other global auto companies could be left in the dust of entrepreneurs who see the parallels with the emergence of a personal computer industry (coming out of garages), a new industry able to rapidly challenge the mainframe manufacturers in the early eighties. A more likely scenario is that advanced design concepts such as the RMI Supercar will be developed and tested through a partnership between start-ups and major automakers. Already many entrepreneurial companies are growing in the market niche created by California's zero-emissions standards, and some are collaborating with the majors.

Amory Lovins claims that the technological foundation for realizing the Supercar concept has been laid. The design challenge is in breaking out of the conventional wisdom of how we conceive and build cars and integrating the breakthroughs already made.

With the Supercar we move from incremental to transformative change, the realm of industrial ecology. At this level we start designing on a clean slate, asking "What do we really need to do to provide the customer utility we're here for?" We open to fundamental redesign of product, production processes, and the very nature of our business. (For additional reading, see Refs. 4 and 5.)

An integrated transportation system. *Amory Lovins also recognizes that even transformative design at the level of individual vehicles gives only a partial, though necessary, solution. A necessary and sufficient solution will only be found at a higher level of design, one that addresses the system in which automobiles function. Supercars and smart highways alone will still leave us with an overall system design burdening the environment via materials and land use. One need only look at the implications of deploying an automobile infrastructure in*

China to grasp the dimensions of this issue. Agricultural land is already being paved over for industrial development. It is degrading heavily from desertification, pollution, and reliance on chemical fertilizers.

Suntrain, an entrepreneurial start-up company in California, has moved design for the environment to the level of system needed for an adequate response to the environmental challenge: intermodal, rail-based transportation. Christopher Swan has designed the technical, business, financial, and political infrastructure for transforming urban and interurban transportation.[6]

Imagine being able to make one phone call to route, schedule, and pay for a trip via public transit that would get you from here to there faster than in your car. Perhaps you start via a van that picks you up at your door, connect without waiting to a subway, transfer to an electric or gas-powered rail car for the main trip, and pick up a rental Supercar to make business calls at the other end. No gridlock. Time to read, tap into the Internet, or work on that unfinished spreadsheet.

Total cost to the individual for using this integrated system for business and recreational uses: 50% of the cost for operating and maintaining a personal vehicle to cover those miles. Environmental benefits: An integrated transportation system such as Suntrain projects would dramatically reduce fuel use, emissions, and resource use. One railway passenger car worth $2 million lasts twenty years, and replaces the mileage consumed by 6000 automobiles worth $90 million. Less urban and rural land would be consumed by the system, and pavement could be removed in some areas.

Is this pie in the sky fantasy? Even without the one-call information system and tight connections, passenger rail transport has increased significantly on selected U.S. routes in the last decade. As with the Supercar, the technologies are fully available now, including self-propelled passenger cars, power plants using alternative fuels, and distributed information systems for system management and customer "travel efficiency." Geopositioning satellites are now used by railways in tighter, more efficient scheduling of trains. Swan says 250,000 miles of rail track are used at roughly 15% of capacity (a sunk infrastructure worth $1 trillion).

With Suntrain we move to the design of institutions and infrastructure grounded in the customer's need to move effectively in the short-haul ranges (up to 400 miles) that constitute the majority of passenger trips. Rather than focus on a specific mode of transportation, the concept addresses the need for an integrated system, linking all modes.

The concept also unifies meeting the customer's business, commuting, recreational, and personal needs.

The Suntrain vision reflects a higher level of design for environment: design at the level of business concept and social system that integrates already present technological innovations into a new solution. Critics often raise the question, "How will we ever get people out of their cars?" If the built-in incentives don't achieve this, then we move to a level of design vital to the transformation in personal lifestyles that sustainability demands. This is creation of the social incentives, communications channels, and means of learning through which people can freely adopt new patterns of behavior.

Defining Industrial Ecology

Definitions

As an emerging field, industrial ecology is still defined in many contrasting ways. Some of the central definitions are displayed below.

> Industrial ecology is the study of the flows of materials and energy in industrial and consumer activities, of the effects of these flows on the environment, and of the influences of economic, political, regulatory, and social factors on the flow, use, and transformation of resources.[7]

> Industrial ecology...may be defined as the systematic study of the interactions between the human economy in all its aspects and natural biological, chemical and physical systems at all scales. The concept of industrial ecology requires that an industrial system be viewed not in isolation from its surrounding systems, but in concert with them. It is a systems view of industrial operations in which one seeks to optimize the total materials cycle from virgin material, to finished material, to component, to product, to waste product, and to ultimate disposal. Factors to be optimized include resources, energy, and capital.[8]

> Model the systemic design of industry on the systemic design of the natural system....industrial ecology involves designing industrial infrastructures as if they were a series of interlocking man-made ecosystems interfacing with the natural global ecosystem. Industrial ecology takes the pattern of the natural environment as a model for solving environmental problems, creating a new paradigm for the industrial system in the process.[9]

IE as a systems framework for design

Differing definitions of industrial ecology converge on one notion: it is a broad framework for design and decision. It provides a systems context for understanding the implications of environmental management across many levels of design. To many pioneers in this field, IE's definitive contribution is moving design from a linear, mechanistic model to a closed-loop system, akin to natural ecosystems.

In our present, linear system we emphasize material throughput as the basis for valuing activity—creating and consuming as the dominant economic activities. Compare this to ecosystems, where production and decomposition are well-balanced, with nutrients recycling continuously to support the next cycles of production. Industrial ecology offers a theoretical foundation to support the transformation to a sustainable industrial system, operating in this balanced fashion.

Industrial ecology implies several distinctive principles:

1. All industrial operations (private and public manufacturing, service, and infrastructure) are natural systems that must function as such within the constraints of their local ecosystems and the biosphere.

2. The dynamics and principles of ecosystems offer a powerful source of guidance in the design and management of industrial systems.

3. Achieving high energy and materials efficiencies in production, use, recycling, and service will generate competitive advantage and economic benefits.

4. The ultimate source of economic value is the long-term viability of the planet and its local ecosystems; without that, present business success is meaningless.

These principles suggest the framework needed in both private and public sectors to transform the industrial system at the level needed. At present the drivers and controllers of change in corporate environmental strategy tend to be regulators, pressure groups, and market forces, along with shareholders. Too often all of these forces are working within the linear rather than the closed-loop model.

Industrial ecology enables the corporate world to work with these socioeconomic forces to more directly perceive the constraints of the biosphere and to design an organic path of change for the industrial system. It provides common ground for defining sustainability by balancing economic needs with ecological constraints.

While many writers emphasize the implications of industrial ecology for manufacturing, especially in waste reduction, others extend its potential span of application much further.

Industrial ecology must subsume all human economic activity, including forestry, agriculture, extractive industries, energy production and use, manufacturing, service operations and processes, and sustenance activities. In doing so, it will also have to address significant culture, technological, and political institutional issues. In fact, part of the reason we find ourselves in our current dilemma is that our systems thinking has, to date, been too limited in both the spatial and temporal dimensions.[9a]

The list of potential beneficiaries of IE also includes governmental agencies, both civil and military, that are responsible for intensive energy and materials deployment.

IE vision and reality

Industrial ecology promises much, but what has it delivered so far? It has stimulated new ways of thinking in a scattering of companies, in a number of major and minor universities, and in agencies like the U.S. Environmental Protection Agency (EPA) and Department of Energy. Some researchers and policymakers are using several IE-based tools like dynamic input-output models, industrial metabolism analysis, and design for environment. Development companies and university researchers are proposing action projects to create "industrial ecosystems" and eco-industrial parks.

At this point industrial ecology's greatest power lies in the whole-systems context for design it offers. This context is valuable even at this early stage of IE development. It raises new questions enabling development of the additional tools needed to manage design across the many levels described at the beginning of this article.

Streams of Exploration in Industrial Ecology

One can see different streams of exploration in industrial ecology, each with its distinctive perspective on the transformation of industrial systems. In this section we will review the aspects listed below:

1. Learning from ecosystems—using principles and dynamics of ecology in design of industrial production and service systems; e.g., multilinear recycling of materials at an industrial site

2. Industrial "metabolism"—perceiving and analyzing materials and energy flows from the biosphere through the industrial system back to the biosphere

3. Structural economics and dynamic input-output modeling—analyzing the impacts of webs of technological change on companies, economies, industries, and ecosystems

4. Design for environment—enabling design of facilities, processes, products, and services with awareness of both ecological and economic costs and benefits across the whole life cycle (See Part 2 of this book.)

5. Management of the interface between industry and natural systems enabling feedback loops to industry for self-regulation

6. Product life extension and the service economy—fundamental rethinking of the appropriate balance between production and service

These streams come together in a holistic, systemic mode of perception and action. They are complementary and are likely to be highly synergistic when applied together (see Fig. 25.2). Furthermore, there is an intrinsic linkage between industrial ecology and the methods of organizational design flowing from general systems theory.

Learning from ecological systems

Throughout human history designers have used natural systems as inspiration for their artifacts. Even in the high-tech era, the heat-seeking Sidewinder missile draws upon the rattlesnake's heat-sensing organ; study of the dragonfly's hovering mechanisms was used to correct certain aspects of helicopter design.

Beginning in the 1970s, designers started to state a larger vision of this mimicking of nature (biomimesis). Victor Papanek's book *Design for the Real World,* for instance, called for systemic modeling upon natural systems, urging the designer to "study basic principles in nature and emerge with applications of principles and processes to the needs of mankind...concerned not so much with the form of parts or the shape of things, but rather, with the possibilities of examining how nature makes things happen, the interrelation of parts, the existence of systems."[10]

This theme is central to the practice of industrial ecology. Initially it has been expressed by identifying key ecological principles, but its fullest development will be in a more systematic approach.

Dr. Robert Frosch, then Vice President in charge of General Motors Research Laboratories, now at the Kennedy School at Harvard, suggested one basis for such a systematic approach in a 1992 presentation to the National Academy of Sciences:

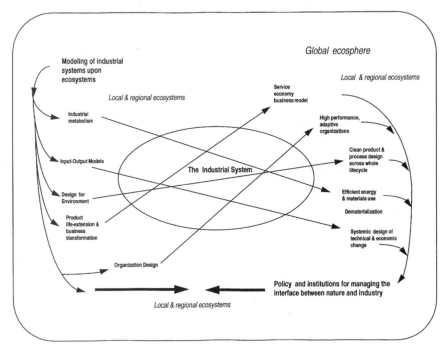

Figure 25.2 Convergent streams: A systemic view of industrial ecology. Industrial ecology is a systems framework for managing the interface between nature and industry. Each IE approach offers a unique and complementary contribution to the task of achieving balance between industrial inputs-outputs and ecosystem capacity. (Organization design is included here because implementing IE will require deep changes in this field.)

The idea of an industrial ecology is based upon a straightforward analogy with natural ecological systems. In nature an ecological system operates through a web of connections in which organisms live and consume each other and each other's waste. The system has evolved so that the characteristic of communities of living organisms seems to be that nothing that contains available energy or useful material will be lost. There will evolve some organism that will manage to make its living by dealing with any waste product that provides available energy or usable material. Ecologists talk of a food web: an interconnection of uses of both organisms and their wastes. In the industrial context we may think of this as being use of products and waste products. The system structure of a natural ecology and the structure of an industrial system, or an economic system, are extremely similar.[11]

Application of natural system principles to man-made systems. Some of the characteristics of ecosystems that industry might usefully copy are listed in the box on page 449. Three of these are then further discussed.

A few natural ecosystem characteristics to be emulated by industry[9,12]

In ecosystems, efficiency and productivity are in dynamic balance with resiliency. Emphasis of the first two qualities over the third creates brittle systems, likely to crash.

In the natural system there is no such thing as "waste" in the sense of something that cannot be absorbed constructively somewhere else in the system. Nutrients for one species are derived from the death and decay of another.

A major portion of energy flows in ecosystems is consumed in decomposition processes in order to recycle wastes for reuse.

Concentrated toxins are not stored or transported in bulk at the system level, but are synthesized and used as needed only by species individuals.

Materials and nutrients are continually circulated and transformed in extremely elegant ways. The system runs entirely on ambient solar energy, and over time has actually managed to store energy in the form of fossil fuel.

The natural system is dynamic and information-driven, and the identity of ecosystem players is defined in process terms.

The system permits independent activity on the part of each individual of a species, yet cooperatively meshes the activity patterns of all species. Cooperation and competition are interlinked, held in balance.

Each member of an ecosystem performs multiple functions as it interrelates with other members.

The ecological niche for any member is the sum total of these interrelationships and the physical, chemical, and biological conditions it needs to live and reproduce in an ecosystem.

In the natural system there is no such thing as "waste" in the sense of something that cannot be absorbed constructively somewhere else in the system. The history of the chemical industry over the last 200 years contains many examples of turning wastes into by-products[13]:

- The Leblanc process (ca 1800) used sodium sulfate, a residual from the manufacture of ammonium chloride (a metal cleaner), to manufacture sodium carbonate (while generating a new waste, calcium sulfide, which later was used in manufacture of sulfuric acid).

- Coal tar was a large-scale waste from gasworks making "town gas" for illumination. German chemists initiated a systematic search for useful by-products, which resulted in development of the modern organic chemical industry. Products from coal tar included aniline dyes, phenolic resins, aspirin, and sulfa drugs.

- Chlorine was originally a by-product of manufacture of sodium hydroxide (lye), with low value and used mainly in water purification. The development of a wide range of valuable chlorine-based organic chemicals turned this around by the 1950s. *However, this "breakthrough" itself generated a new set of pollutants: common CFCs as industrial solvents and refrigerants, pesticides, and herbicides.* This suggests the importance of a larger framework for design when considering how wastes can become by-products.

In the present day, pollution prevention in its waste minimization mode and recycling have prompted many companies in various industries to search for markets for their unutilized products or wastes.

- The U.S. subsidiary of the German chemical and film manufacturer BASF has set up an Environmental Opportunities initiative in its corporate Ecology Department. The mission is to find uses and markets for residual products not currently marketed. The initiative seeks to integrate this practice into day-to-day operations as a way of moving beyond simple compliance to waste disposal regulations. The company develops new revenues while saving on disposal costs.[14]

- US Gypsum is making 100% recycled content sheetrock from synthetic gypsum generated as a by-product of utility flue gas desulfurization. It has been using recycled paper since 1930 and claims to be the largest recycler of waste paper in the United States.[15]

- Wisconsin Public Service and Rhinelander Paper Co. are creating a materials and energy loop whereby the power company will burn paper mill wastes, which together with low-sulfur coal, will power two counties and the paper mill itself. Rhinelander will cut waste to landfill by 25% and save on steam costs.[15]

- The new Boeing Longacres plant in Renton, Washington, uses wastewater from a neighboring wastewater treatment plant for cooling, thus saving on energy and water costs.[16]

- Waste Systems Institute and Pacific Materials Exchange provide on-line listings of "waste" materials available. Such regional or national information networks enable companies to find markets for by-products.[17]

These examples suggest that the ecological principle of linking organisms in food webs where one's wastes are nutrients for others makes good business sense. This move beyond individual plant boundaries raises new design questions: Do we need to modify processes in company A to turn residuals into a product useful in company B? Are there regulatory and liability issues in such a transfer? Do the regulators need to do some redesign? Are we perhaps locking in the use of a hazardous material rather than designing it out of the system?

Note that some interpreters of industrial ecology identify the application of this one principle—no waste in ecosystems—as the total definition of the field. This error leads many to say, "Well, there's nothing new here." Industrial ecology is far broader than this.

Concentrated toxins are not stored or transported in bulk at the system level, but are synthesized and used as needed only by species individuals. An example of this principle in nature: venomous snakes and poisonous plants are very discrete repositories of toxins. (A major exception in nature is where volcanic eruptions may distribute toxins across a wide area. Here, wetlands ecosystems may absorb and ultimately filter large amounts of such materials.)

In industry, AT&T is piloting on-line production of gallium arsenide for computer chips from a chemical precursor instead of shipping this extremely toxic chemical.

Each member of an ecosystem performs multiple functions as it interrelates with other members. An example from nature: During its lifetime a single deer perpetuates its own species by reproducing, encourages new grass and other plant species to grow by grazing and browsing and fertilizing the soil with its waste, and may provide food and energy for a wolf, coyote, or cougar. After death, its remains are converted by decomposers back into the organic compounds which fuel the earth's essential biogeochemical cycles, upon which all species depend for life.[12]

In industry, Quad/Graphics, the largest privately owned printing company in the United States, has aggressively led the industry in pioneering green printing processes and materials. Rather than hold what it has learned as proprietary, the company has embarked on an extensive educational program to encourage other players in the industry, its customers, and end consumers to follow its lead. Quad/Graphics seeks competitive advantage through holding a broad, multifunctional vision of its mission which includes but goes beyond profitability.[18]

Carrying capacity. Ecologists always look at the natural limits in any ecosystem they study. Quality of soil and underlying geology, climate patterns, genetic diversity, and other natural limits define the extent to which plant and animal populations can grow. Unfortunately, this central ecological concept remains controversial when applied to human activity. Technological optimists prefer to think that technical innovation will enable a pattern of continuing industrial growth. Many leaders in developing countries resent concerns about their population growth expressed in industrialized countries. However, some industrial ecology pioneers like Braden Allenby, Robert Ayres, and Faye Duchin make the concept of carrying capacity central to their thinking.

At the level of a company seeking a location for a new plant, the concept of carrying capacity of the local resource base is a vital concept. The plant design team needs to work with awareness of the natural limits of the local ecosystems at possible sites. John Warren of Pacific Northwest Laboratories gives a graphic example: A North Carolina paper mill is located in an area that's great place for a mill *except* that it has more air inversions than any other place in the United States. The air is capped three-fourths of the summer. Review of the carrying capacity of the area would have shown it was not a good location for a mill.[19]

Industrial metabolism studies of energy and materials flows

> 10 tons of active mass raw materials (not including construction materials) per person is extracted from U.S. territory by the economy. Roughly 75% is mineral and non-renewable while 25% is, in principle, from renewable sources. 6% of the total is embodied in durable products. The other 94% is converted into waste residuals as fast as it is extracted.... the tonnages of waste residuals are actually greater than the tonnages of crops, timber, fuels and minerals (because air and water contribute mass to the residuals).[20]

An early foundation of IE work, industrial metabolism, offers strategic designers analytic tools for looking at the total pattern of energy/materials flows, from initial extraction of resources to final disposal of wastes. In the early seventies, Robert U. Ayres at Carnegie-Mellon University, author of the paragraph quoted above, started evolving means to better determine the true costs of materials, factoring in the real value of nonrenewable resources and environmental pollution. This analysis helps give an economic value in the market and the balance sheet of companies to what economists call "externalities." *Industrial metabolism* (IM) studies can be done globally, nationally, by industry, by company, and by site. This is a valuable context for doing environmental audits of facilities or whole companies.

IM analysis highlights the dramatic difference between natural and industrial metabolic processes: in natural systems materials flow in closed loops with near universal recycling; industrial systems are very dissipative, leading to materials concentrations too low to provide value but high enough to pollute. In these terms, an inclusive definition of *waste* would be "dissipative use of natural resources."

An internal corporate IM study might explore an issue like the balance between virgin and recycled materials use, developing a model of materials use, industrial processes, and both environmental and economic costs and benefits. This would enable decisionmakers to evaluate scenarios for change to decrease use of virgin materials.

An external IM study might analyze heavy metals pollution in the larger region surrounding a company's industrial plant, as well as the plant's contribution. Such research could discover that the company's pollution control and prevention efforts have reduced its point source flows to a very low level compared with the nonpoint sources distributed throughout the region. The study would highlight areas where plant performance could still be improved. But it might also indicate that priority for public policymaking should be developing an effective program for dealing with the nonpoint sources through community education, infrastructure, management of government services, and other social measures.

Industrial metabolism suggests several measures of industrial sustainability. Such measures would provide valuable guidance to corporate strategic planning.

IM has been applied to large regional industrial systems (analysis of the Rhine Basin), to specific industries (aluminum), and to specific materials, especially the heavy metals.[21,22]

In Measures of sustainability

The ratio of virgin to recycled mineral resources. "The fraction of current metal supply needed to replace dissipative losses (i.e. production from virgin ores needed to maintain a stable level of consumption) is thus a useful surrogate measure of `distance' from a steady-state condition, i.e. a condition of long-run sustainability."[22]

The ratio of materials recycled to materials potentially recyclable. With regard to materials that are potentially recyclable the fraction actually recycled is a useful measure of the approach toward (or away from) sustainability. A reasonable proxy for this, in the case of metals, is the ratio of secondary supply to total supply of final materials....the recycling ratio in the United States has been rising consistently in recent years only for lead and iron/steel."[22]

Materials productivity. "Another useful measure of industrial metabolic efficiency is the economic output per unit of material input... materials productivity (not reliable for the economy as a whole)."[22]

What if? Dynamic input-output models

Faye Duchin, Director of New York University's Institute of Economic Analysis, has built "what if?" tools upon the foundation of industrial metabolism.[23,24] These dynamic input-output models enable high-level business and policy designers to perceive the broad business, economic, and environmental implications of systemic technical change. Dr. Duchin's input-output models add environmental resource accounts to economic information about the 100 + industrial sectors found in standard national input-output tables. By incorporating a time dimension, she has created a means of analyzing the total impacts of alternative scenarios of industrial change. How would the changes affect the environment, businesses in the target industry, and their major suppliers and customers?

For example: An automobile manufacturer might choose to study the impact on the environment and its own future prospects of a dramatic increase in personal vehicle use in China. The study could factor in such considerations as:

- Choice among material-processing technologies and the associated demand for material and energy resources
- Vehicle efficiency and fuel use
- Emission characteristics and air pollution
- Economic and environmental implications of the new roads and other infrastructure
- Congestion and travel times
- Labor requirements and the capacity of the educational system

The results of this analysis might challenge the practicality and the wisdom of the automaker's dream of a China filled with racing automobiles. The level of increased resource drain, congestion, and pollution might prompt the company to consider an alternative scenario of intermodal, rail-based transportation systems—a scenario that might attract the support of the Chinese government as more appropriate to the transportation *and* environmental needs of China. The resulting strategy for the company might include acquisition of a solar rail car manufacturing business, accelerating R&D on solar- or LPG-powered minivans, and redefining the core business as "providing the means to move people in enormously congested Third World environments."

Is this too radical an expectation? Only if we assume that corporate leadership is incapable of relearning the old truth: the real world is one with a long-term future, not just the next quarter's profits. Dynamic input-output models, along with other IE tools still to be developed, will give leaders lenses for viewing the implications of their decisions in terms of a real world that builds value across the generations.

The Indonesian government is presently working with Duchin in modeling development alternatives that could end the destruction of its rain forests. She has completed studies about other sectors including transportation, the auto industry, and biowaste recycling, and is beginning an analysis comparing the impacts of consumer plastic recycling, source reduction, and biodegradability.

Product life extension and the service economy

Walter Stahel has linked the concerns of DFE with a broader level of design: the rethinking of how manufacturing businesses create value. Stahel, a director of the Swiss Product-Life Institute, argues that closing loops through recycling is only half of the picture. It does not slow the rapid and unsustainable flow of materials and goods through economies. He proposes *product life extension* as the necessary other half and outlines business strategies for achieving it, as well as the dimensions of a service-oriented economy. While his views are transformational in nature, Stahel identifies major corporations, such as Xerox, Agfa-Gevaert, and Siemens, demonstrating the product life extension concept.[25]

Product life extension implies a fundamental shift from selling products themselves to selling the utilization of products, the customer value they yield. This change in the source of economic value to firms, depends upon enhancing product life through design strategies for durability—such as materials selection; modular, readily upgradable systems; and self-repairing components—and strategies for reconditioning and/or remanufacturing. The long-term source of competitive advantage for a company then becomes the ability to provide the needed service through leasing and continuing maintenance and improvement of highly durable material products which it continues to own.

Stahel also considers the larger transition to a decentralized and skill-based service economy that product durability implies. Economic value would be based in utilization (customer satisfaction with the service gained), rather than exchange. Decentralized, labor-intensive service centers would create many skilled jobs for workers no longer needed in centralized, highly mechanized production units. Resource use would be lowered as products no longer moved rapidly from factory to customer to landfill.

The Swiss photocopier company Agfa-Gevaert AG demonstrates that these concepts can be brought down to earth. It leases copiers with a long-term flexible agreement (selling system utilization) which covers all consumables in a price per copy. The company assumes responsibility for product quality and utility over the copier's lifetime. Therefore designers have a strong incentive to use long-life components, standardize components and systems, lower costs of supplies, and aim for ease of repair and reconditioning. "Agfa-Gevaert's interest in product durability is evident: the longer its products can be rented out and the cheaper their operation is, the higher its profit."[26]

Walter Stahel's work represents design at the level where a company asks "What business are we really in?" Wise decisions at this level will have the greatest impact on their environmental performance. But they will need to demonstrate leadership to convert customers from the religion of consumerism.

Management of the interface between industry and natural systems

One way of describing the fundamental task of industrial ecology is to say it will match the inputs and outputs of the man-made world to the constraints of the biosphere. This demands much deeper scientific understanding of ecosystem dynamics, assimilative capacity, and recovery times; the impact of industrial design decisions in terms of location, intensity, and timing of activities; and ecological engineering's use of natural ecosystems as carrier and transfer medium of wastes, or as a cooperative processing component. Industry will need indicators or indices quantifying its impact on natural systems, and it will need feedback systems enabling adjustment of operations in response to real-time information about current environmental conditions.[9]

Development of this interface is neither a trivial nor humble assignment, but neither is it one that any central authority is capable of assuming. Such R&D, and ultimately "interface management," must be broadly distributed throughout businesses, research organizations, and regulatory and policymaking institutions. Dynamic organizational structures and information systems must knit these three sectors into an organism capable of learning and adapting much more rapidly than we now think possible.

Feedback for self-regulation. A specific component of this industrial–natural systems interface has been called Ecofeedback™ by the Dutch industrial designer and consultant, Jan Hanhart. This concept implies business and community environmental information systems enabling feedback loops for self-regulation and environmental management, with real-time response capability.

A full Ecofeedback™ environmental information management system should enable a company's employees to:

- Monitor regional environmental conditions and the environmental performance of businesses

- Track key indicators on global environmental conditions as a guide to long-term policies

- Monitor the total materials flow of the site (its industrial metabolism) against jointly established targets for reducing use of virgin materials and toxics and lowering emissions and wastes

- Monitor patterns of energy usage against targets for increasing efficiency

- Compile comparative environmental performance ratios by correlation of environmentally relevant inputs and outputs to units of product

- Provide feedback that enables plants to adapt in real time to conditions outside environmental performance quality limits

- Provide feedback on cost savings through all of these enhancements

- Share innovations and solve common problems through computer conferencing

- Link environmental quality performance to compensation systems

- Support maximum recycling and reuse of materials within and amongst businesses through a brokering database matching suppliers' resources with customers' needs

To facilitate product and process design, the system would also include information on alternative production processes and materials and the economics of waste utilization.[27,28]

Japanese research on the Ecofactory.   Japanese researchers in the Agency of Industrial Science and Technology have offered a logical analysis of the technologies needed to achieve the closed-loop system ideal. Their report on the Ecofactory appears to be an independent development of an industrial ecology model. The model integrates design of production systems technology—including design for environment at product and process levels—with disassembling, reuse, and materials-recycling technology. These two large components are then linked to control and assessment technology.

The Ecofactory model describes a total system design for closed-loop manufacturing, with the most detailed technical R&D agenda for industrial ecology yet to appear.[29,30] The wish list includes items in energy, design, production, robotics, materials, systems, and information technologies. Specifics such as robotics for disassembly and sorting, materials recognition systems, information systems for concurrent engineering, and many others clearly add up to major business opportunities for those who create and apply them. Companies that pioneer in this field will realize profound cost savings in their own production and can open global markets for these new technologies.

Industrial ecosystems

The broadest application of industrial ecology's analogic way of seeing is to describe manufacturing complexes as "industrial ecosystems." This phrase suggests a web of interaction among companies such that the residuals of one become feedstock for another. The most celebrated example so far is at Kalundborg, a community in Denmark. But one can find other examples, thanks to the historic pattern of the chemical industry described above. Any petrochemical complex can be called an industrial ecosystem, although most are still major sources of emissions. Douglas B. Holmes describes one such complex, the "assemblage" of oil, chemical, and petrochemical industry facilities in Houston, Texas, in the box below, continued on page 459.

Houston as industrial ecosystem.   The Houston Ship Channel is roughly 50 miles long, deep enough to handle nearly any ship afloat, thereby making Houston, an inland city, one of the largest harbors in the U.S.

All the necessary ingredients are present—a deepwater port, oil and natural gas nearby (both on- and off-shore), sulfur (Frasch process mining, both on- and off-shore), salt, and plenty of relatively cheap land. The result: an enormous assemblage of chemical and petrochemical plants and oil refineries. Shoulder-to-shoulder, they stretch for tens of miles on both sides of the Ship Channel.

Much of the raw material is brought into the area by pipeline: oil and gas from south and west Texas, for example. What is more surprising to most people is that most of the products leave by pipeline, too, though some goes out by ship. Natural gas, for example, comes in, is treated (to remove carbon dioxide, hydrogen, nitrogen, and the somewhat larger organic molecules, particularly ethane, propane, and ethylene. Each of these materials is used, if not within the same plant, then by one of the neighboring plants. That is, materials are sold to the adjacent plants, and transferred by pipeline, over the fence.

In this industrial complex, economic forces have caused each company to strive for highly efficient operations, with high yields. Recognizing the value of their by-products (they are not referred to as waste products), they have arranged, wherever possible, to sell these to a neighboring company. This has evolved quite far; there are even closed recycle loops crossing the fences.

The example I remember most vividly from my student days in Houston (late fifties) was the sulfuric acid plant which took in molten sulfur from the local mines, by pipe, made sulfuric acid, which it sold by pipe to all the chemical plants. Then some of these plants, after using the acid in their processes, sold back their so-called spent acid, where it was burned to recover sulfur trioxide, which was then converted to sulfuric acid once again. This material never saw the light of day; made in a reactor, shipped out by pipe, into another reactor, and then back to its birthplace by pipe. Meters on the pipes kept the accountants happy.[31]

An industrial ecosystem in Denmark

"I was asked to speak on 'how you designed Kalundborg'. We didn't design the whole thing. It wasn't designed at all. It happened over time. It's not the kind of thing you can engineer in a moment and drop in place. It takes more time."[32]

One of the favorite cases presented by industrial ecologists is the story of the spontaneous evolution of the "industrial symbiosis"* at Kalundborg, Denmark. This web of materials and energy exchanges among companies (and with the community) developed over the last decade in this industrial region 80 miles west of Copenhagen. Originally, the motivation behind this project was to reduce wastes by seeking profitable uses for them, a traditional business goal. Gradually, the managers and town residents realized they were generating powerful environmental benefits through their transactions.

There are five core partners in the industrial symbiosis:

- Asnaes Power Station—Denmark's largest power station, coal-fired, 1500 MW, employs 600 people.

- Statoil Refinery—Denmark's largest, with capacity of 3.2 million tons, currently expanding by 50 to 60%, employs 250 people (increasing capacity to 4.8 million tons).

Industrial symbiosis can be defined as a cooperation between different industries by which the presence of each increases the viability/profitability of the other(s), and by which the demands of society for resource savings and environmental protection are considered. *Symbiosis* is the living together of dissimilar organisms in any of various mutually beneficial relationships. Here the term is used to mean industrial cooperation with mutual utilization of residual products.

- Gyproc—Plasterboard factory, makes 14 million m² of plasterboard annually, employs 175 people.

- Novo Nordisk—A biotechnological company, producing pharmaceuticals (insulin is the major product) and industrial enzymes; this is the corporation's largest plant in both products employing 1200 people.

- City of Kalundborg—Supplies water and district heating.

Over the last two decades these partners spontaneously developed a network of exchanges which also includes a number of other smaller companies (see Fig. 25.3).

Energy flows. The Asnaes power station traditionally operated at about 40% efficiency. In common with most other power stations, the majority of energy generated went up the stacks. The Statoil refinery flared off most of its gas by-product. Then a series of deals were struck:

- Asnaes sends steam to Novo Nordisk (eliminating need for new boilers), to the city of Kalundborg for district heating, and to the refinery.

- The power plant uses coal and refinery gas to provide electricity, steam, and district heating to Kalundborg (replacing 5000 oil-burning heaters in homes).

- The power plant's excess energy at low-temperature level is used for fish farming, producing 200 tons of fish a year; a greenhouse is planned.

- The refinery provides excess gas to Gyproc wallboard.

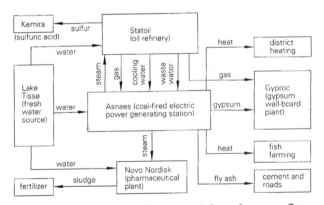

Figure 25.3 Kalundborg. The materials and energy flows among the companies at Kalundborg, Denmark. (*Source: Novo Nordisk.*)

- Statoil built a sulfur recovery unit to comply with regulations on sulfur emission; gas became clean enough to use at the power plant as supplementary fuel.

Materials flow

- Power plant's fly ash goes to cement company.
- Power plant's desulfurization unit produces gypsum which goes to Gyproc.
- Refinery's desulfurization operation produces pure sulfur which goes to Kemira, a company producing sulfuric acid.
- Sludge from fish farm's water treatment plant is used as fertilizer on nearby farms.
- Surplus yeast from insulin production at Novo Nordisk goes to farmers as pig food.

This web of recycling and reuse has generated new revenues and cost savings for the companies involved and avoided pollution to air, water, and land in the region. In ecological terms, Kalundborg became a simple food web, with organisms consuming each other's waste materials and energies. The material below summarizes some of the economic and environmental results at Kalundborg.

Results at Kalundborg

Economic

Total investment in new infrastructure, ca $60 million U.S.

Annual revenues, ca $10 million (conservative, estimate)

Average payback time, 5 years

Accumulated revenue to 1993, $120 million

(Some projects have up to 7 years payback, most are down to 3–4 years)

Environmental savings*

Reduced resource consumption:

Oil, 19,000 tons

Coal, 30,000 tons

---

*All figures are per year.

Water, 600,000 m^3 (out of 3 million m^3)

Reduced emissions:

CO_2, 130,000 tons (out of 4 million)

SO_2, 3700 tons (out of 29,000)

Reuse of waste products:

Fly ash, 135 tons

Sulphur, 2800 tons

Gypsum, 80,000 tons

Nitrogen in sludge, 800 tons

What conditions enabled the industrial symbiosis at Kalundborg to evolve? The web of exchanges at Kalundborg poses an interesting challenge to "designers" who would like to replicate it: it wasn't designed. Novo-Nordisk vice president, Jorgen Christensen says, "We didn't plan it in advance. At the time we were just doing what was profitable and what made sense. The local management of those companies are the actors. Until now we have had no formal organization, no common board or budget. We do what pairs of us think is a good idea."

Christensen identifies several conditions for a new Kalundborg to develop:

- Industries must be different and fit each other.

- The incentive is a sustainable economy; at Kalundborg these arrangements have been commercially sound and profitable; resource savings, environment, and economy have gone hand in hand.

- Development must be voluntary, in close collaboration with the authorities.

- A short physical distance between the partners is necessary for the economy of transportation—many things cannot withstand long-distance transportation (physically, the symbiosis is essentially a series of pipelines).

- The "mental distance" is as important as the physical distance; at Kalundborg the managers at different plants all know each other.

The often repeated story of Kalundborg has stimulated a new breed of designers hoping to find the key to creating industrial ecosystems by intention. In the next section we will explore the design questions being raised in several North American and European projects.

"Designing" Industrial Ecosystems

Kalundborg's innovative exchange of residual energy and materials has inspired a number of efforts to intentionally create industrial ecosystems. These efforts illustrate the design of regional intercompany relations and possible new social institutions to enable and support them. This is a challenging level of design, especially when we remember Jorgen Christensen's caution, "We didn't design the whole thing. It wasn't designed at all. It happened over time." Is it possible to develop a Kalundborg on purpose, or at least to define the conditions that would enable such a complex system to evolve?

There are two complementary streams of inquiry seeking to answer the two questions within this larger one: "What changes within companies are needed to allow participation in industrial ecosystems?" and "What new social institutions and policies will best support the evolution of them?"

The first question is a major theme of much of the early exploration in industrial ecology, especially in workshops and a Spring 1994 conference organized by the National Academy of Engineering. During these events, industrial managers and academic researchers have examined how companies could move toward more closed-loop cycles in materials and energy use. Some key issues addressed include supplier management, design of procurement standards and specifications, process redesign, and total-cost accounting.

The second approach to designing industrial ecosystems is emerging from government, research, and business institutions. The EPA has launched an Eco-Industrial Park initiative; several university research groups are working with existing or new industrial developments in North America to generate industrial ecosystems; at least one business is working with community economic development agencies and real estate developers to plan "eco-industrial parks." (The author is a principal in this firm, Indigo Development.)

These projects, which are discussed below, are addressing a unique set of design challenges spanning technical, economic, organizational, political, and ecological issues.

New Kalundborgs: Several projects

An eco-industrial park prototype. The EPA's Office of Policy, Planning, and Evaluation has taken a lead role in catalyzing development of a prototype eco-industrial park (EIP). Carol Browner, agency Administrator, announced the initiative in a press conference of the President's Council on Sustainable Development (PCSD): "Our Eco-Industrial Park (EIP) project is part of the President's Environmental

Technology Initiative....We will be working with developers, local governments, and planners in communities across the country to identify the most promising development sites."[33] This project was supported by the PCSD's Eco-Efficiency Task Force which designated four EP demonstration projects.

In Phase I of the project a team from Research Triangle Institute and Indigo Development developed "an Eco-Industrial Park generic design concept to the level where its application could be tested in a site or multiple sites."[34] Some questions addressed include:

- How can various levels of government best act to catalyze development of such parks by the private sector?

- How will the developer recruit the right mix of companies to optimize trading of wastes as by-products and to maintain the mix as companies come and go?

- What tools need to be developed to define an optimum mix of companies?

- What is the baseline of relatively certain economic and environmental benefits in the park concept that will reduce risks for developers and tenants in demonstration projects?

- What policy shifts are needed to accommodate development of eco-industrial parks and retrofitting of established parks?

This research will build upon industrial experience in pollution prevention and energy efficiency, as well as spontaneously occurring residual exchange networks such as the Houston Ship Channel network described earlier. The EPA project staff sees industrial ecology and the EIP concept as means of bringing successes in pollution prevention and energy efficiency into a more systemic whole, not as a substitute for them.

Dalhousie University's Burnside study. The Burnside Industrial Park in Nova Scotia is the subject of an interdisciplinary research team in the School for Resource and Environmental studies at Dalhousie University. This effort is the first project inspired by Kalundborg and the industrial ecology framework. The team's work with the large site (including 1200 small and medium-sized businesses) aims to develop principles, guidelines, and strategies for enabling an existing collection of plants to become an industrial ecosystem. An April 1994 project report indicates focus on several key areas:

- Enabling materials and energy cycling among companies through co-location of businesses, a waste exchange information system, and attraction of scavenger and decomposer businesses that typically use or trade "secondhand" materials

- Relating buildings and the park as a whole to the natural environment, including use of passive solar heating in buildings; use of wetlands to filter runoff and sewage

- Making information available to resident companies on materials used, energy required, and wastes generated in Burnside, and creating feedback loops within and between companies, and with park management, and regulators

The Dalhousie project is generating guidelines that will apply to new industrial parks, as well as to retrofitting of older ones.[35]

Cornell University's Ecological Industrial Park proposal.   Cornell University's Work and Environment Initiative has proposed development of EIPs in Rochester, New York, Baltimore and Maryland. The concept includes the development of closed-loop production systems linked to a core resource recovery technology. A unique feature in this project is its new approaches to economic development and business organization. It emphasizes a network model of economic and industrial development in which smaller companies collaborate to achieve marketing advantage and develop joint products.

Another innovative aspect of this project is its support to businesses in developing high-performance work systems, promising more productive industrial organizations. The public-private partnership in this development will have strong participation from labor, as well as industry and economic development agencies.

Cornell's project promises to enhance the competitiveness of manufacturing in North America through the combination of environmental and energy efficiencies and high-performance business practices.[36]

Other communities in the United States and Canada, Europe, and Asia are exploring development of EIPs or redevelopment of "brownfield" industrial parks, sometimes under the names, "green industrial park" or "environmentally sensitive and energy-efficient industrial park." There are also proposals for industrial parks and zones concentrating businesses in the recycling industry. These provide one side of an industrial ecosystem's function, playing the decomposer role to a larger region.

Virtually all aspects of sustainable architecture, urban planning, and construction, and transportation enter into the set of design concepts proposed. The designer's challenge is realizing and testing prototypes drawing upon the idealized model of an EIP that is emerging.

Design challenges in creating industrial ecosystems

Developing an eco-industrial park or a broader regional network is a complex undertaking, demanding integration across many fields of design. Technical design of a plant-to-plant exchange of residual materials and energy may itself be the easiest part. The businesses operating these plants may need to redesign organizational structures, policies, and procedures. Economic development agencies and real estate developers will need to create new strategies for attracting businesses to EIPs. Environmental agencies will need to rethink many regulations and policies. Generalist designers will have to integrate the new thinking in each of these areas into a cohesive metadesign.

For example, the technical task of "designing" an optimal mix of companies using each other's residuals must avoid locking in continued reliance on toxic materials. The pollution prevention solution of materials substitution or process redesign must take priority over trading toxics.

Then the technical process of getting the company mix right must integrate with the economic development and business task of filling a new EIP (not always easy with conventional parks). The "design" may be one that enables the developer or agency to build the mix over time, perhaps with a major anchor company setting the initial constraints to define a next wave of recruitment. The nature of the exchanges that develop will also define a layer of park infrastructure to move the residuals from one plant to another.

Once in operation, an EIP will need a sitewide management system responsible for many new tasks not handled in traditional industrial parks, e.g., maintaining the right mix of companies as individual plants come and go. New businesses with particular inputs and outputs may have to be recruited to a niche, although the interdependence of EIP companies for supplies and/or markets could be buffered by inclusion in a regional waste exchange. The exchange will also be a way of assuring consistency of supply in the face of market-driven fluctuations in generation of needed residuals.

The park management system could assume responsibility (and liability) for management of all surplus wastes not absorbed within the park, a step which in itself would create major cost savings for companies. This raises interesting regulatory issues. Can policymakers design regulatory districts for EIPs parallel to water or sewage districts? Perhaps this could simplify the regulatory task from government and business sides, while the total EIP package improves environmental performance.

A trade-off may be that businesses will surrender some degree of autonomy to sitewide management. This will have to be minimized through such strategies as making the EIP management largely an information-driven system with collaborative self-management by member companies. Success here demands innovation in organizational design within and among companies. Each firm will have a strong interest in the viability and environmental performance of other businesses in their industrial community. This could prompt evolution of the sort of small-town cooperative spirit that enabled the industrial ecosystem at Kalundborg to unfold in the first place.

An EIP management system will be most effective if it operates in the mode organizational designers call "the learning organization." This will be especially important in early prototypes, where fast recovery from inevitable design errors will be imperative. Learnings from such errors as well as successes will enable individual companies and the system as a whole to achieve continuous improvement in both business and environmental performance.

This summary of a few EIP design challenges suggests that the field of industrial ecology will coevolve with other disciplines edging toward a grounded practice of sustainable development.

Benefits to industry

To the companies involved, the eco-industrial park offers the opportunity to decrease production costs through increased materials and energy efficiency, increased waste recycling, and avoidance of regulatory penalties. Increased efficiency will also enable park members to produce more competitive products. In addition, costs once incurred solely by individual businesses—such as the cost of infrastructure, R&D, and the cost of designing and maintaining sophisticated information systems—may be shared by all member businesses in the park. Such industrial cost sharing will help park members achieve greater economic efficiency than their stand-alone counterparts.

These cost benefits to participating companies will increase the value of projects for real estate developers and park management companies.

Benefits to the environment

In addition to the obvious reduction in many sources of pollution and decreased demand for natural resources, the eco-industrial park will demonstrate in a real-world setting the principles of sustainable development. The park's evolution will also result in the creation of even more innovative approaches to pollution prevention and other environmental management technologies. Most importantly, the park will serve as a working model for future eco-parks and other environmentally sound forms of business operation.[37]

Conclusion

For some, this account of industrial ecology may push the limits of this field and of the concept of design itself. Many pioneers are working in a more incremental fashion, identifying the immediate steps for beginning to apply IE in product or process design. But this effort will be most effective in the context of a larger, transformational approach. Incremental change alone is not likely to meet the combined environmental challenges humanity faces. The industrial system itself is going through an enormous transformation even as we attempt to deal with ecological changes of a global scale. Perhaps industrial ecology offers a context for managing both transformations.

We are already in the midst of a major transformation in the industrial system, sparked by technological change, the drive for global competitiveness, and new approaches to management and organization design. Some aspects of this industrial transformation:

- The ongoing information/communication revolution, including

  Automation and computer-integrated manufacturing, increasing the capability for customization

  Electronic data interchange among companies

  Distributed information systems supplanting centralized systems

- Partnering between companies, suppliers, and customers, with tight information links and systems and processes integrated across company boundaries

- Successes with high-performance, self-managing work teams

- The focus on quality, and the development of technology and organizations to support it

- Dematerialization of product (Buckminster Fuller used the word *ephemeralization* to refer to this continual decrease in material input to products.)

- Emergence of the practice of concurrent engineering and life-cycle product analysis

- Rapid industrialization in China, other Asian countries, and some Latin American countries, often accompanied by serious environmental problems

- Growth in production capability running far ahead of market demand in many industries

Each aspect of this transformation presents an opportunity for applying industrial ecology principles and practices.

However, these waves of transformation are now intersecting with the massive restructuring of many corporations, massive cost cutting, staff cutting, mergers, and divestitures. There are deep cuts in middle management and labor. One begins to wonder who will be the customers for these more efficient companies.

One vital ingredient of the industrial transformation to sustainability is perceiving that the viability of any specific company is interdependent with the health of its total setting. The trend toward partnering among companies and with communities illustrates organizations' search for long-term coviability with the larger environment, a search which must extend to questions of economic equity domestically and internationally. Industrial ecology is one natural framework to guide and inform this process.

A frequent concern expressed by critics of industrial ecology is that it suggests a top-down control structure. Nothing could be further from the way ecosystems function, and therefore nothing could be less appropriate for achieving the transition to sustainability. The designers of IE must work in the action mode we practice as members of a jury or participants in disaster recovery: self-organization. The judge does not tell a jury how to conduct its deliberations; he or she simply sets the legal constraints in the case, and jury members organize their own effort to deliver justice.

Complex systems can adapt to the rapid global changes now unfolding only through diverse self-organizing systems, linked by rich flows of information. This discussion of industrial ecology indicates some of the concepts and tools now emerging to guide this task.

References

1. B. Allenby, "Industrial Ecology Gets Down to Earth," *Circuits and Devices,* vol. 10, no. 1, January 1994.
2. M. Renner, "Rethinking the Role of the Automobile," Worldwatch Paper 84, Worldwatch Institute, Washington, DC, 1988.
3. R. L. Klimisch, "Designing the Modern Automobile for Recycling," in B. R. Allenby and D. Richards (eds.), *Greening Industrial Ecosystems,* National Academy of Engineering, Washington, DC, 1993.
4. A. B. Lovins, J. W. Barnett, and L. H. Lovins, *Supercars: The Coming Light-Vehicle Revolution,* Rocky Mountain Institute, Snowmass, CO, 1993.
5. A. B. Lovins, J. W. Barnett, and L. H. Lovins, *Reinventing the Wheels,* Rocky Mountain Institute, Snowmass, CO, 1993.
6. Suntrain Inc. Business Plan 1994 and *Transportation Transformation.* Ten Speed Press, Berkeley, CA, (forthcoming).
7. Robert M. White, "Introduction," *Greening of Industrial Ecosystems,* National Academy of Engineering, Washington, DC, 1994.
8. David Chiddick, testimony before Senate Environment and Public Works Committee, Feb. 23, 1993.
9. H. Tibbs, "Industrial Ecology—An Agenda for Environmental Management," *Pollution Prevention Review,* Spring 1992.

9a. B. R. Allenby, "Achieving Sustainable Development through Industrial Ecology," *International Environmental Affairs,* 1992.

10. Victor Papanek, "The Tree of Knowledge," Chap. 9 in *Design for the Real World, Human Ecology and Social Change,* Bantam, New York, 1973.

11. R. A. Frosch, "Industrial Ecology: A Philosophical Introduction," National Academy of Science, *Proceedings,* February 1992, Washington, DC.

12. Martha Lowe, "Natural Principles for Industrial Ecology," unpublished paper.

13. R. U. Ayres, "Industrial Metabolism," in *Technology and Environment,* National Academy of Engineering, Washington, DC, 1989.

14. *Business and the Environment* (BATE) newsletter, March 1994, Arlington, MA, and personal communication with Steven Rice, manager of environmental opportunities, Parsippany, NJ, BASF.

15. *Business and the Environment* (BATE) newsletter, Arlington, MA, October 1992.

16. Personal communication from David Smukowski, Boeing EH&S Manager, Seattle, WA.

17. *Business and the Environment* (BATE) newsletter, Arlington, MA, February 1992.

18. Quad/Graphics, *Enviro/Facts,* Pewaukee, WI, 1993.

19. "Pollution Prevention Methods: Extending the Concept to Industrial Ecosystems," *Proceedings, Industrial Ecology Workshop, Making Business More Competitive,* Ontario Ministry of Environment and Energy, Toronto, 1994.

20. R. U. Ayres, "Externalities: Economics and Thermodynamics," in Archibugi and Nijkamp (eds.), *Economy and Ecology,* Academic, The Netherlands, 1989.

21. W. M. Stigliani and S. Anderberg, "Industrial Metabolism and the Rhine Basin," *Options,* September 1991, International Institute for Applied Systems Analysis, Luxenburg, Austria.

22. Robert U. Ayres, and Udo E. Simonis (eds.), *Industrial Metabolism—Restructuring for Sustainable Development,* United Nations University Press, 1993.

23. Faye Duchin, "Industrial Input-Output Analysis: Implications for Industrial Ecology," National Academy of Science, *Proceedings,* Feb. 1, 1992, Washington, DC.

24. Faye Duchin, "Prospects for Environmentally Sound Economic Development in the North, in the South, and in North-South Economic Relations: The Role for Action-Oriented Analysis," to appear in *Journal of Clean Technology and Environmental Sciences.*

25. Walter Stahel, "The Utilization-Focused Service Economy: Resource Efficiency and Product-Life Extension," in B. R. Allenby and D. Richards (eds.), *Greening of Industrial Ecosystems,* National Academy of Engineering, Washington, DC, 1994.

26. M. Borlin, "Swiss Case-Studies of Product Durability Strategy," Product-Life Institute, Zurich, 1990.

27. Ernest Lowe, "Industrial Ecology," *Total Quality Environmental Management,* Fall 1993, pp. 73–85.

28. Jan Hanhart, *Ecofeedback,* Rosmalen, The Netherlands, 1989.

29. JETRO, "Ecofactory—Concept and R&D Themes," special issue, *New Technology,* FY 1992, Japan External Trade Organization, Tokyo. Report based on work of the Ecofactory Research Group of the Mechanical Engineering Laboratory, Agency of Industrial Science and Technology.

30. Chihiro Watanabe, "Energy and Environmental Technologies in Sustainable Development: A View from Japan," *The Bridge,* Summer 1993, National Academy of Engineering, Washington, DC. (Sketches Japanese work in industrial ecology beginning in 1972.)

31. Personal communication from Douglas B. Holmes, President, Minergy Associates, former Polaroid engineer and manager, former Chief Operating Officer of Ecological Engineering Associates.

32. Jorgen Christensen, *Proceedings, Industrial Ecology Workshop, Making Business More Competitive,* Ontario Ministry of Environment and Energy, Toronto, 1994.

33. U.S. Environmental Protection Agency, OCEPA press release, April 18, 1994.

34. U.S. Environmental Protection Agency, OPPE, Project Implementation Plan, Eco-Industrial Park, February 1994.

35. R.P. Côté, et al., *Designing and Operating Industrial Parks as Ecosystems,* School for Resource and Environmental Studies, Facility of Management, Dalhousie University, Halifax, Nova Scotia, B3J1B9, 1944.
36. E. Cohen-Rosenthal, "Ecological Industrial Park, Cornell University Work and Environment Initiative," Ithaca, New York, 1994.
37. Research Triangle Park and Indigo Eco-Industrial Park project description, Research Triangle Institute, Research Triangle Park, NC 1994.

Further Reading

Lowe, Ernest, *Applying Industrial Ecology,* a report of the Change Management Center, 1993. Discusses implementation of IE concepts and tools in business organizations. (For Engineering Foundation Pollution Prevention Pays conference, January 1993.)

Lowe, Ernest, "Industrial Ecology: Implications for Corporate Strategy," *Journal of Corporate Environmental Strategy,* Troy, NY, vol. 2, no. 1, pp. 61–65, Summer 1994.

Allenby, B. R. and T.E. Graedel, *Industrial Ecology,* Prentic Hall, Englewood Cliffs, N.J. 1995.

Allenby, Braden R., Deanna Richards, (ed.), *Greening Industrial Ecosystems,* National Acedemy of Engineering, Washington DC, Available through NAE Press Office (202-334-3313).

Ayres, Robert U. and Simonis E. Udo (Eds.), *Industrial Metabolism, Restructuring for Sustainable Development,* United Nations University Press, Tokyo and New York, 1994.

Final Report, Research Triangle Institute Project Number 6050, Volume 1, S. Martin et al., Developing an Eco-Industrial Park: Supporting Research, Volume 2, E. Lowe, et al., Fieldbook for the Development of Eco-Industrial Parks Research Triangle Park, 1995. (To be released as U.S.-EPA cooperative agreement project report.)

Socolow, R., C. Andrews, F. Berkhout, V. Thomas, (ed.) *Industrial Ecology and Global Change,* Cambridge University Press, NY, 1994.

26

Design for Environment in Perspective

One Giant Step for Industry, One Small Step for Life on Earth

Carl L. Henn, CPL, CFP

Senior Vice President
Concord Energy, Inc.
Bernardsville, New Jersey

Introduction

Decisions are made every day by managers, engineers, and industrial design teams that ultimately affect public health, property, and the natural environment. This book has been written to help "front-end" process and product decision makers determine *what* can be done to reduce or eliminate adverse impacts of their activities on society and the earth, as well as *how* to go about it.

It is useful occasionally to reflect upon the reasons *why* we may choose to adjust our goals and change our ways of achieving them. Understanding the significance of why we should change course can have important consequences. It can determine our sense of urgency, degree of cooperation, level of commitment, and depth of satisfaction in getting the job done. Professionals like to know, and should know, where their work fits into the big picture and how much difference it makes.

The DFE Imperative

Why design for environment (DFE)? To impartial observers, the answer is self-evident. Activities that harm people's deserve health, and safety are frowned on by society. Guilty parties deserve to be penalized. Serious degradation and depletion of the water, air, soil, and vegetation of the earth's life support systems is undesirable, increasingly illegal, unethical, unfair, and potentially suicidal.

Industrial processes and products, largely based on fossil fuel and petrochemical technologies, are major contributors to environmental pollution. *Preventing* continuation of this pollution is an important societal goal. *Cleanup* and *control* of pollution are necessary as inter-mediate measures, but they are costly, bureaucratic, and burdensome. Because pollution prevention corrects the problem at the source, it is the long-term solution of first choice.[1] As most of this book attests, DFE is an essential and potentially the most cost-effective means of implementing pollution prevention.

DFE is a logical and critically important response to the environ-mental challenge for most durable products and for many consumer products, particularly for large companies in these industries. Planned waste reduction increases the efficient use of materials and energy. It reduces liability. It increases profitability. It is not only good policy, it is good business.[2,3]

Barriers to Change

If pollution prevention is regularly reported in the United States and Europe to be so beneficial, the question arises as to why more compa-nies aren't doing it.

Many managers and engineers believe that environmental protec-tion increases costs, not that it reduces them.[4,5] This view is generally true for cleanup, control, regulatory compliance, and most waste treatment. Expensive design teams and consultants, as well as the costs and controversies of techniques like life-cycle assessment, are a further deterrent.[6] Equally important, if not more so, traditional capi-tal-budgeting and accounting practices do not fully or fairly display the full costs and benefits of environmental projects. A total-cost assessment study for the U.S. Environmental Protection Agency (EPA) by the Tellus Institute concluded that both business and the environment lose out when traditional accounting practices misrepre-sent the true profitability of pollution prevention options. [7,8]

It is noteworthy that total-cost assessment methods have been available for several years but have not yet achieved widespread acceptance in industry. This is so in spite of the proven advantages of such methods to those companies who have used them. The EPA-Tellus study cites several reasons for this lack of progress, including the resistance of institutional cultures to change, complex methodologies, insatiable demands for data, regulatory impediments, and costliness of studies.

Thus, it cannot be assumed that increased efficiency and cost savings alone are incentives enough to effect needed change. There are always negative rationalizations and barriers to any desirable change. This is the reason that it is imperative to understand more about *why* environmental issues are so urgent.

Given the time it took another commonsense management approach, total-quality management (TQM), to become embedded in the mainstream industrial culture, it could be decades before DFE achieves the pervasive impact required to reduce waste and pollution to sustainable levels. In the meantime, and for an indefinite period, other methods will continue to be needed to control discharges, reduce the use of harmful chemicals, and manage the use of material resources more efficiently.

The Added Value of Life-Cycle Thinking

Life-cycle analytical techniques for various purposes have been employed in government and industry for over twenty years. Only recently has this work begun to take a holistic approach that integrates chemical and energy input-output inventories, environmental impacts and total costs, risks and benefits from conceptual design of products through production, use, recycling, and disposal.[9] The holistic life-cycle approach to materials and product management is both a spatial and a chronological expansion of system boundaries that induces a wider and longer-term perspective in product design, market planning, and resource recovery decisions.[10]

Over the years the *grave* part of the so-called cradle-to-grave approach has been given little serious management attention. It has been considered too far in the future, especially for durable goods, of too little consequence, and usually subject to a choice only between the scrap dealer or the city dump as disposal alternatives in a throwaway society. We have been talking "life cycle" while thinking and acting "life span." Consequently, our industrial design orientation has been focused more on the linear short term for product lives than on longer-term, cyclical (reusable) considerations in the use of materials. Besides, most sellers almost certainly have regarded disposal, even of hazardous materials, to be an end-of-life problem for the buyer, not a design challenge for the producer.

Figures 26.1 and 26.2 demonstrate how this thinking is changing. The differences between the "Old Way" and the emerging "New Way," as depicted in these schematics, are as follows:

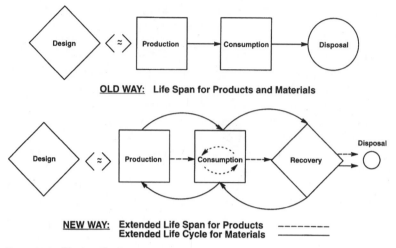

Figure 26.1 Closing the loop.

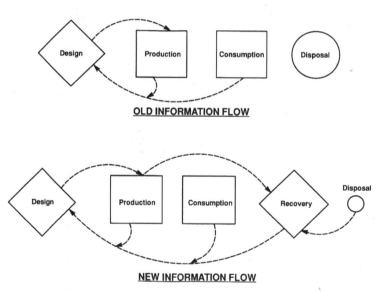

Figure 26.2 Design cycle.

1a. Old way. The lifetime physical fate of most materials, and the unique configuration of those materials in the form of products, have been for the most part inseparable as they have moved through the supply chain to retirement. Usable products don't have life cycles— materials do. Products, even if reused, have life spans, cradle to grave. Materials have life cycles. Materials also have life spans, but only when they go to disposal without having been reused or recycled. When a product (or any material asset) is recognized as no longer usable for one purpose or another, it is then regarded as a configuration of parts and materials that are candidates either for the birth of another product or for the cemetery.

Traditional "life-cycle" design and manufacturing literature has typically depicted the product retirement stage simply as "disposal." In fact, these are linear systems. Linear systems are costly, wasteful, and ultimately exhaust themselves. Only in the last few years have terms such as *recycling, reuse,* or *remanufacturing* been included in life-cycle schematics and analyses, even though it has long been normal salvage practice in the automotive, aircraft, and construction industries, for example, to recover used or surplus parts and materials for reuse or reprocessing.[11]

1*b. New way.* The lifetime supply chain fate of materials is becoming separated from that of products for two reasons: (1) As more materials are being recovered through recycling, they can be used again to produce entirely different products. (2) Many high-tech products become obsolete sooner as a result of fast-moving advances in technology. Such products have a shorter life in the market. These product lives are also called "life cycles," but this usage refers to stages of market life in terms of market share or the rise and fall of sales volume in contrast to the supply chain journey from design to disposal. Such obsolescent products often become disposable goods before completing their movement through the supply chain. They thereby become decoupled from the useful life cycles of the materials from which they are made.

2*a. Old way.* The volume of material that used to be recovered was quite small relative to the volume of material disposed of. Some products could be reused by the original owners or by secondary market consumers for the same or different applications. Some materials have been sold as scrap to producers of the same or different products. Most of the material has been dumped on land or at sea. Feedback to designers from "disposers" has been rare or nonexistent.

2*b. New way.* The volume of material that will be recovered in the future is growing rapidly relative to the volume disposed of. This is a newly identified stage in life-cycle design and management. The number of material recovery and life-extension options is increasing steadily from both a physical and economic standpoint as products are designed for multiple uses and reuses through easier disassembly, improved maintainability, and upgrading by means of replacement modules. Advances in materials science, often modeled on biology, have substantial potential for improving recycling technology and for improving reliable service life during several product lifetimes.[12] More and more purchasing departments have less reluctance to buy products made with recycled materials as product quality improves. Feedback to product and process designers is increasing, especially in some European countries where comprehensive recycling and product take-back regulations are being introduced.

3a. Old way.   Feedback to designers from the factory floor on manufacturability and from customers on product performance and serviceability has ranged from poor to excellent over the years, depending on individual company priorities and practices. With the advent of TQM, quality function deployment (QFD), and concurrent engineering (CE), the amount and quality of feedback to designers has been generally improving.

3b. New way.   The feedback to designers is expected to continue accelerating and improving as life-cycle thinking becomes more prevalent and supplier-producer-customer relationships in the supply chain are tightened by interdependent network operations and mutual environmental compliance and liability concerns. There is a growing extension of perceived producer responsibility for the total impact of processes and products throughout and even beyond the end of usable product life. Every manufactured object casts environmental "shadows" on the earth during its creation, use, and retirement. Stewardship responsibilities and potential liabilities for these shadows endure for the producer and associated supply chain members even as ownership or custody of the object may be transferred many times.

4a.Old way.   Up until now, with some exceptions, the end of first useful life has been given little, if any, profit planning consideration, even for long-life durable goods or infrastructure assets. When material assets are no longer usable for the purpose originally intended, there is a spectrum of material recovery alternatives that generally have not been exploited, systematized, or financially evaluated. The few companies that have done so have reaped substantial dollar savings for their efforts.[13]

Managerial cost accounting and risk assessment have been generally very weak or nonexistent in the area of economically beneficial reuse, repair, remanufacturing, or reconfiguration to more advanced models for developed markets, or to less advanced and lower-priced models for less-developed markets.

Moreover, redesign to upgrade the original product can render the inventory of original replacement parts noninterchangeable with redesigned parts and no longer usable or reusable. The trade-offs and timing between (1) design continuity for remanufacture and reuse of parts and (2) redesign of parts or components to marginally improve product quality or performance may be often influenced more by profit potential in captive aftermarkets than by any consideration of efficient materials usage.

4b. New way.   End of first useful life of products currently poses at least as great a decisionmaking challenge in selecting subsequent life-cycle alternatives as does initial product design. This newly emerging and important stage in life-cycle analysis offers opportunities for design continuity, redesign, possible pollution prevention improvement, and additional profit potential in the remanufacture, refurbishment, or reconfiguration of products and recycling of materials. A second or third life span of similar or different products in secondary, tertiary, or even in primary market segments, can add additional value to materials each time they are reconfigured.

On the other hand, it may be more advantageous in certain cases for a company to generate income from the sale of industrial waste or unusable assets as marketable inputs to another manufacturing operation than it would be to redesign an existing product or process to reduce the amount of waste or unusable assets generated. If such materials were hazardous, this would, in effect, constitute a decision on the part of the original producer to prevent pollution, not by source reduction, but by financially beneficial disposition of the materials to another producer or user and a calculated transfer of risk.

The "New Way," in summary, is simply recognition that there is a fast-emerging, previously obscured stage in life-cycle design. There is a range of cost-risk-benefit, end-of-product-life alternatives, uncertainties, and probabilities that merit system analysis attention. Optimization models of product costs, performance, materials efficiency, and potential environmental impact are required at the resource recovery stage just as they are at the original design stage. A reverse distribution system must be designed.[14] This new stage is actually a window of opportunity in life-cycle design to create more long-term added value in services as well as materials. It can occur many years after the original product or process was designed and can take advantage of all the advances in science, technology, and market development that have occurred in the meantime. In addition, experience in the resource recovery phase can be used to nourish the initial design process in ways up front that will progressively make the resource recovery function more easily and more efficiently accomplished. "Design for service" software for easier product repair and disassembly is already available.[15]

The ultimate goal is to redesign the industrial decisionmaking process to improve the quality and efficiency of life-cycle system performance. Decisionmaking is the critical transformative process where the leverage for producing an earlier sustainable outcome is greatest. It is the process where intelligent use of information technology for decision support can help marry technology and ecology in the development of future industrial systems.

It is more important to improve management and operational system performance than product performance. Ultimately, the latter depends on the former. An effective system lasts longer and is harder to compete against than a successful product.[16]

There are, moreover, two other important aspects of the life-cycle design story that have enormous implications for industrial advances in environmental protection. The first is in the research and development and new knowledge associated with design for environment. The second is required redesign of traditional management systems of accounting and finance that distort economic reality and inhibit environmental progress. Transformative changes in these vital areas of design are essential if the societal goal of sustainable economic development is to be achieved.

Promise and Peril in Conceptual Design

A survey of U.S. corporate environmental managers in 1993 revealed that in 85% of the cases pollution prevention efforts have had moderate to very substantial effects on their company R&D programs. Most of this R&D activity was involved with new or modified processes and material substitutions. Survey results in Europe were similar, with more corporate emphasis on R&D for new product and package designs than in the United States.[17] However, considerable product and package environmental design innovation is taking place in small companies in many industries in the United States, using lessons from nature as a basis for research, evaluation, and product development.[18]

Managers, engineers, and industrial designers regularly make decisions about complex problems involving change, risk, uncertainty, and large sums of money. Should adding consideration of the environmental factor to someone's check-off list or systems model make such decisions much different or more difficult?

The answer is that it certainly does. The environment is not just another added factor. Ecology, biology, geology, entomology, biotechnology, and all the other "ologies" of earth and life sciences, are complex subsystem sciences of a pervasive environmental reality. These systems and their components interact with each other and with human technological and socioeconomic activities in a myriad of constantly changing relationships.

Recent discoveries in subatomic physics, molecular biology, biochemistry, field theory, and chaos theory have completely changed scientific understanding of how nature works. Yet most managers and engineers—indeed, most people educated in the Western world—still base their thinking and acting on the mechanistic Newtonian model of seventeenth-century science. The science has changed, but mainstream economic and industrial mindsets have not.[19,20]

Newtonian and Cartesian-inspired science and engineering have produced a spectacularly successful industrial machine for its beneficiaries in economically developed countries. Machine technologies have revolutionized life on earth. To our dismay, however, we have discovered that the fruits of this remarkable material progress are not all sweet.

At current rates of growth, the environmental impact of our existing petrochemical, fossil-fuel-based industrial economy is unsustainable. Unless we change our established ways of thinking, and accelerate our rate of behavioral change, the economic activities of humankind will inexorably and severely strain the natural life-support carrying capacity of our planet. In some areas it is contended that this has already occurred.[21] Leaders in science and industry are calling for a major change of course.[22,23]

Mechanistic models and mechanical structures have served us well in many ways. They have served us so well, in fact, that the idea of the machine as a design model has been extended and misapplied to economic, social, and political activities with disastrous results. Nationalistic, ideological, and superefficient political machines in Nazi Germany and Stalinist Russia were the ultimate manifestations of a conceptual design idea gone wrong.[24] Not only an idea gone wrong, but a wrong idea.

Social institutions and systems are not mechanical. They are alive. They grow, learn, adapt, and innovate. Unless they do, they deteriorate and die. An economy is not a machine. Yet that is exactly the way we visualize it and describe its behavior.

We want to jump-start the economy, fine-tune it, give it the green light, and fuel a recovery so it won't run out of gas. We tend to imagine it as an engine or a power station of computers and complicated machinery that can be operated from a central control panel. But has anyone ever seen a machine grow? Isn't an economy more like an immensely complex rain forest of countless competing and cooperating organisms, each species seeking its own niche in which it can survive, stay healthy, and reproduce, than it is like an automated factory? Students of evolutionary biology think so.[25]

New lessons from the study of living systems have enormous implications for the way we visualize problems and conduct our affairs. Environmental protection is much more than sorting garbage, saving wildlife, preserving forests and soils, and installing scrubbers on smokestacks, as important as these activities are. It is also about the nature of nature and how nature works. This includes human nature and how and why people make the decisions they do. New studies in quantum physics, microbiology, behavioral science, and social psychology all have something to contribute to environmental R&D and design problem solving, but these findings are generally unfamiliar to most managers, engineers, and design teams. Meanwhile, lack of such knowledge and the outmoded imagery imbedded in the assumptions upon which many decisions are based continues to contribute to some misconceptions in our traditional diagnoses and prescriptions for social and economic progress.

Things look very different to designers who think in terms of organics instead of mechanics, of life cycles instead of life spans, or of interdependent, autonomous networks instead of authoritarian hierarchies. Solutions to many social and economic problems with severe environmental fallout are beyond the professional purview of industrial designers and beyond the reach of green products and processes. But new knowledge in ecology and all the other relevant "ologies" has introduced new requirements in the design and management of organizations, facilities, systems, processes, and products.

New knowledge in scientific "ologies" has impacted the engineering "ilities." The conventional list of system and product performance requirements—reliability, maintainability, manufacturability, transportability, etc.—has become a lot longer, as indicated in Fig. 26.3. We must also now design for dismantlability, recyclability, remanufacturability, reusability, durability, degradability, etc., depending on the type of product or package under consideration. These new design criteria have environmental protection goals of pollution prevention, efficient use and recovery of materials, and the sustainability of industrial operations.

Materials scientists are key players in development and design of sustainable systems. Less virgin material per unit of product can be designed to deliver equal or greater performance.

Dematerialization, miniaturization, and nanotechnology are ways to decouple economic growth from a concomitant increase in the consumption of material resources. The silicon chip is a classic example.

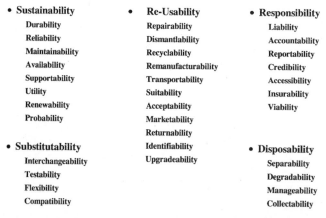

- **Sustainability**
  - Durability
  - Reliability
  - Maintainability
  - Availability
  - Supportability
  - Utility
  - Renewability
  - Probability

- **Substitutability**
  - Interchangeability
  - Testability
  - Flexibility
  - Compatibility

- **Re-Usability**
  - Repairability
  - Dismantlability
  - Recyclability
  - Remanufacturability
  - Transportability
  - Suitability
  - Acceptability
  - Marketability
  - Returnability
  - Identifiability
  - Upgradeability

- **Responsibility**
  - Liability
  - Accountability
  - Reportability
  - Credibility
  - Accessibility
  - Insurability
  - Viability

- **Disposability**
  - Separability
  - Degradability
  - Manageability
  - Collectability

Figure 26.3 New knowledge in the "ologies" produces more project, systems, and product requirements in the "ilities."

Computer chips are very small, highly productive, and made from one of the most abundant materials in the world, viz., sand.

Materials science will not only be concerned with developing new materials or new uses for existing materials. Much work also lies ahead in developing systems-based approaches to material flows, learning more about the industrial metabolism of different materials, and helping to close the life-cycle loop with materials that are easier to recycle and can be used longer for additional product lifetimes.[26] Working together, materials science and effective materials management are critical ingredients of successful design for environment.

Implementing DFE with Total Performance Accounting

If the practice of medicine stands for healing and the practice of law stands for justice, what does business stand for? Surely, one answer is that it must stand for socially responsive and economically responsible decisionmaking that contributes to a just and sustainable society. This includes strategic decisions, marketing decisions, operating decisions, financial decisions, and life-cycle engineering design decisions—all interconnected and all with public as well as private dimensions.

The omission of "environmental" decisions from those just enumerated is intentional. Environmental awareness, like ethics and computer literacy, should be a core value in the decisionmaking process of every industrial and commercial enterprise. Environmental protection should be everyone's concern. It is not merely a technical or legal function, or a segregated responsibility. The key indicator of when this realization takes place will be when environmental performance and costs are not only fully disclosed, but are fully integrated into the financial accounting, cost accounting, and management information systems of large to medium-sized companies. With very few exceptions, this has not yet begun to happen.[27]

Cost, or cost effectiveness, has to be one criterion in any serious systems analysis or design optimization model. For durable goods especially, life-cycle costs are needed. In fact, the world is full of life-cycle cost models. Life-cycle costing was already under way when Earth Day was first celebrated in April 1970. Yet only very recently, over twenty years since the original Earth Day, has work begun to identify and incorporate environmental costs in the design of such models.[28,29,30] Only in October of 1993 did the U.S. federal government issue a directive to incorporate environmental considerations, including life-cycle costing, in federal procurement policy and practice.[31] Little more evidence than this is needed to make the argument for accelerating the rate of necessary change.

Conventional accounting systems seldom capture full internal company costs and benefits of activities related to environmental compliance, control, cleanup, treatment, employee safety, disposal, cost avoidance, exposure to litigation, potential penalties, and fees. Many such costs are intangible, are buried in overhead accounts, and are not attributed to the product or process that generates them.

Defining, identifying, and properly allocating internal environmental costs is an essential first step. Integrating these costs into the company's decisionmaking information system is a critical second step. An EPA North American workshop on environmental accounting and capital budgeting held in December 1993 identified 89 separate action items that should be pursued by various professional, business, government, and academic groups to modify managerial accounting standards and practices to better reflect environmental costs.[32]

Performance and resource utilization feedback to the design function must have the cost data to go with it.[33] Only in this way can designers and others systematically include such costs in the trade-off decisions that are made by companies every day. Only in this way can materials management performance be measured to provide adequate information to designers who use cost-benefit criteria to achieve DFE objectives. An environmental burden per unit of production, per dollar of revenue, or per unit of inventory of specific products or parts would greatly increase the visibility of environmental effects on alternative product or process designs, resource recovery, and profit performance. Savings due to increased productivity of materials designed for multiple recyclings could be calculated. It has been reported, for example, that a component that survives three recyclings generally achieves about a 60% per unit cost reduction.[34]

There are economic and legal forces at work today, in addition to DFE considerations, that have major implications for the resource recovery phase of materials life cycles and product life spans. Recent antitrust litigation and court decisions have weakened the ability of large producers to control the aftermarket for servicing and upgrading their equipment.[35] Greater competition in the after-sales product service and support markets will lower prices of spares and replacement modules. Managerial cost accounting and control, material durability, recycling and disposal decisions, as well as warranty policies, will become more important as "beyond economical repair" practices are driven less by high-margin, predatory pricing.

Total performance accounting is the ultimate step in a financial management and reporting system that is designed for the environment. Total performance accounting is designed for:

1. *Full cost accounting:* Under a full-cost system, companies would identify and disclose all internal environmental costs, plus a grad-

ually increasing amount of the life-cycle costs inflicted upon the public health, property, and the natural environment that can, over time, be reasonably internalized in a company's accounts. Full-cost accounting has many proponents in theory. Some companies are evaluating the idea. Electric utilities, in particular, have conducted extensive studies of the subject.[36,37]

2. *Net added value:* Companies often express pride in their ability to "add value" to resources with their manufacturing and distribution activities. The value added by internal operations, however, says nothing about the external life-cycle costs of the environmental impact of these activities. All of the profit accrues to the producer, who pays only part of the costs. Potential or actual costs of environmental damage should be deducted or internalized to arrive at a *net* added value. This is the true valuation of economic activity. By this measure, products with a negative net added value shouldn't be produced at all.

3. *Investment in values added:* As indicated in Fig. 26.3, design for environmental quality includes the criteria of responsibility, liability, accountability, credibility, etc. Traditional bottom-line thinking has typically viewed production of goods and services as a profit-maximizing, cost-minimizing endeavor. This has encouraged a narrow view of responsibility for employee and customer health, safety, and equity on the part of many companies. Any such additional responsibilities have usually been regarded as added *costs* rather than *investments* in long-term societal acceptability, reduced liability, and market viability. Labor has been typically treated as an economic cost, to the neglect of the value of employees as assets and of the quality of their skills as a return on those assets. More and more, the reality and perception of a company's added value will depend to an important degree on the quality of intangible values produced by its bank of knowledge and integrity. In short, sustainable added value is a function of total values added.

4. *Full-cost pricing:* The Business Council for Sustainable Development (BCSD) has proposed gradual transitions toward full-cost pricing in accordance with the "Polluter Pays Principle."[38] This is a classical market-based method of resource allocation by means of discouraging demand for products priced to reflect heavy environmental burdens. Frank Popoff, Chairman of Dow Chemical, states unequivocally that full-cost pricing, when implemented correctly, will in itself "improve environmental performance more than any other action, program, or regulation."[39]

5. *Stakeholder accountability:* Serious consideration should be given to measuring a company's performance affecting each of its

many stakeholder groups—i.e., suppliers, customers, employees, communities, distributors, lenders, future generations, etc.—in a manner similar to that which is done already in discharging a company's accountability to its shareholders. Stakeholders have conflicting interests and have become increasingly vocal, distrustful, and litigious. But it need not always be that way. For example, companies like Church and Dwight are cultivating the support of expanded stakeholder networks to build brand loyalty and increase the cost effectiveness of their marketing programs. Helpers instead of headaches. Stakeholder management is sure to become one of the most difficult but potentially beneficial challenges of the future for corporate leaders. A well designed total performance accounting and stakeholder partnership system can play a critical role in converting today's complex environmental and socioeconomic problems into tomorrow's business opportunities and accomplishments. Business, stakeholders, and the environment all stand to gain.

Whatever Designers Can Do Professionally Isn't Enough

As we have seen, Machine Age thinking and partial-cost economics and accounting do not conform in many ways to the decisionmaking and DFE requirements of the life-cycle systems approach to pollution prevention, resource recovery, and sustainable development. Current industrial programs of reengineering and restructuring also require rethinking and redesign of the way companies do business and keep score so that the full costs, risks, and benefits of environmental protection can be responsibly evaluated and acted upon.

This potential will not be fully realized, of course, unless life-cycle thinking translates into the practice of life-cycle management. Life-cycle systems analysis and DFE, appropriately applied (back of the envelope in small firms, pin-striped consultants for the *Fortune* 100, and rocket science staffs in Silicon Valley), can make an enormous contribution.

Life-cycle decision tools can be an ally of total-quality management and a contributor to net added value. They can act as an extension cord of producer responsibilities and a cornerstone of total performance accounting and accountability to stakeholders. They are a shoehorn for a longer-term planning perspective, a can opener of the mind, and an important component of business strategy.

Incredibly and regrettably, however, this is not nearly enough.

The reason it is not enough is that the environmental impact of human societies on the earth is caused by more than our polluting technologies and traditional mindsets. The combined effects of exponential population growth, extreme poverty in developing countries, and relentless consumption of energy, fertile soils, forests, fish, and other material resources at unsustainable rates take an even greater toll on the earth's life-support systems than faults in the processes of production. Experience continues to indicate that despite impressive progress in cleaner production and recycling, improvements have been offset by the increase in quantities of items produced, used, and disposed of.

The worsening effects of population growth and per capita consumption anticipated in the next fifty years can only be offset by a *virtual elimination* of the environmental impact of a rapidly growing total output of industrial goods, clearly an unrealistic goal. Every demographic projection shows the population of the earth going from its present 5.6 billion to 8–10 billion by about the year 2030. No reasonably achievable amount of economic development, education, and voluntary family planning will substantially alter this projection. Of the 6 billion people expected on earth less than five years from now, 2 billion will be teenagers who are already born.[40] They will outnumber "baby boomers" 50 to 1.

However "environmentally responsible" producers may become, they are not developing green products for the purpose of reducing the market demand for them. Every company and every country in the world is hooked on growth. Ever greater population pressure and the need for jobs and debt retirement, now make economic growth essential. At the same time, consumerism, pollution, and per capita depletion of resources make it unsustainable. We must keep running faster and faster just to stay in place. Modern society's addiction to economic growth has become a dilemma of menacing proportions: grow or die versus grow and commit suicide.[41]

In the puzzle of sustainable life on earth we haven't connected all the dots. Some of them lie outside the constricted and self-imposed mental boundaries of our technological and economic system models. Many are beyond our planning time horizons. Still others are buried in the self-serving value systems of bureaucratic institutions—public and private. Financial income is more important than social outcome in money-based systems of politics and law. An achievable greening of industrial production alone, a transformation that at best will take decades to accomplish, is not enough to "save the planet." Supply side progress must be matched by a major demand side revolution as well.

The solution to the demand side problem has to start with population stabilization. Answers must be found to sustainably manage a projected real growth in world domestic product from about $25 trillion today to well over $100 trillion in thirty years or so. Either we start to find these answers now in all of the roles each of us play as consumers, voters, and investors, as well as in our roles as managers, engineers, and industrial designers, or else governments in crisis and the corrective forces of nature will do it for us. The choice is ours. The greatest risk is in choosing to do nothing.

There are two resources we can never have enough of. These are intellectual capital and moral courage. A reformulation of quantitative economic growth to qualitative sustainable development will require massive infusions of these intangible but indispensable evolutionary assets. The human brain and the human spirit are unique advantages of our species that have the potential to change our focus from short-term, narrow self-interest to longer-term, enlightened self-interest. Such a change in emphasis constitutes our principal hope for more rapid advancement of the culture of production toward *eco-efficiency*, as well as a necessary global transformation of the culture of consumption and insatiable materials demand to an ethic of *eco-sufficiency*.

On a macro, sociobiological scale, DFE has to stand for "design for enlightenment." We are all learners in the school of sustainability. The only organizations that will have the capacity to change and the resilience to survive in the future will be "learning organizations."[42] We must design them. Not simply grow or die. Change for the better or die.

Increased scientific and environmental literacy on the part of all professionals and its application to decisionmaking in every aspect of working and living is DFE support of the most fundamental kind. If human priorities and values can shift from quantitative growth to qualitative development, sustainable civilized life on earth can become a viable goal and a superior aspiration for everyone. This is *why* we must adjust our goals and change our ways of achieving them.

References

1. U.S. Environmental Protection Agency, memorandum, "Pollution Prevention Policy Statement: New Directions for Environmental Protection," Washington, D.C., June 15, 1993.
2. *The Wall Street Journal*, Dec. 24, 1990, pp. 1 and 17.
3. "Pollution Prevention; Reinventing Compliance, Survey Results: Europe," *Chemical Engineering*, November 1993, p. 39.
4. U.S. Environmental Protection Agency, "A Workshop on Accounting and Capital Budgeting for Environmental Costs," Dallas, TX, Dec. 5–7, 1993.
5. *Chemical Engineering*, op. cit., p. 30.
6. Workshop, "Life Cycle Assessment: From Inventory to Action," Massachusetts Institute of Technology, Cambridge, MA, Nov. 4–5, 1993.
7. A. L. White, "Accounting for Pollution Prevention," *EPA Journal*, July–September 1993, p. 23.
8. J. A. Fava and C. L. Henn, "Life Cycle Analysis and Resource Management," in R. V. Kolluru (ed.), *Environmental Strategies Handbook*, McGraw-Hill, New York, 1993, pp. 582–586.

9. U.S. Environmental Protection Agency, *Design for the Environment,* EPA742F-93-007, Washington, D.C., October 1993.
10. J. A. Fava and C. L. Henn, op. cit., pp. 541–641.
11. H. C. Haynsworth and R. T. Lyons, "Remanufacturing by Design, The Missing Link," *Production and Inventory Management Journal,* The American Production and Inventory Control Society, second quarter, 1987, pp. 24–29.
12. Meeting Briefs, "Materials Science Comes to Life at Boston Gathering," *Science,* Dec. 10, 1993, p. 1646.
13. P. Wengert, President, The Investment Recovery Association, Mission, KS (telephone interview), December 1993.
14. *Reuse and Recycling, Reverse Logistics Opportunities,* Council of Logistics Management, Oakbrook, IL, 1993, pp. 161–176.
15. *Popular Science,* June 1994, p. 48.
16. W. R. Stahel, "The Utilization-Focused Service Economy: Resource Efficiency and Product Life Extension," *The Greening of Industrial Ecosystems,* National Academy Press, Washington, DC, 1994, pp. 178–190.
17. *Chemical Engineering,* op. cit., pp. 31, 39.
18. D. Wann, *Biologic, Environmental Protection by Design,* Johnson Publishing, Boulder, CO, 1990.
19. J. Rifkin, *Entropy into the Greenhouse World,* rev. ed., Bantam Books, New York, 1989.
20. M. J. Wheatly, *Leadership and the New Science,* Berrett-Koehler Publishers, San Francisco, 1992.
21. S. Postel, "Carrying Capacity: Earth's Bottom Line," *State of the World,* W. W. Norton, New York, 1994, pp. 3–21.
22. "Global Warning," *Nucleus,* Union of Concerned Scientists, Cambridge, MA, Winter 1992–1993.
23. S. Schmidheiny, *Changing Course, A Global Business Perspective on Development and the Environment,* MIT Press, Cambridge, MA, 1992.
24. W. Bonner, *What Went Wrong in the 20th Century,* Agora, Inc., Baltimore, MD, 1993.
25. M. Rothschild, *Bionomics: The Economy as Ecosystem,* Henry Holt, New York, 1990.
26. B. R. Allenby, "Industrial Ecology: The Materials Scientist in an Environmentally Constrained World," *MRS Bulletin,* Materials Research Society, March 1992.
27. M. Epstein, "Keynote Address," *Total Cost Assessment Workshop: Considering Environmental Costs to Make Smarter Business Decisions,* Rutgers University, Piscataway, NJ, March 11, 1994.
28. D. Cohan, W. Trench, and M. McLearn, "Beyond Waste Minimization: A Life-Cycle Approach to Managing Chemicals and Materials," unpublished, 1992.
29. U.S. Environmental Protection Agency, "Total Cost Assessment: Accelerating Industrial Pollution Prevention through Innovative Project Financial Analysis," EPA741-R-92-002, Washington, D.C., May 1992.
30. P. E. Bailey, "Full Cost Accounting for Life Cycle Costs—A Guide for Engineers and Financial Analysts," *Environmental Finance,* vol. 1, no. 1, Spring 1991, pp. 13–30.
31. "Federal Acquisition, Recycling and Waste Prevention," Presidential Executive Order 12873 of Oct. 20, 1993.
32. U.S. Environmental Protection Agency, "Stakeholders' Action Agenda: A Report of the Workshop on Accounting and Capital Budgeting for Environmental Costs," May 1994.
33. *Reuse and Recycling, Reverse Logistics Opportunities,* op. cit., p. 284.
34. T. Lent, "Environmental Finance and Accounting—Outline for a Foundation-Laying Conference or Conference Series," unpublished, Berkeley, CA, 1992, p. 5.
35. M. Geyelin, "Xerox Agrees to Vouchers in Settlement," *The Wall Street Journal,* Dec. 8, 1993.
36. Survey Team #4, "Full-Cost Accounting for Decision Making," Task Force on Sustainable Energy Development, Ontario Hydro, December 1993.
37. Final Report, "Accounting for Externality Costs in Electric Utility Planning in Wisconsin," Research Triangle Institute, Research Triangle Park, NC, December 1991.

38. S. Schmidheiny, op. cit., pp. 18–19.
39. F. P. Popoff and D. T. Buzzelli, "Full Cost Accounting," *Chemical & Engineering News,* Jan. 11, 1993, pp. 8–10.
40. P. Schwartz, "Fallout of the Population Bomb," *Rocky Mountain Institute Newsletter,* Old Snowmass, Co, Spring 1994, p. 6.
41. C. L. Henn, "The New Economics of Life Cycle Thinking," *International Symposium on Electronics and the Environment Conference Record,* The Institute of Electrical and Electronics Engineers, Inc., Technical Activities Board, Arlington, VA, May 10–12, 1993, pp. 184–188.
42. P. Senge, *The Fifth Discipline: The Art and Practice of the Learning Organization,* Doubleday/Currency, New York, 1990.

Conclusion

Joseph Fiksel

The Road to Eco-efficiency

This book has described how manufacturing firms all over the world are undergoing fundamental changes in the way that they address environmental, health, and safety management. Many are abandoning their traditional, passive compliance posture and are engaging in voluntary initiatives to improve the environmental performance of their products and processes. This trend has been motivated partly by changing regulations and standards, and partly by increased environmental awareness among both retail and industrial customers. Perhaps the most important factor in changing industry attitudes has been the realization that paying attention to environmental responsibility can actually increase profitability. Companies have recognized that preventing pollution and designing eco-efficient products and processes will generally result in increased efficiency and reduced operating costs.

A number of leading companies have responded to these changes by establishing programs in design for environment (DFE). DFE programs, which usually incorporate design guidelines and other tools, enable product and process development teams to systematically consider design performance issues related to environmental safety and health over the full product life cycle. This book has argued that adopting a DFE approach can enhance the new-product development process in several ways:

- Opportunities for environmental quality improvement can be discovered earlier in the product development process, thus facilitating rapid time to market.

- Environmental issues and their relative importance in various global markets can be evaluated more systematically and with a longer-range perspective.

- Product development practices can become more responsive to stated corporate environmental goals.

Part 2 of this book has presented some practical suggestions for tools that will support implementation of DFE, including metrics and guidelines, requirements for a DFE software infrastructure, and available methods for life-cycle assessment and management. Because of the broad scope and complexity of DFE, the adoption of such tools is essential as companies move from concept to practice.

It is important that the introduction of DFE not introduce burdensome constraints or time delays into product development. Rather, the role of DFE should be to stimulate insights and support creative problem solving. To this end, DFE should be integrated "seamlessly" into the development process, from analysis of customer needs and definition of product requirements to verification that the requirements are fulfilled. Information technology is evolving rapidly to provide better support for product development, so that the vision of a fully integrated DFE toolkit is becoming achievable at a reasonable cost.

From the Prosaic to the Exotic

The practice of DFE ranges from relatively mundane good housekeeping practices, such as minimizing waste on the production floor, to exotic technologies that can convert waste to useful products through physical and chemical transformations. Some DFE approaches can be applied readily and have clear benefits (e.g., energy conservation), whereas others involve difficult trade-offs.

An example of a challenging trade-off decision is in the selection of materials for durable goods such as appliances or automobiles. Metals and plastics are frequently considered as alternatives, and have very different profiles from a life-cycle environmental perspective. Metals are much easier to recycle than plastics, yet their greater weight increases energy demand. Even within the class of metals, trade-offs must be made; for example, aluminum has a higher strength-to-weight ratio than steel, but requires more energy in the extraction and processing stages. In automobile manufacturing, one must also factor in the relative crashworthiness of different materials. Finally, consumer preferences regarding look and feel must be taken into account. For design teams to make such trade-offs intelligently, they will require automated support to assess designs in terms of costs, environmental impacts, and other performance criteria.

As interest in environmental technologies mushrooms, there are many promising developments that may revolutionize the options available for DFE. For example, genetically engineered organisms are being developed that can "digest" waste materials and convert them to harmless by-products. Similar results are being obtained through irradiation of waste streams, high-temperature molten metal baths, and other approaches. Another exotic field that could have enormous environmental benefits is nanotechnology, the new science of molecular-scale devices—undisputedly the ultimate in source reduction. Meanwhile, brand new technologies are emerging for developing industrial products from renewable agricultural sources. For example, the U.S. Department of Agriculture has funded exploratory ventures to develop biodegradable plastic from wheat gluten and granite-like composite from waste newspaper and soybean flour. As we look to the future, human ingenuity may indeed be the saving grace that enables us to avoid the extremists' apocalyptic predictions of environmental collapse.

Vertically Integrated DFE

Earlier chapters have demonstrated that the greatest impacts of DFE often are achieved through initiatives that link the technologies of various companies involved in a production chain. The Kalundborg complex, the DEC/GE Plastics/Nailite partnership, the Baxter Healthcare/WMX collaboration are all examples of this phenomenon. By coordinating the development of environmentally conscious technologies with their upstream suppliers and their downstream customers, manufacturers can introduce significant improvements in both productivity and environmental performance.

Viewed from a life-cycle perspective, a product is part of a larger *system*; namely, the value-added chain from raw materials to end uses. As described in Chap. 5, DFE can introduce design changes that make this overall system more efficient in terms of resource usage or waste generation. Such changes may not be associated so much with a particular product feature as with the industry structure and economic relationships among participants; an example is encouragement of plastic container recycling through industry-government partnerships.

The popular term *virtual organization* is often used to describe systematic cooperation among a network of industrial customers and suppliers. It is well known that sharing of technical information, harmonization of specifications, and integration of business processes will result in improved communication and elimination of redundant or misdirected effort, leading to greater overall efficiency and lower costs. Moreover, strategic alliances among customers and suppliers can bestow a competitive advantage upon each party, allowing them to respond effectively to a dynamic business environment. This is especially true in the electronics industry, where short product lifetimes and rapidly changing technology make fast development cycle time a critical success factor.

An important aspect of customer-supplier cooperation is the development of a robust technological strategy that enables all parties to prosper. Design for environment is becoming a key element of any such strategy, especially since environmental performance is increasingly being viewed from a full life-cycle perspective. For example, the "greenness" of a computer product is determined not only by its power consumption and recyclability, but also by the environmental emissions and resource utilization of the production processes involved in the manufacture of its materials and components. Since electronics suppliers and manufacturers are inevitably linked by the calculus of life-cycle analysis, it makes good sense for them to consider how they can jointly improve the design of the entire "cradle-to-grave" production system.

As an example, Figure 27.1 illustrates the "industrial ecology" of the industry groups involved in semiconductor fabrication and use. Efforts to introduce DFE into any one industry group or company are inevitably hampered by the constraints of the existing markets and infrastructure. Device manufacturers may seek substitute materials that are superior in terms of increased recyclability or reduced energy content, but they are limited by the availability of such materials. Similarly, chipmakers may wish to eliminate certain types of undesirable chemicals from their manufacturing process, but they are constrained by the technology of the process equipment. As a consequence, individual firms may settle for "local optimization," i.e., efforts at source reduction, energy use reduction, and pollution prevention that are within their control.

A more effective and powerful approach is to seek *global optimization* by identifying cross-cutting design changes that promise to decrease the life-cycle cost or increase the life-cycle efficiency of electronic products in terms of resource usage, waste recovery, or other

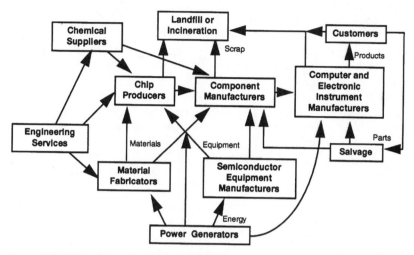

Figure 27.1 Industrial ecology relationships in the semiconductor industry.

important metrics. By lifting constraints and pooling their talents, cooperating companies can focus on innovative technologies that benefit the entire value-added chain. Such innovations might include short-term incremental improvements (such as standardizing the configuration of electronic components to simplify product disassembly at end of life) and long-term fundamental changes (such as introducing entirely new processes that eliminate the use of chemical solvents).

The overall benefits of this type of vertically integrated DFE can potentially be an order of magnitude greater than those achieved through conventional approaches. However, this raises the question of how the benefits should be distributed among the participants in the value chain. It will be important to develop environmental performance indicators that support the measurement of "environmental value added," analogous to economic value added. Suppliers should be recognized not only for their ability to produce components with lower cost or higher quality, but also for their ability to improve the overall environmental profile associated with the product life cycle. Similarly, manufacturers can establish environmental performance targets for their suppliers which are driven in turn by the requirements of their own customers.

Toward Competitive Advantage

Environmental consciousness is much more than the politically correct business trend of the moment. A profound change has occurred in the attitudes of thousands of corporate managers around the world. Having clearly acknowledged environmental protection as a part of their responsibility, they seek to align environmental strategy with business strategy. While this is a noble aim, it presents many challenges.

This book has attempted to characterize the challenges of designing for the environment and described how some companies have addressed them. Each company is unique, and there is no "one size fits all" recipe for successful environmental management. There are, however, certain common elements that can be observed as companies make the transition from the traditional, compliance-oriented approach of the past to the strategic environmental vision of the future.

- *Life-cycle paradigm:* The recognition that environmental responsibility extends beyond the plant fenceline and even beyond the customer's waste bin has led to the ascendance of life-cycle thinking. At a conceptual level, "cradle to grave" has become a cliché. The real challenge is finding productive ways to recover and reuse components or waste materials at the end of a product's life.

- *Cross-functional teamwork:* As environmental performance becomes more important to both product and corporate sustainability, responsibility shifts from environmental staff groups to product and process development teams. Some companies, like Sun Microsystems, have successfully transferred "ownership" of product-related environmental concerns to their engineering group, with the environmental staff acting as facilitators.

- *Integration with quality:* Product and environmental stewardship are embracing the fundamental concepts of total-quality management—measurement and continuous improvement. Armed with the right metrics and tools, companies can readily incorporate environmental values into their ongoing quality programs.

- *Importance of cost information:* In the world "beyond compliance," where environmental quality truly becomes a business issue, companies must trade off the costs and benefits of environmental improvement initiatives. This requires an activity-based approach to "environmental accounting" over the product or process life cycle.

Companies making this transition, in industries ranging from cosmetics to computers, are recognizing that they can derive competitive advantage from environmental excellence. Through designing facilities, products, and processes with an understanding of life-cycle cost and environmental implications, they are discovering opportunities to improve productivity and profitability. There are five major sources of competitive advantage linked to environmental performance:

- *Margin improvement:* Seeking cost savings at every stage of the product life cycle through more efficient utilization of labor, energy, and material resources

- *Market share increase:* Developing global products that meet emerging eco-efficiency standards and are differentiated in the eyes of customers for whom "green" purchasing criteria are important

- *Capital conservation:* Encouraging farsighted design that avoids excessive capital expenditures by anticipating next-generation environmental quality requirements

- *Rapid time to market:* Assuring that key environmental issues are considered as part of the "concurrent engineering" process during the early stages of design, thus speeding up product introduction

- *Enhanced corporate image:* Establishing an image in the marketplace as an environmentally responsible company

This book has demonstrated how leading companies are using the principles of DFE to seek competitive advantage in one or more of the above dimensions. Rather than conflicting with environmental preservation, DFE-based competition enhances environmental quality. Thus, economic forces and environmental responsibility can not only be reconciled—they can actually be synergistic.

DFE is neither a straightforward nor a static discipline, but it is worth the investment. As the pathbreaking DFE pioneers have discovered, the rapid pace of technological and regulatory change will require continuous learning and renewal in the foreseeable future. The road to sustainable development is full of surprising twists and turns, but there are many rewards along the way—for corporations, for human beings, and for our planet.

Glossary

Burden   A change or release to the environment, due to an industrial process, that may have adverse effects

Business enterprise   A managed entity with a defined mission that involves providing economic value to customers

Business process   A sequence of value-adding steps within a business that transform inputs into outputs to satisfy a customer need

Closed-loop recycling   The collection and reuse of waste from an industrial system in a way that contributes to the resource needs of that system

Competitive advantage   A characteristic of a business that enables it to outperform its competitors in terms of financial or other measures

Compost   A stable, humuslike material that results from decomposition of organic wastes through natural, exothermic processes

Containment   A constituent of a material or waste that is a known or suspected agent of risk

Degradable   Capable of being broken down in the presence of certain environmental conditions (e.g., biodegradable implies presence of microorganisms, photodegradable implies presence of light)

Design for (the) environment   A systematic approach to improving environmental performance of products and processes over their full life cycle

Eco-efficiency   The ability of a managed entity to simultaneously meet cost, quality, and performance goals, reduce environmental impacts, and conserve valuable resources

Eco-efficient product (process)   A product (process) that simultaneously meets cost, quality, and performance goals, minimizes adverse environmental impacts, and maximizes conservation of valuable resources

Enterprise   A managed entity that performs functions in pursuit of goals

Enterprise integration   Improvement of enterprise performance through coordination and communication among interrelated business processes

Enterprise model   A conceptual map of the set of business processes that comprise an enterprise

Environment   The surroundings in which a managed entity operates, including inanimate features as well as humans and other biotic systems

Environmental impact   Adverse effects upon human or ecological health and safety due to a product, process, or industrial system

Environmental management   The functional aspect of enterprise management that develops and implements environmental policies and strategies

Environmental management system   Those aspects of the overall enterprise systems, including organizations, practices, and resources, that carry out and support the environmental management function

Environmental performance   The effectiveness of an enterprise at achieving its environmental objectives, potentially including reduced environmental impacts or improved environmental quality

Environmental performance measurement   A process within an environmental management system that evaluates environmental performance through the use of objectives, performance metrics, and tracking systems

Environmental policy   An enterprise's overall aims and principles of action with respect to the environment, from which environmental objectives can be derived

Environmental quality   The measurable attributes of a product or process that indicate its contribution to ecological health and integrity

Environmental report   A document that describes the environmental policy, objectives, relevant activities, and performance results of an enterprise during a defined time period

Exposure pathway   The primary pathway whereby receptors of concern are exposed to a hazardous agent

Full-cost accounting   A system for tracking all of the internal and external costs associated with enterprise business processes, including life-cycle costs due to environmental and other factors

Industrial ecology   The design of eco-efficient industrial systems, involving one or more enterprises, that utilize or mimic the cyclical patterns of material and energy flow found in natural ecosystems

Industrial process   An operation that transforms material, energy, and information inputs into outputs as part of an industrial production system

Integrated life-cycle management   The management of a business in a way that fully considers its life-cycle costs, benefits, and impacts

Life cycle   A sequence of conceptual stages associated with a product, process, service, facility, or enterprise

Life-cycle assessment   A method to evaluate the environmental burdens associated with a set of business processes, assess the impacts on the environment, and evaluate opportunities for improvement

Life-cycle cost management   A method to understand and manage all the costs associated with a set of business processes, including acquisition of supplies or capital equipment, direct labor and material costs, indirect support costs, uncertain future costs, and externalities

Metric   A quantifiable measure of enterprise performance

Nonrenewable resource   A natural resource that cannot be replaced, regenerated, or otherwise restored once it has been used

Objective   A performance target whose achievement can be verified

Open-loop recycling   The reuse of waste from one industrial system in a way that contributes to the resource needs of a different system

Operational metric   A metric that corresponds to a particular business process, and can be tracked through observation of the process

Pollution prevention   The anticipation and elimination or reduction of industrial waste and emissions through product or process modification

Receptor   A human or other organism exposed to a potential hazard

Recyclable   Capable of being diverted from a waste stream and reused in an economically valuable manner

Recycling   Separation, recovery, processing, and reuse of obsolete products, materials, or industrial by-products

Remanufacturing   The manufacture of products incorporating obsolete products or components that have been refurbished

Renewable resource   A natural resource, such as wind power, that can be replaced, regenerated, or otherwise restored once it has been used

Resource   A natural or manmade good that has economic value

Risk   The likelihood of specific impacts associated with a product or business process

Stakeholder   Any individual or group with a vested interest in the performance of a business, including shareholders, employees, customers, community residents, and other affected parties

Sustainable development   Industrial development that meets the needs of the present while sustaining the quality of the environment so that future generations may meet their own needs

System   A dynamic, interconnected set of processes—including business processes, industrial processes, and natural processes—that collectively perform a function

Waste   A material or industrial by-product that has no further economic value and must be discarded

Index

ABOUT THE EDITOR

Dr. Joseph Fiksel is a Principal and Vice President of Decision Focus Incorporated, a consulting firm in Mountain View, California, where he supervises the Design for Environment program. Dr. Fiksel previously directed the Decision and Risk Management business unit at Arthur D. Little, Inc. He holds a B. S. in Electrical Engineering from MIT and a Ph.D. in Operations Research from Stanford.